A LIMITED EDITION COLLECTION

TABLE OF CONTENTS

INN CLOSE PROXIMITY by IDA DUQUE 1

About *Inn Close Proximity* 2

Chapter 1: Julie 3

Chapter 2: ulie 8

Chapter 3: Alex 14

Chapter 4: Alex 19

Chapter 5: Julie 24

Chapter 6: Julie 28

Chapter 7: Alex 32

Chapter 8: Julie 36

Chapter 9: Julie 42

Chapter 10: Alex 46

Chapter 11: Alex 50

Chapter 12: Julie 52

Chapter 13: Alex 55

About the Author 60

Find Ida Duque on the Web 60

CUPCAKES & CARLOS by CARA NORTH 61

About *Cupcakes & Carlos* 62

Chapter 1: Jessica 63

Chapter 2: Carlos 67

Chapter 3: Jessica 72

Chapter 4: Carlos 75

Chapter 5: Jessica 78

Epilogue: Carlos 81

About the Author 84

SEEING RED by ANDI MACDOWALL 85

About *Seeing Red* 86

Chapter 1: Scarlett 87

Chapter 2: Scarlett 93

Chapter 3: Scarlett 100

Chapter 4: Scarlett 105

Chapter 5: Rhett 112

Chapter 6: Scarlett 116

Chapter 7: Scarlett..118

Chapter 8: Rhett..121

Chapter 9: Rhett... 128

Chapter 10: Scarlett...131

About the Author... 134

UN CAFÉCITO AT MIDNIGHT by GLORIA LUCAS......... 135

About *Un Cafécito at Midnight*................................... 136

Chapter 1..137

Chapter 2 140

Chapter 3 142

Chapter 4 146

Chapter 5 149

Chapter 6 156

Chapter 7 159

Chapter 8 165

About the Author... 168

LOST AND FOUND IN MEXICO by CARLA LUNA.......... 169

About *Lost and Found in Mexico* 170

Chapter 1.. 171

Chapter 2 178

Chapter 3 182

Chapter 4 185

Chapter 5 189

Chapter 6 194

Chapter 7 201

Chapter 8 205

Chapter 9 211

Chapter 10 215

Chapter 11.. 219

Chapter 12 224

Chapter 13..228

Chapter 14 231

Chapter 15.. 237

About the Author...242

Join Carla Online...242

OFFSIDES by JENNIFER M. MILLER & JENNA FIELDS .243

About *Offsides* 244

Chapter 1.. 245

Chapter 2... 249

Chapter 3...254

Chapter 4...259

Chapter 5... 263

Chapter 6... 266

Chapter 7... 269

About the Author 272

MERENGUE AND MURDER by D. C. GOMEZ............... **273**

About *Merengue and Murder* 274

Part 1 275

Part 2 285

About the Author 300

MIA'S LOVE by LYNN YORKE **301**

About *Mia's Love* 302

Chapter 1: Afro Blue... 303

Chapter 2: Second Time Around 314

Chapter 3: Fame...323

Chapter 4: Evil Ways...327

Chapter 5: Human Nature 333

Chapter 6: Blue Velvet 338

Chapter 7: Let Me Be Your Angel............................... 342

Chapter 8: Superstar... 346

Epilogue: The Blueprint...355

About the Author 359

Join Lynn Online 359

OWNED BY THE JOCK by IMANI JAY **361**

About *Owned by the Jock*.. 362

Acknowledgement.. 363

Chapter 1: Amy..365

Chapter 2: Tiago.. 370

Chapter 3: Amy 373

Chapter 4: Tiago..376

Chapter 5: Amy 380

Chapter 6: Tiago.. 385

Chapter 7: Amy 388

Chapter 8: Tiago 392

Chapter 9: Amy 395

Chapter 10: Tiago.. 398

Chapter 11: Amy 402

Chapter 12: Tiago 405

Chapter 13: Amy 407

Chapter 14: Tiago 413

Epilogue... 418

About the Author..420

Find Imani Online:..420

FOREVER WITH HIM by ZARIA KNIGHT 421

About *Forever with Him*... 423

About the Author.. 438

INN CLOSE PROXIMITY

Ida Duque

ABOUT *INN CLOSE PROXIMITY*

Julie is completely focused on the success of her brand-new business in Miami. There's only one tiny problem, Alex, the architect her brother's hired to help them.

Too bad Alex promised her brother he'd stay away from her.

Will she let family get in the way of true love or go after what she wants?

CHAPTER 1:
JULIE

"Ahem."

I look up to a black shirt. It has a huge green leaf in the middle. The words *Excuse my bluntness,* on top of it catch my eyes. I raise an eyebrow.

"Yes?" I ask with a polite smile. Is there such a thing as a polite smile in this situation? Sure there is. I work in the hospitality industry. Nothing shocks me. Actually, there are some exceptions: *drunk guests, anyone?*

"You're the concierge, right?" the plant loving customer in front of me asks. Let's call him... Mr. Puffer.

"How can I help you Mr.... sir?"

"You can get me anything I need, right?" He asks, with sunken, tiny brown eyes.

Define anything. "I can *try* to get you anything you need." Although, by the look on his face, he might have already found what he was looking for and more.

Mr. Puffer looks right and left, then leans in conspiratorially. "Do you know where I can find weed around here?" he whispers.

Somehow, I am *not* surprised by his request. "I'm sorry sir, but I can't help you." I reply. "Recreational marijuana is illegal in the state of Florida. It's a misdemeanor. You can go to jail." His mouth opens and closes. "Unless you have a prescription for cannabis?"

He slowly takes a step back, then says, "I'll be back."

I watch him walk away, then turn back to my computer.

I'm the night concierge for a swanky hotel in South Beach, Florida. The cool thing about being a concierge? My days are never the same. From getting exclusive concert tickets for my guests, researching the coolest spot for a proposal, or recommending the best restaurant for you to impress your sweetheart, I'm there. I'm not there for those asking me to babysit their kids. *Dude,* I'm a random stranger with no babysitting experience, you do not want me to watch your kids. Needless to say, my nights are never boring.

On the other hand, can I be honest and say I'm exhausted? This job is grueling. I'm on my feet all night. Some days, my legs are shaky from running and standing for hours on end. Not to mention, the things that guests need at three a.m. and that go from the very annoying to the very ridiculous are enough to make my head spin.

Annoying guests notwithstanding, the salary is not too bad and big tips on this particular shift make up for it. Also, this is only temporary. I'm the proud new owner, (one of them at least,) of a bed-and-breakfast in Coral Gables, Florida. Granted, it's currently a disaster zone, but still, it's ours and I couldn't be prouder and happier. Working nights allows me to be at the bed-and-breakfast during the mornings, while I sleep in the afternoons. I'm tired now, but soon, it'll all be worth it. *I just have to push through it.*

After attending Sunny Beach University, the local university, I started my hospitality career at home in Miami. After a few years in the industry, a large hotel chain offered me a job out of town and I took it. One thing led to another and before I knew it, five years went by. The bad thing was that I was alone. The good thing, also that I was alone. I was able to save a lot of money. A fateful reunion with my best friend over some wine and fast forward to a year later, we bought an old property in a nice area of Miami and came home. This is literally the American dream. Even more so because our parents are Latin immigrants.

Right before I clock off work at seven a.m. I call the hotel's restaurant and order breakfast. The biggest coffee they have is what I want. I give updates and client notes to David, my fresh-looking replacement, including Mr. Puffer, especially Mr. Puffer, then I grab my things and head out.

Once in my car, I eat carefully and try not to dirty up my clothes. I don't have time to change my attire, but I'm hungry. *Priorities.* At the same time, why bother? I'm still wearing a business suit and we're having a business meeting, which means I'm ready to go. It's win-win all around.

Since I drive against traffic, it doesn't take long to drive to the City of Coral Gables and meet my partners and best friends, Leyla, Cristina, Alma, and Maria.

I really, really wish I could go to bed for a few hours, but we need to have a private meeting before *he* arrives. I park and take a huge gulp of coffee.

Half the time I feel that we've bitten more than we can chew, that we're way over our heads and this will be a disaster. I worry that even with all of our combined employment experience, it won't be enough and we'll fail. Not to mention, we're investing so much money.

Granted, it helps that we're dividing everything by five, even so, it's a lot. A lot to change, a lot to fix and upgrade before we open. At the same time, I know in my heart we can do it.

Still standing next to my car, I take a few deep breaths and try to center myself. *I've got this.*

I enter the main house and go around giving (and getting) hugs and kisses on the cheek and I instantly start to feel better. As we gather around the kitchen island, Leyla passes around *croquetas* and *pastelitos*, and even though I just had a huge breakfast, I can't help myself; these smell amazing. I also grab someone's *café con leche* and take a few gulps while we catch up. People are eating, talking and laughing. Yep, now we're ready to roll.

Carlos, Leyla's new old boyfriend and the student dean at Sunny Beach university, is also here. They just reconnected after ten years apart and are having a second chance romance. *Umm, it's like a trope in a romance book.* After a recent episode where we had a theft on the property, he's been stopping by more. He's protective of her, of us. It's kind of nice that he's around.

A few minutes later, I stand up and help Christy distribute papers around.

Good thing at least one of us loves making lists. One of them has our current budget on it. I glance at the number on the bottom and I stop walking, almost slamming into her. It's not looking good. I thought 500K was more than reasonable to fix a kitchen and some bathrooms, but at this rate we're going to burn it all out. *Damn.* "You guys, how can we be so over budget this early in the process?" I ask, looking around at my friends.

"We had to pay for the house's second mortgage and reimburse that guy after his fancy cordless puncher was stolen from here," Cristina says. "Not to mention that guy that used the wrong paint on the guest house and had to re-do it, remember?"

We collectively groan. Painting the guest house was our first little project, but that guy charged us twice for *his* mistake. Too bad we didn't notice until it was too late. To top it off, we can't seem to find a project manager that we can all agree on.

I know we just started and these things take time, but I feel that things are happening at an alarmingly slow pace. Not to mention, rainy season, AKA hurricane season is coming. Even with my limited knowledge of construction, I'm pretty sure that a storm is going to slow or even stop construction.

On the other hand, If I have to talk to every single contractor in Miami to get this project done, so be it.

Our first extensive project is making this kitchen bigger and industrial-ish. It needs to handle volume. We'll also be adding bathrooms in all the rooms that don't have one. The last thing is the pool and gardening.

I have to admit, we got lucky that the property was already zoned for business. We had a loan and a location ready to go in the north of Florida, but when Leyla and Carlos reconnected, we changed the location and came home. Some of us believe that for that alone, this change was the right move. Some of us, *not so much.*

When it's all said and done, this house will be a twelve-room, Mediterranean inspired, bed-and-breakfast in the City of Coral Gables. There's an enormous living room that will double as a check-in space. On the back we have a one-bedroom, one-bath guest house, which will serve as our office. There's also a pool and a very pleasant garden with an immense oak tree and some gorgeous red Royal Poinciana trees. With a little love and pruning, they're going to look awesome. It's been more work than we expected, but I know once we get going it'll be amazing. We just have to push through it.

Unfortunately, we were caught completely unaware of how many permits we needed in order to make this project happen. The city is notorious for being strict. Building permits are required for most types of construction work within the City of Coral Gables.

Have I mentioned we're hospitality industry pros that know nothing about construction or permits? *Yep, that's us.*

Since we're over budget and apparently permits and licenses requirements are now raining down the ceiling... not to mention I really don't want us to get scammed, we need help. *Professional* help.

Thankfully, my brother, Ben, came to the rescue by volunteering his best friend to help us. They met in elementary school and have been inseparable ever since.

The best friend is an architect and co-owner of an excellent local-family business. His family is friends with mine and I know he won't scam us. Not to mention, he's only charging us for materials. He brought his usual fee way down, allegedly. I have to double check this. I wouldn't want to be indebted to the guy for eternity.

The truth is, while I might dislike the guy, and we spent our childhood arguing, I know he comes from a good family, the company is great and for now, that's enough.

he five of us are talking animatedly when there's a knock on the door. Carlos offers to get it and the rest of us wait. It's only a few seconds before I see Carlos walk into the kitchen with the newcomer not far behind. *Alejandro.*

Here we go.

CHAPTER 2:
JULIE

Big chocolate eyes sweep the space quickly, then focus on me. I don't miss the way his jaw ticks a couple of times before we lock eyes.

When I look at him, it takes my breath away. Which is crazy, because I'm supposed to hate the guy.

He's wearing a black sports coat, a gray shirt and dark denim jeans. I hate to admit, he *still* has a nice face. His hair is short and swept back behind the ears, but a little longer through the top. The black curls, casually fingers-combed off his forehead, look effortless. Full lips are framed by a strong jaw.

Full disclosure, teenage me might or might not have had a small tiny crush on my brother's best friend. *Okay. Fine. A big crush.* But then he spoke and those feelings quickly evaporated. Every. Single. Time.

"*Buenos días señoritas.*" He says, with a little wave. My friends say good morning in unison and his face breaks into a slow grin. His smile is genuine. Maybe even a little nice if I'm being honest, not that I would tell that to his face, but still, he's kind of pretty, in an Oscar Isaac kind of way.

I watch Alejandro as he goes around shaking hands. He nods at each of my friends as they introduce themselves.

He glances at me as he's coming my way, but leaves me for last. When he finally arrives at my side, instead of a handshake, I get a kiss on the cheek. "Wait, have we met before?" He teases. He's standing next to me, a twinkle in his eye.

"I think we have." I throw back. "Let me see if I remember. You're an architect. Your family is awesome. You're my brother's insufferable best friend. You're friendly, extroverted, and you have that *rico suave* effect."

His hand is still resting on my waist and I'm rooted on the spot. "*Rico suave* effect? What does that even mean?" His eyebrows dip in the middle in amusement, but he laughs. "Julieta. Nice to see you. It's been a long time."

"It's Julie now. Nice to see you too. Alex."

"Still calling you Julieta."

When I mouth, "still a dick," he grins.

Someone clears their throat and we both turn and look at the group. They're all looking at us. *Already then.* I take a step out of his embrace.

He winks at me and faces the group. "Okay then. I'm Alejandro Peña, but please call me Alex. I am an architect; a good one. I also my own construction firm and I will take care of you guys. Contrary to her opinion, I do not have a *rico suave* effect, but I am in fact, her brother's best friend and he volunteered me for this."

He points at me when he says *brother*, and I raise an eyebrow and turn to him. "He volunteered you? Did you not agree to volunteer for this?"

Alex turns to me. "That is irrelevant. He said to come, so I came. That's how our friendship works." He turns back to my friends and starts walking. "Now, who's the ringleader of this enterprise? *La jefa?*" he asks as he distributes business cards. *The boss?* We all look at each other. We're equal partners and we vote on things. It's a very democratic process.

He glances around the room. "Okaaay, can anyone run me through what you guys have been doing?" He asks as he reaches my side again. He pulls a legal-size notepad and pen out of a laptop bag, then he grabs a stool and gets ready to write on the kitchen island.

It takes well over an hour to tell him everything. An hour talking with us, where all he's done is, pretty much, either ask questions or tell us what *he* would have done instead. This is not my brother's best friend Alex. This is Alejandro, the Architect. *He's an ass.*

Can I kill him? I mouth to Leyla. I motion stabbing with my hands. She mouths *no* and tries not to smile. For the record, he's the only person in the world that can drive me this crazy and I don't even know why.

"Cristina, since you made these wonderful excel sheets, you can be in charge of accounting," Alex is saying.

She's shaking her head. "You can call me Christy. Also, I would rather not be the designated accountant. I don't even like math."

"You'll learn. These excel sheets are great and you guys need a numbers person. Do any of you know an accountant?" Alex looks around the group.

Leyla raises her hand. "My brother's an accountant."

"Perfect. Call him over. We can have him teach Christy the basics." Looking at her again, he says, "You can do the monthly accounting and at the end of the year, hand it over to him and he'll take care of taxes. Tell him it'll be his new side gig." He pauses when he notices her discomfort. "Look, when you guys get going, you can hire someone, okay?" She nods. She doesn't look thrilled but he's right, her excel sheets are super detailed and she's going to do an amazing job.

He looks across the room. "*Señoritas*, from now on, nothing gets bought without consulting Christy, me, and the budget. If you buy something, please keep the receipt. We all agreed?" Everyone nods. "I'll come back tomorrow. We'll go around the house room by room and you guys can tell me what you want. We'll make a list, then in a few days I'll bring some samples or pictures, then I'll buy what we need, get a crew and we'll get started. Questions?"

All of us raise our hands. It takes another hour for him to answer our five-hundred questions.

Finally, he's done. Alex says goodbye to my friends one by one, but lingers a bit with Carlos. After a few minutes of conversation, he walks my way. "Miss Vargas, walk me out?" I nod.

We arrive at his car, but I'm too tired to stand, so I lean on it and wait. I watch as he opens the passenger door, throws in the laptop bag, closes the door and starts pacing in front of me. His lips are pressed together and his arms crossed. I wonder if he's running numbers on his head and just realized what a mistake, he made agreeing to this. I can't help but tap my hands on the side of my thighs and wait.

Finally, I clear my throat. "What are you thinking?" I ask tentatively.

"I'm making a list in my head of the million things I have to do to save your ass." I roll my eyes. He looks at me from top to bottom. "Unrelated, but why do you have a long sleeve shirt, nice pants and high heels in a construction zone?"

"I came straight from work."

He goes back to pacing, slower this time, and glances my way. "You came from work? Where are you working?"

"A hotel in South Beach."

"*Why* are you working?"

"Because I need to work."

"I thought this was your job now."

"You ask a lot of questions."

"I'm a curious guy."

I shake my head. "This will be my job, but not quite yet. I have bills to pay, money to save, contractors to boss around... and now, insufferable architects to annoy. But, yes, eventually that's the plan."

He gives me a lopsided grin. "Well, I hate to burst your bubble, but you're the insufferable one. The only difference is, I'm pretty and you're not."

I gasp. "Oh, my god. Are you listening to yourself?" At this, he throws his head back and laughs. A full-on belly laugh. I shake my head.

He stops pacing and stands in front of me. "I'm kidding. I'm kidding. You know you're beautiful." Turning more serious, he says, "Also, I have news for you. Those are not appropriate for a construction zone."

"Are you kidding me? You're talking to me about inappropriate clothing? What about when you wore that Hawaiian shirt with faces on it?" I pause. "Flowers *and* faces on it? Or, or that one piece romper you and my brother wore, with the pink flamingos on it?"

"Oh my god. That's just me and your brother being idiots at a party. Hang on, you were away. How can you possibly know about that?"

"Yeah, there's this thing called Facebook."

"First of all, what are you? Sixty? Second, are you honestly stalking my Facebook?" he pauses. "Please tell me you're not basing your opinion of me on my ridiculous Facebook feed." *I will never confirm or deny this.*

"Why are you complaining? You're a rich, handsome guy living in Miami with like 20,000 followers and by the way, it's insane that you know that many people." He raises an eyebrow and I keep going. "Actually, I heard from my mom that your mom is complaining that you're single. I'm going to go out on a limb here and guess the problem is that single women meet you, they may or may not sleep with you, but then when they stalk your Facebook feed, they see you with my brother and that's when they realize that you're a man-child who dresses horribly at parties and then they dump you."

"Oh my god. Stop talking. That sounds horrible when you say it."

The fuck? "Don't tell me to stop talking! You're not the boss of me!"

"Are you done? First, who said I'm single? Second, just because I have fun and I sometimes let your brother pick out our clothes, doesn't mean that that's how I dress in real life. And if a woman meets me at a party and judges me solely on the clothes that I'm wearing and not my value as a person, then clearly, I'm better off.

Out of everything he just said, the only thing that sticks out is: *he's not single?*

Sometimes, I have an image in my mind, a cartoon version of myself. It's teenage me. Teenage me falls flat on her face on a couch.

I clear my throat. "If they're ridiculous, why do you post them?"

"It's social media, it's just for fun. I think you're forgetting that we have a family business. A joke or a fun post here or there makes me relatable. And you're judging me on that? How is that fair? I saw news articles about your hotel staff and the strike when you were in Spain. Do I think of you as an HR tyrant? No. I don't, because I know the real you and–"

"Are you serious? There's a strike every other week over there!"

"Precisely my point. Next time you want to know something about me, call me."

"Yes, Mr. Peña. Anything else?"

"Wait, do you have my number?" I shake my head. *"Dame para aca." Give me,* he says and motions to my phone. He glances at me as he inputs numbers on the keypad. I stay quiet.

We're getting digits? This is an interesting turn of events. *He's so hot.* Teenage me is saying as she gets up from the couch. *Actually,* it's more like she's running around and screaming at the top of her lungs. *Oh Jesus. I'm losing my mind.*

As my cell rings, I clear my mind of any thoughts related to him. *Focus.*

"I have to go. *Cualquier cosa, me llamas.* A million things to do if we want to get this thing off the ground." *If anything, call me,* he says.

Teenage me sits down and starts compiling a list of things she wants to ask when she calls him. I don't think she realized this is *not* actually happening.

"I'm sure you can manage," I say.

"Oh, trust me. I can." He takes a step forward and gives me a kiss on the cheek, but lingers for a few seconds. "Bye Julieta."

Teen me wants to swoon like a *telenovela* actress. *Oh boy.*

"Still Julie." I tease. He grins.

I watch as he gets in his car, then I walk back to the house. When I get back in, my friends stop talking. I wait.

After a second, they all start throwing questions at me.... At the same time. "Who is that guy?" asks one, "how do you know him?" "he's hot," "is he single?" Carlos looks at us in amusement.

"Okay. Okay." They all stop talking. "That guy is my brother's best friend. We kind of hated each other growing up. He's always been so... so... smug. I've known him my whole life and I have no idea if he's single. He hinted he wasn't but he probably is, because he's a man-child who wears ridiculous outfits at parties, just for fun. And yes, he's very hot."

Leyla clears her throat. "Can I just say this is the first time I've heard you rant so much about a guy? Does anybody else agree with me?" They all raise their hands. "Anything we should know about? Anything happening there?"

"We literally just moved back home. Can you guys at least wait five seconds? Besides there's nothing happening there and there never will be."

"Never say never," Leyla says and glances at Carlos. "*I* used to say that and now, I'm back home *and* back with Carlos, after ten years! Isn't it crazy?" He smiles sweetly at her. We all look at them. I almost expect us to say, *awwww*, in unison. Thankfully, we don't.

"Leyla, we're all happy for you guys. Really, we are. But this is not the same. He and I met as kids. He's my brother's best friend. We never had anything. This wasn't a thing."

"Did anyone else get a vibe about them?" Again, they all raise their hand. Teenage me fist bumps the air, while she screams "*yes!*"

I need to get a hold of teenage me quickly. Otherwise, she might make me do something really, really stupid. Like kiss him, or worse, sleep with the guy.

CHAPTER 3:
ALEX

I arrive at the office after lunch and immediately go into research mode. After a few hours, I make a list with a hundred items and at least two hundred sub-lists of things that we need. *Fuck this list.*

I drop the list and instead start drawing. I love drawing. The kitchen needs to grow a little and I sketch some ideas and potential layouts. For me, drawing is both a creative and relaxing exercise, so I might as well get started. I want to make sure the kitchen is functional, sustainable and beautiful.

The only reason I'm going through this much trouble is because of my best friend. Because the truth is, his sister gets under my skin in a way I can't even explain. She drives me bat crazy in more ways than one. *She always has.* I'm going to have to find a way to work around her if I want to keep both my sanity and my friendship intact.

My phone rings. *Speak of the devil.* "Hey," my best friend Ben says.

"*Dime*," I reply.

"How did it go?"

I scoff. "Do you really want to know?"

"That bad?

"*Mátame.*" *Kill me now*, I tell him. "We're probably going to spend the next ten years trying to get permits from the city, and that just so that we can start building, but what do I know?" I pause. "Have I mentioned that it's a historic house and now I have like two hundred things that we need to bring up to code?"

"O-kay. I hope that was a joke," he says, concern laced in his voice.

I sigh. "It was. You don't have to worry about it. I'm taking care of it. It'll be done. My team is being assembled as we speak."

"Thanks man. She's my sister and I want to make sure nobody's going to take advantage of her. They got charged twice for paint. I know that if you're there, everything is okay. I really appreciate you doing this for me."

"You forgot to mention that your sister's still a pain in the ass."

I can hear him sigh. I can almost picture him dropping and shaking his head as he does. "Don't start with that. She needs help. Just ignore her. Help her but at the same time, ignore her."

"Help her but ignore her? Sure, that makes total sense." I repeat, almost to myself.

"Alex, we're adults now and I don't want to be in the middle of you two. I'll have to choose you and my family will disown me." He pauses. "Should I talk to her? Do you want me to have my mom talk to her?"

"Nah. I got it. I'm doing research on permits and materials and a bunch of other things. I've already started a couple of sketches for the kitchen, and I have an idea for a cool tile for the backsplash. I'll keep you posted if there's any problems."

"Awesome. I knew I could count on you to help my little sister. Are we still on for Friday?"

"Yeah, sure. I'll see you Friday."

As I hang up the phone, I consider my options. I could back away and disappoint my best friend. Not to mention, it seems that she really needs my help. Option b, stay and work with her, possibly argue about everything, high chance of us killing each other.

Why do I have a feeling my friendship might not *in fact survive this intact?*

***

I went to bed later than usual, drawing and researching. While I was at the house, I took some pictures of the house and I'm already inspired. The house is tucked away in a dead-end street, behind some lush tree and looks amazing from the outside.

I want to give them a comfortable home feeling that at the same time will be an oasis for guests. I noticed no elevators, but we'll make sure that least one room is ADA compliant. All the rooms will be comfortable and beautiful.

The next day, I get up early. I'm exhausted, but by seven am I'm on site, walking around the grounds and making notes.

I've brought Mikaela, my assistant, who's also taking notes. Mikaela is a young architect but super sharp and with great instincts. She'll help me coordinate, not to mention help keep the crazy budget in check. She'll also provide general support. I'm confident that in a few years, with experience, she's going to be an amazing architect.

Like yesterday, I'm able to get into the property with no issues. Stealing from construction sites is a thing. It occurs to me that the first order of business should be to secure this site.

The girls *finally* start arriving by 8am. "Good morning, *señoritas*."

When they all say, "Good morning," in unison, followed by giggles, I grin.

I follow them inside and to the kitchen, where one of them sets down food on a counter, another sets down coffee. By the smell of it, it's Cuban coffee. Somebody hands me one and I happily accept. Then they start eating and talking.

While the girls eat, Mikaela answers calls in another room. I look around the kitchen, take some pictures, and open a few drawers and doors. One of them leads to what might have been a storage or even a laundry room at some point. I can see some pipes. I'm thinking, if we demolish that old storage room I just found, I can make the kitchen bigger.

I stand nearby, make some notes about the kitchen, sip my coffee and watch them. There's at least three conversations going on at the same time. They look happy and comfortable together and for a second, I wonder if they forgot I'm here.

Leyla and Maria are engrossed in a conversation. I have no idea about what. Alma is talking to her cellphone. When she turns it to me and waves, I grin and wave back. She's going to be a great marketing director. Apparently, she's been documenting the process of their little venture on social media. I have to admit, it's a great idea. By the time they open, they'll have more than a few eager fans invested in it and willing to try it out... or at the very least, willing to come out and meet five beautiful women.

Cristina looks at a spreadsheet, glances at the laptop, briefly jumps into Leyla and Maria's conversations and eats. Basically, she's multitasking. How the heck is she able to do all that, I haven't the slightest idea.

Then there's her. My teen nemesis. Actually, no, not really, but I never had a nemesis, and that's a cool word. *Or maybe not.*

Once again, Julieta's wearing a suit. This time, however, it's a skirt suit. When she stands up and starts walking, I can't help notice that her legs go on for miles. When she catches me looking at her, she gives me a glance over, then disappears down the hall. She returns a short while later without her suit jacket and places it on top of the counter, then goes back to her friends.

Julieta has dark brown hair that falls mid-back in soft waves. She's wearing a white sleeveless shirt and I fixate on her arms because, for some crazy reason, her skin seems to be glowing. *What the actual fuck?* I shake my head. At the same time, I can't help wondering what she's thinking because every few seconds, her big brown eyes are directed at me. I can't stop looking at her and I don't even know why.

After a few minutes, she stalks my way and stands next to me. She folds her arms and I wait. "Why are you being creepy?" She says in a low voice as we watch her friends.

It takes sheer force of nature not to look at her and keep my eyes forward. "I'm being creepy? What about you? Glancing at me every five seconds like a stalker. You're the one being creepy."

"You started it. *Creep.*" She fires back at me.

Unable to hold it any longer, I turn to her. "Oh my God, woman. Is there anything you won't argue about? You've been like this since we were kids. Is this why you're single?" Her mouth falls open and she turns to me. Her nostrils flare and she's giving me a hostile glare but for some reason, her angry expression is cute. "Yes, I know that you're single. Our moms talk, remember?"

She looks appalled. "I argue with you because you drive me crazy!" she blurts.

The revelation catches me off-guard. I thought she hated me. Well, as long as we're being honest. "Newsflash, you drive me crazy too! You are too beautiful, too perfect, too... out of reach–" I stop myself. Maybe I don't need to be *that* honest.

When I stop, she too stops, seemingly taken aback. The confusion in her eyes disappears as quickly as it came.

The girls have stopped talking and are all looking at us. *Shit.* I need to stop arguing with this woman. When I turn to her friends, she turns too. "*Estúpido.*" *Idiot.* She says to my ear before she walks away. After a few seconds, the hum of conversation returns.

Crap. Less than five seconds into a conversation with her and I lose it. *This is not good.* We're barely on the second day. I need to put a lid on this unexpected crazy attraction to my best friend's little sister, and I need to do it fast.

After a few minutes, I clear my throat loudly, and they all look at me. When I ask, "Are you guys ready?" They all get up.

Like an orchestra, they move in unison. In a few minutes, they've finished eating, cleaned up the space and seem ready to go.

As we walk around the property, going room by room, I make notes of the cool features of the house, like the dark wood and exposed beams. Immediately, ideas start coming. I'm taking pictures and making notes of things I'd like to highlight. To start with, I'm thinking a few large windows throughout the house to bring more natural light.

As we walk, I notice that Julieta has a huge coffee thermos with her. *Is this how she's still up? With ridiculous amounts of caffeine?*

We're in the last room and I can't help but ask about it. "Nice thermos. What happened? You couldn't find a bigger one?" I tease. "Didn't I just see you drinking Cuban coffee? What are you doing with that thing?" The second the words leave my mouth, I regret them. *Why the hell can't I just leave her alone?*

CHAPTER 4:
ALEX

"Bite me, Alex." Mad at me. Of course, she is.

"Bite you?" I repeat. I consider my opinions.

All the options on my short list mostly end up with her punching me, her four friends punching me, her brother punching me, or worse, somebody stabbing me with a fork. *A fork?* Frankly, it's a disturbing mental picture, *yet* I don't seem to care.

I gently grab her elbow. I slow my pace as we wait for the rest of the group to pass and move to the next room. Mikaela is asking too many questions for the girls to notice us.

Julie narrows her eyes at me and waits. At least I think she's waiting, but I never know with her. "I think you forgot who you're talking to," I say. I have no problem embarrassing her or myself to make a point and she knows this... or should. I get closer to her, "don't tempt me, woman."

She raises her chin but says nothing. I would kill to know what she's thinking.

I realize I'm still holding on to her elbow and I let go. She stays in place *despite* me letting her go. "I dare you to bite me," she drawls.

Uh oh. I did not expect this. Once again, I consider my options. *To bite or not to bite.* Based on her flushed face? I think there's a high probability that she's going to stab me with a fork.

I glance at her mouth; she glances at mine and the room spins. *What the fuck do I do now?*

After a couple of seconds, she walks away from me.

I watch her walk away then I follow her. I'm pretty sure her brother will not take it lightly if I bite her. Even less *where* I want to bite her. I'm going to have to find a way to keep my distance from her.

Once back in the kitchen, it occurs to me that I need to remind all of them to wear appropriate construction attire. This is as good a time as any to do it.

"Ladies, gather around." I wait for them to surround me. "This is a construction zone. I don't want to see anybody in high heels. Starting today, closed-toe shoes or boots. No *chancletas* either." This causes a couple of them to chuckle. "Ah, so you guys have shown up here in *chancletas*?"

"Maybe?" Leyla says.

"Ladies, I saw the closet upstairs. It has like ninety-five pairs of sandals and flip-flops. Do I even want to know why you guys have ninety-five pairs of *chancletas*? At a construction zone?"

"*Que exagerado.* It is not ninety-five pairs," Alma says. "There's five of us here. Each has a few pairs of shoes for emergencies. Do the math."

She thinks I'm exaggerating. *Sure.* "Fine, it's not ninety-five, it's twenty-five." Alma rolls her eyes and Julie shakes her head. "These things can be used as weapons." At this, a couple of them laugh. "Come on, like your mom didn't fling a *chancleta* your way?" I pause while they giggle. "Still. Please guys, no more *chanclas* to the construction zone." I look at them. "Also, I'm shutting the lights here soon. We'll spend this week setting up the guest house but I need you guys to be ready to move. Don't forget your twenty-five pairs of shoes and any other personal things." They all groan in unison.

"You're so bossy. Why didn't Ben warn me that you were a dictator?" Julie says. I consider: *to argue or not to argue?*

I'm serious when I say, "I'm not a dictator, but we have to keep this site safe for you guys and for my crew. I have a job to do. Part of that is making sure that none of you guys fall on your beautiful faces and break your necks, because that would be painful... not to mention, costly."

Thankfully, they don't argue with my logic. "Now, in the next few days, my guys will start arriving. Please be nice to them. If you have a problem, please come to me or to Mikaela and we'll handle it. Comment sexual in nature are not tolerated. Neither by them nor by you guys towards them, but please let me know if any of the guys make you feel uncomfortable. Any questions?" After I answer a few questions, the girls move on to other things.

I start gathering my things. I need to get out of here.

"Okay guys." I look up and look at Alma. "I have a good feeling about this. It's going to be awesome. Can I get a go-team?" She looks around, then starts clapping. "Come on, guys! *Dale!*"

Julie appears next to me. "Is she always like this?" I ask.

"How? Loud, cheerful and positive? Yes, Yes and Yes."

Okay then. Following Alma's lead, we all put our hands in the middle of a circle. When I notice Julie's right behind me, I turn around, switch hands and face her. She looks at me but says nothing. When I put my hand on top of hers, her cheeks flush. Suddenly, my palm is sweaty and tingly. *What is happening?*

I clear my throat, but I keep my eyes on her.

I can barely hear Alma. "Come on, guys! On three. One... two... three..." we all scream,"Goooo team!"

The girls chuckle and I can't help but smile at their enthusiasm. At the same time, I'm having a hard time concentrating. All I seem to be aware of is the beautiful woman in front of me.

I'm forced to look away when Julie breaks contact and the circle dissolves.

After a few more minutes of conversation, I grab my things and start saying goodbye to the team. I tell Mikaela to meet me in the office, then I look for my nemesis.

"Walk me out. I need to talk to you." I say to Julie. She quietly follows me outside.

"What do you have in that bag?" she asks as we approach my car.

"Why? Do you want to see?" She nods and I hand it over.

She rests in my car as she pokes at my bag and glances at me every few seconds.

"A sketchbook, a tablet, a laptop, a camera, a tape measure," she glances at me, "fifty pens and pencils. Do you need to have that many pencils?"

"O-kay, enough of that. Can I have that back, please?" I grab the bag and throw it in the passenger seat then stand in front of her. "Look. I'm sorry about earlier. The truth is, I can't seem to control myself when I'm around you. I'm trying to be a gentleman, but you're driving me crazy."

"You're the one driving *me* crazy."

"Then don't look at me like that."

"Like what?" She asks, eyes wide.

"Like you look at me... I mean–".

"Oh my god. I can't with you. You're so confusing sometimes. Make up your mind. Do you hate me or not?"

"I don't hate you," I blurt. I definitely don't want her to think that I hate her, but how do I even explain what I'm feeling when I don't even know?

"Are you confused? Are you suffering from andropause?"

Andropause? I mouth. She shrugs. "I'm not confused, or maybe I am. I don't know. I– Your brother and I have a hand-off policy" I announce.

"A what?"

"Bro code. No matter how attractive or cool a girl is, sisters are off limits. In middle school we kind of promised each other not to date our sisters."

"Is this a joke?" I nod. "Have I landed in medieval times?" she asks.

"Julie–"

"How do I even respond to that?"

"I don't know, it's just weird, you know? He's my best friend... you're his sister."

"Don't make it weird. It's not his business."

"I think he would disagree with that. He's protective of you, as any big brother should be."

She pauses. Her hand on her forehead for a few seconds while she thinks. "Okay. So, what are you telling me?"

"Look, I had a long night and I'm tired and cranky, but I'm apologizing for my behavior. It won't happen again. We're going to spend a lot of time together. This project will take a year, possibly more once rainy season starts, and I don't want to make things weird between us. I want you to know that I will be respectful and I'll keep my distance. Okay?"

She produces an exasperated sigh. "Question, do *I* have a say in this?"

"A say in what? On whether or not I keep my distance? Do you not want me to keep my distance?" Something like hope springs in me. Which is weird because I never thought about her like *that* until now.

This insane attraction to her is new and well, insane. Growing up, we just argued a lot. She went off to college a couple of years after Ben and I. Afterwards, I went on to do my architecture masters. By the time I came home, we spent very little time together and then she was gone.

She's quiet. "I... I don't know."

"Look, I know that when we were teenagers, I was a jerk. I know that I was a pain in the ass and we drove each other crazy, but this is different. Your brother is like a brother to me. That relationship means the world to me. I promised him I would help you. I told him not to worry. I don't think this–" I move my hand between us, "is the kind of help he had in mind for his little sister."

"Okay. Okay." She pauses. "Are you single?"

"Julieta–"

"Just answer the question!"

I pause before telling her, then decide it's better to be honest. "Yes. I'm single."

"For the record, I'm single too, *but* right now, I really need Alejandro the architect, so we're not going to argue about this because I really, really need your help. Maybe when this is over... we can have a cup of coffee and... talk?"

"I'm sorry, but I'm just not interested in messing up my friendship with your brother by going there with you. Julie, all we did was fight. We're still fighting. It would never work. You get that right?"

She nods. She seems deflated but doesn't argue. I guess she agrees with me.

Oddly enough, half of me expected her to argue, the other half really *wanted* her to argue with me and tell me I'm wrong. That this *could* work.

But she doesn't.

After a few seconds, she says goodbye and walks away.

CHAPTER 5:
JULIE

It's been three months. Three. Long. Months. Since I got shot down. In the words of teenage me: I was publicly demolished, rejected, destroyed. *She's very dramatic.*

I have to admit that the remodeling is coming along fantastically. He really is very good at his job.

Before he started, he made sure we were ready to move the base of operations to the guest house. We did not want to spend a lot of money on it, but it got a fresh coat of paint (twice) and new impact windows. The main room has high-ish ceilings and several windows that let a lot of natural light in.

Luckily, he helped us get high-end appliances at a discount for the small open-plan kitchen and it looks amazing. We also added a single couch along a wall and instead of a dining table, we got a long table. It's made of dark solid wood and it doubles as a conference table, daily workspace and it seats ten, so we all fit comfortably. Honestly, the whole thing looks like a We Work space.

In the lone room, we added a bunk bed and a desk. It could be used to rest or for private work.

Meanwhile, in the main house's kitchen, he demolished an old storage room and expanded it several feet. We also have new electrical work, new floors, more counter space, and cabinets. The new countertops have a very cool backsplash that he handpicked for us. The giant, shining, bronze hood will look great over the brand-new stove. It already looks amazing, and it's not even done. The last thing will be appliances and the kitchen will be finished.

The biggest project is the heating, ventilation and air conditioning system which apparently, it's so old, it's prehistoric. After that, work will start in different bathrooms. Although the backyard will be last, I can't wait to see the Royal Poinciana trees pruned and flowering.

I'm here every day... and so is he. Every. Single. Day. Doesn't he have a job somewhere? Shouldn't he be in his office or helping other clients? At the same time, I feel a weird tension building between us. Sometimes, I can't tell if he hates me or he wants me.

What's worse, these days he barely talks to me. I watch him as he talks with my friends daily, but besides small comments about the project or the team meetings, he barely engages with me. I never thought I'd say this, but I really, really want to argue with the guy.

Today, again, he barely talked to me at the team meeting. Since it ended, he's been talking with Cristy about the budget. All of them are at the table, while I keep glancing at him from the open kitchen.

Fifteen-year-old me wonders if he'll notice me if I throw my huge thermos his way. Maybe hit him on the head with it? Unexpectedly, he glances at me and comes towards me. *Oh, okay.* No thermo throwing needed. Thank God, because my aim sucks.

"Julieta," he says from a few feet away.

I'm about to answer when I spot a gigantic spider and scream. I can't help it. I just hate spiders. While I shake like a crazy person and scream bloody murder, he rushes to me then hugs me. "Julie, Julie. Look at me, it's okay, it's just a tiny spider. You're okay babe."

I look up to see my friends rushing towards us too. Leyla and Cristina run back out again, screaming. Alma and Maria run in and stomp around the floor until they finally kill it. *I think.* If I wasn't so freaked out, I would probably laugh at the craziness.

Alejandro's holding me but he's looking at them and telling them to calm down. After a few minutes, I tell my friends that I'm okay and they all return to our huge table.

Unexpectedly, he grabs my hand and leads me away. I find myself standing in the middle of the bedroom. He quickly scans me, but before I can say anything, he hugs me again. I can feel him exhale.

Teenage me freezes. *He hugged me. He hugged me.*

After a few seconds, I wrap my arms around his waist. When my head touches his shirt, I can't help but smell him. He smells nice. *Fresh.* Like a fresh pile of laundry that I want to run and dive into. Teenage me can't even explain it, it's exhilarating. I take another big whiff, even louder. While he chuckles, teenage me is screaming. *Oh my god. Eekkk!* I think she might have a heart attack.

"Julie."

"How did you know—"

"It's a construction and you're afraid of spiders," he says softly to my ear and holds me gently.

I look up at him. His brow is furrowed. "Wow. I can't believe you remember that." I let my face fall again and snuggle into the crook of his neck.

"I remember everything about you." He says softly before he wraps his hands around my back. They move up and down slowly. "*Julieta.*" He's saying to my ear in a low voice. "Bro code."

"Again with that? First of all, I have nothing to do with your bro code." A wild thought crosses my mind. "Second, since we've already established that we're both single, hypothetically speaking, how do you feel about –"

His eyes are wide, and he gently covers my mouth with his thumb. "Please don't finish that sentence." He glances at my mouth and his thumb moves over my lower lip. When it bounces, he seems enthralled with my lips. "You can't say shit to me like that. Please don't say shit like that," he says after a few seconds, his voice slow, deeper.

I move his hand. "But I can, and I did. We're grown-ups... consenting adults. Have you ever thought we could have some... fun?"

"We've talked about this. It will never work. We would kill each other. Also, let me remind you, this is not the kind of help your brother wanted me to offer you." I hug his waist and snuggle in again. "Full disclosure?" He asks. I nod. "I've thought about it every day for three months."

At this latest revelation, teenage me wants to scream: *Thank you for telling me!* While she runs around the room.

I clear my throat. "What's stopping you?"

"*Tu hermano me va a matar.*" *Your brother is going to kill me,* he says to my ear.

"Who cares what he thinks?"

"I care. He's like my brother."

"But I'm not your sister. We could have some fun." We're still holding on to each other. I take a step back and glance at his mouth. It's only inches away. *Inches.*

"Julieta... don't get in the kitchen if you can't handle the heat. I'm already hanging on by a thread." He lowers his face closer to mine, but then stops abruptly and takes a step away from me.

At that second, I hear my mom's voice and I let go of Alex.

We dash back to the living area just as my mom and brother enter the guest house.

CHAPTER 6:
JULIE

Mom says hello to my friends as she's making her way over to me. "Are you being nice to Alejandro?" she asks as she reaches me. She gives me a hug and a kiss and I hug her back. Walking over to him, she gives him a side hug, which he happily reciprocates.

Wait, what? "What!? Shouldn't you be asking him if he's being nice to me?"

"Hola *Doña*. Tan elegante como siempre." She blushes at his *always so elegant* comment. He winks at me.

I narrow my eyes at him. The fucking nerve.

"You were always so good. Such a good kid." Mom gushes as she places a hand gently on his cheek. "You're almost like a son to us. I know your parents are very proud of you and so are we. I know my daughter and her friends are in great hands with you."

Is she serious? I roll my eyes. I can't decide if she's in love with him or wants to have *him* as her kid. Also, ew. That's a disturbing mental picture.

"*No le digas eso. Se le va a subir a la cabeza.*" It'll go to his head, I tell her.

He's shaking his head. "*¿Estás celosa Julieta?*"

"It's Julie. *Dickhead.*"

"Julieta Maria!"

"*Él empezó.*" I point at him with my hand. *He started it*; I pout. "*Mami,* he's annoying."

Teenage me wonders if we can justify ourselves by saying something like *mami, it's his gorgeous face with the full lips and his fingers-combed hair. Also, the fresh laundry smell. And he's so smart. I just can't help it.* Ummm what would *he* say?

Ben watches the interaction from a few feet away, his eyes narrowed.

Before I can say anything, my friends call my mom over. We walk out while they lead an impromptu tour around the house. Ben follows. I look at Leyla and mouth *thank you.*

Alex and I follow behind. "*¿Estás celosa?*" He repeats in a low voice next to me.

"Jealous? Of you? First of all, why would I be jealous? That's *my* mom. Second, you have your own mom. Leave mine alone."

"I don't know. You look a little ticked off," he says grinning. "I'm not and if I were, it's because you drive me crazy."

"Likewise, Julieta," he says as we walk. We glance at each other a few times, but neither of us says anything else.

We follow the group around the house and finally, end up back in the guest house. Alex and I are still next to each other. I realize now that he never left my side.

I notice Ben is looking at us. A weird expression on his face. Walking over, he asks, "Is everything okay?" "Yes. Everything is great." I reply.

"Do you guys need help around here? Do you need an extra set of hands?"

Why is he asking now? Almost eight months later.

"That's not necessary, I have my crew and we're taking care of it. We're good bro, but I'll keep it in mind," Alex says.

"Okay. Cool." Ben replies, his hands in his pockets. His eyes are volleyballing between us. "Anything I should know about?"

"What do you want to know about?" I ask at the same time Alex asks, "Like?"

Ben says "Okay then." I half expect him to say something else, but he drops it. After a while, Mom, Ben, and Alex leave together.

Why do I have a feeling my big brother might have a bone to pick with me?

***

Every Sunday, we have lunch with Ben. I wake up on Sunday and go food shopping with my mom, then we get cooking.

It's almost the middle of the day by the time he shows up.

"The bed-and-breakfast is looking nice," Ben says when we sit down to eat. "Dad would be very proud of you."

At the mention of our dad, I'm silent for a few seconds. "Thank you." Our dad passed away a few years ago. I'm grateful that I came home and had a chance to say goodbye. It's one of the reasons why I came back home. I didn't want to miss a chance to spend time with my mom.

"Alex is doing a great job..." Ben's saying.

Now what? Do I agree or disagree with my brother? I clear my throat. "He is."

"Anything I should know about?"

I look up from my plate. "What do you want to know?"

He drops his fork and the clattering startles me. "Do you think I'm stupid? Are you sleeping with Alex?" he asks point blank.

"You're way out of line and even if I were, it's none of your business."

I notice the throbbing vein in his neck. *This escalated quickly.*

"It is my business. Did you forget, he's *my* best friend? What do you think will happen when you guys break up?"

I twist my mouth. *Is he serious right now?* "Are you serious right now?"

"Yes. This is not fair to me. At all. He's my friend, but you're my sister. You guys have always hated each other. What am I supposed to do here? Let him hurt you? Let you hurt him? Watch you guys fight and do nothing?"

"There's nothing going on! And once again, if there was, it's not your business!"

"Guys. Enough. *Ya basta.*" *Crap.* I almost forgot mom was here. "Benjamin she's right. Your sister should be able to date anybody that she wants. It's a free country. It's her life, her body." Ben gets ready to argue, but she raises her hand. "Julieta, he has a point. Out of everybody in Miami, you picked *his* friend? Our actions have consequences. Did you ever stop to think about how this would affect your brother?"

"I didn't *pick* him," I glance between them. "There's nothing. Going on. Between us."

"Julie, I like him. He's like a son to me, but he's been part of his family for a long time. We have to think about that. If you guys don't work out–."

"We? I don't remember asking for a vote." I pause. "Look I get it. We're Latinos and we're all in each other's business, but, *once again*, there's nothing going on between us and if there was, it's not your business." It takes a second, then they both start talking at the same time. "Okay. Okay." I raise a hand and look at my brother. "IF, and that's big if I decided to start something with him, I will be sure to give you the heads up."

"That's fair enough," mom says.

He's shaking his head. I can tell that he's not happy, but at the same time, he doesn't have a choice. Finally, he says, "fine."

I can only pray that if I start something with Alex, that it'll work out, otherwise, I might fuck up my brother's longest and most cherished relationship.

CHAPTER 7:
ALEX

After the house incident, where I really, really wanted to kiss her, I had to lie to my best friend and say that there was nothing going on between me and his sister. Which technically it's true. At the same time, I can't deny that I'm crazy about her and I don't know how long I'll be able to hide it from him.

For a change, I spend all day in the office. The day flies by in between meetings and conference calls. I have lunch with my dad. I review drawings. I monitor several projects to see how close, *or far*, they are to completion. I coordinate several teams of people... and I spend all day thinking about her.

Finally, I head home. But first, a detour.

I swing by the house to check on the girls and because I can't wait another minute to see her.

I find them all on the floor of the guest house. "What is wrong with you guys?" I ask, glancing around the room.

"We're tired." Leyla says, at the same time, Alma says "we're broke," and Maria says, "PMS."

They all look at each other, then burst into laughter. I grin.

An idea comes to me. "You guys are depressing me. *Es viernes!* You guys need to get out and blow off some steam. We're going dancing." They all look at me like I grew a second head. "Everybody up. *Dale!*" I clap a few times. The clapping works and they start getting up. I offer my hand and help a couple of them up. "Everybody go home and get dressed. Meet me at the club in two hours. I'll text you guys the information."

Two hours later. I find myself in a club, surrounded by four beautiful women. Carlos is here, he's Leyla's boyfriend and the student dean at the local university. He's smart and super chill. He's also trying to recruit me to teach architecture as an adjunct. To be honest, I don't hate the idea. We're going to get along great.

It's less than ten minutes before Ben and Julieta arrive and for safety purposes, I keep my distance.

This mostly works until she pulls me up for a *merengue*. It's so much fun to dance with her. She can really move those hips, which honestly is not helping my current predicament. When she makes a joke, I laugh, and she winks at me. I'm loving this side of her.

It's amazing how everything gets multiplied by a thousand when I'm with her. She drives me a thousand times more crazy. Dancing with her it's a thousand times more fun. Her jokes are a thousand times more funny. She's a thousand times smarter and prettier than any other girl I've ever been with.

"You look amazing tonight," I tell her while we dance. Because she does. Her hair is in a knot and piled on top of her head, exposing her neck. She's wearing a black sleeveless dress. It's the tightest dress I've ever seen her wear, and it highlights every curve of her body. When she smiles at me, my heart skips a beat.

After a few *merengue* songs. I lead her back to the table where our friends are. We have a few drinks and it's awesome. I congratulate myself for having this great idea. We really needed this.

A while later, I'm in a conversation with Carlos, Leyla, and Julieta when Ben appears next to us. I watch as Ben says something to her ear, kisses her, then turns to me. He asks that I please take his sister home and I agree.

When Ben leaves, she gets a bit closer to me. "What was that about?" She asks.

"Your brother has made alternate transportation plans for you."

She glances in the direction of her brother. "You mean he asked you to take me home because he's ditching me for that girl, who he just met ten minutes ago and will try to get laid?"

"Hey, I'm a great wingman. I fully support any attempts by your brother, or any other friends, male or female, to get laid." She shakes her head. I grin at her.

When a song begins to play, the girls collectively scream and get up. Unexpectedly, Julie pulls me toward the dance floor without asking. Smiling, I get up and let her take me. Frankly, she could take me anywhere and I would go, no questions asked.

After a few more salsa and merengue songs, the next song it's a slow one. Half the dancers leave the dance floor. Her friends included.

I stop moving. She twists her index finger in a "come over here," signal and I try not to laugh but I shake my head. *No.* I mouth.

The truth is that I don't want to slow dance with her. Standing so close to her, it's already making it hard for me to breathe. As I take a step back, she grabs my hands and gently places them on top of her waist, pulls me close, and places her own hands on my shoulders. With heels on, we're almost at face level. "Relax," she tells me. "It's just dancing."

"It's just dancing, but is it really?" I ask. She shrugs.

I can't help but glance at her mouth. She keeps glancing at mine. I feel like a caged lion, trapped, waiting to get out and pounce. Waiting for the bars to finally burst open. *I'm so fucked.*

I take a deep breath and start making a list in my head of all the reasons why I *shouldn't* do this.

She looks at me through eyelashes, then closes the distance between us. When our bodies connect, I lose it. *Fuck this.*

I grab her hand and lead her away from everybody. I don't even know where I'm going, but I don't stop until we're at the back of the club, where the crowd is thinner.

I lean on a column and place her in front of me. Her eyes are huge and she's breathing fast. Without warning, my fingers grab her face. I glance at her mouth. Then I kiss her.

er lips are soft and yielding against my own. When she produces a little moan, I grunt. My heart is pounding in my chest, but when she wraps her arms around me and cradles my neck, I pull her against me. I kiss her harder, deeper, until I'm dizzy with desire, and she melts in my arms.

Apparently, when it comes to her, I'm insatiable. I just can't get enough of her. "Oh, my fucking God. You're amazing." I *have* to tell her because it's the truth. She smiles at me, and in turn, I kiss her again.

I try pulling back a second time.

"Hey there, Mr. Peña," she says sweetly, her voice drunk with desire, right before her perfect mouth breaks into a slow smile. I can't help but smile myself, then I kiss her again, just because.

"Miss Vargas." I pause. "Now we have a problem. I don't know if I can stop kissing you."

"Then don't. I don't mind at all," she grins.

I grin back at her. "I can see that."

I kiss her again. Slower this time. My heart feels like it's going to burst out of my chest. Kissing never felt this way with anyone else before. Kissing *her* it's extraordinary.

"I should probably take you back to your friends. They're going to think I kidnapped you and to be honest, if we keep this up, I might be tempted to really kidnap you and keep you in my house as my slave. Your only job will be to kiss me." This makes her laugh out loud, and I grin at her. "What are you doing tomorrow?"

"No plans."

"Can I pick you up?"

When she nods and before she can say anything, I kiss her again. After a few minutes, we go back to our friends.

At the end of the night, I'm a gentleman and as promised to her brother, I drop her at home safe and sound.

CHAPTER 8:
JULIE

He kissed me. He kissed me. Teenage me keeps repeating. She's completely lost her mind, or maybe I lost mine. I don't even know at this point.

The truth is, I wanted to kiss him so, so badly. I was about to, but he didn't give me a chance. Instead, he pulled me halfway across a crowded club and kissed me like our lives depended on it.

I've never been kissed that intensely or passionately by anybody else before him. When our lips touched, the chemistry was instant. My body was tingling and hyper-aware. He literally took my breath away.

The truth is that it would be impossible to walk away from that feeling. I'm smart enough to realize that this is a once-in-a-lifetime opportunity. This could be something special. I can feel it in my bones.

The next day, I wake up early and start getting ready. I tell my mom I'm going to do some shopping for the bed-and-breakfast and head for the door. "Julieta Maria!" I stop walking and turn back.

"Yes?"

"*Estás jugando con fuego.*" *You're playing with fire,* she says.

"*Mami.* It'll be fine. We're not doing anything."

"Not yet. I'm not stupid. I would have to be stupid or blind to not see what's going on here." She pauses. "Please talk to your brother before it's too late."

"I will."

"Also, for the record, I won't be mad if you give me a grandkid or two... *mejor... una nieta primero.*" She's wistfully staring into space. A granddaughter first, she says. Of course she does.

"*Mami,* please. Don't get too many ideas." She raises an eyebrow. *Too late.* I kiss her goodbye and head out before she can say anything else.

When I walk outside, Alex is waiting.

"*Buenos dias,*" he says, holding a large cup of coffee.

After I hop on, I give him a quick kiss on the cheek. He grins. "Hi. Good morning," I say.

I notice my mom waving goodbye, a huge grin on her face.

Oh boy. The grandkid train has left the building.

After I put on the seat belt, I take the cup he offers and take a sip. It's delicious. I don't know if it's the coffee or the company that's different. "Where are we going?"

"We're going up to West Palm Beach. We're going to swing by an estate sale and check out some antique shops... maybe talk."

Talk? Teen me decides she's going to go with the flow and not overthink it. For once, she's taking this very calmly.

"What are we looking for Mr. Peña?" I ask.

He glances at me, then focuses on the road again. "Well, miss Vargas, if you must know, we're going to look for some Spanish-inspired vintage pieces. Old furniture. I was thinking some old chairs to place around the house. Maybe a couple of mirrors... if we're lucky, a few old books. Just because they're cool."

When I say, "That sounds amazing. I love it," a slow smile spreads on his handsome face.

We spend the morning walking, talking, shopping, visiting old stores and collecting pieces, and also kissing. Any time we get too close, we kiss, like it's the most normal thing in the world for us. After years of fighting and arguing, maybe it should be. Maybe it's time for a change.

Can I just admit I can't believe I'm kissing him? Sometimes it feels like a dream. Teenage me it's in shock. She just cannot believe her luck. After all this time, she's finally kissing him and it's glorious.

During lunchtime, we stop at a small sandwich shop that he swears has amazing reviews. It's a tiny, local family business, and it smells amazing.

After we order, we seat outside under a huge tree canopy. There are dozens of tiny square aluminum tables around us, all occupied by other couples and families.

"These are cute." I say, tapping the top of the table, "we can put a few under the big trees in the backyard."

"That's actually a great idea. I'll find out where to get them and we'll see the prices."

I nod, then unwrap my sandwich and glance at him. He takes a huge bite out of his sub. "Are you ready?" he says when he finishes chewing.

"For what?" I ask, just before I take a bite. *Wow!* It's delicious.

"Are you ready for Alejandro's twenty questions for getting to know Julieta?"

I'm still chewing, but I raise an eyebrow. "Is that a thing? Do you ask other people you're dating these twenty questions?"

"Honestly? This is not a thing with me. I've never done this with anybody but you're not anybody, and I want to pick your brain, so I have a list. Also, full disclosure? I downloaded these off the internet because I had no idea what to ask you." I can't help smiling. He grins at me, then pulls a sheet of paper out of a back pocket and unfolds it dramatically. "Here we go. Ready?"

"I'm ready, Mr. Peña."

"Who's the best superhero in the MC universe?"

I don't know why I was expecting a serious question. I laugh out loud and he grins. "Is this a trick question?" he's chewing, but he nods. At the same time, I can tell he's trying not to laugh. "Let's go with Captain America. You?"

"Iron Man. See, easy peasy." He winks at me. "Next question, do you think the earth could be flat?"

"Oh my god. Be serious." I shake my head.

"It's a valid question. I mean, you could be a flat-earther denier, whatever they call them. I'm trying to determine if you're a sane person before, you know, I commit to anything... Moving on... Who was your celebrity crush as a teenager?"

"Oscar Isaac. Yours?" My answer makes him pause, but he recovers quickly.

"Ashley Green."

"From the Twilight movies?" I ask. He nods. *Interesting.* I look like her. Teen me files that piece of information away for later dissection. What does it say about us that our teen crushes look like us?

His next question is an easy one, "What's your dream job?"

"Owning a business and being my own boss. Yours?"

"Being an architect." He gives me a lopsided smile. He takes another huge bite and afterward, he asks, "What's your biggest fear?"

"I thought you already knew?"

"Right. Spiders. What a waste of a perfectly good question." We grin at each other. "Do you like animals?"

"Some. Cats, dogs, birds... not spiders."

"...spiders," he says at the same time I do. "Of course. Another wasted opportunity."

"I heard that you have a dog," I say, then take a sip of my drink.

"I do. A Golden Retriever. Your brother gave him to me a couple of years ago for my birthday. He's friendly, smart, sweet, and very lovable. *Se llama Zorro.*"

"Somehow that fits you."

"You ready for some serious questions?" I nod. "Do you want kids?" He asks.

"Yes. You?"

"Yes." He pauses. "What's the best part of dating you?"

"Good one Mr. Peña." I pause. "Do you mean *you* dating *me* or dating me in general?"

"Is there a difference Miss Vargas?"

"In this case? The best part of dating me, for you and I guess for me, is that we already know each other and we have history. I love your family, you love mine."

"Are you sure about that?" He teases. I throw a napkin at him. He catches it, smiling. "Okay fine. Yes, your dad was awesome and I love your brother *and* your mom..."

I gasp dramatically, "What? Not me?" I ask in mock surprise.

"Ask me later." He says and winks at me. "What else?"

"I already know that you're a man-child and that at parties you sometimes dress badly. I thought it was because you didn't care, but I'm starting to think it's because you want women to see you beyond the clothes and the title, the money and the pretty face and see the real you. *I* see your value. *You're amazing.*"

He takes a deep breath, clears his throat, then puts his sandwich down and leans back in the chair but says nothing.

"Of dating me in general? Besides sex? I'm very loyal and caring. Actually, I think I'm a great girlfriend." I take a bite and wait for the next question.

He's serious. His brow furrowed. I wonder what he's thinking. Even after knowing him this long, sometimes I really have no idea.

His jaw ticks a couple of times before we lock eyes. I've seen this face a few times these past few months. "Is this your business face?" I ask. Teen me wants to know. He's both scary and hot.

"Do you like me?" He asks.

Why do I have a feeling that one was not on the list?

"Mmm. You drive me crazy, but I do." I answer truthfully.

"Likewise, Miss Vargas." I watch as he crumbles the sheet of paper with the questions and leans forward, then places the paper ball in the center of the small table and leans back again.

I glance at him, then at the little ball, and wait.

For a few seconds, it's like we're the only people under this tree. He's serious when he asks, "Then what are we doing here?"

"*Wow*. That's a heavy one." I take a sip of my drink and give myself a few seconds. "That is... the ultimate relationship question and we're not even in a relationship. I mean–"

"Just go with it. What are we doing here?"

"We're getting to know each other?" I ask. "Right– except we already know each other. I guess the better question would be, what do we want from this?" I move my hand between us.

"I can tell you what I want." He places a hand on his chest. "I don't want a fling with you. I want a relationship. I'm not willing to hide this while I work next to you every day, like there's nothing here. I'm realizing that's not going to work for me. Because there *is* something here. Pretending otherwise, it's just stupid at this point. At the same time, your brother–"

"He's a grown-up. He'll get over it. Can we pretend for a few hours that we're just two people that like each other?" He nods. When I put my hand out, he leans in. He slides his hand in mine, like a handshake, and looks at me, the feeling is everything. "Okay. Okay. How do you feel about dating me, Mr. Peña?"

"Mmm, miss Vargas, I don't think I've ever been propositioned before." He glances at our hands. "I think... dating you is going to be both terrifying and amazing."

"Then do it. Date me."

"Challenge accepted." We grin at each other. "One caveat, we'll have a conversation with your brother. I know we don't need his permission, but we can at least give him the heads up." I agree.

We spend the rest of the afternoon doing more walking, shopping, and kissing. At some point, as we walk, he holds my hand and interlaces our fingers.

I glance at our connected hands.

Strangely, I already feel like we're a couple. We've spent years fighting like an old couple. It's a weird feeling to know we get to *be* a couple. Teen me is digging the word *couple*.

At the end of the day, we stop at the bed-and-breakfast and drop off everything that we bought. I can't wait for my friends to see everything.

The sun is setting by the time we arrive at my house and, like a gentleman, he walks me to my door.

At the door, we kiss like two horny teens, and I love it. I can only imagine what he'll be like in bed. "Good night Mr. Peña."

"Good night, Miss Vargas."

We start kissing again, but when I hear a door slamming, I turn back to see my brother coming our way. *Oh shit.*

"Dude, what the fuck?! You said there was nothing between you," Ben says, looking at Alex, then turns to me. "*You* said you would tell me if you decided to pursue something with him." For a second, he looks so hurt, I feel awful.

"Ben," Alex and I say at the same time, but we're still holding on to each other.

"I can't believe you guys are so selfish. I need both of you to stop this right now. I can't deal with your shit. All you guys ever do is fight. What is wrong with you people?" Before either of us can do or say something, my brother grunts, shakes his head, and storms out.

I let my head fall on Alex's shoulder. "Don't worry," Alex says gently in my ear. "He'll come around. It's going to be okay. He can't be mad at us forever."

I really, really hope he's right.

CHAPTER 9:
JULIE

I spent the next few days calling my brother, to no avail. Then I decide, instead of talking with Ben, I'll talk to Alex. He's been busy with an important client and hasn't been around this week. Mikaela is there daily on his behalf.

I call him a few times, but when he doesn't pick up, I get his address from his mom and head to his house. He opens the door shirtless. Water is dripping from his hair. *Okay.*

"Miss Vargas, what a nice surprise," he says with a big smile. I can't help but grin back.

"Mr. Peña. I'm sorry to show up here. I couldn't reach you and... umm, your mom gave me your address. She said you were busy and sad and that I should come to cheer you up... or something?"

His shirtless state is very distracting. I'm having a hard time keeping my eyes on his. I clear my throat. "Umm, you don't look sad. You look ho–" I pinch my lips.

His face breaks into a slow grin as he grabs one end of the towel wrapped around his neck and dries his forehead. "I'm afraid my mom might be trying to play matchmaker. She likes you. At the same time, you don't need permission to come over. Just call me and come over. Or don't call, just come." He gives me a quick glance over. "Actually, I can come up with at least fifty ways that you can cheer me up."

"Alex!"

"What? I'm being honest."

In that second, a beautiful golden retriever appears at his side, tail wagging. I let him sniff me and offer my hand. After a couple of seconds, I kneel next to him. Now that we're eye to eye, he's licking my face. I can't help but start laughing.

"Okay. He likes you; you just passed the ultimate test." I look up at Alex smiling at me.

"I have something on the stove. Do you want to come in?" I nod. When he offers a hand to help me up, I take it. He holds it all the way in.

Once in his kitchen, I stare as he exchanges the towel with a t-shirt from a nearby chair and puts it on. Sweat pants sit low on his hips and I focus on his stomach muscles as they contract. He winks at me. Teenage me is dying. She's both embarrassed and impressed with his abs.

I sit on the kitchen island and observe him move in his kitchen. "How's Ben? How's your mom?" He glances at me as he cooks.

"I haven't spoken with Ben lately. He won't pick up my calls." Thanks to my mom, I already know that Ben is not picking up Alex's calls either. "At the same time, my mom hinted that she might be okay with this. As long as *nietos* were involved. Apparently, she had a conversation with *your* mom."

"I'm sorry. I'll talk to my mom. This past year, she's been very vocal about her wishes. My sister has no interest in kids and for some reason, my mom seems to think that you and I–" He stops.

"Don't worry about it. I get it."

"Are you hungry?" He asks. I nod.

He cooked a chicken breast with salad. It's simple but delicious and we eat in silence. After we eat, we sit on the couch and he hands me a glass of wine. His dog lays down on the floor next to Alex.

We talk about everything: growing up, our parents, our siblings, our jobs, and the construction.

On the one hand, it's kind of cool that we share so much history. He understands everything about me and knows everybody in my life. On the other hand, it's new. New relationships, like anything new, are exciting. Not to mention, he's fun to talk to and has a lot of stories to share of shenanigans with my brother through the years. I'm learning a new side of him and I love it.

"I better go," I say when I finish the second glass of wine.

"Do you want another one?"

I shake my head. "I think two is more than enough. I have to drive home. Before I go, are we going to talk about the elephant in the room?"

"We're not. We can talk tomorrow. Right now, I'm relaxed and I'm enjoying talking with you and seeing you in my house, with my dog." He lowers his hand and pets his dog.

"Are you drunk, Mr. Pena?"

"Not at all, Miss Vargas. Or maybe I am." He pauses. "Maybe I'm drunk on you."

"Sure, you are. That's funny, Mr. Peña. How many glasses of wine did you have before I got here?"

He's quiet and his brow furrowed. Once again, I wonder what he's thinking when his jaw ticks a couple of times.

"Has anybody told you that your business face is very intense?" I ask.

"A few people have made comments."

"Oh, so this is a thing with you?" I grin. He grins back. "What are you thinking?"

"I'm waiting, while I debate in my head and make a pros and cons list, with fifty sub-lists under."

"Are you trying to problem-solve me Mr. Peña?" I ask. He doesn't answer. "How's that working out for you?"

"Do you really want to know?" He puts his glass down.

A second later the glass tips over, and what little liquid was left falls on the dog. Zorro bolts awake and lands on the couch and on top of Alex, like a giant puppy.

After a few seconds, he starts licking my face. Without intending to, I slowly slide sideways, giggling and laughing while Alex is trying to get the dog off us.

It takes a couple of seconds, but the dog finally jumps down.

Alex pulls me gently towards him and helps me straighten up. "Are you alright?" he asks.

When I turn slightly, his hand is behind the couch for a few seconds before casually landing on my shoulder.

"I'm great. No harm done." I'm still smiling and petting the dog, now on the floor, but with his face on my lap.

Suddenly, Alex puts a little pressure on my shoulder and pulls me closer to him. I glance at his eyes. When he looks at mine, I move an inch closer and wait. Then he kisses me.

He kisses me slowly and deeply, but every second, it gets more intense. Our mouths are locked in a battle of will and passion. Ultimately, I give up. White flags raised, as every square inch of my body slowly melts into his.

"Do you still want to go home?" He asks.

When I nod, he stands up. I take the hand he offers and let him lead me around his home.

We enter a room, but he pauses at the entrance and after a few belly rubs, he closes the door on his dog's face.

I walk to the center of his room and turn to face him. "Aww. You kicked him out?"

"I did. I want you all to myself, Miss Vargas."

"What did you have in mind, Mr. Peña?" I ask as he slowly comes my way.

Without talking, he places his hands on my waist and turns me, hugging me from behind and inhaling into my hair. When he says, "You smell amazing, Miss Vargas," I can't help but smile.

"You don't smell too bad yourself, Mr. Peña." I say as I put my hands on top of his forearms. He kisses the back of my neck softly and I tilt my head a tiny bit.

After a couple of minutes, I can't take it anymore and slowly turn to face him. He's still holding on to my waist and kisses my neck from the front. I reach up and run my hands through his damp hair, then gently pull his head up.

We kiss softly at first, but he slowly speeds up in both progression and intensity.

But it's not fast enough.

In one swift moment, I pull his shirt off. His abs are amazing and I can't help but run my hands over them. When he pulls me close and our hips connect, I have a feeling I won't be disappointed.

Finally, he grabs the hem of my t-shirt and gently pulls it off me. My heart is pounding in my chest. I cling to him as wobbly and unsteady feet and body quickly fill with desire.

In a few seconds, I'm on the bed and he's pulling my jeans off. He starts at my stomach and kisses his way up until we're face to face.

His relentless mouth, molding with mine, is sending pleasure signals along my nerve endings. At the same time, it feels intimate and certain and inevitable. Like it was meant to be all along.

While he reaches for a condom, we make eye contact. Time stops. We connect and it feels like forever is starting now.

CHAPTER 10:
ALEX

I wake up to my dog barking up a storm. She groans and stirs a little, but doesn't move. I smile. For a few seconds, I can't believe she's mine.

I clear some hairs off her forehead and kiss the top of her head. "I'll be right back. Don't go anywhere." Her eyes are still closed but she gives me a slow smile.

I get up, take my dog for a walk and get back in bed with her. Before my body fully hits the mattress, I start kissing her again.

I can't stop kissing her. She's a thousand times more interested in my kisses than anybody I've ever been out with, and it's a thrilling feeling.

It's wild to think I might have found the one person who is not afraid to argue with me, put me in my place, but then share this incredible intimacy with me and kiss me like she kisses me. Without reservations but full of craving, lust, desire and longing and everything in-between.

I lay down next to her and pull her close.

Although this just started, I can't even imagine going on a date with someone else or kissing anyone who's not her. Even less, sharing my bed with anyone else. At this point, it's unfathomable.

"Good morning Mr. Peña." She says sweetly and my body perks up in attention. "You know, if you wake me up like that every day, I might never leave this bed."

At her words, I laugh. "Good morning, Miss Vargas. Are you hungry?" She nods. "To be honest, I'm starving," I say. "But first—"

I grab her arms and she squeals in delight. I kiss her again and again and again. I really can't help it. I make love to her and I completely agree with her; we might never leave this bed. Frankly, the idea doesn't scare me at all. I can see it clearly in my head, us sharing this bed, and eventually filling it with kids.

A few hours later, we're finally in the kitchen eating. Mostly, because we're starving and we have no more energy left. She's standing next to me in her underwear, wearing my shirt, no pants, and I smile at myself.

After we've eaten, my dog needs to go out again. "Go. While you take him. I'll clean up," she says.

"Okay. I'll be right back." I give her a quick kiss, then grab the leash. "Close the door behind me, please."

A short while later, we're back home. I'm about to knock on my door when I hear a car behind us. I turn to see Ben parking behind my car. Before I can react, Ben quickly comes out of his car and heads my way. *Crap.*

"Alex, wait up." He says as he walks my way. "Can we talk?" He stops for a second to say hi to my dog. "Hey, buddy."

"Uh, sure. What's up, bro?" I ask, as he's straightening up.

"I want to apologize. It's just that you know... You and my sister... it would never work. It's not personal, I know you're a nice guy, but you guys have never gotten along. You just argue too much. It's better for all of us if you guys just don't..."

He's going on and on about why it wouldn't work between me and his sister.

Half of me agrees with him. We did spend most of our lives fighting. The other half is infuriated on our behalf that he won't give us a chance. Even more so because he thinks it's up to him.

Would this be a good time to tell him I've already slept with his sister? That I might be falling for her?

"... and after the b and b is done, we'll go back to normal. You know what I'm saying?"

Right. *Normal.* Sure. Do I even know what normal is without her? I have a feeling my *normal* has her in my life and he's not going to be happy.

"Ben. We need to talk. There's something you should know." As I'm saying this, my dog wanders off. We both follow him with our eyes as he follows a smell close to the cars. "Julie and I — Something happened last—"

"Is that my sister's car?" He interrupts. He glances at me, then back at the car again. "It is, isn't it?" Before I can say anything, he turns and knocks on my door.

"Ben, wait."

It's less than five seconds later before Julieta opens the door. Still in my shirt, still no pants. *Shit.*

It takes a second before her face registers what's happening. Her eyes are wide. Her shoulders hunch and she shrinks away. I hate that she feels this way.

I make eye contact. I want her to know that I feel for her, for me. That it's going to be alright.

I try again with her brother. "Ben. Listen to me."

He glances at me briefly. His face is flushed, and he's baring his teeth.

When he turns to her and points a finger at her, I react by pushing his hand down. "Hey, knock it off." Honestly, at this point, I don't care that she's his sister. He's not touching her in this state.

I notice his aggressive stand and realize, a second too late, that he threw a punch. When his fist slams into my face, I stagger back.

Julie lets out a scream, then covers her mouth with her hands.

Instinctively, I grab my face. At the same time, my dog reacts.

Zorro growls, his body is stiff, and he's leaning forward as if ready to pounce. He lets out a loud warning bark. *Shit*. My dog mauling my best friend in front of his sister is not going to win me any points with him. I'm already on his shit list.

I grab the dog with both hands, kneel down, and tell him to calm down. He does. While I'm talking with my dog, and before I can say or do anything, Ben gets in his car and leaves.

I stand up and hold her in my arms. "Don't worry. It's going to be fine."

Unfortunately, I don't know if I believe that. For the first time it occurs to me, I'm not sure it will be.

***

The next few months are a blur.

We start dating. We're officially dating because I can't not date her. I want her mind, body and soul. Besides, at the end of the day, it's only up to us.

We're already in each other's lives, but we're getting to see each other in our most unguarded and vulnerable state. The truth is that I feel a whole level of comfort with her.

Not to mention, we work great together. We're honest with each other. If she hates my ideas, she lets me know. If she wants something that is not architecturally sound or I think will not work, I'm not afraid to shot it down. We're getting really good at brainstorming ideas together and the project is all the better for it.

Incredibly enough, since we started kissing, we've completely stopped fighting and arguing. Now, all we do is kiss.

Six months go by. The year ended and a new one started. We've fallen into a nice rhythm. Both with the project and with our relationship. We regularly have dinner with our moms. I join her and her mom for lunch on Sundays and it's really great.

There's a lot of kissing and mind-blowing sex and while at the beginning I was wondering if this was just physical, as the months go by, I can't stop thinking that this is something more. This is special and possibly the forever kind.

Except for the fact that Ben never shows up to any invitation, and that he's stopped talking to us, I would say that life is great.

It sucks that I can't talk to him. I can't share anything with my best friend. In twenty years, we've never let this much time pass without talking. It's been months. I honestly thought he would have come around by now, but now I'm not so sure and it's really starting to worry me.

CHAPTER 11:
ALEX

We're outside the guest house having our first argument.

This project is way behind schedule. Rainy season didn't help. Now a few of the guys are out with a bug and construction is down to a grinding crawl. Half the projects are on pause here and at the firm. I had several VIP clients complain to my dad and now *he's* pissed at me. *Shit.*

I'm pacing. Finally, she stops in front of me and stops me. "You should have called me earlier," I say.

"You're mad at me for not calling you earlier? And you're telling me a year later?" She glances at me. "Honest question, why would you expect me to call you? You were friends with my brother. I think you're forgetting that before this, you were not my friend."

"I'm friends with your brother and your family. My dad would have been more than happy to help from the beginning. You know this is what we do for a living."

"Dude, if you can't do it or don't want to do this anymore, just let me know. I'll find somebody else."

I go back to pacing. *Fuck.* I stop in front of her. "*Relajate* okay. I never said I didn't want to do it. I'm just saying it's taking way longer than we expected. I have clients complaining and my dad is pissed at me. I'm fucking stressed out, okay?"

"Fine. I'll make it easy for you. Alex, you're fired."

I stare at her, my eyes bugging out of my head. She's completely lost her mind. "You can't fire me. You didn't actually hire me. Ben hired me to–" I stop mid-sentence.

She pauses too. After a few seconds, she hugs me and I hug her back. "What is going on? Why are you so crazy today?" She takes a step back, and looks at me.

"There's a lot going on. I drive myself crazy at work and you drive me crazy. That's double the crazy."

She gives me half a smile that doesn't quite reach her eyes, then steps away from me. She rests on a wall, her arms crossed. "What is the problem? I know it's not the construction. You do this for a living. What is the problem?"

I take a deep breath and think about it. "I don't know. I'm tired and stressed and my go-to person is your brother and I can't talk to him about this." I move my hand between us. "I can't talk to him about anything. It's driving me crazy." I lean on the wall next to her and cross my arms. We're hip to hip but facing forward.

"You know what? Maybe we need to stop seeing each other. Let's take a break."

I look at her. "Julieta—"

"I don't know what else to do here Alex. It's like there are three people in this relationship and one of them is missing and until he's back, we can't be whole again. So, let's take a break. Besides, I'm busy with this and you have your own family business to take care of. You've already spent enough time here—"

I stand in front of her. "Is that what you want? You want to end this?" She doesn't answer. "Wow. I did not see this coming. You're going to do this to me now? On top of everything?"

"Look, he doesn't want us to be together. You're miserable. My mom is miserable. I'm miserable because you guys are miserable... I mean— maybe if we take a break, he'll talk to us. We can try to fix that, then come back to this."

"I can believe you're suggesting that."

"I'm at the end of my rope! You're not doing anything about it, so unless you have any ideas..."

I take a deep breath. "I'm not going to argue with you right now. I don't have the mental capacity to argue with you right now." Right now, I'm too freaking tired and stressed and frustrated to have any ideas. "Mikaela will take over. I'm out."

"Alex! Alex!" she screams behind me, as I walk away from her.

I feel like shit, but there's no other choice. The alternative is to have a huge argument with her that will surely fuck everything up.

CHAPTER 12:
JULIE

I basically just broke up with him. Possibly. Maybe. Teen me is bawling and wants to chase me with a bat for doing the stupidest thing ever. At the same time, *he* walked away.

I spend the next couple of weeks focused on the bed-and-breakfast and my job at the hotel. I figured, if I focus on that, I won't have time to think about the fact that my brother hates me and that I just broke up with the man of my dreams.

I'm miserable without him but the worst thing is that he didn't even argue with me. He just left.

Since then, he's barely shown up to the bed and breakfast. His assistant is there every day and as nice as she is, she's not him.

As the days go by, I feel my job as a concierge, extra draining. I don't know how long I'll be able to keep this up. The idea of quitting is looking better by the day.

It's four am and Mr. Puffer is back. I'm two hours away from the end of my shift. *Just two hours. I can do this.*

This time, he's really... puffed. He's extra mellow today, but for some reason, he's also extra flirty and creepy.

He stands in the lobby and watches me. I keep an eye out while I wait to see if he actually needs something. Finally, he comes over.

"Hi." Mr. Puffer says. "How are you?"

His eyes are tiny. *Can he even see me?* "How can I help you?" I ask with a semi-polite smile.

"I was wondering, do you know of... an escort service?" Once again, he's surprised me. I didn't think *that* was what he was thinking.

"No. I'm sorry. Maybe you can search for one online. From your room." I offer.

"Are you available for... a date?" He wiggles his eyebrows at me.

"Excuse me?"

"Uh, what?"

Oh, my freaking God. "Do you not see me working? I mean look at my tag." I point to it. "It says, concierge, do you see the word escort anywhere here?" Now that I've started, I can't seem to stop. "Every time you come down here, you have these random requests. Do you even have a job? Or are you just a random drug dealer?"

"Uh..."

"I am so sick of people who think they can come here... all this entitlement... I mean, if you're a drug addict, go to a program or something. Stop hitting on women. Especially women that work hard and are trying to make an honest living. If you're just rich, stop spending money on drugs!"

"Uhhh..." I can't tell if I've shocked him, or he's just too *puffed* to reply.

David, my co-worker, materializes out of nowhere and rushes to me. "Julie? Is everything okay here?"

"No. Everything is not okay here. This, this puffer, just propositioned me." The look of horror on the puffer's face it's priceless. For the first time, his eyes are huge.

David gasps. "Julie, take a break. I'll help our guest."

"Fine. I'm out. This is not how men are supposed to be. Nice men get jobs and love their careers and love their moms. They have nice friends, loyal friends. They don't go to hotels, alone, and out of their rooms in the middle of the night to preposition to complete strangers... while high!"

"Can you wait for me at the office and we'll talk about this," David says.

"You know what David... I quit!"

While Mr. Puffer and David stand there with their mouths open, I grab my things and leave as quickly as I can.

***

I drive home and sleep. When I wake up, I feel much better. I go to the bed-and-breakfast and I tell my friends everything.

Throughout the day, I think about Alex. He loves his job *and* his mom. He's a nice human being. He doesn't do drugs and he knows me. He really does. He feels like my best friend, my lover, my cheerleader. I can take on any challenge with him by my side. It feels like there's no way I would fail and if I did, that's okay, too.

I want to have everything. I want love, a career, and a family. But at the same time, I want to give *him* everything. I want to surrender everything in exchange for his love. *That doesn't even make sense,* teen me is saying, but I digress.

I'm so sick of waiting. Hasn't he realized that we belong together?

How many days or months am I supposed to wait for him? How much time does he need?

Teen me is ready to hit him in the head with a bat, if that's what it takes to bring him to his senses.

I grab my phone and start calling people. Then I go looking for a bat.

CHAPTER 13:
ALEX

I guess she misses me and truth be told, I miss her too. I miss her soo fucking much. She keeps calling me. I keep calling Ben and round and round we go. It's a vicious cycle and I don't know how long we'll be able to keep this insanity.

All *I* know is that I need to talk to Ben as soon as possible if Julie and I are going to have a chance. I really, really miss her. I miss talking to her, hearing her talk, more than anything, touching her and kissing her. I don't think I can go another week without her. At any given time, I'm less than five seconds away from calling her and begging for forgiveness for walking away from her.

Finally, after a couple of weeks of calling and leaving message after message, Ben agrees to meet me at the university basketball courts.

I arrive early and start shooting basketballs with Tom, Keith, Matt and Kyle while we wait for Ben for a three-on-three game.

Like us, they've known each other their whole lives. If Anybody understands the dynamics of my friendship with Ben, it's these guys. I know they'll just get it.

The six of us regularly play basketball together, and this is a last-ditch attempt at reconciliation with my best friend. Thankfully, it seems to have worked.

While we wait, and as we dribble the ball and warm up, we talk. I can't help but tell them everything (mostly.)

"I don't have a sister so I can't put myself in that position, but I think you should have sat him up, invited him for a beer, and come clean," Keith says.

"That's the lawyer talking," Tom teases. We all laugh.

Keith shakes his head, and then looks at me. "It's true though. You know I'm right. Just talk to the guy."

I take a deep breath. He's right. In hindsight, I probably should have said something or had a conversation much sooner.

"I don't know. It's tough. I have sisters and as their big brother, I would probably blow a gasket. What would bother me more than anything is that he lied... then I guess I would probably come around." Tom admits.

Keith looks at his brother, Kyle. His eyebrows up in amusement and he address him. "Kyle? What do you think?"

"I have no comments..." Kyle has a guilty look on his face and we all look at him. "What?" He asks.

Tom raises an eyebrow. *Do I even want to know?*

"Anything you want to share?" Tom asks and the rest of us holler and laugh.

Matt throws the ball at Tom, distracting him. "I don't know what the big deal is. I mean, he's my friend for a reason, right? If my best friend wants to date my sister and they love each other, who am I to say no?"

I stop, hands on my waist. "That's a good point Matt, can you tell Ben that?"

"Tell me what?" Ben asks, walking in. We all turn towards him.

After that exchange, Ben barely talks, but we play for a few hours. In the end, I'm sweaty and exhausted, but I feel much better about this whole thing.

To be honest, I'm just about ready to put this behind us and move on.

Neither of us is saying anything while we're sitting on the benches watching the other guys play.

"I want to say that I'm sorry that I didn't tell you anything. I get that she's your sister and I probably should have manned up and told you. I feel that I fucked up our friendship, but that was not my intention." I start.

He exhales. "I'm sorry that I hit you. I was just pissed off. You haven't fucked it up yet."

"Look, the truth is, I didn't know it was going to lead to anything. There was no way to know. When I saw her for the first time at the bed-and-breakfast, I knew I liked her, but I had no idea I was going to fall in lo–"

His water bottle stops mid-air. "Wow. You love her? Like you love her, love her?"

"I do. She drives me crazy, but I do."

He shakes his head. "There's nobody good enough for my sister, but if I had to choose. You're at the top of the list."

"Thanks man..."

"One thing though."

"Yes?"

"I don't want to know or talk about your sex life. I don't want any details, and if I see you hooking up with a girl, I'll be telling my sister."

"That's fair enough."

"Also, we've done a lot of crazy shit over the years–"

"My lips are sealed–" I hear steps and look up. Suddenly, she's in front of me and my heart wants to leap out of my chest.

I pause to look at her. I have no idea how she found us.

She points at me. "You! Stop ignoring me! If you don't want to be with me, then tell me to my face that you don't want to be with me. *Me tienes loca* and by the way, I can't believe you're letting me go because you're scared of losing *him*." She points at Ben and he raises an eyebrow.

I'm about to say something when she turns to her brother. "And you, stop meddling in my life. It's none of your business who I sleep with. Stop being so childish and stop eing mad at him. He's miserable. I get it, that's your best friend, and I'm sorry that we went behind your back. I know we hurt your feelings, but that does not give you the right to tell me who I can or can't be with, so stop it."

I get up and start walking toward her. "That's interesting, I didn't think anybody could *not* let you do anything." My best friend chuckles and she narrows her eyes.

"I'm not done. I can't deal with your drama! You two are worse than me and my friends! You're like two hormonal teenagers in middle school!"

"Julie–" I try again as she's back ranting to her brother. She's wearing a ponytail and no makeup. She's flustered and beautiful, and I can't wait to have her in my arms. "Julie–"

"... and by the way, fuck you and I'm telling mom you're being an asshole." She turns to me again. "And I'm going to tell *your* mom that you're ignoring me."

I try not to laugh. "Julie... Can I say something?"

"No..." She looks at me again. Her eyes are watery and she looks just about ready to lose it. When she turns and runs out, my heart breaks. I can't let her leave like that. I don't want to.

I turn to him.

"O-kay. She must be PMSing," he says and we chuckle. "Are you going to go after her?" he asks after a brief pause.

"Do I have permission?" He nods. "I need you to understand. If I go after her I'm keeping her."

"Look, nobody deserves my little sister *but* if I had to choose, there's nobody else I would rather have as a brother-in-law than you. Now, can you please get her before she tells on us? Our moms are going to kill us."

Laughing, I go toward him and we clap each other in the back, then I grab my bag and run out after her.

Breathing fast, I catch her just as she reaches her car, then I drop my bag on the ground and stand in front of her. "Julie–"

She slams the door to her car and wipes a runaway tear with the back of her hand, before she turns to me. "You son of a b–"

"I know, I know, I'm sorry. Don't leave."

"You walked away from me but if you think for one second–"

She won't let me talk. I can't think of any way to stop her, except... "I'm in love with you."

When the words leave my mouth, they immediately stop her in her tracks.

"If you can just stop for one second and let me talk–" I say. I take advantage of the fact that she's too stunned to speak, and I kiss her. It takes a few seconds, but finally, she kisses me back. When she melts into me, I know I'm right where we need to be, with her in my arms.

"You should have led with that!" she says, punching my chest.

"*Ow*. I know. I'm sorry. But you're not letting me talk."

"Why would I let you talk when you're being–"

I raise a hand. "I know you missed arguing with me, but I need to say something."

She crosses her arms. "Fine! Talk!"

I gently untangled her arms and grab her hand. "First of all, I'm sorry for walking away. It had nothing to do with you. When I saw you that first day on the site, I thought you were beautiful. As the weeks went by, I didn't see you as Ben's little sister. I saw you as this amazing woman and slowly, I fell in love with you."

"I'm in awe of your passion and determination and work ethic to make this massive project work for you and your friends. Please don't be mad at me. I needed to talk to him and fix it because I don't want to stop kissing you."

"I thought I had a great life, but it turns out, my life is a thousand times better with you in it. You fulfill me in ways I didn't think were possible. I want to do the same for you. I want to give you passion and love and happiness."

Tears are streamlining down her face. I pull her towards me and I hug her. When she wraps her arms around me, I bury my face in her hair.

"I'm in love with you, Mr. Peña," she finally says, her voice cracking.

I pull back and kiss her again and again, then grin at her. "Likewise miss Vargas. Likewise."

The End

***

Did you enjoy the story? Don't forget to leave a review! Also, sign-up for my newsletter for a free story, deleted scenes & bonus content, and updates on my next release. Sign up for Ida's newsletter here.

ABOUT THE AUTHOR

Ida Duque writes sweary, sweet with heat, romantic comedies with a Miami flair. Actually, if she's being honest, it's more like loud, crazy Miami-infused romcom. Her books feature smart sassy women who love life, family and each other and are hoping to find true love. Also, there's kissing...lots of kissing!

A native of a beautiful island in the Caribbean, these days Ida lives in South Florida with her husband and two kids, one of whose future plans include becoming "the boss of Miami." Seriously. Ida's loving every minute of raising her but will welcome parenting tips on dealing with aspiring dictators. There are currently no playgroups in their area organized for fiercely independent kids also interested in political machinations and autocracy.

FIND IDA DUQUE ON THE WEB
www.idaduque.com

Check out Ida's other Sweet with Heat Romantic Comedy
The Humor of Love
The Academy of Love
Christmas with the Dean (Carlos & Leyla's story!)

CUPCAKES & CARLOS

Cara North

ABOUT *CUPCAKES & CARLOS*

Cooking, coaching, and many mishaps is what brings two high school teachers together in Cupcakes & Carlos.

CHAPTER ONE:
JESSICA

It was my first day as the long-term substitute teacher for the Life Skills class that my mom referred to as old-school home economics. The regular teacher, Mrs. Munoz, gave birth to triplets and decided to remain home for the rest of the year. As a person desperate for a job since the bakery I tried and failed to operate closed down, I was more than happy to fill in for this particular class.

"Hello everyone, I'm Jessica Howard, I will be filling in for Mrs. Munoz for the rest of the year." I smiled brightly at the classroom full of students looking at me like I just announced I came from another planet and would be conducting experiments on them shortly. I cleared my throat. "So...uh. Let's...go around the room and...tell me who you are and a little about why you signed up for this class."

I smiled brightly at the girl in the front row and she turned her head and ignored me. The silence grew to an unbearable pressure on my and I knew my face was beginning to turn red with it. I was about to speak when a voice in the back of the room had me sighing with relief.

"Hey. I'm Miguel." He raised his hand in a wave. "I took this because I need good grades to play ball and I was told this was an easy class. So." He shrugged.

Several students laughed and I asked, "Who else took this for an easy grade?"

Most of the class raised their hands. It was out of sequence, but since there were people who did not raise their hands, I asked, "And what about you?"

"Me?" she asked. I nodded. "I took it because I need to know how to take care of my grandparents. They took us in, and...I thought this would help me. You know. Help them."

I nodded. I took a mental note to ask her later what else I could make sure we covered in here that might help her. What else I could do. I asked, "And your name?"

"Nikita." She wasn't a smiler for sure.

"It's nice to meet you, Nikita." The rest of the class introduced themselves without much difficulty and I learned a lot about them and their perception of what this class would be about. Since it was only two weeks into the school year, I had all of Mrs. Munoz's lesson plans and syllabus to draw from, but I knew some of them needed more.

I also knew how to get introductions rolling in the rest of my classes. By lunch, I was feeling both exhausted and like I had a new purpose in life. When I entered the faculty lounge, I didn't get the sense that was the vibe most of these teachers had.

"Hi." I beamed.

A couple people looked over at me. One older woman with a head full of gray hair indicated I should come sit next to her. I did because at least she was welcoming. She smiled and asked, "How is your first day going, sweetheart?"

She was talking to me like I was a kid. I tried not to feel offended, since she was obviously up there in age, but still. "Well. I'm excited."

"Good. Good." She nodded in approval. I was afraid what I now knew to be a wig was going to come right off. She looked down the large conference-like table at some of the other faculty and said, "It's nice to see someone happy to be here."

"Give her a week." One of the male teachers said as he toasted me with his coffee cup and left.

"I didn't make it till the end of my first day." A red head pointed at me and then added, "But it comes and goes. You have one of the fun classes. Something they don't have to take seriously, so it may be different for you. Isn't that right, Ms. Edna?"

"Music is not something to take lightly, Rebecca." I gulped.

Yikes!

Then, I gasped. Fortunately, low and unnoticeable to the glaring women still at the table. I blinked and hoped my face was not turning red with the sudden heat rushing over my cheeks.

"Hey hey! How is everyone today?" He smiled and I gulped.

The redhead, Rebecca, straightened her back and pushed her assets out as she did. "Hey, Coach. Great. How's the team looking this year?"

"Awesome." He was all energy and joy. He was also gorgeous.

Ms. Edna, the music teacher was even all smiles at him as she said, "Now that is a man who understands music."

He laughed and I tried to control my smile at that response. What was it about him?

"In my day..." She started as she got up. "They didn't make 'em like you in my day."

My goodness! I bit my lips not to crack up laughing at how fresh she was being.

"Awe. You are too kind." He winked at her. "Now," he said as he looked at me, "Who is this new person you seem to have taken a liking to?"

Um.

Ms. Edna patted my shoulder and said, "A sweet one." Then she looked over at Rebecca and said, "Not like some of our other faculty."

He chuckled and playfully scolded her with an, "Awe, now. Keep the family feud out of the breakroom, please."

Family...well, that made a bit more sense as I looked between them. Some mixed heritage on Rebecca's part, but now that he mentioned it, I could see the face structure, the body type. That was made easier as Rebecca stood up and said, "Come on, Gran. I'll walk you back to the music room."

"You can walk yourself back to your own classroom." Ms. Edna was not someone I wanted on my bad side.

Once the door closed, the coach said, "Whew. That's usually the worst of it. You'll get used to it. I'm Carlos. You are?"

Who was I? I blinked at him a few times and said, "Life skills."

His smile was bright and the playfulness in his eyes only made me blush deeper. I corrected, "Jessica...Jessica Howard. I'm filling in for Ms. Munoz."

"Oh man! She had the twins?" he seemed both happy and sad if that were possible.

I nodded. "Yes. I got the call last night asking if I was ready to fill in for the rest of the year."

He grabbed his chest and winced. "No. No way. How could she do this to me?"

My brow went up and I was highly offended by his reaction. It must have shown on my face because he said, "Not that I don't think you will do fine as the sub. I just...we had a special relationship."

"Like...how special?" My brow quirked. He laughed.

"Not that special. She would always make cupcakes for our games. It means a lot to these kids to have that extra attention. I suggest her class to a lot of my players and kids who need it because she cares. They need real skills, and she makes learning fun. You got big shoes to fill." He looked at my feet and then said, "Well, maybe only in the metaphoric sense."

I balked.

He chuckled again. "You play sports?"

No. "Maybe."

"You look like you could handle yourself." He nodded as he continued to assess me. "Volleyball?"

Nope. "Some."

He lit up. "I knew this was going to be a great year!"

"How's that?" I asked.

"We need a coach for the girls' team. You know the game, right?" he asked. I gulped and nodded. It was either admit I lied in an attempt to impress him or keep lying and go look it up as soon as he was out of sight which is what I had planned to do.

I added, "I've never coached and that was a really long time–"

"I got you." He pulled the coffee cup from under the dispenser and took a sip. He made a sour expression and said, "You get used to it."

I didn't even know what to say.

He did. "I'll email you the information. I'll let Principal Carter know you are stepping up for volleyball. It will all work out."

With a smile I couldn't say no to, he headed out the door. I just blinked at the now empty faculty space and took the first bite of my sandwich. I had only a few minutes to eat before I needed to be back in my classroom.

What a first day!

CHAPTER TWO:
CARLOS

It was her second day of teaching and I suspected the students were going to be a bit rowdy, but I did not expect them to start a fire. That was the thing about working in a school that had lots of needs. She was a mess. Counting her students for the fourth time as the fire department handled the oven fire that was out, but the smoke set off the alarms and now...*Ay, Dios Mío!*

I put one of my seniors in charge of my class and headed over. "Hey. You all right?"

She looked at me and I could see she was holding back tears. "I took roll. I had twenty-eight and now I have twenty-six. I don't know where the two students are."

"Which ones?" I asked and looked at her clipboard. I read the names and smiled. "I got it."

She looked up at me and the tear streaked. I smiled. Something crazy ached inside me when I looked at her, but that tear just...kicked me in the chest. I was serious as I said, "It's going to be okay. They are okay. Trust me."

I motioned for one of my players and he ran up to me, "Yes, Coach?"

"Go get Paris and tell him if he is not with this class in three minutes, he is not pitching the entire season." I was serious and he knew it.

"Shit." He took off running.

I knew those two students were an item, so they probably just snuck off to have some time alone. Not uncommon, but she was too knew to know all that. I watched as he went straight to the pit, or the area the students liked to congregate in because it had limited visibility from a distance due to the location, the overgrown landscaping, and the lack of care or concern for what could take place there by the administration. I assumed the last part since they would have cleared the shrubs and trees if they did care or had funding for it.

Paris was a sprinter and he was not waiting for Manuella. I looked at him and said, "Don't do that to anyone, ever. Understand?"

He looked from me to Jessica and realized how upset she was. It was a shock to him. I understood that. Like many of these kids, he didn't have a whole lot of people invested in him beyond his ability to throw a baseball. I coached three teams at this high school. Two more than any other high school coach around. One more than our neighboring rival where they had the same population of students.

Paris said, "I'm sorry. I thought you saw us walk that way."

"I'm just glad you're both okay." She smiled at him and the look of guilt on his face made me pat him on the back as he headed to get Manuella and congregate with the rest of his class.

Jessica looked at me and said, "Thank you."

"I would say you could thank me by baking me a cake, but–" I laughed as her pretty lips rounded in shock. She smiled, snickered, and then nodded.

The fire department were loading up and the principal was on his way over.

"He's going to fire me on my second day." She was gripping the clipboard tightly.

"Don't worry." I assured her.

Principal Carter rubbed the back of his neck as he approached and said, "Well. We need a new stove. Apparently that one has been a fire hazard for a while. We were lucky you put it to use or it may have happened when no one was here. We could have lost the whole school."

He saw someone horsing around beyond us and said, "Hey, you two. Come over here."

He was not going to apologize or stay to hear her response. I was. "So...sorry we have a crappy stove and see...not your fault."

"So you want that cake then?" she asked and her smile and pink nose from the crying was touching.

"Maybe." I looked at the students around us because they were getting quieter. She may not have noticed that, but I did. They were watching. Always. I looked at the crowd and said, "Okay, back to class."

The grumbles made me laugh, but the students here usually listened to me. It was a rough year for my first one, but after that, most of the time, I loved this job.

***

I didn't really expect her to make me anything. Truly. However, when Tuesday and Wednesday came and all she gave me was a shy smile as we passed in the halls, I started to think I had imagined those little sparks of interest I was feeling.

I hadn't really paid attention to a woman in that way in a while. Not since Camila. I walked down the hall toward my classroom and considered the superstar athlete and the girl at his side. That was once us. Camilla always thought I was going to go pro in one sport or the other. Maybe become the Mexican version and modern day Bo Jackson. I knew sports, but I liked living here, near my parents. With the exception of my abuela, most of our family was in Mexico or throughout South America.

I thought Camilla and I had the same plans, but all the time she was talking about building a family, she meant with a professional athlete making millions of dollars and traveling the world. I was sulking by the time I took a seat at my desk. I was not my usual upbeat and happy self the rest of the day.

That rolled over into practice.

"Coach!" I turned to look at the young superstar running toward me with a huge smile on his face.

"Hey." I forced a smile to mine.

"I got in!" He handed me his phone. I looked at it. He was getting early acceptance to the school because they wanted him locked in and on that team.

"You sure you want to commit? This is the start—"

"Yes! Of course. I've wanted to go there since I was a little kid. Yes. This is it! The one!" He was practically bouncing.

I nodded as I handed the phone back to him and said, "Congratulations. You worked hard for it, but—"

"I know, Coach. No slacking. I have to maintain in order to stay in. I know." He was serious and I gave him a genuine smile this time. "You've drilled that into us since freshman year."

"Well. Glad to know it stuck." I gave him a hug and patted his back. He needed it. Like many of the students at this school, he was missing a full-time parent and the one he had was working double-time to make up for the single parent income. "Tell your mom we expect to see the food truck at the third game."

He laughed and nodded. "Okay. Yeah. Thanks, Coach. For everything."

I watched as he turned and then ran toward the parking lot. His mom made sure he had a vehicle as soon as he could get a license since she couldn't always shuttle him around to practice and games.

By Friday, I was back to my usual self, not letting my past get me down and not expecting a certain new teacher to follow-through on baked goods. This is why I was surprised to find multiple boxes of cupcakes on my desk.

The note read:

I couldn't decide on one cake and my neighbors were no help other than keeping the cake I brought to them to try out. So. I hope the team likes variety and maybe you can tell me which one is your favorite?

All of them. They were all my favorite and I hadn't even opened the first box yet.

I carried them to the cafeteria where my favorite lunch lady let me keep things for the team.

"Look at that! I thought you said you weren't getting the good luck cupcakes this year." Mrs. Esther smiled at me.

"I didn't think we would, but I guess our new life skills teacher is going to pull through for us." I was entirely too excited about that.

She gave me a look and I could feel my face turn about the color of the red apron she was wearing. She laughed and said, "I thought so. Oh, honey, she is a sweetheart. Did you know that she came to let me know a few of the students have some allergies and issues that impact what they can eat. She doesn't think it is diagnosed, but thanks to the questions in class, she made that guess. I put in for some new options. I mean, we won't know for sure, but I know that school breakfast and lunch is all some of these students get around here."

I nodded. "I know."

It was part of the reason I had this space in the refrigerator and another space in a cabinet for protein bars and other stuff I could easily hand off to my players without them being embarrassed though everyone around here knew ninety percent of the school was comprised of students experiencing economic struggles in one form or another.

"I can't wait for Diversity Day this year." Mrs. Esther was back to her clipboard and whatever she was looking at on it.

"Um, what?" We didn't have diversity day. Every day at this school was diversity day in the sense that there was a mix of racial profiles, but a consistent lack of income.

"Fundraiser. New thing the district put together and your new favorite cupcake maker is planning on taking some of her students to the finals in the food category." She looked at me and said, "Guess we may win state at something."

I balked and then cracked up laughing. Our team was really good, but we had never made it past regionals. "How is one day going to get them to state?"

"It begins on diversity day, big fundraiser at the country club." She gave me a look and I cracked up again. Our kids were not members for damn sure, but the venue meant the attending crowd was interested in throwing some money at these kids. "They are taste testing and the schools with the most votes on the specific foods get to go to state. The team that wins gets a scholarship for each participant to one of those culinary arts colleges."

"Well damn." I blinked at her. "I guess I better up my game or they might start hanging up their cleats and tying on some aprons."

She laughed and pointed as if to say, bingo.

I had a renewed interest in these cupcakes. Maybe they would not be so great. Maybe.

CHAPTER THREE:
JESSICA

By the end of my first month, I was exhausted, exhilarated, and totally crushing on the coach. I realized this was not just my imagination. I was getting more obvious about it becasue one of my students said, "You should go for it."

"Um." I looked over at the sophomore adjusting her shirt so it showed a bit more cleavage. I had never been that bold as an adult much less as a teen. "I'm not..." While I tried to find the words to lie, she stopped messing with her clothes and looked at me.

When nothing came out to finish that statement, she giggled and said, "Look, everyone loves Coach. I mean, if my mom wasn't mean as a snake, I would want him to be my step dad." She looked at the man laughing with a group of students at the end of the hall near his classroom. "Of course, not for the right reasons."

"Oh my God!" I put my hand over my mouth. She burst out laughing and I shook my head. "Stop. That is not funny. You are going to meet–"

She rolled her eyes up and then stuck her tongue out. "Come on. Let's not pretend like I have options." She looked around the space and shrugged her shoulders. "This is my life and it always will be."

I had to be careful here so I said, "Maybe." She looked over at me. "But maybe not. I mean, if we win, you could go to school to become a chef or a baker or–"

"You think we can win?" she asked.

And in a very un-teacher-like fashion I looked her directly in the eye and said with every bit of conviction I felt, "Hell yeah."

Her eyes lit up and she said, "Yeah?"

I nodded.

"Okay. I'll...join the cooking team."

"Yeah?" I was trying not to get myself too excited.

"Yeah. I mean, I was going to play volleyball when they said you were coaching, but...I'd rather do this." She smiled at me and I could barely explain how much that statement meant to me.

"Okay. I'm glad to have you on the cooking team. Now, we need other students who really like to cook." I looked around and so did she. I had a recruiter for this and unlike the volleyball team, my cooking students stood a good chance at winning.

After school that day, I changed over into my coaching clothes and headed toward the gym.

"Hey, Coach!" I heard his voice, but it took me a minute to realize he was calling for me.

I turned and laughed, "Not used to that yet."

He smiled that warm smile and nodded. "You'll get used to that being your first name to lots of people by the end of the year."

"At least two teams." I laughed.

"Yeah. About that. How uh...are you sure...uh..."

I laughed. "I am way more confident in my coaching ability in the cooking aspect than I am in that gym."

He nodded. "Okay. I just...these kids get used to winning or losing. And...both become a burden."

I thought about that. "Thanks." Then I bit my lower lip and said, "Coach."

His cheeks tinted and I thought about that bold sophomore and quickly added, "You said you would help with this." I indicated the gym behind me. "Like...over dinner or..."

I was not confident on this court for damn sure.

He smiled brightly and said, "Yeah. That sounds great. We should wrap up this practice by six. Seven sound good?"

"Sure." I nodded. I wasn't sure how to proceed so I added, "I can cook."

He laughed. "Yeah. I know. Do you want to cook or go out?"

I blinked a few times and decided, "I'll cook. That way we won't be rushed so someone else can get the table."

"Here." He handed me his phone. "I'll text you when I'm on my way."

Feeling super nervous, I handed it back with my information in it and said, "Awesome."

He really smiled then and said, "Totally."

I blushed so deeply, but was saved from more embarrassment as my girls came giggling and talking down the hall toward the gym. They made some whistles and cat calls that had me frowning at them and saying, "Be professional, ladies. Come on. Two more laps for disrespecting Coach Carlos."

That had them grumbling and him giving me a raised brow as if that surprised him. I didn't want them turning into...well, they couldn't very well complain about people doing that to them if they were going to do it to others, right?

CHAPTER FOUR:
CARLOS

"I want to meet her." I regretted telling my mom where I was going instead of coming over for dinner as she just asked me to.

My silence revealed more than any words I could have said if I could find the right words to begin with.

She laughed and said, "Oh, I definitely must meet this girl. Bring her to dinner tonight."

"I can't. I told you, I was invited to her house. How would that look if I then said, no lets go to my parents house instead?" I rubbed my forehead. Why did I answer the phone? I knew she would want me to come over. They lived one neighborhood away from me and that was still not close enough for my mom. We didn't live in the school district I taught in. I often felt guilty about that, but at the same time, I had my parents close by and they had to be near their businesses as well. My dad owned multiple Mexican restaurants that he had built from a food truck which he still preferred to operate himself and most of the time. My mom owned and operated two child care centers rated the best in the state for early childhood education.

I hated to admit that in the finance department, I definitely needed them more than they needed me. They came to this country, embraced opportunity, and then made their own dreams come true. As an only child, I benefited from both of their choices. Once I was old enough to really listen, I could go to work with either one of them. I had summer jobs not a summer job and both the restaurants and the childcare centers helped solidify my love of teaching and homemade foods.

"We will come to your game next week." She pulled me from my thoughts with that statement and I realized I missed some of her conversation as I drifted down memory lane.

"Mom." I didn't even have an accent but they both did though I had to listen closely to hear it in my dad's speech or when he was in the restaurants around people who spoke Spanish. He said in business it was important to know who one was talking to and become a chameleon so they could see what they needed to see to invest. That had served him well and them too through the years.

"I can't wait to meet her." There was nothing left to say. No argument to make.

I simply said, "I'll see you next week."

She was happy as we said our I love yous as we did not like to say goodbye in my family. I looked down at the outfit I had changed into and decided it was entirely too much for a dinner at her house. I didn't want to give her the wrong impression. I didn't want to get the wrong impression. This was not a date. We did not establish this as more than two colleagues meeting to discuss coaching tactics over dinner.

At her apartment. In her space. I changed three more times before settling on a school t-shirt and jeans. Very casual and comfortable. I did stop to pick up a bottle of wine and then thought better of it and went through the drive thru to pick up two of the ridiculously expensive fall drinks at a coffee shop. I had seen her with one two mornings ago and...shit. I was in over my head because I wasn't even sure what I was doing here.

I pushed the buzzer for her apartment and the door clicked. I was so nervous it was ridiculous. Once at her door, I was about to knock when it opened and the smell of fresh baked something wafted past her and wrapped around me like a seductive cinnamon rolled glove. "That smells amazing."

She giggled and said, "Thanks. I was trying something new for dessert."

"Dessert first. I like it." I entered and held up the drinks.

"You're not kidding!" She laughed as she reached for the one I offered to her. "These are so bad, but soooo good."

She put the straw to her lips and closed her eyes as she took a long drink. The sigh as she opened them had me a bit uncomfortable. I hadn't really been turned on by a woman drinking a beverage before. I was now. Had been since that door opened. I took a drink of mine as we moved to the table she indicated as she closed the door behind me.

One more drink and she said, "I'm going to be up all night now. The combination of this caffeine and the sugar. Whew. I hope you are prepared for a long night, Coach."

I took another sip of the drink that would no doubt increase my energy level since it packed quite the punch. I could see why she picked one of these up near the end of the week. I might start grabbing one now and then. "I think I can last as long as you need me to."

We both just sort of stared at one another and then her pink cheeks lifted in a smile as she said, "Well, that may be all night."

So glad I was sitting. "I have no place else to be."

This was not just my imagination and no matter how much part of me was all about resistance...the moment she pulled those cupcakes out of the oven, I knew I was done for.

CHAPTER FIVE:
JESSICA

"I'm so excited to meet you." I shook the hand of the woman looking at me like I was crazy, but I was really excited to meet his parents. Especially at a game where we could cheer them on and talk without him being right there with us. I could get to know them, they could get to know me and since I was head over heels in love with their son, I wanted to make a good first impression.

"Manuel." His dad was much more laid back and seemed less surprised by my enthusiasm. "Let's get to our seats." He indicated with his arm and I moved toward the stands. I could hear him whisper and I knew three words from the college Spanish classes I had taken, but that was it. Amiga which I knew was a friend who is also a girl, but may or may not be used in the context of girlfriend. Mijo which I knew was son. And finally, si. Which I knew as yes. So, with all of that context, I knew I needed to crack open those textbooks again. I also knew that the Spanish I learned in college was formal, derived from Spain, and not universal because each region and country still had their own accents, terms, and...yeah. I would not be holding any bilingual conversations right away.

Carlos had told me everything about them. Everything. We spent the entire night talking about our lives and when he learned I had failed at my bakery, he told me how his dad started with just a food truck and now owned multiple restaurants. He didn't make me feel the shame I had felt around pretty much everyone else in my life that I had a business and it failed. It cost me all of my savings and was why I lived in an apartment and took the first job that was offered, teaching.

"So, are you from around here?" his mom asked.

"I'm actually from the East Coast, but I always wanted to live on the West Coast so when I went to college, I came out here and...I've been here ever since." I smiled, but she was studying me pretty intently.

"And adventurous spirit." His dad, on the other hand, smiled at me.

"I thought so. I uh...am a lot more cautious about my adventures now. In fact...I think I found my calling." I looked out toward the field as they announced the game would be starting soon. "I love teaching."

"So does our son." His dad was amazing. His mom was still eyeing me.

She finally asked, "Where is your family?"

"All over. My mom is in South Carolina. My dad New York. My siblings from their second marriages are either still at home with their respective families or in college in other states." I gulped. "I...don't have a close family. Not like he does."

That was a problem for her. I could see it clear as day. I understood it. Just couldn't change my own circumstances and there was a time when I wanted to. But not anymore.

"Do you want children?" she asked point blank and I was a bit surprised at the bluntness.

His dad chuckled and said, "I see you plan to take my advice."

She waved him off and said, "I want to know this woman my son did not bring to dinner to meet us."

I blinked. "You wanted me to come to dinner?"

"Yes. I want to know who you are." She was serious.

"Well, I...didn't know I was invited to dinner." That hurt, but I would ask because I was sure he had a reason. I hoped he had a reason. Maybe he didn't want to be there for the grilling I was about to get if this opening conversation was an indication of how the night was going to go. "This...after this game, the dinner would be the first time we went somewhere public together. It's...new. The start. But...yes, I do. I would like to have a family. I wish I had a big family, and technically I guess I do, but...I don't live one neighborhood away from anyone. Family is very important to him. He was clear about that. I was clear that despite my background, I am very much on that same path."

As if that was all she wanted to know, she smiled and said, "Okay. You don't think he needs to be a professional athlete and move away or teach at the college and move away. He is not going to move away."

I failed to hold back the giggle. "No, ma'am. I don't want him to move away and he does not want to leave."

It was as if the world had been lifted off our little space in an instant as she said, "Okay then. And you will come to dinner next week."

His dad smiled and winked at me. I nodded. Yes. I would come to dinner next week and every week if they would have me. "Absolutely."

The game went well and the team won. Dinner with his parents went even better. When it came time to bring this night to an end, I didn't want it to end.

"I have cupcakes." I teased.

"You're going to make me double my workout." He patted his flat stomach and smiled. "What kind?"

"Your favorite." I opened the door and stepped back into the apartment.

"I think they are all my favorite now." He stepped forward and the tension between us increased.

"Makes it easier to plan that way." I stopped moving as he shut the door and then stepped into my space. "I want to make a lot of plans with you."

He smiled down at me and then leaned in until our lips touched. This was the start of the rest of my life. The rest of my life with cupcakes and Carlos.

EPILOGUE:
CARLOS

"Mijo!" I picked up my two year old son and watched my four year old daughter throw a ballet slipper at her six year old brother playing his video game instead of getting dressed.

My house was filled with laughter, screaming children, one barking dog, and a cat that just jumped from the kitchen counter to perch on top of the refrigerator in a wise decision if there ever was one.

"Cat!" he pointed and Whiskers, rightly aware that this child was a squisher, hissed.

"Be nice, Mr. Whiskers." I then looked at my son and said, "You, too. You have to be gentle."

He roared with laughter and in the process of trying to squeeze my neck also head butted me. This made him laugh again, but ensured I would need some acetaminophen in my near future.

"Abuela's here!" My daughter only had to say one of two words and the entire house come to a simmering pause just waiting for one of the grandparents to come through the door.

She opened it and said, "Why isn't everyone ready?"

As if I had not asked this question already, everyone, including my cat chasing, head butting toddler, began to do what needed to be done. My mom moved over to me as my toddler checked his own diaper bag to make sure he had the toys he wanted.

She hugged me and then patted my cheek and said, "It's going to be a great night."

I smiled and nodded. "Yes. It is."

When we arrived at the school, we were entering through a magical space that I knew took a lot of time and energy because I had spent a lot of time and energy doing some of this decorating. The reason, besides my daughter, was waddling toward me with our fourth and final child due sometime this month. This was it for us. When we talked about a big family we thought six, but we both agreed if we hoped to hold up as well as my parents as we aged, this was the stopping point.

She moved to hug me and said, "Look who came to see it."

I turned to see four more grandparents entering the room. "Wow."

Her parents, both sets, made an effort which meant the world to her, to me, and our kids. They would never be as close as my parents, but apparently being a grandparent changes how people vacation these days.

All the greeting said, it was time for the play, but first, I had to sneak off to the reception area afterward because I knew they would be gone before I could get one if I didn't take one right now.

I heard her giggle and say, "Oh, Coach. That is a penalty if ever there was one."

Icing on my lips, cupcake in hand, I had to admit, "I'll take the penalty."

She made her way to me and scooped a finger of icing off to eat. I frowned at her, "Hey. Flag on the play."

"I'll take the penalty." She smiled up and I leaned down to kiss the love of my life. This woman who had stumbled into a teaching position, then a coaching one, then when our cooking team made it to state, she became an curriculum developer and trainer for a culinary arts program that stretched across multiple schools. She didn't just teach in one place anymore and she got to train other teachers. Still, our school was her home base and while she relinquished the coach apron to our original life skills teacher, she did not give up the volleyball one.

She touched my forehead and asked, "What happened here?"

"Your son."

She laughed. "Well, time to go watch your daughter."

"My daughter." I teased because she was such a daddy's girl and we had another boy on the way so yeah, that little girl was going to be spoiled forever.

"Do you think it's fair she will be the only girl?" she asked as we headed to the seats.

"Yes." I nodded and laughed. "I do." Fair or not, that was the situation.

"We could adopt though." She looked up at me.

I hadn't thought about that with us turning them out every two years on our own. "Okay."

I nodded. Sure. If in two years we wanted another, we would adopt one.

"I love you and your gigantic heart." She leaned against me.

"And I will always love you." I kissed her forehead. "Though I could love you more if you let me grab one more cupcake."

***

Hope you enjoyed Cupcakes and Carolos.
Be sure to leave a review!

ABOUT THE AUTHOR

Cara North is the long-time multiple-subgenre, romance pseudonym for Tonya Nagle, PhD. As a faculty member at multiple institutions of adult learning over the past twenty years, having a pen name was key to keeping her identities separate. Today, you can find everything under one website and additional pen names for YA and non-romance centric sci-fi and fantasy. She is a USMC veteran. She loves writing short stories for anthologies and connecting with her readers.

Find More At

www.creativewritingwithdrnagle.com

SEEING RED

Andi MacDowall

ABOUT *SEEING RED*

When a lie brings on more controversy that she doesn't need, Scarlett is forced into a fake marriage with her childhood rival, Rhett. The deal is one year, they pretend to be married and in the process try not to fall for each other.

CHAPTER 1:
SCARLETT

"Yeah, Mom I'll be there." I groan, strolling out of Neiman Marcus, swinging a few bags in one hand—a new cocktail dress and epically gorgeous designer shoes—and a mocha latte in the other.

The shopping trip is Mom's bribe du jour and insurance that I'll be in attendance at their thirty-fifth wedding anniversary ball. The talk of the town and that's what cautions me.

"Don't huff at me. It's not too much to ask all of our children to be there, is it?" Emotional blackmail is her forte. I prop my phone on my shoulder, looking for my car. Stopping at the curb, because I can't find it.

The sign at the exit reads, East wing. Dammit, I went out the wrong way. It's at the other entrance and according to my gold bangle watch, I have forty minutes to get to my appointment, so I haul ass in the other direction.

"Right. I don't want to bring undue attention to myself. For my sake and y'alls."

I'm completely turned around. There are two exits out of the store, I take the far one and end up in the other parking lot.

"You can't hide forever." I don't think she means it to, but her tone is condescending like I'm a child. Only I'm not a child and this is a big deal. It affects my career, my future.

The reason she sees it as an overreaction is that she's content to be a mom and wife. The first Lady of Ebony Cove, but she doesn't have a desire for a career. And thus doesn't understand my need for one.

Ultimately though, Mom's right. Ugh, that physically hurts to admit. The more I hide, the more they talk, and it becomes a vicious cycle that reincarnates itself over and over. I'm just not sure I'm ready to face the world again. Even if it's limited to Ebony Cove.

"Besides, it's all in your head. I doubt anyone remembers your little incident at all."

Okay, I was on board before that comment. She always takes it one too far.

"Incident." I say, scoffing.

The nerve of her to make light of my public humiliation, cementing the idea that she truly doesn't get it. I inhale again before I blow a gasket. I have to remember, it's not her world. She limits her exposure to social media. Not seeing the value in it or in having a career at all.

New York was good for me in a lot of ways. Giving up my inheritance kept me humble. I had to depend on myself. My skills, my prowess. Learn to work hard, think bigger. More than that, I found my passion and now this incident as she so casually calls it may dismantle that dream forever. But I can't explain this all in a simple phone call.

"Mom, I didn't spill wine on my dress at a gala." Though admittedly, that would be embarrassing. My arms flail as I speak, making an exaggerated gesture. "TMZ filmed my breakdown for freak's sake. And the entire world labeled me the psycho and him the victim, even after he cheated on me." The whine in my tone makes my ears ache, but this is so unfair.

Oh why did I leave Mexico?

It was heavenly, hard bodies everywhere, barely clothed. Tequila flowing like rivers and best of all, not a soul recognized me. Not like here. Three days back and tongues are already getting a workout. Small town gossips itching to get their fix like my life is some damn reality show.

Mom's quiet. That's never good. She stays that way for a while. After an unknown amount of time, she says,

"Rhett is back in town. Have you seen him? He'll be there tonight." The lift in her voice startles me, changing the subject and not a good one at that.

Not this again. I take a drink of my coffee, savoring the chocolatey goodness on my tongue. Looking both ways, I cross the street, half distracted by the thought of him being there.

Can we really be civil? Historically, that answer is a no. I guess we'll see.

"I know. Makes sense, as it's his parents' anniversary too."

Our parents are best friends and have been for decades. When we were born they named us after the iconic lovers. A guarantee we'd fall in love and get married. At least that was the plan. Leave it to us to spoil the whole thing.

"You know he's in the Navy."

"That's nice." I laugh, gulping through a dry patch in my throat. Ignoring the thump of my heart at the notion. Military men turn my body to mush.

The uniform, those rippling muscles. Authority in every word they speak.

Now I can't breathe, because of Rhett. No. I force memories from our youth. The scrawny goth kid with more bone than muscle and picture his lanky body in uniform. No way he's changed that much.

"Mmm hmm. Not just in the Navy. He's a SEAL. And handsome. You're both adults now. I think it's time you bury the hatchet."

"Between his eyes? Now that's a plan." I say in my snarkiest tone, with a wide grin at the thought. Silence again. "I'm at my car and have to go. I'll see ya tonight."

I set my coffee on the roof of the car—a rental—and press the key fob to open the hatch. After I hang my dress and shoes in the back, I slam the hatch down in time for a familiar blond-haired woman to cross right behind it.

Eliza Johns.

We were besties in high school. Officers together on the drill team. My first lieutenant in the *Scarlett Squad*. Since then, the thrall has gone out of our relationship. In high school, I was one of *those* girls—popular, ruling the school. It was my kingdom and I its queen. That's all ancient history now.

"Eliza." I address her, but she rushes right past me, focused on her phone. I know she heard me as she was only inches away a minute ago. About three cars away, she halts and backtracks to where I'm standing, next to my vehicle.

"Lettie. I'm so sorry. Didn't see ya there, hon." Sure she didn't. She's a terrible liar. "How've ya been?"

Either she's taken up residence under a rock. Or she doesn't actually care, and this is an attempt to extract a nugget from me to feed the rumor mill. I'm betting on the latter option.

Every town has a ring leader. The one that supplies the gossip. My guess is she's the self-appointed queen. "I heard about that unfortunate business with Derrick Jonas." she says.

Derrick is a famous country singer, not related the brothers. I knew it.

She's casting her net, hoping to catch something. A little tidbit she can exploit. I can't abide this probing, so I shoot back.

"Great. Never better. Can't wait for the party tonight."

"Oh, what he did, that had to be mortifying." She gasps, covering her mouth, practically clutching her pearls. If she were wearing any. Her whiney twang comes out thick as molasses and counterfeit as a three-dollar bill.

"No, it felt great. Really, I recommend it sometime," I sneer through a strained smile. Glancing at my watch, I shift in place. I really don't have time for this.

My hair appointment. The perfect excuse to get out of here with my dignity intact. She digs through her purse for her sunglasses. Even though it's overcast to cover her eyes. Probably so I can't read her like a cheap tabloid. Give her a day and she'll have the entire town buzzing about the latest gossip like the glory hound she is.

Eliza clears her throat as my distorted reflection bounces back at me, shielding the windows to her obsidian soul.

"Well it's been fun." I inch away and she follows me. "I have to go." I grab my coffee and stand by my door, hoping she'll take the hint.

"Oh, you're attending the ball." The tone of her voice pitches higher than before. Genuine shock sweeps over her features as her eyes nearly pop out of her head and her mouth drops open. I cross my arms, glaring hot coals at her, leaning on the fender.

"Bless your heart, darlin." I say in a sickening sweet tone, biting back the urge to rip her to shreds. "You honestly thought I'd miss my parents' anniversary party?"

I close my eyes and puff out my lips. Mom is right. It's like a blade in my heart. But it's true. I want my phoenix moment, but I'm resisting the process.

For the last few months, I avoided the pain, opting for numbness. Only I can't rise from the ashes if I won't endure in the fire.

I swing my car door open. Her pasty complexion grows pink around her shades as she glowers through the nearly opaque lenses.

"Well, I just thought after what happened on TMZ that you'd be too embarrassed to show your face." She stammers, she was not expecting me to fire back.

"You'd like that, wouldn't you?" I squint at her, tilting my head.

She fans herself in the blistering heat, waving her massive bridal set in my face. It's big enough to put a dent in my window.

"Oh, honey. I just am concerned about your well being. I snagged my Timothy years ago." Eliza crinkles her nose. More fake sympathy. Why?

"It must be hard to be pushing thirty." She leans into my ear and whispers. "Single." Stepping back, she shrugs, wearing a half-clenched smile but feigning concern. "You know what they say. Always a bridesmaid, never a bride."

I slam my car's door and pace forward so she and I are inches apart. That's it. The gloves are off. "Well congratulations. Smart starting young, get that first marriage out of the way. That way you're still a young enough to snag man number two. You know when he tires of your bullshit and cheats?"

Her mouth drops open. Good. "How dare you say that?"

"Who else but a bitter woman would relish in another woman's suffering? Things cooled off already? Did he finally see you for the callous, vicious person you are? That's too bad. Beauty may be only skin deep, but ugly is down to the soul."

I verbally nuke her. It's Chernobyl with words, leaving her a radioactive pile of rubble.

And by the way, she casts her gaze on the concrete, rather than meet my eye again, tells me I'm sniffing at the right tree.

She scoffs, getting in my face. "At least I can keep my man happy. That's why he ditched you for the supermodel."

White smoke comes out of my ears as I dig my nails into my palm, suppressing the desire to pound that snarky smirk right off her face.

"I am married." I blurt out. Okay, where am I going with this? To hell, never mind I'm already there. Where am I gonna find a husband? No worries for now. I shove the thought into the back of my mind. I'll worry about that later.

"You're what?" She shifts her weight and cocks her head. "Really? When? Where did you meet him?"

"Yes, it was while on vacation, in Mexico." I picture Mario Lopez in his younger years as I describe my fake paramour with a shit-eating grin. "He's a rebel. Bad boy on a motorcycle with tricks int he bedroom that makes me think he moonlights as a stripper."

One lie gives birth to more lies and pretty soon I'm the mayor of Lieopolis. In super deep like to my eye-balls, but my pride won't let me back down.

"Well, I can't wait to meet him then. Surprised your parents said nothing of you eloping."

I swallow, fighting the knot lodged in my throat. "They wanted to wait till after the ball."

CHAPTER 2:
SCARLETT

In the hotel's bar and lounge, I'm ready to get loaded.

Normally, I'm a fruity drink kind of girl. Give me a margarita or sex on the beach as in the drink. Anything with an umbrella and more parts fruit than alcohol.

Not tonight.

Tonight is a hard liquor kind of night, but I can't shoot it straight, so I opt for the next best thing.

"Vodka and Sprite."

"Let me guess, you're here for the masquerade?" His Spanish accent is sexy and refreshing. Reminds me of Cozumel. Oh, how I wish I was there now.

A hot older man with dark skin flashes me his pearly whites and hazel eyes. He's wearing a white button-down shirt that's cuffed at the elbow, revealing a few tattoos.

Another peeks out above his collar.

My formal gown cuts in all the right places, offering up the swell of my breasts on an altar of silk. On display for any ogling eyes. But that's it, no touching. I drum my irritation on the mahogany bar. I can't even openly flirt.

I should be in the ballroom, but I can't bring myself to cross the threshold. For twenty minutes I stood there like it was at the edge of a cliff with a five hundred foot plunge. One step forward and I'm a goner. Later I'll make an appearance, do the supportive daughter thing and duck out early to avoid gratuitous inquiries.

While I wait for my drink, I study my reflection in the mirror backing of the bar, propping up my chin on the edge of my upturned fist.

The dark red color is new. Glad I let Mandy, my hairdresser, talk me into the dye job this afternoon. Earlier, I walked right past mom, and she wasn't the wiser.

Incognito in crimson. I like it.

Mandy pulled it into a low chignon. Classy and understated. My theme for the night. Other than my lips—which could use a touchup—my make up is holding up well. My eyes are a different story, though. Worn, weary and no matter how I dress them up with this gold ornate mask, there's an obvious sadness I hope only I can see.

For the last few months, I've focused on the anger for the incident, but I haven't grieved. I loved Derrick, and he forged my love into a weapon and stabbed me in the back with it. The biggest betrayal didn't come from my enemy. It never does. And I haven't processed that part of the hurt yet.

"Here ya go. On the house." The bartender winks as he sets my drink before me. Guess the sparkle isn't completely off this diamond.

***

RHETT

I should be in the ballroom, dutifully receiving guests and enduring the idle chit-chat that nearly sends me into a murderous rage.

And I fully intend to, after. After a drink or five, to dull my senses, so I keep my tongue in check. Where alcohol agitates some, it loosens me up. Allows me to endure the inane chatter of the debutants in Ebony Cove.

My stint in the Navy thickened my skin, and left me with little patience for the shallow pursuits that the well-to-do in this town concern themselves with. The bitter rivalries that have no basis in real world meaning. It's more trivial than celebrity tabloid bullshit.

The concierge at the front desk directed me to the hotel lounge and bar. Perfect. I step in the glass doors. It's low key. A quiet piano plays in the background. Now we're talking. Reminds me of the smoking and brandy room in my parents' place. Minus the smoke. Dark wood and burgundy bathed in electric candlelight.

The Golden Age of Hollywood. Clark Gable and Vivien Leigh. *Rhett and Scarlett*. The originals, not our cheap imitation. I love black and white movies.

There are a couple of men at a table to my left, deep in conversation. An older gentleman watches a football game on the tv with subtitles to the right.

And dead center is a woman drinking alone. Gold mask, black cocktail dress with no back, and sparkling heels.

The style of her hair screams vintage Hollywood with a modern edge. She stands out in a good way. In a mask, so she's either taking a break from the festivities or avoiding them altogether.

My kind of woman.

At the bar, I slip off my uniform jacket. Which, to the average observer, is a tux jacket with gold stripes on the sleeves in the rank of lieutenant. By all appearances, it's a Navy issued monkey suit.

After I drape it over the back of my chair, I order. "Tequila, por favor with lime. And whisky on the rocks. Top shelf for both. The oldest whisky ye got." I revert to my native tongue when around other Spanish speakers. In Texas, there's an abundance of them.

"Where are you from?" The bartender asks.

I grin, I get this a lot. "Here. Well, mostly. But my mother is from Scotland."

"Tu Hablas espanol?"

"Aye." I chuckle, tapping on the hardwood. Every time I meet new people, I have to relay my life story, but I don't mind. I'm proud of my heritage. All of it. "Spanish, English and Gaelic. My dad is Colombian and Mexican. My mom is Scottish, but I was born here. I've spent a great deal of summers in Scotland and lived there for a few years."

He grins. "I'm David. That's awesome. Don't think I've met a Scot around here in a while. My mom is from Colombia. Dad is Mexican. That's an interesting combination with the Scottish." He grins. His accent is almost non-existent, but I can tell he's a native speaker. "We could be cousins. I was in the Navy too. Not an officer, but I took this job after I did my time, until I finish school. Damn, listen to me telling you my life story. I'd love to trade sea stories some time. Oh, by the way, what kind of tequila? I got Cuervo, Patron, 1800..." He lists off.

"No worries. Navy men are rare in Texas, being landlocked and all. Patron reposado, but just a shot." I like a smooth tequila I can sip, but whisky is what I'm craving. "Also Macallan whisky. Aged after twenty. Thirty is better if ye have it."

"Certainly coming right up." He throws the bar rag over his shoulder, bringing back memories.

Before I joined the Navy, I tended bar, much to the chagrin of my parents. But I did it for the experience and to meet girls. The ladies went crazy for a man pouring the drinks. Though I didn't spin them around like in the movie *Cocktail*, I held my own. Come closing time, I took many to my bed. It's how I met my ex-wife, Jessica.

Born into a wealthy family, they expected me to attend college, then become a lawyer or other respectable profession. Which I did, minus the respectable profession, at least in their eyes.

So I partied at university and enlisted in the Navy right after. A terrible disappointment to my father even after making it through BUDS and becoming a S.E.A.L. as an officer.

The gorgeous mystery woman is reading something on her phone, oblivious to our conversation happening right next to her, completely immersed. I adjust my mask, assuring it's not going anywhere, and take the stool next to her.

"I'm..."

She cuts me off with a raised finger, but doesn't so much as glance in my direction. Her scarlet lips move with the words on her screen—then, without warning—she lays the phone down and addresses me.

"Sorry, I was in the middle of a passage. I wanted to read the end."

Her voice is delicate, like butterfly wings. Soft and demure with a British inflection. I prefer the roughness of the Texas girls' drawl, but her voice leaves me spellbound.

She flings me a cursory glance and locks on.

"Uh.. I'm." Is all I can get out of my windpipe. It's suddenly bone dry. My mind goes effectively blank, and I stammer when I try to speak while she stares blue topaz at me in utter silence.

"I'm Andres." I damn near choke on the word. My middle name.

"I'm Maeve."

"Maeve and Andres." I whisper under my breath like we are an iconic couple.

"What did you say?"

The bartender cuts in, right as I go to answer. "I apologize we're out of Patron but here's a thirty-five-year Macallan."

I take the tumbler and say, "Thank ye. Whatever the lady is having. Put it on my bill."

She flushes a lovely shade of pink, turning to hide her smile. "Thank you. I'll get... the next round."

I spin the crystal tumbler in my hand, fixate on the amber liquid inside, and take a drink.

"I'll not hear of it." I lean in her direction, getting a whiff of jasmine and vanilla, and my heart hits new heights.

She tilts toward me, a few inches away, and says, "You'll not only hear of it. You'll accept it because it's a deal breaker. It's only fair. I intend to drink you under this bar."

"Bad week?"

"Been better. This week has been a definite contender for the shittiest week of the year. Maybe my life. No, that was three months ago when my fiancé cheated on me and I confronted him at my work. I lost my job too."

Sadness wells in her Caribbean blue eyes like a beacon drawing me in. All I want to do is scoop her up in my arms and comfort her.

Her confession digs up old skeletons that haunt me now, too. "Could've been worse."

Not to piggyback on her pain, but maybe give her reassurance she's not in this shitstorm called life alone.

Her eyes sparkle with curiosity, narrowing on mine with nothing more than interest.

"How so?"

A cynical half-smile escapes me. "You could've been married," I say, through a final swig, emptying the glass and set it down, expelling a satisfied sound. "For five years."

I flinch at my own words and the memories that flood my noggin. "My last cruise was the final nail in the coffin of my marriage. No one bothered to tell me. No warning. No call. No note. Just a cleaned out condo. Empty shelves and drawers. Come to find out she was banging the neighbor."

She spits out her drink and releases a humorless laugh, drawing her brows together. "Oh Andres I'm sorry." Maeve drags a manicured fingertip across my chin, right below my lip, and tilts her head. "Truly I'm sorry."

I slowly shake my head, joining her for a hearty laugh at my expense, taken back a little at how much I adore nearly every sound she emits.

She scrunches her adorable nose, downing another gulp. Clasping my shoulder, she lightly pats it, and I shift uncomfortably in my seat from the electricity that flits through me from simple contact.

Twice she's sent my body off in a frenzy and I've been in her company for less than ten minutes. There's a sublime elegance to her movements, not loud and boisterous. Her understated appearance and mannerisms are like a crisp, fresh breeze.

"Okay, you win. At least I found out the bastard was a cheat before I permanently attached myself to him."

She raises her glass to mine and we clink them together.

We spend the next hour laughing and joking about our epically bad taste in mates. It's a balm for my battered soul.

"My mom drives me crazy. I'm barely divorced, and she wants me to settle down again right away." I lament. "Prattling on and on about grandkids. I dinna ken. I tune her out a lot. She's a feisty wee thing, though."

Maeve grazes her finger over mine, and goosebumps raise all over from that minor contact. There's nothing inherently sexual about the way she brushes over my skin, but the reaction to her is.

"Maybe we could pretend to date. Then she'll stop setting you up. I would hope."

I focus on her mouth as she speaks, lifting the corners again. Now I want to kiss her. Feel those plump lips against mine.

"We could pretend to be engaged." I say, upping the ante and holding my breath, expecting her to storm off or shut me down.

Instead, she giggles and I want to kiss her more than I did a second ago. It's a beautiful melody, melting my heart.

For an inexplicable reason, I'm drawn to her and I suddenly grasp why moths love flames.

The danger, the blinding light that consumes you until you're embers or ash. But before all that, there's unspeakable heat. She may consume me in a great ball of fire, but what a way to go.

She gets a mischievous glimmer in her eyes, arching a brow. "We could pretend to be married. It would solve everything."

It's a bluff; it has to be. So I call it, daring her to fold. I tilt my head, gripping my glass. My vision concentrates there now. "Fake marriage. Interesting. How would that work?" I ask. "Wait before you answer that. Are you drunk?"

"No." It's short, almost combative, but she's serious.

"You pray-tend to be my husband..." Her twang slips out as she cocks her head, and she doesn't notice her faux pas, so she continues. "It would solve your problem."

Wait, I know that voice. It hasn't changed since high school. I throw down a hundred for the drinks as I process this impossibility. *Scarlett*. Scarlett just asked me to be her fake husband.

CHAPTER 3:
SCARLETT

"Let's go," he orders, grabbing my hand, whisking me out of the bar before I can object. Not that I do.

Outside the hotel is a small park. Not much more than a stone walkway and some trees. I slide my feet out of my shoes and traipse barefoot through the lush, damp grass. His legs are longer; he takes smaller strides so I can keep up.

Enormous oak trees form a canopy overhead. I crane my neck to take in the fullness of it. In the daytime, I bet this is great to shield visitors from the sun with much-needed shade in the heat.

A newly painted cream wrought-iron bench is at the center of a stone walkway that cuts through the manicured green. The branches above dance in the slight breeze, playing peek-a-boo with the stars. Street lights sift through them, casting shadow puppets on the concrete around the bench.

"Can you stop for a second?"

He obliges, halting in place long enough for me to slip my heels on, braced on his brawny forearm. After that, it's only a few more steps to the bench.

"Sit."

Another order.

There's not a hint of ask in that word, but for some mystifying reason, I lower myself onto it. His back is to me, so he can't see. It's strange how I'm compelled to obey his commands. This man, with the deep booming voice, whom I hardly know anything about. Our chat was the most fun I've had rehashing my breakup with Derrick. And I haven't laughed like that in ages.

Andres unties his mask and shoves it into his pocket. "What is the real reason for this subterfuge? Scarlett."

My real name. I blink a few thousand times, waiting for my brain to catch up. The timbre of his voice is deeper than I remember.

Flying to my feet, I nearly trash one of my heels when I land on them in a fluid movement. My heart pounds wickedly in my chest. His name burns in my lungs before I let it escape my lips. *Rhett.*

He has his back to me, so I can't confirm. The reverberation of his words bounce around my skull. I give myself another minute for it all to solidify in my mind.

There's no way.

Right now, I'm wading in a river of denial. It can't be. My thoughts aren't coherent or complete anymore. I'm backing away while fascination grips me. This man, hotness personified, can't be the pimply faced skinny kid from high school.

Exhibit A, he's enormous, with stacks of dense, corded muscle. Exhibit b, that voice. It makes my knees J-ello and my blood run super hot. Deep, rich like a well-aged wine. Speaking of well-aged, the years have favored him.

And now I have to see for myself. My throat constricts as I lift my fingers excruciatingly slow to his shoulder. I take a deep breath and spin him around—which, given the mass of his torso—I can't do it without his cooperation. So he's a SEAL.

"Rhett Cortez." Saying his name brings on a smile, but I flatten it out before he notices.

"In the flesh. Your highness," he mocks, bowing. "Nice to see ye again, love."

Fire crackles beneath my skin as anger and lust wrestle in my thoughts for top billing. I can't hide the flush coloring my cheeks. So I tell another lie. Focus on the parts of him that don't turn my grey matter to ooze.

I scowl at him, hugging myself. Kevlar to protect my heart, but he's armor piercing ammo. Bound to get through. "Devil... in the flesh." I correct his initial statement, bristling while I rub away goosebumps he invokes.

It's not logical, I know. We both lied. We both pretended to be other people. But somehow, in my mind, his deception is far worse.

What reason does he have to hide his identity?

He dips down to my level with a devilish grin. "I never claim to be a saint."

Restlessness consumes me, but I stick to that spot, mired. It's disconcerting, how *not* disturbed I am by all this. I mean I'm face to face with my arch nemesis. Geez, we sound like Batman and Catwoman. He's more of a cross between Mario Lopez and Gerard Butler with a physique that would put the Rock to shame. The artist who fashioned him took his time. The detail is exquisite, like he's carved from stone.

Irresistible.

That is until he opens his mouth.

Glaring razor sharp daggers at me, he unbuttons the cuffs of his white button-down shirt and slowly rolls them up. Revealing labyrinthine art inked into his naturally tan flesh, winding around his bulging forearm. Rhett, closes in on me. I shut my eyes softly, lost in the scent of his whisky and obsession for Men. I'd recognize that anywhere. The way it blends with his personal chemistry creates an intoxicating fog surrounding as he presses me into his hard body.

"I'm waiting for an answer."

"Um."

God he smells good. Gripping his shirt, I bury my face in the cotton garment. Just inebriated enough to let him take me home. It's foolish. This man cares nothing for me, but I want to do something utterly foolish.

No.

Now I have to get away, because I'm at the verge of crossing the mother of all lines. He must have amped up pheromones, because the visions that dance through my head right now are anything but demure. Or polite. The electricity streaking between us isn't real. But I want to pretend for one night it is.

This ends now. I'm trembling, fighting with every fiber in my being to push off him. And at least one part of me is completely boycotting that idea. He's not budging either, not holding me but he makes no effort to move. Guess I have to do all the heavy lifting.

This is a lie. A cruel, vindictive lie. I lift off him, newly incensed and once again have full control of all my faculties. Rhett clutches my arm, part to spin me back to him and part to keep me from stepping in the grass.

It's considerate. Ugh.

No, don't be sweet.

My mind races, rehashing our conversation with a fine tooth comb. A stone lodges in my chest, then sinks in my gut. Everything. I told him everything.

This is a sick joke.

Ply me with libations and then pump me for information. That's all he wanted to pump me for. There's a sudden, sharp pang of disappointment, and it rattles me further. Parking on the bench, I cradle my head in my hands while I melt down inside. Damn Vodka. Damn Russians for making the Vodka and damn hot bartender for letting me drink it like water.

Salty rivers stream down my cheeks, I can't stop them. Rhett is towering over me, and I peer up at him, wet eyes and all.

"Did you set this up?"

He doesn't even flinch. "Do I look like a damn babysitter? Why the hell would I want to put myself through that torture on purpose? If I'd known, it was ye. I would've run the other way screaming." he snarls. It's an actual freaking growl like a wolf and I can't breathe. *If my body would take a break from the lust fest, that would be great.*

Oh, it's on, back on my feet I stomp toward him.

"Yeah right. You just wanted to get me to spill all those juicy tidbits. Why else would you lie and give me a fake name?"

"Are you serious right now? How old are you Scarlett? Still playing fucking childish games? And for the record, you lied too." He closes the gap between us, leaving only a sliver of air.

"That's beside the point." I lift my chin, turning so he can't see the look of guilt on my face.

"No, it's the whole bloody point. Ye still think we're in high school. For the damn record, I haven't spoken to Lizzie since high school. Almost fifteen damn years. Contrary to what ye may think, I've been overseas fighting wars. I'm not interested in your petty rivalries. Or this pitiful, spiteful school age bullshit. And by the way, I hope ye have me in a sweet condo where I'm living rent free in that pretty head of yers."

I'm reeling from the force of his words, which hit right between the eyes. It's a cheap shot, but not more so than mine. My entire freaking body flushes red-hot and not from lust or anger, but from embarrassment. Because he's right.

He's got the back of my knees pinned to the bench. I panic inside, a deep all consuming shiver rocks my form. "Is this the part where you tell everyone I threw myself at you? That I lied? That I caught my ex fiancé banging his slut on my car."

"I'll do no such thing, but I want the truth. Honesty would be yer friend right about *now*, lassie." he blows through clenched teeth.

In all the years I've known him, he's never called me lassie or lass. It's intimate the way he says it, like we're in a lovers spat. The inflection in his tone makes my insides mush, and I can barely stand. I plunk down on the bench, staring up at him with wide, teary eyes.

There is no more charade. I let him see all I've kept buried until now. The uncertainty, the agony and, most of all, the vulnerability.

Not to manipulate him. It wouldn't work anyway, but because a small part of me trusts him. Okay, I have to, but I can't explain why. Thank God Rhett isn't half as petty as I am.

He lifts a finger to his lips. Someone is joining us from behind.

CHAPTER 4:
SCARLETT

"We have a visitor." Rhett declares, pointing at the swinging gate. A feminine silhouette strides toward us, but I can't make out who it is. The rhinestones on her a black evening gown catch the light from the street lamps. It's pretty, like a starry night. Her face comes into view, Eliza. Okay, I'll admit, she has good taste... in clothes.

I rush to my feet; slinking behind Rhett. Gripping his shoulders, I attempt to disappear inside him, pressing my cheek into his strong back.

"Ready to fess up yet? What's this about? I canna help if I don't know," he says over his shoulder.

"You'd help me?" I blink at the prospect, perking up just a bit.

Of course. He's a professional hero, maybe that's how he gets his jollies. Rescuing poor girls that dig their own graves with a shovel in hand. I don't have the luxury of time to imagine every scenario, so I nod, rubbing tear stains into his shirt.

"Okay fine. I told Eliza I was married. She threw out the line and hooked a sucker... fish."

"That's it?" He chuckles and damn it all to hell. It's freaking sexy. I smack his shoulder blade and he doesn't even flinch.

Smart move, handing him a weapon loaded with ammunition.

"Well, I wouldn't expect you to understand. You have little of a reputation to save."

"Ye ken. If you want me to do ye a favor. You might try to show me some respect."

"I *am* trying."

I cross my arms with my elbows in his lower back. The man is a mountain.

Rhett twists and grabs me, forcing me to his side. His skin warms against mine as I struggle to get behind him again. "Listen to me, stand tall, hiding will only make it worse."

"How do you do it?"

The words drizzle out slowly as I lean into his muscular frame, glancing at his hypnotic eyes for a second between questions. It's all I can take, they are like lasers that see right down to my soul.

"Do what?" He tucks a stray lock behind my ear.

"Pretend you don't care."

"Oh, it's not an act, love. I really don't give a shit. Ye and yer ilk haven't crossed my mind in some time. Real world, remember? War. Blood. Guts. Want some advice?"

I turn my neck to roll my eyes. Whatever. "I guess."

"Why does what she thinks have such an impact on ye?"

"That's not advice."

"I'm getting to that. Now. Answer the question."

There is no give to the man. Everything is black or white, like a chess board the pieces either help or harm the cause.

"Because she can ruin me. Rumors destroy lives in a small town."

Rhett grips both my arms and leads me further into the park in a private corner. Eliza's phone distracts her for a second and she stops to take the call.

"Do ye really believe anything that woman can say will ruin ye?"

"Yes." I grip my throat to confirm that weak ass voice came from me. What happened to me?

"How?" He inquires, focusing all his attention on me.

I glance at her behind us quickly and meet his intense gaze, answering with a shrug. "Scarlett how? Can she end your non-existent business? You can live off your inheritance and never have to work. So why does she threaten you so much?"

Rhett is making way too much sense right now. It's grating on my nerves because he's popping those illusion bubbles one by one. "Because she has what I want."

Eliza is still busy on her phone, while Rhett interrogates me like it's his profession. Damn he's good.

"What's that?"

"A husband, children. Success."

An authentic shocked expression covers his features as his jaw drops open. "Okay I want a family. Children and I want my business. I want it all. I see women like her and I'm jealous. I was always the best. The fastest, smartest and strongest. I had the most skill. Now I'm playing catch up and have a huge handicap."

"What yer personality?"

I glare at him, he has to keep picking at that scab doesn't he? After a weighty exhale I bite my bottom lip. *Do I look as shitty as I feel right now?*

Almost as if he reads my mind he says, "Ye look gorgeous. Ye may be a mess, but ye're quite a bonny one. A beautiful devastation." In an odd way that is the nicest thing he's ever said to me. It's almost endearing. "Trust me on this. Stop letting those that have nothing to offer ye decide how ye view yerself." He dips down to my level. "That's an order."

I should be offended but I'm flattered and the way he delivers that command has my entire being humming.

A few more minutes later, Eliza is off her phone and treading toward us. Plastered on is a fake smile as she clicks her heels on the stone heading our way.

No doubt she's here to rub her perfect life in my face. Rhett is right, and I take a second to marvel at this rare occurrence. I let all these people define me, but they don't pay my bills. They don't support my dreams. Hell, they probably didn't subscribe to my YouTube channel.

"Well, there you are."

Eliza's sing-song tone literally makes all the little hairs stand straight up and pins and needles tingle throughout my form. The feeling when an appendage falls asleep, that's what rampages through me.

Epic timing murphy.

Eliza. *Anything else you want to spring at me? A nuke? Random solar flare?*

I'm quaking in my designer shoes until he loops an arm protectively around my waist, so he has my ear. "Follow my lead. Oh, and... you owe me," he whispers.

"Lettie, you sly devil. When we spoke earlier, you didn't tell me you snagged this hunk right here," Eliza says, flashing him a brilliant grin. Unbelievable, she's openly flirting with my non-husband.

I force a smile, waiting for Rhett to dispute her claim. Instead, he says, "We wanted to be respectful of our parents. We planned on skywriting it next week."

I smack him lightly with my hand. "Don't tease her, honey. Truthfully, it's so new. I... Can Can hardly believe it myself," I say through an overly wide smile, suppressing the tears that gather behind the threshold ready to be freed.

My heart flies at a million miles a minute, threatening to beat right out of its confinement. I'm committed now. Can't stuff this genie back in the bottle.

"Wait, a minute." She shifts in place, gesturing her question before it leaves her lips. "I thought you were in the Navy. Where did y'all reconnect?"

She's casting that wide net again, hoping to snag us in a lie.

"Vacation. We got married in Mexico after visiting my grandparents," he says and I nod.

It's scary how in sync we are as he nails the pillars of the lie with little direction from me. Rhett grins, squeezing me tight into his stonewall of a chest and says, "Scarlett and I buried the hatchet. Luckily not in each other and we found out we have a lot in common."

Damn, he's good at this. Not sure that's a plus or a minus in his column. Or what I'll owe him after bailing me out. Eliza scrutinizes his statement but doesn't argue.

"Well, I spoke to your parents. And they said y'all need to find a place and I have the perfect one in mind. I can take you on a tour tomorrow."

We shake our heads simultaneously, dismissing the idea. "No, we don't need a place." We insist in unison.

Her eyes narrow in suspicion. Clearly, we have much to discuss before pulling this off. "So y'all are living with your folks on what is basically your honeymoon?"

Rhett plants a gentle kiss on my temple. "She's right, love. We canna stay at my parents' forever."

Good save.

"Right." I let a breathy sigh disguised as a laugh loose, blowing through my words. "Sure. Tomorrow."

Eliza hands me a business card and is gone. I give myself a minute or two for my mind to wrap around all this and for her to clear the vicinity.

Once she's out of earshot, I flip around to find his ice-blue eyes, squinting like he's too bright for me to look on directly. "You could've hung me out to dry?"

He crosses his beefy arms, almost in indignation. I'm genuinely shocked he didn't play that card. "I could have."

I swallow with barely any moisture in my throat to complete the action. He has done something most can't hope to accomplish, rendered me speechless.

"Um... Why didn't you?"

His eyes burn through me like hot pokers but there's no real heat in them but there is a hefty dose of scorn. "I'm not as petty as ye."

Turning my head, I take my licks. I deserve that.

Rhett's eyes glitter in the moonlight, with an arrogance that irks me a bit. "Is that gratitude beaming in your eyes?"

No, not giving in that easily. *It was, cocky bastard.* Now contempt burns in them as I wish they could reduce him to ash. No I don't. As much as it pains me to admit, and it kills. I need him.

But I can't fall at his feet; I'm not made that way. Instead I fold my arms, guarding my heart and tap my foot on the concrete. "You can't help yourself, can ya? You... just.. have to be an asshole."

He tilts toward me, and our lips nearly touch, and he breathes mint into them. "Princess. Ye havena see me be an asshole. Would ye care for a demonstration?"

Those eyes shouldn't keep me enthralled, but they do.

I huff, storming off to the parking lot. Not believing my luck, or lack thereof. Why him? Why did it have to be him? *Karma you bitch.*

He trails behind for a microsecond, then picks up his strides to match mine and catch up.

After we exit the gate he hooks my arm and spins me to face him.

"Where are you going?"

I ignore him, scanning the cars. My car is around here somewhere. Time to take off and away from this nightmare. I rummage in my clutch for my keys and let out a frustrated scream. The valet has my keys. I grunt, shoving past him. "Away from you."

"We're married, remember? If we don't make an appearance the gossip mongers will run with their own version of this situation. Besides, if we're to pull off this ruse we need a meeting of the minds. I'm doing this for ye."

I slam both palms into him, fueled by the raw rage at this whole situation, but he doesn't move an inch. It's like trying to knock a skyscraper off its foundation.

"I hate you." I say, unconvincingly. "What do you get out of it?"

"A favor."

I scrunch up my face. "Ew, I'm not doing that with you."

He smirks, twisting an unruly ribbon of my hair around his finger. "I love how your dirty mind works, love, but that's not what I'm referring to."

I yank the lock, slipping it through his fingers. "What then?"

"I'll let ye know later," he says, rubbing his thumb over his plump bottom lip and I want to kiss him.

I need rules. Boundaries. Before I lose my damn mind.

"No kissing on the mouth. No dating, except for a couple events. You may be affectionate to keep up appearances."

"Well thank you for that permission. And it's yer loss." he dips down so his lips graze my ear. "I'm a fabulous kisser. Though it's better this way. Wouldn't want you to get hooked on me." He flashes me that boyish grin and the icy encasement around my heart thaws a little.

"No sex." I stutter. My bottom lip quivers as my lower region fights to keep that on the table.

"Ye don't sound committed to that decision. Are ye sure?"

I'm not, but I can't let myself get sucked into his vortex. This is a business proposition. Not a segue to a happy ending.

"And we have to stay together for what? A year?" I cringe when I say that because it may be a deal breaker. Like it or not, I need his cooperation.

"A year? Deal."

The wind whips through the space between us, taking with it any hint of animosity from before. Whatever he wants in return must be monumental for him to agree to those terms. The look on his face says everything. I'm a mess. "On second thought, you are in no shape to face anyone. I'll venture the shark tank for ye. Ye go ahead to your parent's house. I'll pick you up in the morning."

Once we get to my Audi, he opens my door, holding it while I get settled.

"You can't tell anyone. Promise?" I say in a timid voice.

"Promise." Rhett lays his hand over his heart. "On my honor as a SEAL."

"Good... Wait, are you really a SEAL?"

"Aye. I am."

"Okay, I'll give you that one. That's hot. Rhett, what favor do you want?"

He pecks my hand and shuts the door. "Not tonight, Scarlett, but I'll keep my end of the deal."

Before I speed off, I text my mom, "I'm gonna kill ya." I know it was she who told the world. Eliza lit the match, but I'm certain mom was the one who let it spread like a wildfire. Another text. "We need to talk when you get home."

CHAPTER 5:
RHETT

"You're gonna love this one," Eliza says, as we follow her up to the charming, but large, old house. I hope so, considering this is the tenth house that she's taken us to today. After I escorted Scarlett to her car last night, I had a little talk with my mom and hers. The story goes, Eliza sniffed around the party to discover who Scarlett's mysterious man was. Her mom played along and with mine hatched a plan to tell everyone we got married, locking me in unknowingly to this falsehood, but it may work out perfectly. I want to prove that I've set down roots for this job and what better way than to be fake married.

I get it, the training is nearly a year long, and they want insurance that I'm calling Texas home for an extended amount of time. Ironic, since the actual job will send me overseas.

The others were brand new, and Scarlett hated them and nit-picked every little crack and dent in the house, saying they were too cookie cutter and lacked character. I pegged her wrong, figuring she'd jump for the modern house with mucho amenities. Instead, she's smitten with this farmhouse in the middle of the sticks.

I take in the surrounding scene, still not entirely believing my luck. Scarlett, next to me, on my arm in a white little number—grazing her curves just right with those scintillating heels from last night. Her outfit is light enough to catch the slightest breeze and lift off those gorgeous thighs, giving me a better peek. If I wanted one. Which I don't, and I avert my eyes in a vain attempt to resist her.

Classic Scarlett, she has to have a bit of sparkle, but I don't mind. Her legs are phenomenal, toned to perfection, which is not a huge departure from high school. Now I'm glad I opted for loose khaki shorts, which will hopefully camouflage any evidence of her effect on me.

We take a quick tour of the outside of the house that I think she'll settle on. That we'll live in, if she gives her seal of approval. Not as husband and wife. But as... I honestly don't know.

The blazing afternoon sun peeks from behind the clouds, warming up the stagnant air.

No breeze.

No relief.

Whatever has Mother Nature hot under the collar, the rest of us are about to be cooked alive.

Eliza's in a Pepto-pink suit that looks more like Elle Woods than Joanna Gaines. Her champagne locks shine bright in the sun. She's brilliant, but her Achilles heel is the inability to keep a secret. In her career, though, she's a pro.

"This one is on a good stretch of land. Five acres. But I warn ya, the house needs some work. You can get it for a steal if you're willing to hire a contractor. It's larger..." she trails off, flipping through the stack of papers on her clipboard to get the exact details right.

"Horses." Scarlett exclaims and makes a beeline for the dilapidated stable. Clearly, it's intended for horses and it's in utter shambles. There are holes to patch on the roof. Walls need to be replaced. That's just what I can see from here. I can only imagine the work the inside of the main dwelling will require.

Eliza continues, "Yes, it says here there is a modern tornado shelter, but the house was built in 1970. And..." She hands me a flier—the listing—with the rest of the details.

1970. *Wow!* I slow my steps to read the pertinent information. "It's almost 4000 square feet." I read aloud, almost shouting to Scarlett. "And a partial renovation."

That can be more a headache than it's worth, but maybe a project would be beneficial. My jaw drops when I see the price. It's got to be a mistake. "150,000?" I ask and Eliza nods an affirmative.

"And they'll cover closing. They want a quick close, and they bought it for a little bit of nothing. So even at this price, they'll make a killing."

I've been toying around with the idea of an investment property. This may be the perfect fit. Scarlett spins around in circles like a child in the grass, then walks backwards to address me. "This place is amazing."

I nod, biting my cheek to keep from laughing at her whimsy. Can't let on that I like her. Playing her arch nemesis is far too much fun. But when he plops down because she's too dizzy to stay standing, I can't help but get a warm feeling in my chest. It spreads to my fingertips. Her antics are adorable, bringing me straight back to our childhood.

She's still in the grass, tearing it out blade by blade, peering up at me with a half-squint to not get blinded by the sun. And it's like my lungs forgot how to breathe and her goofy grin is the lost instruction to resume. I step back, my chest and heart going off the rails. This isn't happening. I did not just get winded because of that girl's smile.

Only it wasn't Scarlett, the grown woman that I saw, taking on the mannerisms of a child just now. She was Lettie, my high school tormentor and fuck it all, she never looked prettier. For a split second we were back in school, back in a suburban jungle.

Lettie stands, brushing off her backside and my mouth is suddenly dry like I swallowed a mouthful of cinnamon. Again I struggle to breathe. Water is all I need, like the wetness from her mouth. I drift to daydream and snap myself out of it. What? No. I most definitely don't want to kiss her... a lot.

Denial, thy name is Rhett.

Baseball. Puppies. The house. Right, we're here to see a house. I refocus, beating down my libido with a yardstick and pretend that the most stunning woman on Earth won't be sharing a roof with me.

She's occupied, so I gently tug Eliza to the side. Ultimately, the house really should be mine. And stepping away, gets more blood to flow North again.

This woman has a way with me. Always has. All cards on the table; I don't hate her. I pretend to hate her. I lie to myself that I ever could.

I've tried. For every nasty comment in high school. For every time she used me to climb the social ladder by making me her verbal punching bag. But it's hopeless. Hating her requires more strength than I have, but I'll pretend and hope this ends up meaning something.

I doubt after our little ruse has run its course, Scarlett will want to live here indefinitely.

And I'm not afraid of getting my hands dirty.

Now I can't speak for the princess.

Before I can complete the inner commentary, *her highness* slips off her heels and hands them to me, flashing me a snarky grin, "You don't mind holding my shoes, do ya? Peasant."

Her words get breathy as she climbs the horse pen which stirs up a cocktail of conflicting feelings in me when she lands on the other side ankle deep in the mud.

This is a side of her I've never seen, and it's truly astounding.

"Peasant?" I raise my voice so it carries over the distance to her.

"Well, since you insist on calling me your highness. That makes you my subject. Doesn't it?"

"Touche."

CHAPTER 6:
SCARLETT

The dumbfounded look on Rhett's face is absolutely priceless. He stares at me like a unicorn horn grew out of my forehead.

"Are you okay? You look a little overheated."

He's in a t-shirt and khakis. A must, on this unusually hot Texas day. It's winter in theory but we're expecting a high in the nineties. Summer is drunk and keeps showing up uninvited.

He blinks a few times, shaking his head like this is a dream he's trying to wake from. "Sure, I never knew you to enjoy getting dirty."

Too easy to exploit.

"Do you like dirty girls?" I say in a sweet tone, teasing him. After all, we're supposed to be newlyweds.

Flirtation is part of the job description. His darkly tanned skin turns a lovely shade of red at my remark and he clears his throat. "Umm."

He's on the ropes; time to finish him. Let him know I'm a force of nature. A raging inferno, not some delicate flower that will wilt from the slightest criticism.

At least not anymore.

And it pisses me off, he writes me off as a lazy debutant. So easily he forgets I was captain of the dance team. Practices were, on average, ten hours a day. During competition season, all bets were off.

I lean on the highest rung of the pen, resting my chin on my hand, eyes locked on him as say, "Rhett, you've never known me. Not the real me. Your assumptions only serve one end. To make you look like an ass. Which I'll admit you're good at."

I shrug and straighten my back, then climb the fence and straddle it. His eyes darken unmistakably as he stares raw lust at me with my shoes in his arms. His strong, masculine jaw stiffens and I suspect the same in more secret places.

No sex. That's my rule. I lift my chin to the open sky, marveling at my stupidity. *Easy, a piece of cake.* His slacks tighten around his erection and I avert my eyes, wishing I hadn't taken sex off the table.

Swinging my leg over and hop back down as Eliza rejoins us. In a few minutes, I'm in his arms again.

I can't show hatred for him, not if this is going to work. Besides, he's doing me a favor. So I'll settle with driving him to madness with lust.

Drool streams down his chin, and I swipe the area with my thumb. "You've got something right here, honey."

He throws me a weary look and we stroll to the house. It's large with some nice amenities. I curl my arm around his as we step on the wrap-around porch. This place is gorgeous. Designers tend to see things others can't. They picture the finished product with all the renovations. Where he got this idea that I have an aversion to hard work. I'll never know, but it's time I correct that right now.

"I know you think I'm being picky. But this is a better value. In the long run it would be the better purchase. Despite all the work it needs. I'm up to it if you are?"

CHAPTER 7:
SCARLETT

Six months later.

"Eggs. Milk. Flour. I can't find the oil."

I drag out those ingredients, setting them on the granite counter, dusting the excess flour off my hands. Now where's the oil? I ransack the kitchen. Flipping open cabinets, I dig through the pantry.

No oil. We must be out. Or maybe we didn't buy it before we moved in. I can't remember.

Damn. I should've confirmed before I started breakfast. *Is it actually essential to have oil in pancakes?*

According to Google, no. I flip through Pinterest and a few recipes later find a substitute. Only to look up and see the bottle of cooking oil mocking me from atop the stove. I grit my teeth, swearing under my breath. No substitute needed now.

I measure and stir the ingredients into a mixing bowl. Normally, I don't eat breakfast. Not that I'm actively on a diet, but my appetite doesn't fully develop until a couple hours after I wake up.

Typically, I satisfy the first morning rumble with coffee, but Rhett mentioned them this morning before he hopped in the shower. And I haven't thought of anything else since.

He keeps me on my toes as the man never idles for a significant amount of time. More or less, we've gotten along these last few months. Which is odd. A few fights here and there, but nothing Earth-shattering. And hand to God, I'm starting to like him.

I turn up the radio while I pour the pancakes into the frying pan. Taking in a little Miranda and Carrie, raising hell and taking names on the radio.

"Scarlett."

Echoes of my name ring in the air. I turn toward the sound. Not entirely certain I heard that correctly. At least, I think it was. I twist the volume down so I can hear better. After a minute or two, there's not another sound, so I turn it back up.

Heavy footsteps pound into our ceramic tile and I look over to Rhett standing in the kitchen with my bathrobe wrapped around his waist. "Did ye use the last towel?"

"Yes. Oops. The floor was slick, so I used it as a bathmat after I was done. And I forgot to replace it. Sorry."

"Scarlett, are ye bloody kidding me?" He's seething but calming as the minutes pass when he realizes I made breakfast. His hard, muscular torso rains excess water all over the kitchen floor and I don't hate it.

A lump materializes in my throat, and I struggle with my next breath. His Michaelango worthy body has me damn near tripping over my feet to step back to the stove. I turn, hiding a smile with my bitten lip, trying not to bust out laughing.

After flipping the rest of the pancakes onto a plate, I turn off the burner. "You're welcome."

***

His muscles ripple and tense with all the unspoken words between us. The tension solidifies more by the minute. A blend of frustration radiates from him with a healthy, lusty glow as he stares into my eyes like he's finding his way out of a maze, and the uncertain glint tells me he's not confident in his ability.

There's a glimmer that I never noticed before. A sparkle of admiration, and I must be imagining things, because it appears as enjoyment. Sounds of silence cling to the air but neither of us move to speak.

I shake my head harshly like I'm trying to perish him from my thoughts. "Did you need something?" I say through rapid blinks.

Immediately the scowl returns as recognition sparks in his eyes. I'm guessing whatever was on his mind when he came into the kitchen. "Yes, come with me. Please."

His teeth clench as he struggles to remain convivial despite his harsh glare and rigid posture with a curled fist. So tight, as if he's got a death grip on his last shred of sanity.

We end up in the bathroom. There's toothpaste on the sink, water puddling under his feet and the tile all around us.

"And what is this mess?"'

"My makeup." I shrug in a failed attempt at being cute to defuse the situation.

"Really? Why is it all over the counter?"

"I was making breakfast, and I forgot about it, sorry. But I have to go meet someone this afternoon about a possible job. I'll take care of it when I get home."

He stifles a pain-filled, humorless laugh as he retreats to the closet to dress. "Very well. I'll be home late. I'm training with some guys I worked with."

That gets my attention, and I plead with my eyes to come. "And you're not gonna introduce your wife?"

"Why, so ye can flirt with them and make it awkward?"

"Precisely." I bob my head, practically bouncing in place.

He gets right near my face with an exaggerated mouthing no, shaking his head.

"You don't want me." I mutter under my breath, unintelligibly.

"What was that?"

"Nothing." I sing-song. "Well, I better be going."

Before he can utter another sound, I'm out the door.

CHAPTER 8:
RHETT

The next day, Scarlett wanders into the kitchen and leans over the granite counters in my shirt and, I assume, shorts, somewhere under it. Though I'm secretly hoping I'm wrong. It hits a few inches below her glorious ass. This is my personal hell. Does she have a pool going on? How long will it take before Rhett loses his mind?

She bends over to grab a dish out of the bottom cabinet, and I get a full view of her barely there shorts.

I release a weighty breath, puffing out my cheeks. This is torture. After she pours us both coffee, she rests her elbows on the counter next to where I'm sitting.

"Thank ye. I appreciate it." She smiles, it crinkles the corners of her eyes and thumps my heart at a significant uptick.

"So Rhett. We've not had much time to get to know each other. This has been quite the project."

She tightens her brows as she downs her first drink. "This coffee. Is it from your grandfather's farm?"

I blink a few times, shocked as shit she remembers. "Yes. In Colombia."

"Wait. I thought you were Mexican."

"I am as well as Scottish."

"Well, that's obvious."

Scarlett flutters her lashes and a beautiful pink fills her cheeks. Which strains my throat, like I'm sucking oxygen through a rapidly closing straw. In the last few weeks, she's laid off the incessant jokes at my expense, settling with driving me out of my gourd with lust.

"26 years we've known each other, and you didn't know I was Colombian too? On my father's side, of course."

Now she flushes for another reason altogether. She rises stiff as a board. "Well, I hated you. Didn't seem like a detail I needed to know."

"Past tense?" I ask. "As in, you don't anymore."

Her blush intensifies and spreads as she spins with her back to me. "No, I still do."

"Really. Ye haven't insulted me or made a snarky remark all morning."

"Give me a second. I'm not awake. I haven't even finished my coffee."

"Admit it, you like me."

"Never."

I'm on my feet and plant my hands on either side of her, trapping her against the counter and our lips graze. "So if I kiss you right now. Ye'll do what, lass?"

"Sma... ck yo... u." she whispers into my lips, but her voice quivers. Not even she believes those words.

"Worth it." I declare, but I pull back and grab my coffee, leaving her hanging.

Her luscious lips part in surprise and I toss her a wicked grin as I saunter off to take a shower, but stop at the threshold. "Scarlett."

She's in a daze, her eyes glossed over. Dark, needy, and drunk with desire, but I can't give in. "Uh hmm."

Speechless. Interesting. "Remember that favor you owe me?"

Her face burns red-hot. Any mention of our agreement is a surefire way to piss her off. I pace back to her, stopping a few feet short. Out of arm's reach, just in case. She grits her teeth, crossing her arms and now she's a fortress.

"Yeah."

"I'm cashing in tonight."

Scarlett covers her opened mouth. Her mind races. I can see it in her eyes. I study every micro-expression she gives me. After a few moments of silence between us, she giggles. "No way. I'm not sleeping with you."

"Correction, you *do* sleep with me." I finger her chin, and her eyes flutter close. Her chest moves with her labored breathing. Is this more anger? Or something sexier? "I'm not asking for sex. Is that all you think ye're good for?"

"No."

"We have dinner with a security company that's moving in. They are big time. Good news. If I get this job. I won't always be around."

Her face falls visibly and my heart bumps up a notch or two. It's fleeting; she corrects straight away.

"That's great. I mean for you. You won't have to put up with me all the time."

"A true blessing, indeed," I say, but I don't have it in me to pretend she doesn't light my fire. That I'm not excited beyond words; my days begin and end with her.

"That's the deal. A year that is now halfway over. Enough to further our careers and not get caught in the lie. If we separate after a couple months, no one will believe it's real."

Right, that.

"So, are we on for tonight?"

"A deal's a deal, right?"

***

SCARLETT

He leaves me in a cloud of his manly scent. I'm a coward. The last six months with him started off rocky but for the most part, have been incredible. Respectfully, he has kept his distance. And like an idiot, I keep up the pretense I want him to. But I don't. Last night I dreamed this was real. That the feelings between us were something tangible, like a honeysuckle nectar I could live on.

This morning when he cornered me at the counter and leaned in, I was certain he'd kiss me. But he pulled back. Chickened out. Maybe I read him wrong or my incessant teasing him has turned him off permanently.

Well, I'm not putting myself out there just to get turned down. I'll wait for him to make a move or not. I don't care. Except I do.

Our dining room has a massive table. It's wooden and fits the organic feel of the house while keeping the farmhouse charm. Fixing up a house isn't much different from planning an event. And I miss decorating a venue. Miss planning out someone's wedding or Bar mitzvah.

For the last few months, this home has been my project to dress up pretty, but I'm ready to coordinate events again and matriculate in public again.

Rhett enters the house, covered in muck as he slinks past me. Probably hoping I don't notice the footprint trail of mud through my freshly mopped floors. I follow him to the bathroom.

"Dammit. Can you please not drag every grain of dirt in the yard through the house? Is it too much to ask you not to muddy up the floors I just cleaned?"

I'm pacing in front of the closed door, trying to shake off this mounting frustration. But it resurfaces as a tremble in my extremities.

Why am I nervous? This is his opportunity. We're not even a couple, but I shoulder the weight of the evening too. He climbed out on that high limb for me. The least I can do is ensure he makes a good impression. And as much as I hate to admit it, I like him. Maybe more than like him.

"Rhett." I swing the door open to a naked man standing before me. My eyes dart to his erection and I can't avert them. He flushes and covers himself, but stays in that spot, trembling.

"Aye. I'm sorry."

I'm not letting this go. Today I busted my ass to get the house in order and he tracks mud all over the kitchen. But his remorseful expression eviscerates my sullied mood. He's impossible to yell with those weepy eyes and stunningly gorgeous body just aching to be touched.

His apology sucks all the oxygen from my fury, and I stare at him. Not ogling his body anymore, but fixing on his eyes.

"Alright, I better get it cleaned up before dinner. It will be delivered in about thirty minutes. Since the oven is still not working."

He nods, still stunned by my presence. I don't say another word and exit the room. When all I want is to jump in his arms and do this for real. But all I need is another one-sided relationship.

Thirty minutes later, the doorbell rings. Uber Eats is delivering Chinese food. His favorite. Not mine. I prefer Mexican.

He emerges in black jeans and a button-down shirt. My heart skips a single beat as my breath takes off like race horse at the starting pistol and I fan myself to cool down

"Love. Ye okay? Ye look positively feverish." He crinkles his eyes as he lays the back of his hand across my forehead which only spurs me on more. His boyish grin sinks my sarcasm ship and I can barely get a word out.

"Just hot from cleaning up your mess." I playfully glare at him, but it's not genuine irritation even. Yes, it irked me, but I can't deny all he's done.

"I love when you clean. It's a treat to watch you bend and reach. Teasing me with all the goodies. I can't have."

"You like when I tease you? When I resist you?"

Rhett cocks a brow. "Aye I do."

"Why is that?"

"Because when I win ye over. It will be a greater victory."

I scowl, tightening my arms over my chest. "You really are a pig. Misogynist."

"Am not. A misogynist thinks women can't think for themselves. Think they are empty-headed simpletons who belong in the kitchen, serving them like slaves. I ken fine well ye're capable, and I want to see ye succeed."

"Why is that?"

"Because I want to conquer the best. That's the only time it's a true victory."

"You think this is a contest?"

"If it were ye dinna stand a chance. And when I win, you will beg me to kiss ye. Ye will like it."

His lips are a work of art. Perfectly shaped and, if I'm being honest, so is every square inch of him.

"This means war."

"Bring it. When I win, we go on a real date, and you admit you don't hate me."

"Never. But I'm not plotting your demise anymore. Or where to hide the body. Does that count?"

"Maybe." he says, twinkling his eyes in a puzzled expression. "Ye really aren't?"

I giggle. "No way. Who else will muck out the stalls?"

"Well, it's nice to know I'm good for something."

"Okay, what about *when* I win?"

"What do you want?" Tough question when all this started the answer would be "out of this nightmare" but now I'm dreading the end of the next six months.

"I don't know. Out of our proposal so I can take jobs out of state."

I slap a hand over my mouth, immediately I regret those words, but it's a genie bottle moment again and worst yet, it's true. I miss working. My dream was to work at the Plaza, planning first class events, turning that venue into a wonderland.

His grin fades fast, not what he wanted to hear, but who are we kidding. This. Us. It's all a pipe dream. In reality, we don't work.

He boxes me in against the table, moving in like a lion in the Serengeti. "Terms?"

Easy, the first one to seduce the other wins. Bed. Wait. No. I'll never be able to walk away if I let that man in. He claims too much of my mind already. Like half a hemisphere is decorated in his image now. Anymore and I'll be trapped in this town forever.

But still I throw down the gauntlet. "First to kiss the other wins. To give in."

He licks his lips and I'm about to yank out my white flag right there. Damn when did he start turning my crank so readily?

Rhett dips down so that slightly moistened lip, barely brushes my heated cheek, hot, wanting. Do I really think I can walk away from this unscathed? Stupid. I'm a moron. I swallow down a materlizing knot. Tiny hairs raise all over my body as his warm breath dances on my cheek and I give in to a daydream of that mouth devouring me. After a few excruciating, maddening moments he steps back, pleased with himself. Crinkling his gorgeous forehead he says, " Too easy. I practically have you begging me to consume ye right now. I said I want to a challenge."

"That's not true," I lie, straightening my spine, stiffening it to a breaking point. Trying with every cell in my body to pretend that's not true, but the drool on my chin tells a contrary story. He swipes it with his thumb. "Love ye have something right here." I scowl at him, shoving his hand away, crossing my arms to give me space to collect myself. It's useless, but it's the only tool in my box I have left to hide my insane attraction to this man. "Fine. First one to say the L word loses."

"Loser?" I ask, in a sassy tone.

"No, I love you. Because that means there are real feelings."

"That's the bet. You'll lose because I'll never say it." Not even I believe my own line of bullshit and what if Rhett really feels something for me. That's crazy. Anyway, that's tomorrow's problem.

"We'll see." He flashes me that panty-dropping boyish grin and I'm not liking my chances anymore for victory. "One more rule. No manipulation. Meaning don't say something you don't mean in order to get the response you want. Understand?" Damn. Honesty, integrity. I truly didn't believe that was in his DNA. I nod, because my pipes aren't working.

Rhett leans in surrounding me in familiar scents and hooks my chin.

"Love, because I haven't said it before. The bastard is blind and stupid to cheat on you. On behalf of every other male. I'm sorry for all of it. But most of all, he didn't cherish what he had." He frowns and gives me space I didn't ask for.

I smack him on the shoulder before he's out of my reach. "Hey you just said no manipulation."

He brushes the hair from my face, then brings a thumb to my bottom lip. The look in his eyes I can only describe as love. His skin glows. "I meant every word. Ye'll learn if ye give me a chance, that while I'm willing to lie for you, I'm not willing to lie *to* you. That is a promise."

My throat dries instantly and I'm practically panting. A thirst fills my mouth, one only he can quench. But I can't give in, get lost in him. Not when I'm close to returning to the work I love.

The bastard, he knows how to be competitive. And now I don't want to win. *Oh shit.*

CHAPTER 9:
RHETT

Dinner with Brice and Noah went great. I should hear soon what they decide. In the meantime, I took a position at Copeland Security.

Scarlett emerges from the bedroom. I almost won the bet last night. Stubborn lass, she refuses to say it, not because she doesn't feel it. But more so, she doesn't want to lose. The three words are on the tip of my tongue, but I can't give in. Losing her would gut me now, but if I really love her, do I want to hold her back? Her dreams are the crux of who she is, her identity.

"Buenos dias." I curl around her. The last few months are everything I want in a relationship.

"What does that mean?"

"What, you didn't take Spanish?"

"Yeah, but Billy Thompson did my homework, so I didn't learn anything." She shrugs. I knew it and I chuckle inside.

I roll my eyes. "Why am I not surprised? Means Good morning. Madainn mhath is the same in Gaelic."

"You speak three languages?"

"More or less."

Her phone rings, and she excuses herself to answer it. I grab my bag of work gear and head out of the house to drop it in my truck. Right before I reach the exit, I step back because I forgot my phone and stroll to the bedroom to retrieve it.

"Oh wow. You want to hire me?"

Scarlett's voice whizzes through the air from the room. I don't want to interrupt, so I spin on my heel to leave. Only to hear. "New York. I'd love to."

My heart sinks and my stomach turns. This we have means so little to her she'd agree to a job clear across the country without so much as a head's up? If I hadn't rushed back in for my phone, would I even know?

I love her, but I can't stand in her way. So I'll tell her to go the only way I can. I'll lose the bet.

***

SCARLETT

This is it.

My dream job back in NYC offers me a position. I impressed them with my presentation months ago and will overlook the TMZ fiasco. This will put me on the map again. Followers. Everything I dreamed up on that beach in Mexico.

"New York. I'd love to... But." I stall, staring at my reflection, not believing what I'm about to say. I love Rhett. Oh, my God. I love him. I don't want to leave him.

My heart sinks to my gut. A preview of the void without him. I can't fathom the real thing. Bad enough, his job will drag him from me if he gets it intermittently, but I can't bring myself to say yes.

"I can't." I finally finish the thought. "It's a great opportunity, but I don't want to relocate." Then inspiration sparks. There is nothing like that here. I'll start one.

"Scarlett, how about we give you a couple of weeks to think it over? We're not in a hurry. You may change your mind." Her tone reeks of disgust with the last word. No need to think about it. They have my answer. "Thank you Maryanne. I'll consider your offer."

Rhett barges in the room as I hang up, looking hopped up on a designer drug. He's pacing and distraught, but no need. I'm ready to lose the bet. I can't deny how I feel anymore.

"I can't do this."

"What are you talking about? This. I know I agreed, but I can't handle your quirks."

I close the distance between us. "Quirks? Like what?"

"You always leave an empty jug of milk in the fridge. With like a single sip. And your makeup is all over the counter. I'm used to order and you thrive in chaos."

"You can't be serious." I scoff, hoping this is a bad joke or an elaborate skit he cooked up.

"I love you, Scarlett, but that's not a reason for us to be together. You win. Now you can pursue your dreams, which don't include me. You don't need me."

The pain in his eyes when he says I don't need him slices into me. I blink back tears, with a gaping hole in my heart, because he made an assumption and was so willing to give me up.

"If you'd given me a chance to talk, you'd know that I was planning to turn it down. But you made it about you. I was gonna lose the bet, but if you really want me to go, I will. Since I won, I'll be leaving tonight."

Rhett grips my arm. "What?"

Tears fall now, massive crocodile tears create wet spots on my cheeks. "Because I may be selfish, but I would never want to let you go. And I want a man who will fight for me. If something you overheard made you think I didn't want you. And you can make that decision without me, then I don't matter to you as much as you do to me. And I can't do that again. I can't be the only one fighting for a relationship. You did precisely what you accused me of." He wags his head, backtracking at breakneck speed. "And you're right. We get on each other's nerves. This failed experiment is over. Goodbye Rhett."

CHAPTER 10:
SCARLETT

Six months later...

"Honey, I'm home." That's right, I live alone. I kick off my heels and my puppies sigh as they sink into the plush rug. Mom gave me a stipend to furnish my apartment. It looks amazing. The opposite of the farmhouse charm at Rhett's but it suits a city girl with a light palette in modern decor like I raided an Athropologie store.

It's courtesy of WedWorx my new employer. A shoe box compared to Rhett's place.

Today was a nightmare and all I want to do is soak in a hot bath and drink a bottle of wine from the bottle. I pop the cork and toss my blazer over the back of the couch. Murphy had a field day with this event. One disaster after another. I check my phone. Mom called twice three days ago. What the hell?

My eyes are closing on their own, but this has to be serious, so I press her name. "Scarlett. Can you answer your phone?" *No hello, nice.* Sixteen-hour days are catching up with me and I keep drifting. "It's Rhett."

I bolt up. Sleep is the last thing on my mind now. His name is like a brand across my chest. That wound is still scabbing over. "What about him?" I say with more snark than I intend.

There's a painfully long pause. "Well, he was at his new job and was shot."

I hang up the phone, my legs waver for a second before they go out from under me and I crumple into a ball on the floor. The room spins. Her last words are on a loop in my mind. I can't hear past them. Tears rain down my face as I clutch knees, bringing them under my chin. He's gone, and I never got to tell him. After a few minutes of weeping and several deep breaths as I press her name again.

"Scarlett." My heart stands still, not daring to beat until I know the verdict.

I squeeze my eyes shut, refusing to be in this moment. I can't do this. Devastation reverberates through me like an earthquake, shaking my very foundation. I'm sobbing, my lungs ache and burn, my face soaked from the deluge of emotion. Stupid girl. My pride did this. Cost me love, real love. Love that overlooks the imperfections or even learns to adore them. Devastation hits me so hard I can't breathe.

Silence. She's giving me time to gather my thoughts and join her again. "Mom. This is my fault. I didn't tell him. I avoided it because I was afraid of losing myself. If I gave in. Now I can't." I whine the last few words in desperation. "Why didn't I tell him?"

"Didn't tell me what?"

Rhett. I jerk my eyes to my door where he's filling up the empty air at the threshold. I must've not locked it in my exhaustion. I blink at him. Alive. Safe. Though bandaged up and leaning on my door jamb.

"Mom. I have to go. Rhett is here." I lower my phone and let it drop on the floor.

"I thought you were dead. And you let me go. You let me walk away from you."

"Shut up." His chest moves rapidly with his breathing while he inches toward me.

"How did you find me?"

"I said shut up. Can ye let me bloody talk? If you'd let me go first, ye wouldn't have ended up here."

"Well, if you had fought for me, I would've never left. And what are you doing here?"

"Fighting for you. And I'm not taking no for an answer. I'm going to marry you. I'm going to kiss you and love you, and there is nothing you can say to change my mind."

"What if I don't want you to? What if I irritate you? Or push your buttons. What is the line? When will you stop loving me?"

"Death."

"What?"

"Death, that is my line. When I'll stop loving you. Even then, I'll beg God for more time."

"I thought I annoyed you and you hated me?"

"Have you not learned one damn thing? Hate and love aren't opposites. They are cellmates. They're bitter companions like a buddy cop film. Hate is a breath away from love. A kiss. The passion that fuels hate can spark a love inferno. I had to hate you, to love you. You drove me out of my mind with your quirks."

"Yeah, I know." I drop my chin.

"No, I mean, when you were gone there was no makeup sprawled across the counter. The milk was always full and my bed was made the way I liked it. And I missed it. I missed your pillows taking up the whole bed. Every one of those quirks was another reason to love you and I do. And I will never let you go again."

"What are you saying?"

Rhett kneels at my feet and brandishes a gorgeous sapphire cushion cut ring. I hate diamonds and I'm floored, he remembered. "Marry me. For real. Forever. Live with me in our farmhouse until you kill me in my sleep."

I chuckle. "I won't kill you."

"Right, you need me to muck out the stalls."

"Yeah, I don't want to do it."

"Is that a yes?"

I nod, too choked up to speak until I manage to croak out a weak, "Yes, but can we renew our vows?"

"No. I think it's time we come clean. A fresh start. Rip out the old foundation and pour a new one."

"Then yes. I'll marry you."

The end for now.

***

Enjoy the Seeing Red? Be sure to leave a review! Also, sign-up for my newsletter for a free read, exclusive sneak peeks, and updates on my next release.

ABOUT THE AUTHOR

Andi is a poet at heart as well as a songwriter and musician. Storytelling is her passion, whether it's crafting an intricate story or a clever turn of phrase in a song, she's always looking for a new way to spin a yarn. Her thrillers (written under Andi Herrera Grant) are ripped from the headlines and she hopes to bring awareness through prose about difficult subjects. When not writing, she's strumming her guitar, raising her five kids or hanging out with her husband who inspires most of her heroes.

Want to chat with Andi, win prizes and be the first to see all the sneaks and exclusive content of Andi's newest work? Sign up for Andi's newsletter here.
Visit Andi's website here.

Read More of Andi's Books:
Andi MacDowall
Every time You Leave
Heroes with Heat and Heart Volume 2
Shades of Love

Andi Herrera Grant
Saved by the Everyday Hero

UN CAFÉCITO AT MIDNIGHT

Gloria Lucas

ABOUT *UN CAFÉCITO AT MIDNIGHT*

Julieta and Cesar were childhood friends. Friendship eventually gave way to romance but when Cesar decided to take a break from college to travel Europe, Julieta's obligations forced them apart. Ten years later, a chance encounter gives them the opportunity to try again.

Julieta wanted to bottle this moment forever. *Well,* she thought. *Maybe not* this *moment. The moment before this one.*

Cesar sat before her, naked except for his boxers. She was fully dressed and sat with one leg crossed over the other, their late-night breakfast and her coffee growing colder by the minute.

Earlier, at her request, they had gone out to watch a matinee at the aging theater near their town center. It butted up against the dying mall they used to frequent as teenagers. Cesar had whistled and commented on its appearance. His breath came out in puffs, the wintery air refusing to give way to spring, despite it being mid-March.

"Crazy how quickly things change, no?"

She nodded as a wave of nostalgia settled onto her. "I remember getting all dressed up just to come here."

"I remember that, too. And your weird goth phase." He stuck out his tongue at her.

"Oh my God, Cesar," she said, putting her hands momentarily over her eyes. "I was trying to forget that! Now I'm going to wake up in a cold, anxious sweat every other month thinking about it."

"I think I still have pictures."

"On pain of death, you will give those to me or burn them!"

He tickled her ribs and she screamed. "Never. Also, I'm not scared of you. I can just tickle you and that's it. Game over." He poked her rib again.

"Stop it!" she laughed. "Quieres un puñetazo?" She mimed punching him in the face.

"Why are you so violent?"

"It's not violence. It's tough love."

After the movie, they held hands on the walk to the car and he stopped her before she reached the passenger side. He kissed her gently and took her face in his hands. "You're never allowed to choose a movie ever again."

Julieta burst out laughing. "What? Y por qué?"

"That was like the worst movie—"

"It was not the worst—"

"It absolutely was."

She placed her hands on her hips. "You can't sit there and say you haven't seen a worse comedy."

"It's okay," he said, his voice low. He kissed her nose, then lightly on her lips. "You don't have to apologize. If you *really* want, I'll let you make it up to me." When he kissed her again, she bit his bottom lip playfully and he laughed. "You're so mean."

Twenty minutes later, they were in his apartment, making a line of clothes to his bedroom. They collapsed onto the bed, desperately hungry for each other, as if making up for the lost years. Afterwards, body singing, she had fallen asleep and woken up well after the sun had set.

Alarmed, she sat up and checked her phone. It was a little after 1 a.m. which gave her almost three hours to get ready for work. She collapsed back onto the bed and rubbed her face. With a sigh, she forced herself up.

Cesar rolled to his back and stretched. "Guess we needed a nap."

"Must have."

He watched her searching the floor for her belongings. "Where you going, babe?"

"I have to go to work at four, remember?"

"I thought you were going to play hooky today." His tone was teasing. When she leaned over him to fish her bra from the folds of the sheets, he ran a hand over her hip.

She giggled and swatted his hand. "You're a bad influence. No hooky today. We're short staffed."

"I feel like you're always short staffed." He yawned.

Julieta sighed. "Yeah, true. It is what it is, though. Anyway, I have to go so I can shower and get ready at my house."

"I thought you had some scrubs here."

"I used those last time and forgot to grab another set. But I can linger a little bit. And tengo hambre. So, if you're feeling nice you can feed me. Oh, y café porfa."

His chuckle was warm and low. "Un café at midnight like always."

"It's after one."

"Close enough."

Julieta paused to admire his form as he walked to his dresser. He pulled on a set of boxers and then wandered to the kitchen. She followed, diverting from the path only to collect and don her t-shirt and pants.

As he started on eggs and toast, she brewed a strong batch of coffee.

"I'm going to pass on the coffee," Cesar said.

She waved her hand. "I figured. I only made a little."

He sat their plates on the small kitchen table and took a seat. She joined him, coffee cup in hand. She took a tentative sip and set the mug down.

"Thanks." She smiled.

"Of course."

They ate in silence for a few moments before Cesar cleared his throat. And that was where Julieta wanted to stop time. She wanted the comfortable silence of a midnight breakfast to remain locked in her memory, a snippet of time tucked away to access forever like a picture in a locket. When the time was right, maybe when she was old and the grief of it all ebbed away, she'd slip it out and watch the beautiful moment of two young lovers sharing a simple meal while the world around them slept.

His dark, brown eyes met hers and she felt should could drown in his gaze. She studied the lines of his face, the fullness of his lips. She thought of them curled up in his bed and him kissing her finger tips before pulling her close. She thought of the nights when desire felt like a fire burning hot in her belly and the subsequent days of finding the marks of an enthusiastic lover.

"You see this mark here?" she'd exclaim. "That's where you bit me."

He'd grin at her. "Yeah? Well, I have matching scratch marks." He'd shake his head when she'd gasp and begin apologizing. "No regrets."

But their relationship was deeper than physical. For all their differences, they understood each other. There was so much she would do for him. But one thing she could not. And so, when he asked her what he had asked a decade prior, her heart dropped. Once again, she was going to break his heart.

They met in elementary school, his entrance notable only because he had moved to the district mid-year. One day, the door opened and an adult ushered a child into the room. A quick introduction was made and he was shown to his seat. It was at the opposite end of the classroom and Julieta quickly turned her attention back to her drawing. She didn't think much of the gap-toothed boy until the day he asked if he could show her a trick with his chocolate milk. She had narrowed her eyes but agreed.

"I can smile and drink the milk and not open my mouth a lot."

She titled her head. Encouraged, he grinned and threaded his straw through the space two missing teeth had left behind. He tried to drink deeply from the brown-and-white box but had overestimated the amount of milk left behind. The loud slurp earned him a frown from one of the teachers supervising their portion of the cafeteria and elicited a disappointed look from the boy.

Julieta found the swift changes of his face from elation to surprise to disappointment so comical that she squealed with laughter. He flashed her a sheepish smile and it was then she knew they would be friends forever.

"My name is Julieta."

"I'm Cesar."

In middle school, her father found a job in a different state. They were crushed and vowed to remain faithful pen pals. Those days, one of her favorite pastimes was checking the mail; the other was writing letters. His were typically short and to the point. Hers were long and tended to ramble. But he told her he liked them and sometimes he would tuck in little notes from their mutual friends. They made plans for a giant reunion, the date and whereabouts unknown. She'd smile as they planned it all out, down to the type of cake they should get; but as the months ticked by, she lost faith that it would ever happen.

Then, life intervened and her father's work contract ended at the end of its second year, without the option for a renewal. She kept their return a secret. When she spotted him at school on the first day, her eyes lit up. His backpack was slung on one shoulder and he was walking with a small group of people. Carefully, she jogged to him and jumped on his back.

"Guess who!"

In her mind, the act was playful and cute. He'd catch her legs like one does when giving a piggyback ride. He'd gasp and set her down. She'd give him a big hug. Mutual friends would be excited to see her. New people would be introduced.

In reality, she had not accounted for his backpack. Nor had she thought of the consequences of jumping onto an unassuming person, best friend or no. As soon as her hands touched his shoulders, he began to turn. She had pushed downward to provide herself extra momentum on the jump but his simultaneous pivot knocked him off balance and he began to fall just as her feet left the floor. The kids on each side of him turned toward the commotion, their own faces registering shock.

The subsequent crash was ugly. Cesar landed with a loud *oof*, followed immediately by his backpack, Julieta, and the weight of her backpack. Gasps sounded around her and several teachers ran over to assist.

After they were helped up, Julieta shot Cesar a shy look from under her lashes. He had grown a lot since the last time they had hung out in person. Adulthood had touched the edges of his boyish face. Her face felt as if it were on fire.

Cesar touched the side of his head and crinkled his nose. He grinned at her. "Hey."

Her heart was still pounding but the amusement in his face calmed her. She smiled and then winced. The taste of copper filled her mouth and she realized she had split her lip. The vice-principal arrived, his mouth in a deep frown. "What is going on here?"

Cesar would tease her for years afterward. "I think that's the fastest anyone ever got in-school suspension ever. But that's when I fell in love with you, you know. Every clumsy part of you."

She'd laugh, scoff and claim she wasn't *that* clumsy. He'd roll his eyes and kiss her. But that had been before, when they thought life was simple and love conquered all.

Cesar cleared his throat and shifted in his chair. Sensing a change, Julieta frowned and set down her fork. "What's up?" she asked.

He flashed her a quick smile. "I was offered a job."

Julieta's heartbeat quickened. "Oh? That's great. Were—were you looking? Is the one you have now..." She hesitated. "Is it a bad fit?"

"I guess I'm always kind of looking for better opportunities." He shrugged. "But this one pays a lot better. And it's more responsibility, so it'll look great on a CV."

"Oh." Too late, she realized she looked disappointed. "That's great. I'm—I'm happy for you." She hoped her smile looked genuine.

He laughed self-consciously. "Yeah. Well, there's one little snag. Maybe. Maybe not."

Julieta heard the ticking of his wall-mounted clock. The hum of his refrigerator turned on. She felt an eternity pass before he finally answered the question hanging in the air.

"It's...it's in California."

Her mouth parted slightly and her stomach dropped.

Quickly, he reached out for her hand. She let him hold it but didn't squeeze back. "You should come with me. I know it's kind of a sudden request, but...you should! I've lived in this part of Cali and it's kind of nice. Weather's better than here at least. March feels like spring."

She smiled politely and withdrew her hand. "I still have school and my internship."

"Yeah, but this position doesn't start until after the fall. You'll be done by then."

She shook her head. "Sure, but what about my abuela? I don't think my mom and dad can support her alone. Her health is declining."

He made a noise in frustration. "One of the things I love most about you is your loyalty. And how caring you are. But...but you have to think about *you*, too, you know? You can't live being the one in charge of everything forever. Have you ever put yourself first? Like, what do *you* want to do? Where do *you* want to live? Where do *you* want to travel?"

Julieta pulled her hand from his grasp and grit her teeth. "Maybe some people have that luxury..." His eyes hardened at the stab but she pushed forward. "But others can't afford to let people down."

"Oh, and so *other* people just let themselves be used up?"

She stood abruptly. The chair complained against the floor and he looked startled at the noise. She walked toward the front door and he followed, grabbing her hand to stop her.

"Let go of me," she hissed.

"Jules. C'mon. Please. Let's talk about this."

"There's nothing to talk about! I can't move to California! I can't drop everything."

"You're not dropping anything! I don't start the new job until after you wrap up your program. And you can still help your family just not every day. And, to be honest, it's not your responsibility to take care of your whole family forever. I mean, you've admitted your grandmother isn't going to get better. Maybe it's time to hire a nurse. Or something."

Julieta frowned and bit her lip, the back of her eyes hot with the threat of tears. Her thoughts turned to her grandmother.

***

The rattle of dishes being handled sounded momentarily from the kitchen. Julieta looked up from the computer screen and sat silently, waiting. It was late; a glance at her watch told her it was nearing 1 o'clock in the morning. The due date for her paper was quickly approaching and she had stupidly picked up an extra shift at the hospital Saturday. She wouldn't have time over the weekend to do much but double check references and formatting; and then cross her fingers when she hit submit Sunday evening.

A dog started to bark somewhere in the distance. With that, she began to type again, periodically frowning and looking through her notes.

"Why do they insist on making generic names so weird?" she grumbled, flipping through her medication reference guide.

The clinking started again. *Okay. I did hear that earlier.*

She sighed, pressed save twice, and stood. Her room felt unsteady. "I've been sitting too long." The feeling ebbed quickly and she left her room, noting the stale, yellow light spilling from the kitchen. Someone was awake.

"Amá?" Julieta's voice was low as she made her way down the hallway. She stopped short when she found the kitchen empty. Briefly, the childish fear of ghosts swept through her body. She exhaled an amused laugh. *Too many energy drinks, Julie. You're going crazy.*

Then, the idea of an intruder flashed in her mind's eye. Their neighborhood was relatively safe, but that didn't mean the occasional break-in wasn't reported. Every night before bed, her father made sure to check all the windows and doors. If he knew he was working late, he'd text her a reminder.

She chastised her paranoia. Why would someone trying to rob the place make noise and turn on the lights? Unless he was an idiot. The thought made her crack a smile. Though, she didn't consider herself superstitious, it was difficult to control her imagination when it felt like the entire world was sleeping.

A cold hand gripped her wrist and she yelped, yanking it hard as she spun around.

"Ay, mijita, que paso?"

Julieta gasped and steadied her grandmother. "Oh, Wela! I'm so sorry. I heard noises from the kitchen."

Her grandmother, Alma, frowned, her face pensive. "O, sí, mijita. I was going to ask you: Do you know where my cup is?"

"What?" Julieta's heartbeat was still racing. "Cup?"

"Sí, the one your grandpa gave me. Remember?" Alma clasped her hands in front of her expectantly.

Julieta tilted her head. "Your coffee mug?"

Alma's eyes lit up. "Uh-huh, that one! Do you know where it is?"

"I—maybe. But...Wela, it's like 1 o'clock."

Her grandmother smiled. "I like to make sure my Ignacio has un cafécito before work."

Julieta's heart sank. She never knew how to handle her grandmother's memory. Especially not alone in the middle of the night.

"Oh. Um, Wela...I think it's too late for coffee. Everyone..." She paused, unsure if she should let her grandmother assume her late husband was included with 'everyone.' She cleared her throat. "Everyone is asleep. Are—are you having trouble sleeping?"

Alma frowned and looked at the floor. "Oh. Pues, a little. I don't like sleeping by myself." She looked around. "Where's my cup?"

Julieta took her grandmother's hand and smiled. "Sabes que, Wela? I think maybe some tea would be good. I'm going to make some manzanilla, okay? Go sit at the table and I'll heat the water."

After the tea was brewed, Julieta stirred in some honey and set the mugs in front of her grandmother and herself. Alma placed one of her hands on top of Julieta's. The skin looked paper thin, its frailty made more obvious by swollen veins and arthritic knuckles. "Gracias, mija."

"No problem, Wela. I needed something warm before bed, too."

Silence enveloped the kitchen as they sipped the warm beverage. Another glance at her watch told Julieta it was approaching two in the morning. Fatigue hit her in the chest. The paper would have to be finished the next day. *Technically, today,* Julieta thought, wryly. *I should have brewed myself a coffee.*

"Mija?"

Her eyes felt heavy, but she turned her full attention to her grandmother.

"Where's my—"

She wasn't sure if Alma was going to ask about her late husband again, but the thought made her panic. If she wanted to sleep before work, she had to get her grandmother to bed, and talking about Ignacio would make that impossible.

"Your cup? You're holding it. I made tea." Julieta smiled brightly. "Do you want a little more?"

Alma blinked and looked at the cup in her hands. "Uh, no, mija. Thank you. I'm sleepy."

"Okay, then. Let's get you to bed."

Cesar brought her hands to his lips. "Come with me."

"But what about *my* work?"

He sighed. "I thought you were looking to go elsewhere, too? After your program is done, you wanted to move to a clinic, right? Stop the hospital grind and get more time with your patients, right?"

Julieta shrugged. "I mean, yeah, but I meant *here*. I have more connections and I'd be close to my family. Moving to California means starting all over."

"You know that's not true. People can network from everywhere. And I'm sure that your place would give you tons of recommendations. They love you there."

A stab of guilt flashed through her. She hadn't told her work she was looking to go elsewhere. Most assumed she'd finish her program and at most switch departments. The idea of putting in notice almost felt like a break up. Some of her best friends worked in the hospital.

***

Julieta yawned, her eyes watering. She heard Eve laugh and gave her a sheepish grin afterward. Eve had just returned from a patient's room and joined her at the nurses' station.

"Need more coffee, Jules? I'm tired just looking at you." Eve's long black hair was tied into a droopy bun. At 4'11" tall, she was the only staff member in the cardiology unit that was shorter than Julieta. Even so, she was affectionately called 'Mom' by most of the staff. After 20 years of being a nurse, she held more weight than most of the newer doctors.

"Sorry," said Julieta. She rubbed her eyes. "Went to bed late. My grandma woke up a bit confused last night."

Eve's smile dropped. "Oh, I'm sorry."

"It's okay." Julieta shrugged. "It's not too bad most of the time. She asks for her purse a couple times in a row. Sometimes she gets really irritable, but like...in a way that's not like her. But there's been a few times—not that many—where she's been so confused that she thinks Welo is still alive. And that," her voice trailed off. After a moment, she cleared her throat. "It's hard to deescalate."

The phone rang before Eve could reply. Julieta gratefully answered the phone and relayed the message.

Eve took the report and then arched an eyebrow. "I'm serious about the coffee, though. Go run to the break room really quick."

"Mm," said Julieta, suppressing another yawn. "Not sure I want another lovely chat with Mary."

"Psh. I think she's busy with Dr. Murtagh. Plus, if she has an issue with it, I'll tell her I told you to."

"I don't think that's how that works."

Eve narrowed her eyes and crossed her arms. "What's she gonna do?

"Anyway, I have to finish charting and then room three needs a vitals check, room four needs meds. Once I'm up and running around I'll feel better."

"Alright, well, I offered. If you fall asleep standing up again—"

Julieta burst out laughing. "I have never fallen asleep standing—"

"Uh-huh. Well, anyway, get a nap in between today and the weekend." Eve crossed her arms. "I heard you're picking up another shift. Again."

"Yes, *Mom*, I did." Julieta suppressed a smile at the chastisement. "Gotta whittle down this college debt!"

Though the hospital was impressive and patient satisfaction was decent, staff shortages were common, and the hours could be brutal if given the chance. Management constantly reached out for people to work doubles or cover the less desirable shifts. It made for ample opportunities to earn overtime. The paychecks could be beautiful. But on the other hand, if one didn't push back every now and again, the hospital was happy to consume every spare moment of its staff, like a vampire sucking the life source out of its victims. The lay person thought a medical degree and hospital employment meant plenty of money. What they didn't see, was the majority used the money to pay back gargantuan loans with unforgiving interest rates.

"Yeah, I know. But if you work yourself half to death..." Eve paused and rapped a finger on the desk.

"I won't. What! Don't look at me like that. I won't. Pinky promise." Julieta smiled and suppressed another yawn.

The rest of the shift went by unremarkably, minus one altercation with an old man who tried to cop a feel when she attached electrodes to his torso for an EKG. Her rebuke earned her a grumbly cackle. She retold the story in the locker room to Eve and Olivia, her friend from the oncoming shift. They shook their heads.

Olivia rolled her eyes as she tied her hair back into a bun. "I hate some of these dusty, old men. Thanks for the warning, though. If he's still here, I'll take Diego in with me. I always seem to get stuck with the perverts." She smiled brightly. "Oh! In completely unrelated news: you both are invited salsa dancing next weekend. I know you picked up an extra shift, Jules, so that's why you are absolutely forbidden to get any extra overtime next Saturday, okay? Okay."

Julieta opened her mouth to protest and Eve covered with a hand. "We are in!"

Olivia giggled and clapped in excitement. "Awesome. Wear something pretty. I gotta go."

Eve dropped her hand and Julieta slapped her playfully on the arm. "What if I have a test that weekend?"

"We both know you don't. Have some fun for once, yes? All work and no play makes for a great path to burnout."

"That's true." Julieta chewed on her cheek. "You're right. I need me-time."

"And what screams me-time better than tequila and salsa dancing with some hot men? Maybe I'll find a sugar daddy." Eve shook her hips and they laughed.

The idea of cramming in a night out with her friends in between work, classes, and helping out with her grandmother felt slightly overwhelming. But Julieta knew her friends were right. There had to be a break somewhere in all of the tedium of hard days and harder nights. On a whim, she detoured to a new boutique before going home and bought a bright red dress.

She smiled at her reflection as she modeled the dress to herself. "Well, now you have to go, Julie."

Julieta sipped on an energy drink on the way to *Melanie's* the Latin night club Olivia had chosen for Saturday night dancing. Her grandmother had had an episode that had left the entire family without sleep the night before. The short nap she was able to take earlier in the day felt inadequate, but she hoped her friends' energy would be contagious, like a telepathic jolt of motivation. And, if not, the energy drink would help.

She nervously smoothed out the front of her dress after paying the Uber driver and stepping out of the vehicle. The line to enter kept growing and she rushed toward the back of it, self-consciously gripping her small black purse.

"Hey!" The voice was accompanied by a hand that firmly gripped her upper arm. She whipped her head toward the sound, eyes wide. It was Olivia.

"Oh my God! You scared me half to death!"

Olivia threw her head back and laughed. "I was afraid you wouldn't stop in time. You looked like you were on a mission! I love your dress, by the way."

"Oh," Julieta looked down, as if noticing her attire for the first time. She grinned. "You said to wear something pretty. I just bought it. It was a little pricier than it needed to be, but—"

"Pshh, you need to splurge on yourself every now and again. Anyway, c'mon. We're right here." Olivia led her to the middle of the line where several of their friends were waiting.

Julieta flashed a concerned face at the rest of the line. Heat rushed up her neck. "I don't want to cut the line."

"You're not cutting," Olivia said, waving away her concern. "We were saving a spot for you. Plus, it's not like you're the only friend who was late. I've seen people wedge in front and behind us because they were joining a group."

When no one complained, Julieta relaxed and embraced the rest of their group. Eve, Ruby, Beatriz, and Celina all took turns embracing her. They chatted excitedly until it was their turn to flash their IDs at the bouncer. His dark eyes studied their faces a moment, matching each face with the card presented. He nodded in silent affirmation and they marched inside. Women had free entry before midnight, so after presenting their IDs once again to the balding man standing behind a booth, he scrawled a black X with permanent marker on the back of their right hand.

The dance floor had a scattering of couples and there were numerous empty tables.

"See? I told you if we get here early, we'll have plenty of places to sit." Olivia raised her voice over the music.

Julieta nodded even as she wondered how 11 o'clock at night could count as early.

Pulsing bass slowed and gave way to the rich, reedy sound of a lone accordion. The sound reverberated through the crowd and those on the dance floor paused at the transition. Slowly, percussion and trumpets were added and after the sound of a record scratching, both the cumbia and electronic beats dropped.

Beatriz squealed. "Cumbias are my favorite! Let's go snag a table and then go dance!"

Olivia answered Eve's questioning look. "They'll play salsa, too. Tonight's one of those variety nights. They'll play everything. Lezz go!"

After claiming a table, Beatriz and Ruby ran to the dance floor, yelling their drink orders over their shoulder.

"What'd they say?" asked Celina.

Eve shrugged. "Tequila shots. That's what they said."

"You're evil," Olivia said, cackling.

"I'm just being helpful. We're here to relax, right? Get loose?" Eve moved her shoulders side to side.

"Exactly. And who better to teach us all about the art of being loose women?" Celina batted her eyes at Eve as she hooked an arm around her.

Eve gasped. "You little bitch. I hope you know I've always hated you."

Olivia and Julieta burst out laughing.

"Ay, que mala. I was just playing."

"Plus, it's not like you needed any pointers. Your little black book looks like a dictionary."

Celina screamed as the rest burst into laughter again. "That doesn't even make sense, puta. Do dictionaries even have names?"

"Fine," conceded Eve. "Then, like one of those baby name books. *Over One Thousand Best Names*. Maybe you can publish it and I'll pass it out on the maternity wing."

When the waiter returned, the women were still laughing. Julieta wiped an eye and made a waving motion toward the table. "We're okay," she said, her voice barely a squeak. Amused, he left the drinks and promised to return to check in on them.

The music transitioned from cumbias to a bachata. Shortly afterward, Ruby and Beatriz returned.

"Oooh, did you order my rum and coke?" Beatriz asked, scanning the drinks.

"Bitch, we cannot hear you over this music as you run away," Olivia said.

"We got you both vodka and cranberries." Julieta pointed to the drinks to her right.

Ruby shrugged as she sat and picked up one of the glasses. "That works." Beatriz sat heavily next to her.

"I was going to get you guys tequila shots, but I was outvoted."

"Well, I appreciate you, Evie. Although, I don't know if we're at that part of the night yet." Beatriz pushed her behind her ear and drank deeply from her cup.

"What part?"

"The part where drinking tequila straight sounds like a good idea."

The group laughed and finished their drinks while they chatted about work, chastised each other about talking about work, and then segued into Beatriz's relationship problems. Their waiter returned and the group ordered some wings and a round of drinks.

"Why do you always find the worst men?" Ruby asked, frowning, her arms crossed in front of her.

Beatriz groaned. "I don't know. It's a curse, I guess. But, I mean, he's trying."

Eve crinkled her nose. "Is he, though?"

"This is why I'm so glad I'm not straight. These men ain't shit," Ruby said. Her face reddened when she realized the waiter had walked up to the table with their orders as she finished her complaint. Julieta stifled a giggle.

"Well, it's not like women can't be assholes," Celina said. "Case in point." She held a hand out toward Eve, palm facing the ceiling, like she was presenting a prize on a game show.

Eve slapped her hand away.

Beatriz snorted out a laugh. "We love you, Evie. Well, anyway, let's not think about Jorge tonight. He can be categorized as a work topic. Off limits." She downed the rest of her glass.

Julieta pressed her lips into a smile as Eve leaned over to whisper in her ear. "Money she's crying about him before last call."

Eventually they found themselves on the dance floor again. The club had filled with more patrons and Julieta felt as if the crowd moved their bodies along the pulse of the music, like buoys that obeyed the guiding hand of ocean swells. Either the extra bodies, alcohol, or both made her body feel flush with warmth. Perspiration formed along the edges of her hair. She used her fingers to rake the sides of it up away from her face and spun, hoping that would elicit a pseudo breeze that would bring extra relief.

Her elbow connected with someone's face. Even over the music, she heard a cry of offense. She gasped and stumbled, her hands dropping and reaching out wildly, as if she could use the air to steady herself.

A strong hand grabbed her arm and the world dropped from under her.

Cesar.

"Hey, Jules. That's a hell of a hello." Cesar rubbed a hand over his mouth and Julieta's stomach flipped as she realized he was the face her elbow had connected with. He was grinning. "You look great, by the way."

She realized her mouth was open and closed it. She shrugged. "Thanks. Um, you look nice, too." A beat passed. "Why are you here?"

He laughed. "Still the same ol' Julie." He used his thumb to indicate behind himself. "Gabe invited me."

She smacked him on the chest. "That's not what I meant."

Cesar made a show of wincing and stepping back. "Porque eres tan mala? First you uppercut my face—"

Julieta laughed. "I did not uppercut anything. I was hot—"

"You do look hot," he said, his eyes focused on hers.

Her lips curled into a small smile in reaction to the flirty tone of his comment.

"And then," he said, rubbing a hand on his chest, "after the simple assault—"

Julieta barked out a laugh. "My elbow barely touched you."

"—I remained the gentleman and steadied my attacker after she lost her balance because she can't fight in heels."

"Oh, trust me, I can fight in heels. I just wasn't fighting."

He laughed.

"Who's this?" Ruby's voice cut through their banter.

"Oh!" Julieta startled and saw her group of friends had stopped dancing and gathered behind her. "Hey. Sorry. This is Cesar. He's...an old friend." She didn't check for his reaction to the title. "We grew up together. He moved away not long after we graduated high school."

"About two years afterwards," he clarified. Julieta forced a smile, still facing her friends.

Eve appraised them both and Julieta couldn't help but feel as if her friend could read everything about their past as clearly as if it were written out in simple terms and stapled onto her forehead. "Oh, neat. What brings you back?"

Julieta turned toward him this time, wondering if he'd continue the teasing or answer directly. Cesar smiled. "Work, actually. Though, right now this is more pleasure than business. Up until the assault."

"Assault!" Eve's eyes widened.

"He's exaggerating," Julieta replied, her hands on her hips.

"Just a simple elbow to the jaw," he said, shrugging.

When Ruby stole his attention by asking another question, Beatriz leaned close to Julieta. "I'd assault him, too. Wow. You two really just friends?"

Julieta laughed. "We met in 2nd grade. I feel like I've known him off and on since then." Movement from her peripheral stole her attention and she realized he was excusing himself. An emotion fluttered through her chest, though she couldn't name it. She wasn't sure if it was nostalgia, longing, regret, or simple relief.

Her friends began dancing again, but she realized she was now distracted. It took all she had to not look around for him.

Why would he come by again, anyway? You broke his heart a thousand years ago and then topped it off with an elbow to the face. Julieta didn't know if she wanted another drink or Tums.

As it happened, less than an hour later, Cesar reappeared with his friends. By then, Julieta had done her best to pretend he hadn't mysteriously reappeared into her life and alcohol had made her feel extremely brave. When he took her hand, she didn't wait for an invitation. She glanced back only once and saw Eve's grin of approval.

When the night ended, her friends were quick to bid their goodbyes and Julieta found herself alone; or rather, she found herself standing outside next to Cesar as she fumbled with her phone to order a ride home.

"Do you work tomorrow?"

Julieta stole a glance toward Cesar. "No. Why?"

He shrugged. "Just wondering." When she narrowed her eyes, he burst out laughing. "Why do you always look so suspicious?"

She couldn't help but grin. "I'm not suspicious. I'm just—there's implication behind that question."

"Oh, yes? And what would that be?" He closed the gap between them and she could smell the mild spice of his cologne.

The urge to kiss him, fall into him, was unbearable. She took a breath. "I don't know, but knowing you it's probably a bad decision."

He let out a disappointed sigh and smiled at her. He brushed a loose strand of hair out of her face. "Still always overthinking."

A stab of offense coursed through her. She took a step backward. "I'm not overthinking. I'm being practical." She shook her head when he opened his mouth. "I'm serious. This is a bad idea. It didn't end well last time and—I mean, do you really want to—"

Cesar cut off her thoughts with a kiss and with that, Julieta felt like she was 20-years-old again, young and dumb and naïve. And she didn't care. All she wanted was to spend one more night pretending responsibilities weren't a thing.

"You said you had a day off tomorrow, right?"

This time, Julieta just smiled in response and he ordered a cab. When they arrived at his apartment, they made their way to his bed, leaving a trail of clothes from the door to the room. His mouth left a trail of fire from her neck to her navel. Before he made his way further south, she said it again: *This is a bad idea.*

He paused and she felt his breath hot against her abdomen. "Doesn't mean it's wrong."

After their meeting at the club, they fell back into the natural rhythm of their previous relationship. There had been no discussion of their previous break-up nor their reconciliation. Looking back, Julieta knew it was because they had hoped the other had changed. Cesar had hoped she had changed enough to set down responsibilities. She had hoped he had changed enough to slow down. It appeared neither would get their wish.

She walked back to his kitchen table, sat, and took a large swallow of lukewarm coffee.

He followed and took a seat, folding his hands expectantly in his lap. One thing she had to credit him for was his ability to know when to wait for an answer.

Her thoughts wandered to one of their dates.

On a whim, she had suggested they go karaoke at a hole-in-the-wall she liked. It still allowed smoking inside but she explained the trick was to arrive early. After singing a few off-key songs and sharing an appetizer, she noticed the bar was getting crowded.

"As a nurse, I can confidently say this amount of second-hand smoke is shaving at least a couple minutes off our lifetime."

"Probably. I know a place we can go that's smoke-free," Cesar said, his hand creeping up her thigh.

Julieta laughed and her look turned flirty. "Is that right? Does it have live music, though?"

The next singer's track began. "I don't really know how to sing," the woman slurred, swaying slightly. "But if you're drunk enough, you can do anything, right?" A few patrons whooped.

When she started singing, Cesar cringed. "Well, she answered *that* question and it's a resounding no." He shot Julieta a look. "Well, I can't promise this quality of live music..."

"Ay, no seas malo," Julieta said, swatting his arm. "C'mon, let's go."

She blinked back to the present. "Do you remember that karaoke bar we went to last month?"

He nodded.

"It's not usually my type of place but the patrons are nice, even if some nights they smoke too much, and you get a lot of chances to sing." She tapped her fingers against the table and took a breath. "My fiancé—*ex*-fiancé—took me there. That's how I found out about it."

A corner of his mouth tugged downward but otherwise his face stayed neutral. "Oh. Fiancé. That's—I didn't realize you had ever been engaged."

"I didn't know whether to mention it when it happened. And maybe that's how I knew it wasn't going to work out." She shrugged. "Either way, he was a great guy. Just maybe not the right one for me."

"Have you ever been engaged?"

Cesar shook his head.

"Why?"

He frowned. "Uh, I—I just haven't."

She picked at a fingernail. "I only bring up my ex because I think it says two things. One, that if I'm being honest with myself, the reason I broke up with him was probably because of you."

Cesar's eyebrows raised. "Me?"

"I love you. More than I probably should." She shook her angrily when he began to speak. "Wait, no. Stop. Before you say anything. The *other* reason I broke up with him is because I keep choosing men who are wonderful and great but...who aren't a good match with me. I keep..." Her voice broke but she rushed forward. "I keep proving that love isn't enough. And that's a heartbreaking thing to find out.

"I can't move to California with you. And it's not a reflection of how much or how little I love you. It's a reflection of the responsibility I have to my friends, my family, my career. But mainly myself."

"Julie..."

"No, stop." She stood again but this time gently, taking care to not scratch the chair against the floor again. "I can't. Just as much as you can't stay. Because that's the alternative. You could stay with me. But you can't."

And with that, she fled the apartment, the tears finally flowing free when she crossed the threshold.

She composed herself before entering her house in case her grandmother was awake and wandering about. Mercifully, no one was awake and she was able to shower, change, and leave to work without incident.

At work, Eve eyed her suspiciously but Julieta managed to fend off any prying questions. She didn't have the energy to explain her heartache. After her long shift, she went home, turned off her phone, and barely made it onto her bed before sleep swallowed her whole. When she woke, the previous day's conversation with Cesar came flooding back to her and she cried. Why did she ever accept the invitation to go out dancing?

The deli was busy and waiters bustled to and from the tables. Ruby and Olivia had invited Julieta to lunch and she accepted only because she had declined the last two invitations.

"Finally, we got you out from under that rock," Olivia said, her smile genuine. "We've missed you."

"I know," Julieta said. "I've just been busy."

"Always busy. Girl, you make me tired *for* you." Ruby laughed.

"Tell me about it. That's okay, though. Once school wraps up, it'll be a lot better. Just gotta grind for a few more months!"

Olivia nodded. "Almost there, chia. And then you really are okay staying here?"

"As opposed to what?" Julieta frowned.

"Moving in with Cesar."

Julieta exhaled a small laugh. "Yeah. Funny thing is I would move in with him. Just...not all the way to California."

Olivia shrugged. "I get it. You're such a great daughter. But...you looked so happy with him. I...I was really rooting for you guys."

"Ugh, I know. I know! But I just—I can't. For a million reasons."

Ruby raised her eyebrows. "I feel you. And I agree with you. *He* could stay. I mean, that's as equal to a sacrifice as he's asking you to make. You know?"

Julieta let out a breath of air. "Well, anyway. How are you guys doing?"

"Good." Ruby's face lit up. "I met someone."

"Oooh, really! What's her name?" Julieta perked up at the news.

"Fatima. We've only been going out a couple weeks but so far, she's amazing." Ruby grinned.

"You got to fight with someone at least one good time to see how they really are, though," said Olivia.

Ruby cut her a look. "Let me have my fun, damn it."

"Alright. My bad." Olivia put her hands in the air, palms out. "My bad."

"Well," said Julieta, "I'm excited for you. Anything fun and exciting for you, Oli?"

"Eh. Same ol', same ol'. But I can't complain much. Could be worse." She paused and then gasped. "Oh, did you hear?"

Julieta's eyes opened wide. "Oh, geez. No? I don't know? Someone died?"

Ruby snorted. "No. Olivia's just dramatic."

"Shut up. No, I'm not. Anyway, Beatriz finally dumped what's-his-face!"

"Manuel? Noooo." Julieta was delighted by the news. "Good for her. About time."

"Yeah," said Olivia. "And apparently his bitch ass kept begging her to give him another chance and blah, blah, blah. She had to block him everywhere."

The trio laughed.

"Well, good. Serves him right. He didn't deserve her." Julieta smiled. "I need to text her soon."

"You do! And we need to go out to Melanie's again soon," Olivia said, clapping her hands together lightly. "There's a cumbia night coming up. That's always fun."

A memory of dancing with Cesar flashed in Julieta's mind. She pressed her lips together into what she hoped was a smile. "Yeah. Would be fun."

"God, at least sound believable." Olivia stuck out her tongue.

Julieta giggled. "I meant it. I promise. We do need to go dancing soon."

"Great, it's a date. And push comes to shove, I'll kidnap you for the night. Deal?"

"Deal."

Lunch continued with more details about Ruby's new girlfriend, discussions about work, and promises to get together soon. Julieta embraced her friends and drove to her house. She had enough time for a nap before going in for her evening shift. With the end of school in sight, she allowed herself up to two extra night shifts a month.

In her room, she stripped down to her underwear and t-shirt and slipped under the covers. Her thoughts turned to Cesar. They still texted and had met up a few times, but she was doing her best to provide distance for herself. His upcoming departure was looming and she felt it acutely. Every time they met, it felt like opening an old wound.

She thought back to their breakfast, to the moments before he had told her he was moving away again. Before she slipped into the blackness of sleep, she held tight to the image of his face, smiling and beautiful, the love of her life.

***

Julieta's dreams were muddled and fading quickly. Groggily, she searched for her phone and glanced at the screen. It wasn't time for her alarm to go off and she frowned.

What woke me up?

A sharp rap at her door answered the question immediately. "Julieta!"

Her mother's voice sounded desperate and she bolted upright? "Si, Ma? Que paso?" Julieta rushed to the door and opened it. "Ma, what is it?"

"Your wela! She's gone. I can't find her, mija. The door was unlocked and I don't know where she went. It's getting dark." Her mother's eyes were filled with tears.

"Where's Dad?"

"Looking for her. I don't know what to do."

Julieta's heart felt like it was in her throat but she took a deep breath. She couldn't panic if she wanted to be helpful. "It'll be okay, Ma. Have you called the police yet?"

"Yes, I called 911."

"Okay, great. Then we already have a ton of help. You said Dad went looking for Wela already? Do you know where?"

Her mother shook her head. "No. I don't know. He took the car. He's probably going up and down the blocks. He told me to stay here in case she comes back."

"That's a good idea. Are you okay by yourself if I look, too?" Her mother nodded quickly. "Okay. Then, I'm going to get dressed and look as well. I'll call some of my friends. We can search on foot. Maybe she wandered into a backyard or something."

"Okay, mija, be careful."

"I will, Ma. Stay by your phone. If Wela comes home, call me. If— *when* we find her, I'll call you to let you know. Okay?" Julieta kissed her mom on the forehead and rushed outside, blinking back tears.

She called work and let them know she wouldn't make it in. She sent texts to her friends. Messages immediately poured in.

I'll be right there.

Her heart swelled with the support even as her hands shook. "No," she chastised herself. "You won't think the worst. Wela is fine. We will find her."

She looked at her phone and dialed. He picked up on the first ring. "Cesar..." She burst into tears.

"Julie? What's wrong? What happened?"

It took her a few tries to explain it to him.

"Are you at your house?"

"I'm walking down the block trying to see if she wandered into someone's backyard."

"Okay. I'm on my way."

Everyone arrived within minutes of each other and they walked the neighborhood like a grid. As night enveloped the world, Julieta felt herself grow more desperate. The group searched hidden areas with flashlights and knocked on doors. Apologetic neighbors shook their heads at the description and promised to keep an eye out.

Each block yielded nothing. Julieta checked her phone obsessively, wondering if she had missed a call or text that would inform her that her grandmother had been found. But it stayed stubbornly quiet.

The image of her grandmother spending an entire night outside alone and confused was terrifying. She clenched and unclenched a fist on the hand that wasn't holding a flashlight. Cesar noticed and walked over to her. He took her hand in his and squeezed it.

"Hey," he said. "We'll find her." A tear fell down her cheek and he hugged her. "You believe me, right? We'll find her. I know we will."

She pressed her face against his shoulder and nodded. She pulled away and straightened her form. "I'm good. Let's keep looking."

The search party continued, periodically accompanied by neighbors, though eventually the hour grew too late to keep knocking on doors.

Julieta's phone rang and startled the group. She pulled it from her pocket and almost dropped it. "Hello? Yes? Hello?"

"Mija." It was her father. "They found her." Julieta felt so relieved she almost fell. "I already told your mom. I'm on my way home to pick her up."

"Wait, pick who up? Wela is at home? Or you're picking up Mom?"

"Wela is in the hospital."

Julieta blanched. "Oh my God. Why? Is she okay?"

"Si, mijita. She's fine. She got on the bus or something and ended up getting let off somewhere strange. When the cops found her, she had a cut on her leg or something. So, they took her to the hospital to check her out."

"Oh, I see." Julieta placed a hand on her heart and sighed. "Okay. Did she go to *my* hospital? Or a different one."

"Yours."

"I can be there soon."

"No, mija, it's okay. You don't have to. They're discharging her soon and we can take her home right away. I'm just getting your mom because she would kill me if I didn't."

Julieta chuckled wearily. "Okay. Alright. Well, I'll see you guys soon, okay?"

She ended the call and turned to her friends. They faced her expectantly. She grinned. "The cops found her." A small cheer erupted. "I know. God, you guys, I'm so grateful for you all. Thanks so much."

Tears flowed down her cheeks and she noticed that many of her friends were also teary eyed. They all embraced and said their goodnights. Once everyone started toward their cars, Cesar fell in step next to her.

"Thanks."

He glanced at her. "No problem."

"You didn't have to come but I'm glad you did."

"Don't be ridiculous. Of course, I had to. I love you and I care about you. And this is your wela we're talking about."

Julieta smiled. "Well, still. Thanks."

When they reached her house, he kissed her. "Goodnight, Jules."

She watched him start toward his car. "Wait." He paused and looked back. "Do you want to come in?"

He knitted his brow. "You sure?"

She nodded, shrugged, then nodded again.

He laughed. "Well, only because you're so certain. And because I'd love to say hello to your wela."

"I think she'd love seeing you again." She took his hand and they walked to her room. She stripped down to her underwear and t-shirt again. He joined her in the bed and stroked her hair until she drifted off to sleep.

The month following the elopement of Julieta's grandmother, was filled with numerous discussions about hiring a part-time nurse to help with her daily routine and safety. A security system with chime alarms on every door and window was installed. The future was uncertain but the family did their best to plan around the complexities of caring for a loved one with dementia. Providers passed them pamphlets advertising memory care units.

Julieta's mother was adamant against the idea of having others care for her. Julieta herself was unsure. In the meanwhile, an in-home nurse would be helpful.

A warm breeze played with her hair as she sat on the park bench. She worked a fingernail with her teeth as she scrolled through her phone. Images of a new memory care unit looked up at her. Smiling nurses sat alongside smiling residents. The option to schedule a tour flashed on the screen.

"You're deep in thought."

Julieta glanced up and smiled. "Maybe it's because someone's late."

Cesar grinned. "Not late. Making an entrance."

"How do you make an entrance to a park?"

"Like this." He bowed and produced a bouquet of flowers from behind his back.

She giggled. "Awww. Okay, fine. I forgive you."

"And also, I bought like a hundred tacos from the taco truck down the street for our picnic. They had tacos de lengua, de barbacoa, de asada..."

"Ooh, really?" Her eyes lit up.

"I ever tell you you're a complete fat kid?"

"Listen, man, you eat more than me. So, you have zero room to talk."

He shrugged. "It wasn't a complaint. I like some squish."

"I'm squishy?"

"Only in the perfect places."

"Love handles are perfect?"

"Yes! They're the best. Come here." He pulled her from her seat and kissed her. "And also, this." His hand wandered to her butt.

She batted him away. "Hey, sir. This is a family-friendly place."

He grinned. "You're right. I apologize."

"Where are my tacos?"

He snorted. "I should have known. Straight to the point. I set it all up right there on that table."

"Oh, wow!" She raised her eyebrows. "So, you were here a couple minutes before you came and said hey. How'd I not see you?"

"Hence, my deep in thought comment."

"That's fair." She opened the paper bag and pulled out packs of tacos wrapped in aluminum foil. "Geez, you were right. This is a lot."

"I skipped breakfast on accident."

Julieta laughed and they sat, partitioning the food and drinks. As they ate, they spoke of everything and nothing. A few birds flittered overhead and vanished. The breeze began to pick up and Cesar jumped up, running behind a clump of napkins that blew off of the table. She stuffed the rest in the paper bag, afraid they'd also escape with the wind.

When he returned, he placed a hand on his side and made a face. "Don't run with a full stomach. That was dumb. I should have left them."

"Well, Mother Nature appreciates you for not littering." She smiled. "I'm sorry about your tummy."

He sighed. "Yeah. Well, at least it's a nice day."

Her smile froze slightly. The warming weather reminded her that their time together was limited. Fall was approaching and with it his departure. She turned to watch a couple kids throw a ball around. A lump formed in her throat and she drank from her soda bottle to try and clear it.

Cesar placed a hand on hers. "Hey."

She turned toward him and set down her drink. "Hey."

"I want to ask you something."

She sighed and closed her eyes. "No, don't do this again, Cesar. I can't go with you. And I just—I just want to spend as much time with you as possible because—"

"Will you let me talk first?" When he had her attention, he nodded once, satisfied. "Okay. I wanted to ask you to move in with me."

"Wait, how is that different?"

"I'm not finished."

A dog began to bark and they were momentarily distracted.

He shifted in his seat. "Will you move in with me? Not in California. But here."

Julieta opened her mouth, then closed it. Her brows furrowed. "I'm confused."

"I love you, Jules. A lot. You're it for me. You wanted to know why I had never gotten engaged? Because I've never found anybody like you. You are smart and funny and stubborn and beautiful and a little bit of a pain in the ass."

"Hey! I will cut you."

"And violent."

"I am not violent."

"And delusional." Cesar laughed when she smacked his arm. "See? Anyway, what I'm saying is I would be a complete idiot if I walked away from you or let you push me away. I talked to the company who offered me that new position. And they have a branch close by I could work semi-remotely from. I'd have to work a bit of a swing shift but your hours are crazy, so it's nothing we're not used to. And I am extending the lease at my apartment and—"

"Yes."

"What?"

Julieta smiled. "Yeah, I'll move in. Although," she held up a finger, "we have to talk about the closet set up."

"What? Wait, are you already trying to claim extra closet space?"

"I have a lot of scrubs. And if you work remotely, you won't even need that many clothes."

"See? Pain in the ass."

She laughed. "You know what—" He cut her off with a long kiss. "Never mind."

"You want to go check out *our* place? We can rechristen it."

A wave of excitement coursed through her. "Our place. That sounds nice."

The End

***

Enjoy the story? Be sure to leave a review! Also, sign-up for my newsletter for a free read, exclusive sneak peeks, and updates on my next release.

ABOUT THE AUTHOR

Gloria Lucas is an emerging author who primarily writes Literary Fiction. She has published numerous short stories and personal essays, including *The Man Who Turned into a Mountain*. She is a Navy veteran and mother of four. When she isn't working or writing, she enjoys spending time with her family, hiking the Appalachian Trail, and visiting karaoke bars. To learn more and stay up-to-date with upcoming releases, visit her site glorialucas.com.

Her debut novel, *How Deep the Ocean,* is scheduled to be published November 2022.

LOST AND FOUND IN MEXICO

A Romancing the Ruins Novella

Carla Luna

ABOUT *LOST AND FOUND IN MEXICO*

To score a spot on a reality dating show, travel influencer Sofia Sanchez needs a quickie divorce from the sexy archaeologist she accidentally married in Vegas. But when she tracks him down at his dig site, deep in the jungles of Mexico, resisting him proves more challenging than she ever imagined.

CHAPTER 1

Four Years Ago

Being born at the tail end of December meant Sofia Sanchez always lost out on a real celebration. Her birthday was lumped in with one of the big Sanchez family holidays—Christmas Eve, New Year's Eve, or Three Kings Day. Totally unfair, since she was the type who loved the spotlight.

This year, however, she couldn't have asked for better timing. Because her twenty-first birthday just happened to fall on the first night of a "wild girls' weekend" in Las Vegas. No longer bound by the limits of her crappy fake ID, Sofia could drink, gamble, and party the night away. Three nights, to be precise, all funded by her friend Yasmin whose family was so wealthy they owned four houses, two yachts, and a stable of horses. Not only had they paid for the girls' posh limo ride from San Diego to Vegas, but they'd also booked them in a deluxe Tower Suite at the Bellagio.

Now, sitting at the hotel's upscale Lily Bar & Lounge with her two besties, Sofia stirred her ridiculously expensive mojito and scanned the area for potential hookups.

"Just to refresh you both on the rules of this weekend's challenge," Yasmin said, waving a glittery fingernail at them. "You have three nights. At least one of them should be spent in the arms of a gorgeous guy."

Elle groaned. "Can't we just enjoy each other's company?"

Yasmin rolled her eyes. "Nope. We've spent too many nights at the apartment watching Hallmark movies. This is our chance to let loose."

"This weekend has to be memorable," Sofia added. "Not just on Instagram, but in real life." Unlike Elle, she was fully on board with Yasmin's challenge. She loved taking risks and embracing adventure. Anything to avoid ending up like her boring older sister, Olivia, who spent most of her time holed up in the college library.

"The only rule is that you have to check in via text before you end up in someone's bed," Yasmin said. "That way we can make sure you're safe."

"Nothing about this is safe," Elle muttered. "How about we go to Cirque du Soleil instead?"

Squinting across the lounge's darkened interior, Sofia spotted a group of guys clustered around the bar. Four men about their age, casually dressed, looking like they were in Vegas for a little fun. "Check it out, ladies. Serious hotties dead ahead. You two with me?"

"I'll pass," Yasmin said. "They look like frat guys. I'd rather find an obscenely wealthy businessman. Someone tightly wound on the outside but a tiger in the sack."

Elle shook her head. "Sounds like a good way to get murdered. Or get an STI."

Sofia patted her shiny gold wristlet. "That's why I always bring condoms with me. Besides, the guys over there look harmless. If they act creepy, then I'll move on. But you never know unless you try."

One of her personal mantras. In her twenty-one years, she'd rarely turned down an opportunity. She'd tried skydiving, cliff jumping, paragliding, and surfing, and she'd once taken an impromptu road trip along the Extraterrestrial Highway through the Nevada desert because she'd been dating a guy who believed in UFOs. Not the wisest move in the middle of August, but definitely unforgettable.

As she stood, she wobbled a little, slightly unsteady from the combination of two mojitos, one round of birthday shots, and a pair of precariously high heels. But despite her petite stature—barely five feet one in stocking feet—she'd learned to hold her liquor. She smoothed out her sparkly gold minidress and adjusted the birthday tiara perched atop her dark brown curls. "I'm going in."

"Yes," Yasmin squealed. "Get it, girl."

Sofia left their table and approached the pack. Her plan was simple: engage them in some light conversation, flirt a little, score a free drink, and then decide if any of them were worth pursuing.

She slowed her pace as she got closer, only to freeze in her tracks. Her breath hitched. Though she wasn't familiar with three of the faces, one of them was instantly recognizable.

Javier Castillo.

Only the hottest, most desirable bartender *ever* to work at El Marinero, her family's Mexican restaurant in San Diego. She and Javier had spent last summer working together when she'd waited tables to earn money for college. During his first week there, she'd turned on the charm, hoping to lure him into bed. Though he was clearly into her, he refused to take the bait. Not only was she the boss's daughter, but he couldn't offer her anything long-term. After the summer ended, he'd be leaving for grad school.

To which she'd replied. "I'm fine with short-term."

Given how prominently he'd featured in her sexual fantasies, she would have settled for a few months of no-strings sex.

But instead, he'd offered friendship. To her surprise, she'd had a blast with him, hanging out after their shifts ended and exploring San Diego's late-night scene. When he'd left in September to start grad school at the University of Chicago, she bid him farewell with a heavy heart, unsure of when she'd ever see him again. Since he didn't do social media, she couldn't even stalk him online.

But now he was here. In Vegas, of all places.

What were the odds?

She should have been playing roulette. With this kind of luck, she could have put all her money on red and come out a winner.

She took a moment to savor his mouthwatering appearance. He was the total package: dark, curly hair, a firm jaw with a hint of stubble, broad shoulders, and light brown skin just a shade darker than hers. Impressive biceps peeked out from under his short-sleeved button down. She wanted to run her fingers over those muscles. Or brush up against his ass, which looked nice and firm in a pair of jeans.

She inched closer. Though she meant to address him in a husky, come-hither manner, her voice came out as more of a squeak. "Javi?"

At first, she thought he hadn't heard her above the din of the bar. But then he turned his head. His eyes widened. And he smiled. A slow, sensual smile that made her insides churn like a carnival ride.

"Sofia Sanchez? What are the odds?"

She let out a pent-up breath. "I know, right? That's *exactly* what I thought."

"I should try one of those slot machines. Put in a hundred bucks. Because clearly, luck is on my side tonight."

Yes. He was just as pleased as she was. That boded well. "What are you doing here?"

"Bachelor party weekend."

He was getting married?

Her disappointment must have been painfully obvious because he chuckled. "Not me. My buddy Tyler. We go way back." He pointed to the tall, blond guy to his left who was built like a quarterback. "What about you?"

"My friend organized a girls' trip to celebrate New Year's Eve. And my birthday." She gestured to her tiara. "I just turned twenty-one."

"Happy birthday. That means I need to buy you a drink, right?" He gave her a grin so devastating that it sent shivers dancing along her spine.

"Yes, please. I'll have mojito."

As he introduced her to his buddies, she beamed winningly, assuming he'd want her to stay and chat with the group. But once their drinks arrived, he hustled her off to a red velvet couch at the other end of the lounge.

Seated beside him, her bare thigh pressed against the rough denim of his jeans, she was so overcome by his physical presence she could barely breathe. She inhaled his scent—a mix of spicy soap and sandalwood—and tried to center herself. "What about your friends? I don't want you to ignore them."

"Trust me, they won't mind. Tyler didn't plan a bunch of activities. He just brought us here to have fun."

That sounded a lot like her weekend. Except Javier wasn't *like* her. For someone who was only twenty-three, he was surprisingly mature. Back in San Diego, he'd told her he'd already mapped out the next ten years of his life.

But maybe tonight, he'd be willing to veer off course. After all, this was Vegas, where the usual rules didn't apply.

Rather than suggest they jump into bed immediately, she decided to start on a more conversational note. She'd work up to the sex part. "How's grad school? You just finished your first semester, right?"

"It's great. Studying archaeology full-time, learning from world-class professors—it's exactly what I hoped for. But you know what the best part is? Meeting other grad students who are just as excited about pre-Columbian archaeology as I am. Makes me feel like less of a nerd."

She nudged him. "You're not a nerd."

"You called me one."

"Only after you gave me a fifteen-minute lecture about the evils of Spanish colonialism when we visited the Junípero Serra Museum. It was a lot."

"Fair enough. But you know what I mean, right? I feel like I've found my people."

She should have been thrilled for him. Instead, his words chipped away at her self-confidence. Did that mean she wasn't one of his people? Maybe he'd fallen in love with a brilliant archaeology student.

"Have you met anyone special? Like a girlfriend?" She cringed at how needy she sounded, but she wanted to get the question out there. No sense lusting after him if he was already taken.

"Nope. I'm trying to focus on my classes. No girlfriends, other than this one woman who keeps haunting my dreams. No matter how hard I try, I can't get her off my mind."

Sofia took a swig of her mojito, hoping the alcohol would lessen the ache pinching her heart. Even if Javier hadn't connected with the woman of his dreams yet, he was already fantasizing about her. "Is she an archaeologist?"

He tapped her nose with his finger. A gentle boop, like the kind he'd done when he'd teased her at El Marinero. "She's you. Even after all this time, I'm still dreaming about you."

"Me?" Her pulse raced. "But...you didn't want me."

His warm chuckle sent a rush of heat surging through her. "Oh, I wanted you. I just knew better than to act on it. On my first day of work, your dad took me aside and warned me not to mess with you. He was very intimidating."

She almost choked on her drink. "You never told me that."

"He asked me not to. But it wasn't just him. I had a plan in place and couldn't risk a big romantic entanglement, not with someone I cared about. But resisting you wasn't easy."

She licked her lips, tasting lime and mint. "I wanted you so badly. It was fun being friends, but..."

But she'd wanted more. And in the two months they'd spent together, she'd fallen for him. Hard. Which wasn't like her at all. She was used to instant gratification—intense flings that burned hot but fizzled out quickly. Something about the slow burn of Javier's friendship had sparked a different, more intense set of feelings.

"I won't lie—I had *so* many fantasies about you." He placed his hand on her thigh.

The loud drumbeat of her heart threatened to drown out everything around her. As she clamped her hand over his, a spark rushed through her entire body, right down to her perfectly polished toes. "What kind of fantasies?"

He leaned in closer, his warm breath tickling her ear. "If I tell you, I won't be able to take them back."

She tried to block out the buzz of the crowd and focus on him. His full, sensual lips, turned up in a sly smile. His dark eyes, capturing hers with the promise of mischief. The feel of his hand, pressed against her bare skin.

"Tell me," she whispered.

"In one of them, you were on your knees, naked, while I plundered that sweet little mouth of yours. In another, I had you on my bed, legs spread wide, tasting you until you screamed out my name. I had you in the shower. Up against the wall. I imagined you bent over the bar at the restaurant, moaning as I drove myself deep inside you."

Holy. Shit.

Even the chilly air conditioning couldn't douse the flames he'd ignited inside her. Setting down her cocktail glass, she rubbed her hands over her face, trying to clear her mind. Too late. The images were already flooding her brain. A throbbing ache built up between her legs. The urge to touch herself and relieve the pressure was all-consuming.

He pulled away. "Too much? Sorry. That was exceptionally crude."

"Are you kidding? I'm so turned on right now." She grabbed his hand. "What are we waiting for?"

"Those were just fantasies."

"But they don't have to be. Right? Do you have your own room?" Her heart raced so fiercely she thought she might explode if she couldn't act on any of his suggestions.

"We're staying in a suite, but I scored one of the private rooms."

"Perfect. Let's go."

He swallowed, clearly uneasy. "This is probably a bad idea."

"Why? You don't work for my dad anymore."

"I'm heading back to Chicago in three days. Right after I get there, I'm leaving for a dig in Mexico."

"And I'm about to leave for a semester abroad in Spain. So I'm not looking for commitment. Just a little fun. Don't you want this? Don't you want *me*?" She couldn't handle it if he rejected her again. All she was asking for was three nights. There was no way a tiny fling like this could derail his carefully thought-out plans.

For a moment, she swore she could hear her older sister's voice in her head, cautioning her against acting so rashly. *You sure you can handle this, Sof?*

Of course she could. Even if she'd fallen in love with Javier last summer, she'd known it was one-sided. She hadn't expected him to share her feelings then, and she certainly didn't expect it now. Instead, she could accept this gift for what it was—a weekend of smoking-hot sex with a guy she'd dreamed about for months. Sure, she might be heartbroken when he left, but the steamy memories would be worth it.

When he hesitated, she palmed his cheek, caressing the rough stubble. "Please, Javier. We're in Vegas. And I'm here for three whole nights."

He let out a ragged breath. "Me, too."

"Then let's enjoy all of them." She gave him a sultry smile. "You want me on my knees? Spread out on your bed? Then take me to your room and we can act out all your desires. Except the fantasy where you're banging me over the bar at El Marinero. Though, I agree, that would have been unbelievably hot."

What did it matter if his feelings were driven by lust rather than love? The sex would still be incredible.

He tossed back his drink and flashed her a devilish grin. "Let's do it."

She brought out her phone. "Just gotta send a text." She took a photo of them together and sent it to her friends: *Going up to Javier's room for a night of fun. Top that, bitches!*

CHAPTER 2

Sofia braced herself against the white marble sink in the bathroom of Javier's room and took a deep breath. Normally, she wasn't the type to overthink her actions. If she wanted something, she went for it, regardless of the consequences. Now she was worried she'd been too hasty.

Javier had been fantasizing about her since last summer. For all she knew, he'd built her up to be this amazing sexual goddess. What if she didn't live up to his expectations?

A knock on the bathroom door made her jump. "Sofia. You okay?"

"Yes. I'm great. Fine! Super!"

Javier's voice was soft. "We don't have to rush into this. If you want, we can hang out, order room service, and watch TV."

She opened the door tentatively. She'd stripped down to her lacy black bra and matching panties but hadn't gone any further. Javier sat on the edge of the bed, waiting. Though he was still dressed, he'd already turned down the covers.

When he saw her, his mouth fell open, like a cartoon wolf with his tongue lolling out. He stood and grabbed a quilted bathrobe from a hook by the bed. Advancing toward her, he brandished it like a shield. "If we're just going to hang out, you might need to wear this. Otherwise, I'll have a hell of a time resisting you."

His honesty made her laugh. She cocked her hip to the side. "You think I'm sexy?"

"Of course you're sexy. I thought you were sexy even when you wore that ridiculous peasant blouse and red frilly skirt at El Marinero."

God, how she hated that outfit. "Is that when you imagined bending me over the bar and having your way with me?"

His mouth quirked up in a smile. "Among other times, yes."

"Okay, then. You can put down the robe because I'm not going to need it."

Gathering her courage, she closed the distance between them. She unbuttoned his shirt, then eased it off him. One of his shoulders displayed a tattoo she'd never seen before, a Maya symbol that looked like a sun. As she brushed her lips against it, she longed to discover if he had any other hidden tattoos. She ran her hands along the firm muscles of his chest, loving how warm and solid he felt. She wanted to touch him everywhere, just to make sure he was real. When she reached beneath his jeans and stroked him, he groaned in response.

"That feels so good," he said. "You can't imagine how many times I've dreamed of this."

She looked up at him. "Just so you know, I might not live up to all your fantasies."

"Right now, you're wearing almost nothing, and we're alone in a hotel room. I'd say you're doing just fine. Do you want to keep going?"

She loved that he was *asking* her. Clearly, he wanted her, but he was willing to let her set the pace.

"Yes, please." She gave a nod toward the nightstand where she'd left her wristlet. "I even brought condoms with me. A lady always comes prepared."

She unzipped his jeans and pulled them down around his ankles. He kicked them off, revealing a pair of tight boxer briefs, the bulge of his erection visible against the dark fabric. She traced her fingers along the outline of his dick, enjoying the way he shuddered. She was tempted to sink down to her knees and fulfill his first fantasy, but he placed his hands around her butt and lifted her up. Giving a squeak of surprise, she clung to him as he carried her over to the king bed.

Sitting on the edge, he pulled her onto his lap, so she was facing him. She ground against him shamelessly, loving the hard feel of him between her thighs. Taking care not to pull on her hair, he removed her tiara and set it on the bed. Then he threaded his hand through her curls and kissed her. She tangled her tongue against his, tasting rum and mint, sweet and delicious. As his kisses became more demanding, his fingers tightened on her hair, sending tingles of desire racing through her.

When she broke away to catch her breath, he regarded her a look of adoration. "You're so incredible, Sofia. I'm not worthy."

"You're totally worthy, you sexy archaeology nerd. I want you with all my heart."

"I have to warn you, this first time might be quick."

"Oh really?" she teased. "Then we'll have to do it a lot more times."

He flipped her onto the bed, so she was lying on her back atop smooth silken sheets. Then he was leaning over her, the warmth of his body palpable even before he reached out to touch her. Her breath caught as he pulled aside the lace of her bra and lowered his head. He took one nipple into his mouth and sucked on it hard.

It felt so good. So wickedly, sinfully good. But she wanted more.

She unclasped her bra and wiggled out of it, giving him full access to her breasts. He worshipped them, kissing, licking, sucking, until she was lost in the heady rush of sensation. She guided his hand between her thighs, desperately wanting him to satisfy the ache building up inside of her. "I need you to touch me. Right there."

"With pleasure." His mouth never left her breasts as he dipped his finger under her panties and stroked her. Softly at first, until she moved her hips in encouragement, causing him to press deeper, in a steady rhythm. She moaned as he hit the right spot with the perfect amount of friction.

"Yes. Like that. *Yes, yes, yes.*"

The orgasm barreled over her like a freight train, so intense it took her breath away. She arched her back and cried out his name, only to tense up again as his touch brought her to the edge of ecstasy once more and sent her tumbling over. Gasping, she came again, the waves of pleasure crashing through her like an ocean current. She gave a blissful whimper, her muscles loosening as she relaxed in his arms.

He smiled down at her with a bemused expression. "Damn, Sofia. How could you ever think you wouldn't match my fantasies?"

"But I haven't done anything yet. I'm lying here and letting you do all the work."

He grinned. "I love being in control. Watching you come is a total turn-on."

If he liked taking control, then she was more than happy to accommodate him. But she also wanted to give him something in return. She grabbed her wristlet from the nightstand.

"I think you need some pleasure, too. I've got enough condoms to last us a while."

"But I haven't finished with you yet. I need to taste—"

"You will. I promise. We have all night. Right now, I want you buried deep inside of me." She locked eyes with him, willing him to concede. As much as she loved being the recipient of such generosity, she wanted him to share the experience.

She shimmied out of her panties and waited as he removed his boxer briefs. Unwrapping one of the condoms, she took her time sheathing him. Then, when they were both naked, he drove himself inside her. He was bigger than she expected, filling her completely. She wrapped her arms around him, bringing him closer.

She nipped at his ear, speaking to him in a harsh whisper. "I want you to fuck me senseless. Rough, hard, fast, however you want it. We can take it slower next time."

His warm laughter rumbled from deep inside his chest. "Keep talking like that and I'll be lucky to last five minutes."

She loved that he could joke about it, that he didn't take himself too seriously even though the heat between them was ghost-pepper hot. She grabbed his butt and urged him on, moaning as he pounded himself into her. It was hard and rough and frantic but so damn good. She angled her hips, wanting to get the pressure just right, and cried out as the sensations built up inside of her. Seconds after she hit her peak and let out a wail of unbridled rapture, his lusty groans followed.

He collapsed on top of her, laughing. "That was unbelievable. But way too quick."

"It was perfect. For a first time." She flashed him a saucy grin. "On our next go-round, I might hold you to a higher standard."

"I'll do my best, mi corazón."

My heart. The words made her shiver with delight. Whether or not he loved her, right now, she felt like he did. Cradled in his arms, she couldn't imagine a better first night in Vegas.

The best part was, they still had two nights left.

CHAPTER 3

A persistent buzzing woke Sofia from a deep slumber. Mindful of her pounding head, she turned and groped for the phone on her nightstand. But when she dropped it on the floor, she didn't have the energy to reach for it.

Screw it. Whoever it was, she could deal with them later. Spotting a half-filled bottle of water on the nightstand, she guzzled it gratefully. Anything to ease the painful dryness in her throat. As she set the bottle down, she caught sight of the digital clock beside the bed, mocking her with its bright red numbers. 9:45 a.m.

Was it morning already? *Too soon.*

She rubbed her eyes and took a quick self-assessment. Yes, she was brutally hungover, but she was also naked, with a gorgeous man lying next to her.

Her first night with Javier had been off the charts. Sexy and intense and scorching hot. The second night they'd taken things more slowly, making love in a way that was sweet, tender, and unforgettable.

Unfortunately, last night—their third and final night in Vegas— they'd had too much to drink, which meant their New Year's Eve shenanigans were a hazy blur of memories. She could vaguely recall doing shots at a rooftop lounge, dancing at a club, and watching fireworks explode over the Strip.

And having sex with Javier. Lots and lots of sex.

If her foggy brain served her correctly, he'd taken her up against the wall. And on the poufy gray couch at the other end of the room. And on the bed. Not on the floor, though. Hotel carpeting was just too icky.

When her phone buzzed again, she grabbed it off the floor and shuddered at all the notifications. Six New Year's Eve messages from her friends back home, two voicemails from Yasmin, whose call had woken her earlier, and a slew of texts from the extended Sanchez family, who had rung in the New Year at El Marinero.

Rather than deal with any of them, Sofia set her phone back on the nightstand and snuggled closer to Javier. Even if she was dehydrated, exhausted, and in desperate need of coffee, she could think of something she needed even more. Since this was their last morning together, she didn't want to waste it.

She kissed his shoulder. "Javi? Sweetie? Wake up."

He opened his eyes and brushed her tangled curls away from her face. "You're insatiable, you know that?"

She giggled. "I know."

"How can you possibly have any energy left? I'm wiped."

She reached beneath the blanket and stroked him. Nice and hard. "Seems like part of you is wide awake."

He speared her with a look of pure lust. "That's because you look as delectable as ever."

The low rumble of his voice flooded her with a rush of heat. "Would you like a taste?"

"I would. But let's get these covers out of the way." He flung aside the sheets and eyed her hungrily.

She stretched out seductively, pleased at the way his gaze roamed over her figure. After that first night, she'd lost all her inhibitions around him. It was impossible to be shy after he'd spent so many hours exploring her body.

She still couldn't believe she'd run into him. Or that they'd gotten to spend three whole nights together. Truly, this weekend was the kind of magical, meant-to-be coincidence that only happened in movies.

When he reached for her, she caught the gleam of metal on his left hand. Odd. She grabbed his hand and examined it. "Where'd that ring come from? Did you win it?" At some point last night, they'd had a riot playing a giant claw machine, where the prizes were jewelry and poker chips.

His brow furrowed. "I'm not sure."

With a growing sense of trepidation, she examined her own hand. An identical gold band graced her ring finger. "What the fuck?"

Javier rubbed his hands over his face. "Please tell me we didn't succumb to the oldest cliche in Vegas. We weren't that drunk, were we?"

It had to be a joke. Their friends must have pranked them.

But that would have taken a *lot* of planning on their part.

With trembling hands, she snatched up her phone again. Since her own memories were too jumbled to recall, she'd have to rely on her obsessive desire to document every aspect of her life. At first, the photos were harmless. The two of them posing in front of the fountain outside the Bellagio. Drinking cocktails at Chateau Rooftop. Doing shots with another couple. Serving as witnesses at that same couple's wedding at The Little Vegas Chapel on the Strip.

Huh. She didn't remember that last part at all.

The next few pictures provided all the evidence she needed. Her and Javier exchanging vows beside an officiant dressed in a shiny gold jacket. Grinning like idiots as they stood under a neon "Just Married" sign. Displaying their rings as though their impromptu wedding was something to be proud of.

It was true. She *was* married.

Though she was shocked as hell, she wasn't as upset as she should have been. Despite the sheer lunacy of what they'd done, she couldn't suppress the tiny thrill of pleasure coursing through her. She might have fallen for Javier last summer, but this weekend had sealed the deal. She was well and truly in love with him.

She just hadn't told him yet.

Javier placed his hand on her shoulder. "Is it true?"

She handed him the phone. "See for yourself."

He groaned as he scrolled through the images. "Fuck me. This is a nightmare."

Definitely not the response she'd been hoping for.

Sofia shrank away from Javier, unnerved by his stormy expression. A knot of raw emotion clogged her throat. True, they'd made a huge mistake, but it could have been worse. At least they hadn't gambled away all their money.

Or had they? She wished she could remember everything they'd done.

Javier turned the phone toward her. "Who's that other couple with us? Are they friends of yours?"

Peering at the image, she dove deep into the swamp of her murky memories. "No, I think we met them at Chateau Rooftop. Then they convinced us to join them when they took a rideshare to the county clerk's office to get a marriage license. But I can't remember much after that."

All during the ride, they'd kept drinking. Doing shots of tequila. Or vodka. Either way, the alcohol had done a number on her memories.

"Dios mío," Javier said. "They must have talked us into getting married, too. But why were we so stupid?"

The anger in his voice made her flinch. Wrapping her arms around her middle, she tried to control her churning stomach. "I wouldn't call it stupid. More like impulsive. We were drunk and wanted to have fun."

"It's not fun if it ends up ruining our lives." He thrust the phone back at her. "You didn't post it on your Instagram, did you?"

She frowned, her earlier hurt replaced by irritation. "Of course not. That's a carefully curated account." Back when she was a senior in high school, she'd created SoFood SoFia to highlight the seafood specialties served at El Marinero. Over the next three years, she'd broadened it to include foodie delights from restaurants all over Southern California. She loved finding hole-in-the-wall places that served fabulous dishes but had yet to be discovered.

Once she'd acquired over thirty thousand followers, she'd promised herself never to sully it by posting drunken selfies. As much as she delighted in spontaneity, she wasn't about to mess up her brand.

But if she'd been drunk enough to end up with a ring on her finger, she might have been equally careless with her posts. She opened the account and gave a sigh of relief. Her last photo was an artistically framed shot of the Chocolate Sin Cake she and Javier had shared when they'd eaten lunch at Hell's Kitchen in Caesar's Palace.

"We're good," she said. "I think we're the only ones who know."

They had to be. If she had revealed the truth on social media, her phone would be blowing up right now. She eased out of bed and scanned the room until she spotted the final piece of evidence. She grabbed the paper from the coffee table next to the couch and brought it back to bed with her.

Sure enough, it was a marriage license between Sofia Sanchez and Javier Castillo, issued in the state of Nevada last night at 10:15 p.m.

"So, it's real?" he said. "*Fuck.*"

She blinked back tears. "I'm sorry. Is it really that awful?" She didn't want to cry in front of him, but she hated feeling like she was nothing more than a massive mistake.

"You don't actually want to be married, do you? You're only twenty-one."

"I know." She sniffed and wiped her eyes. "But maybe it's meant to be. This weekend was unbelievable. And we ran into each other purely by chance. There are hundreds of hotels in Vegas, but we're staying in the same one. That's not just a coincidence. It has to mean something."

He released a ragged sigh. "Oh, Sofia. This isn't meant to be. We're both in school, and we live two thousand miles from each other."

All valid points, but that didn't stop his words from shredding her heart to ribbons.

"Think of our parents," he said. "Can you imagine how they'll react?"

The thought doused her romantic notions like a splash of ice-cold water. For all the impulsive shit she'd done, she'd rarely been punished. Since she was the baby of the family, her parents usually let her off with just a lecture.

This time, they might not be as understanding.

"If my folks find out I got hitched in a Vegas chapel, they'll be furious," he said. "No one in my family has ever gotten married without a big Catholic wedding."

"Same," she whispered.

As she imagined the fallout, her optimism vanished. Forget about fate. This marriage had the potential to derail her entire life. "I'm supposed to leave for Barcelona in a week. Do you have any idea how hard it was to convince my parents to let me take a semester abroad? They'll never allow it once they find out about this."

Never mind that all the arrangements had been made. Her father was stubborn as hell. He'd not only force her to spend the rest of her junior year in San Diego, he'd probably demand she move back home.

"We need to get this annulled. Or get a divorce. Or something." Javier's dark eyes bore the slightest hint of remorse. "No offense."

"None taken." Even if his initial reaction had wounded her, she was now firmly Team Quickie Divorce. Anything to keep her parents from learning the truth.

As if by unspoken agreement, they both started searching on their phones. Sofia's buzzed with a text from Yasmin. *Wake up girl! Left you 2 messages already. The limo's picking us up at 11:30. Meet us in the lobby and don't be late!*

Eleven thirty? It was after ten. That gave her a little over an hour to clean up, pack her stuff, and figure out how to nullify a marriage.

"We could get an annulment here in Vegas," Javier said. "But I don't think we'll have enough time. I'm flying out at one."

"I'm leaving at eleven thirty. And it's New Year's Day. I'm sure nothing's open."

"Right." He resumed his search, only to let out a huff of frustration. "There's a lot to wade through, but it seems like our best bet is an uncontested divorce. Something quick and cheap. But I don't have much time to look into it. Right after I get back to Chicago, I'm leaving for that dig in Mexico. I'll be working there all semester."

Sofia longed to console him. Anything to bring back the fun, sexy man she'd spent the last three nights with. "How about I take care of it?"

"Are you sure?"

"Absolutely. There must be places that handle this stuff online. I don't know how much it costs, but I can do some research once I get home. Does that work?"

His dour expression gave way to an affectionate smile. "That would be great. Thanks. You won't tell anyone, will you?"

"Hell, no. Not even my sister."

He clasped her hand and brushed his thumb across her knuckles. When he spoke, his voice was tinged with regret. "Sofia, I'm sorry."

"Don't be. This isn't what either of us wants. Not right now."

"I know. But I could have reacted with less hostility." He raised her hand to his lips and grazed it with a tender kiss. "I'm not sorry we got together. You're an amazing woman. Maybe if we weren't still in school, and if our lives weren't headed in different directions, I might be willing to give this a try. I really like you."

She flashed him a weak smile. "I like you, too."

Liar. She was in love with him. But now wasn't the time for heartfelt confessions. She didn't want him feeling guiltier than he already did.

"It's for the best," she said. "Go have fun digging up ruins in Mexico. Have adventures."

"You too. Have a blast in Spain. I'm sure you'll make the most of it." He leaned over and placed a soft kiss on her lips.

She kissed him back, then got up and retrieved her clothes. She took the marriage certificate with her, but when he offered to give her his ring, she shook her head. "You keep it."

If nothing else, it could serve as a reminder of their three nights in Vegas.

CHAPTER 5

Present Day

Sofia's spirits lifted at the sight of the Santa Monica Farmer's Market. Even if she'd woken far too early, she was determined not to let her stress and exhaustion get the best of her. She didn't want to waste her morning, not when the three-block spread of produce and flowers offered numerous photo opportunities for her popular Instagram account, SoFood SoFia. Though the market was already crowded with people flocking from stall to stall, they gave off a positive energy. Even the temperature was comfortably mild, the cooler weather due to the "June gloom" so prevalent in Santa Monica during the early part of summer.

But even as Sofia delighted in the vibrant colors and textures around her—the baskets of bright red strawberries, the dark green heads of lettuce, the bunches of light purple lilacs—she couldn't focus. When she stopped to photograph a vendor selling goat milk products, her hand shook so badly she couldn't frame the shot. Whether it was nerves or caffeine, she couldn't say. Maybe that third cup of coffee had been a mistake.

Her older sister, Olivia, placed a gentle hand on her arm. "Hey. You okay?"

"No," she snapped, then immediately regretted her tone. But she couldn't summon up her usual go-with-the-flow attitude. "I thought I'd hear back from the show by now. The producers said they'd contact me by nine, and it's already ten thirty."

When her phone buzzed with an email notification, her heart constricted, but it was just an ad. *Damn you, Old Navy.*

Olivia picked up a bar of goat milk soap from the display and inhaled. She offered it to Sofia. "Take a sniff. Lavender's supposed to have a calming effect."

"I don't think a bar of soap's going to do the trick. I'm too wound up about yesterday's audition."

"Didn't you say it went really well?"

"Yeah. I totally nailed it."

"Then what's the issue? Seems like you're a slam dunk for a reality show. Your account has a ton of followers."

"True, but I don't want to get my hopes up. Not yet." After Olivia offered her the soap again, Sofia gave in and inhaled the scent—a fragrant mixture of basil and lavender. Soothing, to be sure, but it didn't help. She wouldn't be able to relax until she'd heard back from the show.

Since graduating from college three years ago, Sofia had been building up her brand as a social media influencer. Her biggest gamble had been to broaden the focus of her online persona to include international travel. Though she'd struggled a little at first, she'd slowly accrued sponsors as she worked her way through Europe, the Mediterranean, and North Africa.

Lately, however, she'd hit a plateau. When the producers of the reality show *Recipe for Love* had reached out to her, she'd jumped at the chance to audition. What better way to promote her brand than a show that embraced cooking *and* dating? She'd made such a positive impression during her Zoom interview that she was invited to Los Angeles to audition in person. A week later, she'd flown to L.A., crashed at her sister's apartment, and tried out for a coveted spot on next season's show. Now she was waiting to learn whether she'd made the cut.

A male voice behind her made her drop the soap. "Are these enough avocados?"

She turned and glared at Olivia's boyfriend, Rick, a six-foot tall, muscular hottie, who towered over the two of them. "Damn it, Rick. You startled me."

"Sorry. But you're really jumpy this morning." He handed Olivia a bulging paper sack. "Well? Do I need to get more?"

Olivia peered inside the bag. "Not unless you're making enough guacamole for an army." She set it inside her cloth tote bag. "This should do for tonight. Your next assignment is to buy a pound of Roma tomatoes. They need to be slightly firm, but with a little give. Make sure you smell them first. That's how you can tell they're ripe."

He placed a quick kiss on the top of her head, then grinned at Sofia. "Kind of bossy, isn't she?"

"The worst," Sofia said. But as Rick headed toward the tomato vendor, she couldn't help but smile.

One of the benefits of spending time with her older sister was watching her glow when she was around Rick. Up until last summer, Olivia had never been the type to cut loose. But when she'd reconnected with her first love, Rick Langston, at an archaeological dig in the Mediterranean, she'd embraced her fun, adventurous side. The two of them had been inseparable since they'd returned to California together last fall.

"You're making guac tonight?" Sofia asked. Other than her cousin Rafael, no one in the Sanchez family made better guacamole than Olivia.

"I'm teaching Rick how to make it. The boy has zero cooking skills, so I've been schooling him. Let's just say it's a slow process."

"But you love it, right? It's gotta be kind of sexy, heating things up with Mr. Hottie in the kitchen." Sofia gave a little pout. "I'm kind of jealous."

"How is that possible? Didn't you have a fling with a spicy Moroccan chef when you were in Casablanca? You said the hot oil wasn't the only thing that was sizzling." Olivia snort-laughed.

"Ziyad was a lot of fun, but it wasn't meant to last. None of them ever do." Despite the smoking-hot sex, Sofia hadn't connected with Ziyad on a deeper level. The same could be said for all her hookups.

"I didn't think you wanted any strings."

"I thought that, too. But being around you and Rick is making me crave something real. I'm twenty-five, so maybe it's time I committed to an actual relationship, even if I have to work for it."

Olivia gave a dreamy sigh. "When you love someone, it's worth the work." She paid for the soap, tucked it in her tote bag, and led them past three more stalls until she found a citrus vendor. "But if you're looking for a relationship, do you think a reality dating show is the best place to find someone? Aren't those shows all planned and scripted?"

"I wouldn't be doing the show for love. Just exposure. But you never know when fate might step in. Maybe I'll meet my soul mate."

At one time, Sofia had thought she'd found him when she'd reconnected with Javier in Vegas four years ago. But their passionate weekend hadn't led to a lasting relationship. All she had left was a string of steamy memories.

She pushed Javier from her mind and focused on the future. "If nothing else, spending the next few months in L.A. would give me time to explore some new projects."

"What kind of projects?"

The idea had been simmering in Sofia's brain for a while, but she'd been too busy traveling to focus on it. "I want to create a series of foodie videos, incorporating recipes from both sides of our family. Being in one place would give me time to work on them. And if I'm not jetting from country to country, I might have a better chance at a real relationship."

As much as she loved her nomadic lifestyle, she'd been on the go for years. Maybe it was time to switch things up. How great would it be if she could transform her life for the better *and* find someone to share it with?

She angled her phone to capture an impressively stacked pyramid of blood oranges but startled when it buzzed. She peeked at it, her heart pounding in double-time. The world froze as she stared at the email notification. "It's them. What if they turn me down?"

"Do you want me to read it for you?"

Sofia passed her the phone. Unable to calm her galloping heart, she clenched her hands together, offering up a silent prayer.

Please say yes. Pick me. I'm perfect for the show.

Olivia took a step back from the stall and started reading. "Hi Sofia. We had a great time with you yesterday. You definitely have what it takes to star in *Recipe for Love*. Unfortunately..." Her voice trailed off. "Sorry. Should I keep reading?"

Sofia's heart sank. She thought she'd prepared herself for the possibility of rejection, but the knots coiling in her belly indicated otherwise. She stumbled back until she found a quiet spot behind the citrus vendor, where the crowd wasn't as thick. After taking a few deep breaths, she tried to infuse her body with a sense of calm.

Don't stress. It's just one show.

"Keep reading," she said. "What did they say?"

"Hold on." Olivia's brow pinched as she stared at the phone. "They mixed you up with someone else."

"What?" A rush of indignation raced through her. How could they confuse her with *anyone*? She was a freaking unicorn.

"Here. Read it yourself." Olivia handed the phone back. "Apparently, the team did a background check and found out you're married, which means you're not eligible to be on the show. Sounds like a screwup on their end."

As Sofia read through the email, her stomach pitched again, worse than the time she'd been caught in a squall on the Aegean Sea.

Any thoughts of aspiring to a tranquil state vanished as her heart rate climbed into the stratosphere. "I can't believe it."

"Just call them. Tell them they got the wrong Sofia Sanchez."

She wished that were true. Because the reality was more than she could take right now. "The thing is..." How could she even say it? She felt like such an idiot. "I...um...I got married four years ago. In Vegas. But I thought I was divorced."

"You're joking, right?" Olivia said. "Is this part of the show? Are we secretly being filmed?"

I wish. Sofia read through the email a second time. It had to be a bad dream. A huge glitch. She couldn't possibly be married.

Could she?

She gulped past a dry patch in her throat, barely able to swallow. All of a sudden, the crowded market was too much. "I'm feeling kind of dizzy. And queasy. I think I need to sit down."

"Deep breaths, okay? Whatever this is, you can handle it. But let's get you out of here first."

Sofia appreciated that her sister wasn't demanding answers, even though she probably had lots of questions. "Where should we go?"

Olivia pointed to the entrance of the market. "If you head toward Wilshire Boulevard, then walk a few blocks south, there's a small park with benches overlooking the beach. Go there and take a breather. I'm going to tell Rick to head back to the apartment, and I'll join you in about ten minutes. Okay?"

"Sure. Thanks." Still clutching her phone in a death grip, Sofia navigated through the crowds, only breathing freely once she'd made her way to the park. She found an empty bench, brushed off a fast-food wrapper, and sat down. She wrapped her arms around herself, suddenly chilly from the breeze coming off the Pacific Ocean.

It can't be true. It just can't be.

Fifteen minutes later, Olivia came to join her, carrying a couple of smoothies. She sat beside Sofia and passed her one. "Mango-papaya. It should help calm your stomach."

"Thanks." She took a grateful sip of the sweet, fruity goodness. "What did you tell Rick?"

"Just that we needed a little sister time together. I sent him back to the apartment because I wasn't sure how much you wanted to share."

"Thanks, Liv."

After a few sips of smoothie, Sofia recounted her weekend in Vegas. Though it pained her to reveal how foolish she'd been, she didn't make any excuses for her behavior. Nor did she brush off the incident like it was no big deal, which was her usual move whenever she screwed up.

To her credit, Olivia didn't chastise her. Instead, she waited until Sofia was done before speaking. "Sounds like an epic weekend. Why didn't you tell me about it?"

"Honestly? Because I was embarrassed that we fucked up so badly. Plus, it was all so weird." A wave of sorrow washed over her. "You want to know what the weirdest thing was? When I found out we were married, I wasn't that upset. I was in love with Javier. And the sex was incredible. Plus, he's a great guy. But he wasn't happy about it at all."

"Aw, Sof, I'm sorry. But you have to admit the timing sucked."

"No kidding. Thank God he talked some sense into me. He made me realize the whole 'just married' thing could screw up our plans, like his dig in Mexico and my semester abroad."

"Was that right before you left for Barcelona?"

"Yeah. And he was about to go on this big archaeological expedition. Since he was leaving first, I offered to take care of the divorce. But divorce lawyers are pricey as fuck, so I found an online service that was way cheaper. They said they'd handle everything for three hundred bucks plus the filing fee. I texted Javier right before he took off, and he sent me his half of the money."

At the time, she'd been pleased that she'd taken care of it so efficiently. Now she wondered if she'd screwed up.

She continued. "Since the divorce wouldn't be finalized for six months, I put it out of my mind. Or I tried to. That semester in Spain helped a lot. After I got back that summer, I got an email telling me the divorce was final. I let Javier know, and that was it."

And I never heard from him again.

Other than a text thanking her for arranging the divorce, he'd never reached out to her. She'd tried texting him a few times afterward, but he hadn't responded. Though his silence had hurt like hell, she'd forced herself to move on with her life.

Olivia's brow furrowed. "Then why did the producers of the show think you were still married? Do you think the online service messed up the paperwork?" She gestured to Sofia's phone. "Do you still have the email they sent you when they confirmed the divorce went through?"

Sofia nodded. Though her inbox was a cluttered mess, she'd had the foresight to flag the message when she'd received it. She did a quick search and pulled it up. "Here it is. See?"

Olivia took the phone. "You went with a service called EZ-Divorce? Don't you think that sounds kind of sketchy?"

Sofia glared at her. "Maybe? But I didn't have time to do a ton of research. The site seemed legit, and they had a bunch of testimonials from former clients."

Though now that she thought of it, those testimonials could have been fake.

"Sorry," Olivia said. "How about I send them an email? My guess is that there was a paperwork glitch."

"Thanks." Sofia took a refreshing sip of smoothie and tried to tamp down her escalating sense of dread. Until another horrifying thought hijacked her brain. "What if Javier is married by now? That would make him a bigamist."

Olivia gave a slight laugh. "He's not married. I would have heard about it if he was."

"You're still in touch?" Sofia fought back an irrational surge of jealousy.

"Sure. We were in a bunch of classes together, remember? We graduated the same year."

Sofia remembered. Olivia had been the one to introduce Javier to the family when she'd invited him over to dinner as part of her archaeology study group. She'd also helped him land the bartending job at El Marinero. But since she hadn't been interested in him romantically, Sofia had been free to pursue him without violating the almighty "sisters before misters" rule.

She tightened her grip on the clear plastic cup holding her smoothie. "Does...um...does he ever mention me?"

"Not really, but mostly we talk about academic stuff."

Harsh. In all likelihood, he hadn't thought about her since that weekend in Vegas.

She, on the other hand, had never gotten over him, no matter how hard she tried. Over the years, she'd had her share of impulsive hookups and scorching-hot flings. But none of those men had ever touched her heart the way Javier had.

Sometimes when she was alone at night, she let her mind drift back to their glorious weekend together. But the way she'd felt with him—so alive, so passionate, so much in love—now felt like a distant dream.

She bit her lip as the sting of tears prickled her eyes. "I guess I'm not as memorable as I thought."

Olivia set Sofia's phone on the bench and placed a hand on her shoulder. "If it helps, he follows you on Instagram."

She perked up. "He does? I thought he didn't do social media."

"He doesn't. But he keeps up with SoFood SoFia. He told me last year that he was impressed you'd visited so many countries."

That made her feel marginally better. But only marginally because he'd never once commented on any of her posts.

When her phone buzzed with an email notification, her heartbeat accelerated. She grabbed it off the bench only to explode in frustration. "Address undeliverable. What does that mean? Did you type in the wrong address?"

"No. I just replied to the email they sent you. But maybe that's not the right address for correspondence. Let me look them up. What's the website again?"

"EZ Divorce dot com." Even as Sofia said it, she couldn't dislodge the uneasiness skittering along her spine. Olivia was right. That name sounded sketchy as hell.

"You sure?" Olivia asked. "My browser didn't turn up any hits. It just says 'Sorry, the page you were looking for does not exist'."

Don't panic. Do. Not. Panic.

Which was exactly what Sofia wanted to do. But as she scrolled through her emails and Olivia searched every permutation of the name, the truth hit Sofia like a smack upside the head. The service no longer existed. She now suspected the $300 fee for "the Platinum Package," in addition to the $435 court fees, had been for nothing.

She started spiraling into panic, her heart racing faster, her breath coming in shallow gasps. *I've been married for four years. And I had no idea.*

"Do you think I was scammed?" she asked.

"I don't know, but we need to figure out your next step. Maybe Araceli could help. She's a paralegal."

Thank God Olivia was thinking clearly because Sofia's mind was a jumbled mess. She'd completely forgotten that their cousin Araceli worked for a law firm. "Can you call her? Like, right now? She's in my contacts."

"Sure." Olivia grabbed Sofia's phone, punched in the number, and put it on speaker.

To Sofia's immense relief, Araceli answered on the second ring. "Hey, Sofia. How's it going? Are you back in California now?"

"Yeah. I came back to try out for this reality show called *Recipe for Love*," Sofia said. "Have you ever seen it?"

"Oh my God," Araceli squealed. "I love that show. Did you catch last season? I was seriously rooting for Chandra to win, but that bitch Simone kept sabotaging her, and—"

"Can you hold that thought?" Sofia asked. "Right now, I have a legal problem, and I need your help. But you have to keep it under wraps. Do you have a minute to talk?"

"Um...sure. You didn't break the law, did you? My firm doesn't deal with criminal cases."

"Nothing like that. Olivia's here with me, so I put you on speaker."

"Okay," Araceli said. "Let's hear it."

Taking a deep breath, Sofia recounted everything, starting with her drunken marriage in Vegas and ending with the morning's shocking discovery. When she finished, she waited for her cousin's response, only to be met with silence.

"Araceli?" Sofia asked. "You still there?"

"Yeah. Wow. This is the juiciest piece of gossip I've heard in ages, but I won't breathe a word. In the meantime, hang tight for a sec. I'm going to run a check to see if I can find the service you mentioned."

Sofia's jaw tightened as she waited anxiously. After five agonizing minutes, she couldn't take it any longer. "Find anything?"

"Nope. It's like the place never existed. Were there any documents attached to that last email you got from them? Like an actual decree of divorce?"

"No. But I didn't follow up, either. Once I texted Javier to let him know the divorce was final, I wanted to forget it ever happened." Not that her decision had blocked out the pain. But over time, she'd managed to push the memories into a tiny corner of her mind where they didn't hurt as much.

"Got it," Araceli said. "My guess is that this service was either a scam or they went out of business. You're never going to see that money again."

"Fuck," Sofia muttered.

Why hadn't she followed up? All she'd gotten was a lousy, two-line email with no attachments. But she'd been so determined to put the incident behind her that she hadn't questioned the legitimacy of her divorce.

"The money's not the issue," Olivia said. "It's a sunk cost. The bigger problem is that Sofia's still married. What should she do about that?" A seagull flew toward them and perched on the edge of the bench, but she shooed it away.

Sofia ran her hands through her curls, which were now hopelessly tangled from the breeze blowing off the ocean. "I'm such a fucking disaster."

"Don't be so hard on yourself," Araceli said. "Stuff like this happens all the time. I can help you file the divorce. Honestly, you should have come to me right from the start instead of dealing with some shady online service."

"Sorry," Sofia said. "I was trying to keep it quiet."

"I'll draw up the paperwork and make sure Javier gets served," her cousin said. "As long as he signs the papers, we'll be golden. You'll have to pay the filing fee again, but I promise you'll get that divorce."

Just what Sofia needed—another charge on her overloaded credit card. But it had to be done. "Thanks. I appreciate it."

"It shouldn't be too hard to reach Javier, since he's getting his PhD at the University of Chicago." Olivia said. "But Sof, maybe you should call him first to warn him. That way he won't be blindsided when he gets the papers."

Sofia's stomach clenched at the thought of his reaction. She could only imagine how pissed he'd be when he found out he was still married.

"Olivia, do you have his address?" Araceli asked.

"Yeah, hang on," Olivia said. But as she scrolled through her phone, she let out a groan. "I was wrong. Javier's not in Chicago right now."

"Where is he?" Even as Sofia asked, she knew she wouldn't like the answer.

"He's back in Mexico, working on a dig at Calakmul. It's a Maya site in the Yucatán Peninsula, but it's deep in the jungle."

Sofia resisted the urge to let out a primal scream.

Seriously, universe? What did I do to deserve this?

"If he's in Mexico, it's going to take longer to serve him the papers," Araceli said. "There are a lot of rules involved with serving someone in a foreign country, and the process can take months. Sorry."

Sofia let out a huffy breath. "Fine. Then I'll go there and do it myself."

As painful as it would be to see Javier again, she needed to own up to her mistakes. And she needed to do it in person.

If she had to track him down in the jungle to make things right, then so be it.

CHAPTER 7

Sofia's trip from Los Angeles to the Hotel Puerta Calakmul had been an epic journey, involving a flight to Cancún, a long-ass bus ride, and a shared taxi.

But she still wasn't done.

From the hotel, she had to travel another forty miles to reach the Maya site of Calakmul. Since the ruins were located deep in the rain forest, the only way to get there was by joining a group or hiring a guide. Not wanting to waste time on a lengthy tour, Sofia contracted with the hotel to arrange for a personal guide. All she wanted to do was get to the site, locate Javier, and have him sign the papers.

On the morning of her reunion, she woke before six, too anxious to sleep another minute. She used the extra time to primp. Even if she'd be spending the day in a hot, humid jungle, she wanted to look her best when she greeted her husband. Once she was ready, she grabbed a granola bar and went down to the lobby to wait for her guide.

As the minutes ticked by, she tried to calm the nervous energy surging through her. She'd planned this whole trip so hastily that she hadn't stopped to question the wisdom of her actions. Immediately after talking to Araceli, she'd contacted the showrunner for *Recipe for Love* and explained the situation as best she could. Thankfully, the producers had given her a chance to turn things around. If she could get the divorce papers signed and filed within the next two weeks, she'd still have a shot. Though the divorce wouldn't be final for another six months, she'd be single by the time the show aired.

With that goal in mind, she'd booked her flight and plotted her route to Calakmul. Rather than let Javier know she was coming, she opted for "controlled spontaneity." But now she wondered if she'd acted too hastily. Was surprising him at his dig site really the best move?

Olivia had warned her against it. "Don't you think you should call him first? Even if his cell doesn't get service, he'll have a satellite phone. Or you could send him an email. He probably checks his messages whenever he goes into town to get supplies."

Sofia refused to listen. What if Javier was furious with her? She'd have a better chance of convincing him she'd genuinely screwed up if she told him face-to-face.

She glanced at the clock above the hotel's front desk. 9:15 a.m. Her guide should have shown up by now. Already, four other groups had left for the ruins. She was debating whether to hit the restroom and check her appearance again when one of the hotel clerks motioned her over to the desk. "¿Señorita Sanchez?"

"Sí. ¿Qué pasa?"

"Lo siento, pero Tomás no vendrá esta mañana."

Her stomach twisted into a knot. This had to be a bad omen. "What's wrong?"

He switched to English. "Engine trouble with his Jeep, Miss. Best not to risk it. You wouldn't want to end up stranded in the jungle."

Definitely not. Even so, the hitch in her plans only made her more jittery. "Thanks for letting me know. Can you make arrangements with someone else?" She waited patiently as he perused the screen in front of him.

When he looked up again, his somber expression was hardly reassuring. "I'm sorry, but all our guides are contracted for the day and have already left. The best I can do is arrange for a guide the day after tomorrow. Would that work?"

The longer the delay, the more her anxiety would fester, but she didn't have a choice. "Sure. I'll take whatever you have."

"Oh, wait." He brightened. "There is one group that hasn't left yet. Perhaps you could join up with them. They'll be leaving for Calakmul soon."

Thank you, fated goddess. She beamed at the clerk, offering him her full wattage smile. "Perfect. Muchas gracias."

Convincing the group to include her shouldn't be too hard. She'd just turn on the charm. If that failed, she'd offer them money. Surely they could make room for one more person?

She settled into a wicker chair and scrolled through her phone, checking to make sure she hadn't missed any urgent messages. Once she left the hotel, she'd be off the grid for the day.

"Sofia Sanchez. Isn't this a lovely surprise?"

The sarcastic voice set her teeth on edge. She glanced up in apprehension, only to lock eyes with one of her nastiest rivals, Wilhelmina von Boemel, aka Wander Willa, a tall, snotty, trust-fund brat with a sleek mane of platinum-blonde hair. Like Sofia, Willa was a travel influencer, but she wasn't content merely to promote herself. Instead, she tried to sabotage her rivals by spreading nasty rumors, using fake accounts to post insulting comments, and urging her trollish followers to do the same.

For years, Sofia had tried her best not to spar with Willa. She wasn't about to start now. She pasted on an ultra-fake smile. "Hey, Willa. Small world, isn't it?"

Willa got right in her face. "What the fuck are you doing here?"

Harsh. Even for Willa that was an extra level of hostility. Sofia drew back, wincing at her rival's powerful coffee breath. "Just a little sightseeing. Why?"

Willa lowered her voice to a murderous hiss. "This is my gig, got it? I spent months setting up this deal with the hotel."

"They're sponsoring you?"

"Naturally. Approaching them was sheer brilliance on my part. Everyone goes to Chichén Itzá and Tikal, but they bypass the ruins at Calakmul. I plan to show those idiots what they're missing. This hotel is ideal since it's the closest one to the site."

"Makes sense." Even if Sofia didn't like Willa, she could respect the hustle. "What did you think of the ruins?"

"Haven't been yet. We'll go as soon as our guide gets here."

Sofia fought back a groan. This had to be the group the clerk had mentioned. As Willa turned to greet her entourage—a burly, bearded cameraman and a petite Latina woman who bore the harried look of a personal assistant—Sofia battled her growing sense of panic. If she didn't take action, the group would leave, and she'd lose any hope of getting to Calakmul today.

What to do? Wait two more days or beg Willa to include her?

Who was she kidding? Her reunion with Javier couldn't wait.

She got to her feet. "Any chance you'd have room for one more?"

Willa barked out a laugh. "Like I'd ever help you?"

"I can pay you. I also promise I won't post any content—not about the site or the hotel—until I'm back in Cancún. I'm not trying to compete with you."

Willa tilted her head to the side. "Why the urgency?"

Sofia hated showing any vulnerability, but she had no choice. "I need to find someone who works there. An archaeologist." When

Willa stared her down, Sofia caved. "He's my ex, and I need to talk to him."

"You came all the way out here to track down your ex? That's pathetic."

"Please? I'd rather not wait."

Willa glanced at Sofia's stomach. "Are you pregnant with his kid?"

"No! It's something else." Sofia clenched her hands, hoping Willa wouldn't ask for more details. She'd sooner eat glass than reveal her Vegas mistake to her archrival.

"Fine. But it's going to be a long day. We're making photo stops along the way, and we're not leaving until the site closes at five. Two thousand pesos. Non-negotiable."

That amounted to a little under a hundred dollars. An outrageous price, but worth it to get the trip over with. Tomorrow, Sofia could relax at the hotel pool, secure in the knowledge that she'd accomplished her task. "Thanks. I appreciate it."

Hard to believe, but today was going to suck even more than she'd thought possible.

CHAPTER 8

Once Willa's guide, Jorge, arrived, he led the group outside to a battered green Jeep. The drive to the ruins took them over a rutted road that cut through the Calakmul Biosphere Reserve, a huge swath of protected rain forest extending for hundreds of miles. The thick canopy of trees overhead made Sofia feel like they were driving through a leafy green tunnel. When a sudden rain shower sprang up, she barely felt it under the heavy foliage. The air was thick and humid, giving off the pungent smell of dense vegetation and tropical blooms.

Along the way, Jorge stopped the vehicle to point out the wildlife: tapirs, coatis, toucans, parrots, and spider monkeys swinging through the trees. When Willa stepped out of the Jeep to take pictures, Sofia joined her, enthralled by all the photo opportunities. Even if she couldn't post any content now, she could do it once she got back to Cancún. The trill of bird calls and persistent buzz of insects added to the atmosphere.

When they arrived at Calakmul, Jorge parked in a small lot next to the Visitor Center and led them to the center of the site. While he explained its role in Maya civilization, Sofia stared at the ruins in amazement. She'd visited a lot of archaeological sites during her travels, but she'd never seen anything like these monumental step pyramids. Carved out of thick gray stone, they towered above the treetops.

Despite the sweltering temperature, Jorge insisted on taking them to the top of the highest temple. As Sofia followed Willa's cameraman, who was drooping in the heat, she was grateful not to be carrying anything heavier than a messenger bag. The trek up the carved stone stairs was a sweaty slog, but the view was worth it. From this vantage point, Sofia could spot a few other structures poking out from under the jungle canopy. Hard to believe an entire city had once existed here, containing thousands of people. So much of it had been swallowed up by the thick rain forest.

Once they descended from the pyramid, Sofia reapplied another coating of bug spray to ward off the persistent mosquitoes. Time to quit stalling and focus on her mission. Before leaving Los Angeles, she'd asked Olivia to research Javier's dig site. Her sister had discovered the site wasn't anywhere near the monumental structures that formed the core of Calakmul. Instead, it was in an even *more* remote location, two miles away. Olivia had advised Sofia to go to the Visitor Center for help in locating the excavation.

"I'm not sure if they'll give you access to his site," Olivia had cautioned. "I don't think it's open to the public."

Yet another reason she'd suggested Sofia contact Javier before heading to Mexico. But Sofia had a plan of her own.

She took Willa aside. "I'm going to track down my ex. What time should I be back?"

"Meet us in the parking lot by five at the latest," Willa said. "Otherwise, I'll leave without you."

"No worries. I'll be back long before that."

After waving goodbye to the group, Sofia returned to the Visitor Center. Inside the building, two clerks were stationed at the main desk. She approached the younger of the two, a hottie with a scruffy beard and a name tag that read "Pedro." Flashing Pedro an adorable smile, she told him she was a graduate student from UCLA studying Maya archaeology. She had arranged to meet with Javier Castillo to tour his excavation site, but since he'd neglected to show up, she needed a ride there.

Though she'd been prepared to offer up a bribe if necessary, Pedro agreed without hesitation since he needed to drop off supplies. Sofia followed him outside to a rusty black truck and hopped in.

So far, so good. Despite the morning's setback, she was still on track. But as the site faded into the distance, her nerves kicked into high gear.

No doubt about it, Javier would be upset when she revealed the truth. But *how* upset?

And could she handle his anger without dissolving into a sobbing mess?

Pedro took them along a rough, bumpy road, stopping at one point to move a fallen branch from their path. Once they reached the excavation site, Sofia recognized the familiar elements. Large trenches cut into the earth. Fragments of stone walls. Buckets, tarps, shovels, and picks. A mix of college students and local laborers scraping at the dirt with their trowels. On the other side of the site, faded canopies shaded a couple of makeshift lab tables. Beyond them were a cluster of tents, along with a few hammocks stretched between the trees.

As two of the laborers approached the truck to help unload it, Sofia thanked Pedro and hopped out. Shading her eyes, she scanned the site until she spotted Javier working at one of the lab tables.

She allowed herself a brief, blissful moment to observe him before he took notice of her. He was alone, his eyes focused on the laptop in front of him. He looked as scrumptious as she remembered. If anything, he'd gotten *more* handsome.

Javier Castillo. My husband.

No, her soon-to-be ex-husband. Even if the sight of him sent butterflies fluttering through her ribcage, she couldn't let her memories steer her off course.

She approached the table with hesitant steps "Javi?" Her voice came out in a breathless rush, but it caught his attention.

His eyes widened. "Sofia? Is that you?"

She gave him a broad smile. "It's me, all right. In the flesh."

He stared at her, mouth agape, obviously stunned that she'd materialized out of the jungle. "I...I can't believe you're here."

"I thought I'd surprise you. Looks like it worked."

"Is this for your account? Are we being filmed?" His look of astonishment gave way to a roguish grin. "I'm not at my best for the cameras, all sweaty and dirty. Whereas you look as hot as...I mean...you look...stunning."

"You like my outfit?" She'd opted for style over practicality—an adorable khaki romper, a jaunty leopard-print scarf, and a twill safari hat. Her only concession to the rugged terrain was her sporty Teva hiking boots.

He laughed. "Absolutely. You look like a sexy safari guide."

A thrill of pleasure shot through her. He'd called her *sexy*. That had to be a good sign. Maybe this reunion wouldn't be as painful as she'd imagined.

"I didn't bring a camera crew. Just little old me. I..." Even if she'd traveled thousands of miles to tell him the truth, she needed to ease into it. "I don't know if you've been keeping up with my account but—"

"Sure. I check it when I'm in town. You were in Morocco last month, right?"

"Right. That was my last stop before heading home to California for a bit. But now I'm traveling through the Yucatán Peninsula. Olivia told me you were working here."

"I'm glad you came to visit. Calakmul's an underrated gem." His brow furrowed in confusion. "But how'd you get to this part of the site? Our dig's off-limits to tourists."

She gnawed on her lip, then flashed him a cheeky smile. "I may have lied and said I was a graduate student with an appointment to talk to you about your site."

His dark eyes danced with amusement. "That's the Sofia I remember. Since you're here, do you want the full tour?"

Nice. He wasn't even angry that she'd finagled her way onto his dig. She was tempted to reveal the true reason for her visit, but she didn't have the heart to break the news yet. At the very least, she could wait until he'd shown off his excavation.

"I'd love a tour. I've learned a lot about archaeology during my travels. I even visited my sister when she was digging in Cyprus last summer."

When he came around the table to join her, her breath caught at his nearness. She'd forgotten how much his height and physical presence overwhelmed her. He'd been muscular before, but she didn't remember him looking this built. Working in the field had done wonders for his physique.

"I saw the pictures you posted from Cyprus. Looked like a great project." He took her arm to lead her around the site.

She shivered under his touch. He gave off a protective vibe. Like he could keep her safe, even if a wild jaguar sprang out of the bushes and attacked them.

He pointed to the largest of the trenches, where a long stone wall was visible. "Right now, we've been focusing on Trench B because of the structural remains we found there. This whole area was a residential settlement, probably dating as far back as 500 A.D.—the start of the Classic Maya period.

"The central core of Calakmul, the part you would have seen when you entered the site, contained the ceremonial aspects of the city: the palace, the temple, the ball court, and the acropolis. But for this dig, we're more interested in learning about daily life in Calakmul before its abandonment in 1050 A.D., and we're still trying to determine why it was abandoned."

She nodded, glad she'd had the foresight to read up on Maya civilization during the plane ride to Cancún. She'd learned about their temples, their rituals, and their complicated calendar with its elaborate hieroglyphics.

"This is amazing," she said. "I can't believe you're in charge of it all."

He chuckled. "Not really. I'm just running the show for a bit. Professor Alvares, from the Universidad Autónoma de Campeche, is leading the dig. But he's been gone this past week because his daughter's getting married in Cozumel. Dr. Molina—he's our assistant director—would normally be in charge, but he had to head into the capital to deal with some paperwork. He's setting up next year's excavation."

After Javier showed her around the site and introduced her to the crew, he invited her to join them for lunch. As they sat under a cloth canopy, dining on tamales, black beans, rice, and papayas, she enjoyed their tales of life in the field. Since they only went into town once a week to shower, do laundry, and restock their personal supplies, this dig was high on the hard-core scale. Not exactly Sofia's cup of tea. Though she'd dealt with plenty of rough conditions during her travels, she'd never gone a full week without showering.

By the time lunch was over, Sofia couldn't stall any longer. A torturous ache tugged at her heart. Javier had been so pleased that she'd come all this way just to visit his site, when in reality her motivation was far more selfish.

She waited until the others had returned to their trenches before she pulled him aside. "There's something I need to talk to you about."

He placed his hand on her arm. "Sure. Everything okay?"

"Not exactly. Can we talk alone?"

He led her back to one of the lab tables and gestured for her to sit across from him. As she did so, a spider monkey with mottled black and gray fur dropped down onto the table. She yelped and scooted away, almost falling off her chair in the process.

Javier laughed. "That's Bingo. He's a mooch but totally harmless. He always shows up when I'm doing lab work because he knows I have a weakness for dried banana chips."

Sofia took a few photos of Bingo, then set her phone to the side. Before she could speak up, Javier favored her with a warm smile. "I still can't believe you came all the way out here. This site is way off the beaten track."

"It was worth it to see you." She meant it. She just wished she didn't have to deliver bad news at the same time.

He regarded her with a tender expression. "Thanks. I missed you, Sofia. You're every bit as beautiful as I remember."

She wanted to bask in his praise, but she felt too much like a fraud. She ran a hand through her curls. "I'm kind of a mess. The humidity's murder on my hair, and I'm all sweaty."

"I'm coated with a layer of dirt after spending half the morning digging, so I've got you beat."

On him, it looked pretty good. She released her breath in a whoosh, trying to control the ragged beat of her heart. *Just tell him.*

"I came out here because I...um...I applied to be on this reality dating show called *Recipe for Love*. Have you ever heard of it?"

"Heard of it? My mom loves it. She and her sisters watched it all last season. They were so mad when Chandra got kicked off." He glanced around. "Is that why you're here? Are you filming a segment where you revisit your old flames?" He made a show of smoothing out his hair.

I wish.

"No. I'm being considered for next season. My audition went really well, and they love SoFood SoFia, but..."

"But what?"

"But I found out I wasn't eligible because I'm still married. *To you.*"

CHAPTER 9

Sofia expected Javier to respond in anger. Instead, he started laughing. Full belly laughter that brought tears to his eyes.

"You had me, Sofia. Nice one." He turned and peered at the dense bushes behind them. "Where's the camera crew? Are they hiding back there?"

She wiped a layer of sweat from her forehead. Her voice wobbled. "Sorry, but it's not a joke. After I auditioned for the show, I got an email from the producers. They told me I wasn't eligible because they'd done a background check and found out I was married."

Now Javier wasn't laughing. Or smiling. "That's not possible. You made the arrangements right after we left Vegas. Then you texted me that summer and said it was a done deal. Were you lying?"

"No! I honestly thought we were divorced."

At this point, it would be easy to blame everything on the shady service she'd used. But Sofia knew she should have followed up. At the very least, she should have asked for a copy of the divorce decree. All she'd done was push the news into a dark corner of her mind in the hopes of blotting it from her memory.

Bingo approached Javier, but he shooed him away. "So, what happened?"

His expression was so grim she could barely get the words out, but she told him everything, cringing as she admitted that EZ-Divorce might not have been as legit as she'd assumed.

When she stopped talking long enough for him to respond, his voice was an angry growl. "If this is a setup for the show, I'll be pissed as hell."

"It's not." She fought back a surge of tears, wounded by the rage in his eyes. "I'm not sure what happened, but I'm guessing I was scammed, or the place went belly-up."

"Just how much research did you do, anyway? Did you ever think to ask for referrals?"

"May I remind you that I only had *six days* to deal with it? I didn't have time to do an in-depth study!"

Javier raked a hand through his hair. "I can't believe this. I almost got married last year."

"You were engaged?" She made no attempt to hide the shock in her voice.

He raised his eyebrows. "Not that it's any of your concern."

"You're my *husband*." A ridiculous response, but the thought of Javier loving someone so much he wanted to marry them—*for real*—hurt her beyond measure. Even if she'd had her share of steamy flings, she'd never considered marrying any of them.

"I didn't know it at the time!" He banged his hand on the table, causing Bingo to shriek and skitter away. "I thought I was divorced."

"Did you tell her what happened in Vegas?"

"No. I never told anyone." He rubbed his forehead, as though the conversation was giving him a headache. "You?"

"Not up until now. But only two people know, and they promised they'd keep it a secret. I realize now that I should have followed up after I got that final email, just to make sure everything went through. But my life got busy. Ever since I graduated college, I've been traveling nonstop."

"Right. Enlightening the world with your oh-so-important takes on food and travel. Because that's what we need right now, isn't it?"

"Hey! Don't shit all over my profession."

"It's not a profession. You travel on someone else's dime, take photos and videos, and call it a day. You're not contributing anything."

The words bit into her like a thousand tiny paper cuts. She'd heard similar takes from some of her snarkier relatives, but the words stung more coming from him. "At least I'm not playing in the dirt like a kid, trying to study a civilization that died off a thousand years ago!"

Aware her voice had risen, she cast a glance over at the excavation site. A couple of students were watching them. When she scowled at them, they looked away.

Javier's jaw tightened. "So, what's our next step?"

"My cousin's helping me out. She's a paralegal, so she drew up the paperwork. She'll make sure the divorce goes through." Sofia reached into her messenger bag and placed the papers in front of him. "Here. Sign in all the places I flagged. As soon as I'm back in the States, I'll file them. I don't want this marriage any more than you do."

"Because it might destroy your reality show career? Now there's a worthy profession."

"Don't be so fucking judgmental." Hadn't he just told her his mom loved the show? Or had he turned into one of those stick-up-the-ass academics who thought popular culture was a waste of time?

He grabbed a pen and signed the papers with a flourish. "Make sure you let me know when it goes through. For real, this time."

She snatched the papers back and stuffed them in her bag. "Why? In case you want to get married again?"

"Because I don't want to be married to you," he snapped.

Ouch. She glanced at her watch. 1:45 p.m. Still plenty of time to get back to the main site before Willa left. "Can you give me a ride to the Visitor Center?"

"Not during the middle of a workday. Carlos can take you when he and the other workers leave at four."

Not ideal. She'd be cutting it close if she wanted to get there by five. "Um...are you sure you can't—"

"Four o'clock. Take it or leave it." His murderous expression suggested he was totally done.

"Okay. Thanks."

"Glad to oblige. Now if you'll excuse me, I've got work to do." He stared her down, as if waiting for her to leave.

"Fine. I'll just go wait...over there." She pointed to a spot in the shade, at the edge of one of the trenches.

"Goodbye Sofia."

Even if she hadn't expected him to be happy, the whole exchange was thoroughly soul-crushing. She'd always tried to live by the mantra "good vibes only," but Javier had bestowed some spectacularly bad vibes on her.

Two hours later, when she left the excavation site with Carlos and the other laborers, Javier didn't come to see her off. *Jerk.*

Don't obsess over him. You got what you came for.

Carlos dropped her off at the Visitor Center before heading down the road that led out of the Biosphere Reserve. She walked over to the parking lot, where she found Jorge's Jeep parked in the shade. She leaned against it and scrolled through the camera roll on her phone. If nothing else, she'd gotten some great pictures. But she was hot, tired, and heartsick. She couldn't wait to get back to the hotel, take a long dip in the pool, and indulge in an icy margarita.

When Willa returned with her lackeys, she appraised Sofia with a withering look. "You're a mess. I hope you weren't trying to win this guy back."

The most Sofia could manage was a faint smile. "Nothing like that. Just needed to settle a few things. I'm ready to head back whenever you are."

"I need to film a little more content before we leave, so sit tight," Willa said.

Sofia plopped down on a large rock, her mind drifting as Willa filmed another video. No matter how hard she tried to envision herself playing a featured role on *Recipe for Love*, she couldn't stop brooding over her argument with Javier.

Give yourself time to recover. Once you're back in L.A., you'll be able to move on.

After the last of the tourists trickled out of the site, Pedro locked up the Visitor Center for the night. He waved to her as he and his companion drove off. By now, Sofia was getting antsy, eager to put Calakmul far behind her.

At 5:30, Willa declared she was done. Though Sofia knew better than to offer up a critique, she thought Willa's video seemed dull and uninspired. She waited as Willa and her entourage climbed into the Jeep. But before Sofia could clamber into the backseat, Willa barked out a command, and the door slammed shut. Jorge started the engine.

"Hey!" Sofia pounded on the door. If this was Willa's idea of a joke, it wasn't funny. Especially after the day she'd had.

Willa smirked. "Sorry, bitch. Did you honestly think I'd help you out? You can find your own way back." She flipped Sofia the finger then yelled at Jorge.

Jorge gave Sofia an apologetic shrug, but after Willa ordered him to leave, he drove off in a cloud of dust.

What the hell?

It had to be a joke. Willa just wanted to humiliate her. Any minute now, she'd order Jorge to turn the Jeep around.

Or would she?

Setting her dignity aside, Sofia ran after them. After ten minutes, she had to stop. Bracing her hands on her knees, she gasped for breath. Sweat trickled down her forehead, but she didn't bother to wipe it away.

She was stuck.

CHAPTER 10

Clearly Sofia had underestimated her rival's mean streak. Now she was alone at a centuries-old archaeological site. In a jungle where jaguars roamed after nightfall, seeking out easy prey. And she was so far off the grid her phone couldn't get a decent signal.

Now what?

She'd have to go back to the dig site. Even if the local workers had left for the day, she'd seen tents, which meant Javier and the other students were living on site. Surely one of them had a vehicle. They'd have to, in case of emergencies. If Javier refused to help her, she'd bribe one of the students to drive her back to the hotel.

She pulled out the crumpled map she'd picked up at the Visitor Center. One side of the map focused on the touristy areas, but the other provided a broader overview of the entire site, including all the roads leading in and out. She tried to orient herself, remembering Pedro had driven east along a narrow dirt road. Once she found it, she began walking along it, keeping an eye out for movement in the bushes. Her senses were on full alert as she listened for growls, snarls, and other big-cat noises. But the only predators that disturbed her were the mosquitoes. She slapped her arms and doused herself with another coating of bug spray.

A creepy howl sent a jolt of adrenaline racing through her. Were the ghostly occupants of Calakmul taking offense at her for trekking through their abandoned city? Still shaking, she looked up into the trees and caught sight of a few howler monkeys. Then she broke out laughing. The whole situation was so ridiculous it defied description.

Even if she was stuck in the jungle, foraging her way back to a guy who hated her, she was having an adventure. She started filming herself, laughing in self-deprecation as she recounted her experience. She didn't mention that she had come to Calakmul to get a divorce, only that she was tracking down a lost love and had failed miserably. Her subscribers would love it. They always enjoyed it when she bemoaned her epic fails in the romance department.

After forty minutes of traipsing along the narrow, rutted road, she spotted the site. By now, she'd drained her entire water bottle.

She was sweaty, thirsty, and exhausted but proud she'd found her way back.

Nailed it.

The excavation crew sat at the picnic tables eating dinner. Sofia's mouth watered at the scent of grilled peppers and onions. She hesitated, anxious at the thought of humbling herself in front of Javier, but she didn't have a choice. As she approached the group, he spotted her. His thunderous expression made her stomach clench up. Before she could advance any further, he strode over to her and grabbed her arm.

He lowered his voice. "What the hell are you doing here?"

"I...um...things went a little sideways. I missed my ride. I mean, she decided not to take me back to the hotel. I shouldn't have expected her to be nice because we're rivals. But even so, she should have honored our agreement. I paid her two thousand pesos, and it was *not* meant to be a one-way trip."

Javier held up his hand. "Enough. I'm not interested in your half-assed excuses."

"Sorry. But I need a ride. It's getting dark, and the site's closed, and everyone left, even Pedro. Do you think someone could drive me back?"

He let out a groan. "Professor Alvares has the Jeep, and Dr. Molina took the truck when he went to Campeche. He won't be back until the day after tomorrow."

"The day after tomorrow?" she yelped. "How can you survive without a vehicle? What if there's an emergency? What if someone falls and gets injured?"

"Then we'd call for help. There's a satellite phone, but it's for real emergencies. Not because some diva got into a catfight and lost her ride."

Sofia crossed her arms. "I am *not* a diva. And it wasn't a catfight. More like a snub. Or a big diss. Either way, she's going down. Even if I'm all about good vibes, this—"

"*Stop.* Just stop." He let out a pained breath. "I can't believe I'm saying this, but considering how late it is, you're better off spending the night here."

"You have an extra tent?"

"No. You can stay in mine. I'll just tell everyone..." He rubbed his hands over his face. "Shit. What am I going to tell them? I said you were a grad student."

"They don't need to know your business. If they think we're hooking up, then who cares?" She cast a jealous glare toward the group, which included two women. "Unless you're hooking up with one of them?"

"I don't pull that shit in the field. It gets too messy." His shoulders slumped in resignation. "Since you're here, you might as well join us for dinner."

Pushing past her discomfort, Sofia greeted the crew again. She put on a brave face, joking about missing her ride like it was no big deal. No one asked about her relationship with Javier, though she was certain they were brimming with questions. After all, she'd shown up unexpectedly, claimed to be a grad student, and was planning to spend the night in Javier's tent. But they treated her respectfully, whereas Javier spent the entire meal scowling at her.

Darkness fell quickly in the jungle. Other than a few camping lanterns to provide illumination, the area around them was pitch-dark. Javier explained that they used a generator to provide electricity during the day but shut it off at night.

Once everyone retreated to their tents, she followed Javier to his. Unlike the other pup tents staked out in the small clearing, his was a spacious dome tent, the kind that could hold four or five people. Inside the tent, the funky odor—a mix of sweat and unwashed socks—was a little off-putting. She wished she had a scented candle to diffuse the smell, but an open flame might not be the wisest choice inside a nylon tent.

She set down her messenger bag in a corner. "This is pretty roomy. Is it just for you?"

"Yep. I used to have a smaller one, but I bought this last year when my brothers and I went camping in Baja. It gives me more space to spread out."

"Sorry to cramp your style, but I didn't expect this."

He raised his eyebrows. "Your friend just abandoned you? That seems harsh."

From his tone, she suspected he didn't believe her. Maybe he thought she'd returned because she was desperate for another chance with him. *Hardly.* Not after she'd trekked all this way to secure a divorce.

"Willa's not exactly my friend. It's just..." She sighed, too worn down to launch into a lengthy story. "It's not important. Is there somewhere I can use the facilities?"

He reached into a knapsack and handed her a thick metal flashlight. "Here. You'll need this. There's a sign just past the tents. Follow the path and you'll find the spot. But be careful." He frowned. "Do you need me to come with you?"

And watch me pee? No thanks.

She eased out of the tent, zipping it up behind her. Using the flashlight, she found a handmade signpost reading "This Way to the Shitter." *Lovely.* It led to a crudely built wooden shelter enclosing a pit toilet, like an old-fashioned outhouse. Though it was outfitted with toilet paper and hand sanitizer, it was still dark and creepy. She couldn't shake the fear that a snake might crawl up the toilet and bite her in the ass.

As she was leaving, she turned off the flashlight, wanting to experience the full darkness of the jungle. It was a game she and Olivia used to play when they'd gone camping as kids. They'd sneak out of their tent, shut off their flashlights, and view the night sky in all its glory. Except here, the thick trees blocked out the stars.

A rustling in the bushes made her heart seize up. She froze, scarcely daring to breathe. Trembling, she stepped a few paces backward. When the rustling came closer, she screamed and ran, dropping the flashlight as she sprinted away.

She didn't care that she was going in the wrong direction. After the terrible day she'd had, she wasn't putting herself at the mercy of a ravenous jaguar.

Javier's voice rang out. "Sofia! Where are you going?"

Had he been following her? Stalking her to make sure she didn't do anything stupid? She was about to tell him off, but the rustling got louder. Shrieking, she backed away and stumbled over a roped-off area. Her foot tangled in the rope, and she tumbled backward.

Javier yelled. "Sofia! No! Stop!"

Too late. She was falling.

Free-falling right into the center of the earth.

CHAPTER 11

Sofia was falling.

Careening downward like Alice in Wonderland, with no idea where she was headed. She screamed and flailed her arms, hoping to find something she could grab on to. As she caught the damp scent of water, she took a deep breath and braced herself for impact.

She hit the water with a splash and plummeted under. As she sank into the chilly depths, she kicked out, hoping to propel herself off the bottom. But there was no bottom.

Swim, damn it.

She swam to the surface and emerged, gasping for breath. A quick assessment made her heart flood with relief. No broken bones. No painful injuries. And even if she was trapped in an underground lake, the cool water was a refreshing change from the sticky heat of the jungle.

"Sofia! Are you all right?"

Javier's voice came from somewhere above, but she couldn't see him. Inside her watery hellhole, the darkness was all-encompassing, even inkier than the night sky. She kept herself afloat by treading water, but the heft of her hiking boots weighed her down.

A bright light shone down upon her, so fierce she had to shade her eyes at the intensity. When she opened them, she stared up in shock. She was in an underground cavern, far below the surface. Above her, the cavern walls were sloped at the sides and filled with craggy rock formations, stalactites, and twisted vines. Way up at the top was the hole she'd fallen through, which looked about ten feet across. The sight of bats spiraling overhead made her shudder. Somehow, she'd ended up in a bizarre sinkhole that resembled a cross between the Batcave and the Upside Down.

"Sofia!" Javier called out, his voice thick with agony. "Sofia! Answer me! Please! Are you all right?"

"I'm fine! Just...stuck." The distance to the top was easily twenty or thirty feet, and she couldn't see any way to reach it. No ladder, no rope, no stairs.

"Hang on, okay?" Javier said. "We have a system rigged up. Let me round up the others, and I'll come get you. There's a ledge off to one side. Can you see it? If you climb onto it, you can rest. Just be careful."

The concern in his voice almost brought tears to her eyes. Even if she'd screwed up spectacularly, he didn't sound angry. She spotted the ledge he'd mentioned, cut into one side of the cavern. She swam over to it and hoisted herself up. The craggy rocks scraped her shin, but a section of the ledge was smooth enough to sit on. She let her legs dangle in the cool water until something brushed against her ankles. Piranhas? Underwater demons? Either way, she wasn't taking any chances. She pulled up her feet and tucked them to the side.

From above, Javier's voice carried as he yelled out instructions. Within fifteen minutes, he appeared above her, wearing a rock climbing harness, while the others lowered him down on a rope. As he made his slow descent into the cavern, Sofia watched in awe, surprised by how comfortable he seemed. Clearly, this wasn't his first foray into this underground lair.

When he reached the ledge, he yelled up to the top. "All good! I'll call up when I'm ready." He sat down beside her. "Are you okay?"

Before she could make a joke about falling straight to hell, a flood of emotion washed over her. What if she'd hit the cavern wall instead of landing in the water? What if she'd fallen onto one of those scary-looking stalactites? A sob choked in her throat, rendering her speechless.

Javier enfolded her in his arms. "I'm sorry. I didn't think you'd end up at this part of the site."

"I wouldn't have, except I heard a rustling in the bushes and some scary growls. I freaked out and ran in the wrong direction. Sorry." She felt like such an idiot, especially since she was making up the part about the growls. For all she knew, the animal in the bushes could have been harmless.

"Don't apologize. I should have warned you about the cenote."

"The see-what?"

"The cenote. It's a natural sinkhole made from collapsed limestone. Like an underground cavern filled with water. The peninsula's full of them."

"They're like swimming holes, right?" One of the day trips offered by the hotel included a visit to a couple of cenotes. But the caverns in the photos were outfitted with rope swings, ziplines, kayaks, and steps carved into the stone. They looked a lot friendlier than this place.

"Right. Some of them have been developed for tourists. They're popular in the summer. But others are closed off because they're not safe for the public. Like this one. We roped it off because we've been exploring it during the excavation. The Maya viewed cenotes as a gateway to the underworld."

Talk about creepy. "So, definitely like the Upside Down, then."

He chuckled. "Maybe, but we haven't encountered any demons. Although we found human bones that probably came from sacrificial rituals. And lots of artifacts, including intact pottery. We've been documenting the remains with an underwater drone."

"That's amazing." Here was a facet of archaeology she could relate to. "I'm sorry I insulted your job before. What you do is incredible."

"Thanks." He smoothed a wet strand of hair from her forehead. "I'm glad you're okay. I was so worried when you fell in."

"Why? You hate me. Wouldn't this be an easy way to get rid of me?"

"I don't hate you." He let out a lengthy sigh. "If anything, I was deeply in love with you. But I thought it was over. Having you show up out of the blue—and tell me we're still married—threw me for a loop."

Her heart raced. He'd been in love with her? Why hadn't he ever told her before?

She wanted to ask for more clarification, but now wasn't the time. "Sorry I didn't give you any warning before I showed up. I should have called or sent you an email. That's what Olivia would have done."

"I'm glad you just showed up. It's better this way." As a couple of bats swooped down from the top of the cave, he tightened his grip on her. "Let's get you out of here. If you need to head back to your hotel tomorrow, I'll contact Pedro. He can arrange a ride for you."

She wasn't thinking about the hotel anymore. Now that she'd gotten over her initial shock at falling into an underground cavern, she was more curious than frightened. The thought of exploring it appealed to her adventurous side. "Are you going to do more investigating here?"

"We have one more dive scheduled tomorrow. After that, we'll start packing up the dig site. You caught us at the tail end of the season."

Perfect. She gave a shiver of excitement. Easing out of his arms, she graced him with her sweetest smile. "Can I dive with you? Please?"

His laughter echoed off the cave walls. "Are you serious?"

"I'm totally serious. Exploring a gateway to the underworld? If it wasn't on my bucket list, it is now." A semblance of her old spark fired up inside her. She loved this kind of shit.

"You're really something. But we use scuba gear, and—"

"No problem. I got my scuba certification two years ago, when I was in Italy. Then last fall, I spent a day exploring the ruins of an underwater shipwreck in Turkey." She derived immense pleasure at the stunned look on his face. "I've also been spelunking in the Pyrenees and rock climbing in Sicily."

He brushed his hand across her face, the softness of his touch sending her heart soaring. "You're just full of surprises, aren't you?"

"So? Can I go?"

"You'll need to follow my instructions. No messing around. Since it's technically a burial ground, we can't disturb the bones or the artifacts."

"I'll play by the rules. I promise."

"And if you decide to stay, you'll have to wait until the day after tomorrow to go back to your hotel. Is that okay?"

Since she had the room for three nights, it wouldn't be a problem. Paying for a place she wasn't using was a slight annoyance but worth it for a brand-new adventure. With Javier. "It's okay. If you can put up with me."

"I think I can manage." The affection in his voice warmed her heart.

He unclipped the harness and adjusted it around her. "Let's head up to the top. You can go first. Once you're up there, leave the harness clipped to the rope and tell the others to lower it back down."

As the students hoisted her up, Sofia's breath caught in a mixture of fear and excitement. She covered her face when a bat flew toward her but resisted shrieking in terror. Only after she was back on solid ground did the tension ease from her body. Though she was dripping wet, she was alive and unharmed. And tomorrow, she'd get to go exploring with Javier.

After the students brought Javier up to the surface, he thanked them but didn't offer a word of explanation. Instead, he hustled Sofia into his tent, bringing a small camping lantern with him. The light cast eerie shadows on the walls, but she no longer felt any unease at being stuck in the jungle all night.

She'd be safe with Javier.

CHAPTER 12

Seated on a pile of blankets in Javier's tent, Sofia fluffed her wet hair with a towel. "Do you have anything I could wear until my clothes dry off?"

"Hang on a sec." Javier rooted through a duffel bag and took out a t-shirt and a pair of shorts. After he passed them to her, he stood and backed out of the tent. "I'll wait outside while you change."

She cast him a bemused smile. "It's nothing you haven't seen before."

"True. But I don't need the temptation."

Did that mean she could still tempt him, even after four years? She fought back a surge of longing. *Pull yourself together. You're here to get a divorce.*

Once he left, she removed her boots, shucked off her wet outfit, and set everything to the side. Though Javier's t-shirt hung almost to her knees, it was clean and dry, giving off the faint aroma of laundry detergent. Maybe she'd take it with her when she left Calakmul to have a tangible reminder of him.

"You can come back in," she called out.

Javier returned, zipped up the tent, and sat across from her. As he took in her appearance, a wry smile played at the corner of his lips.

She flushed under his scrutiny. "What? I know I look ridiculous. Your shirt is four sizes too big."

"You, ridiculous? Never. Do you need anything else? You can borrow my sleeping bag if you want."

Even after her cleansing dunk in the cenote, the humidity still weighed on her like a thick blanket. "I'm good. But I'll take a pillow if you have one."

"Sure." He passed her one, then reached into his pack and pulled out a half-full bottle of tequila and a couple of tin cups. "Want a drink?"

"Thanks. Just a little." A shot of tequila sounded like the perfect way to take the edge off, but the last thing she needed was to get drunk and do something she'd regret. Like trying to convince Javier they should have wild, passionate sex.

The sharp bite of the tequila was so strong it made her cough, but the burn of the alcohol filled her with a warm glow. When Javier's eyes lingered on her figure, she met his gaze brazenly. Bad move. Being alone with him in an enclosed space only made her more aware of his physical presence. Her pulse raced as she imagined his full lips claiming hers. Or his strong hands stroking her bare skin. She wiped her forehead as a rush of heat surged through her. Time to switch focus.

"Can I ask you something?" she said.

"If you're trying to hit on me, forget it. I'm a married man."

That got a laugh out of her. "I was curious about what you said earlier. That you were engaged. Can I ask what happened? Or is it too painful to talk about?"

He shrugged. "It's not that painful. In the end, it was for the best."

Because all along, you still wanted me?

Obviously not. Even if he'd kept up with her account when he was on the grid, it was clear he hadn't thought about her much since Vegas.

"Remember when we worked together at El Marinero?" he asked. "How I told you I had my life all planned out?"

"Sure, I remember." She ticked off the items on her fingers. "Get a PhD in Archaeology, lead a few digs, land a tenure-track job at a university, and settle down with a family. Right?"

"Yep. I know it sounded intense, but I needed to stay focused. It was hard enough turning my back on my dad's landscaping company, but I also took a huge risk by studying archaeology instead of something stable like law or business. I didn't want to screw up."

"I get it." Though she'd admired his goals, she'd also thought they were a little inflexible. She couldn't imagine mapping out her life with such detailed precision.

"It was all going well until I met you at El Marinero. You didn't fit into my plans."

She gave him a sassy grin. "But you wanted me anyway."

"Can you blame me? Resisting you took every ounce of willpower. Then Vegas happened and all my fantasies came true." He reached over and twined his fingers with hers. "That weekend was amazing, but I never thought I'd end up married."

She squeezed his hand in return. "Neither did I."

"After I left Vegas, I told myself I'd get back on track."

"Is that why you never answered any of my texts?"

"Sorry. I knew if I backslid, I'd be a goner. The only thing I allowed myself was the occasional peek at your Instagram. You seemed to be doing well, so I figured you'd moved on."

Even if his logic made sense, it still hurt. But she said nothing, letting him continue.

"During my second year in Chicago, I met Teresa," he said. "She checked all the boxes. Smart, driven, an academic like me. We were such a good match that I proposed a year later."

Sofia blinked quickly, trying to stem the tears welling up in her eyes. He'd married her on a drunken whim, but he'd *chosen* to marry Teresa. "Did...did you love her?"

"I thought I did. But I think I loved the idea of her, and the stability she offered. Unlike me, she wasn't chasing a crazy dream. She was a brilliant financial analyst. With her skills, she'd be able to find work wherever she wanted. But honestly? As much as we talked about the future, there was something missing."

There had to be because he hadn't mentioned passion. To Sofia, that was just as important as stability.

He continued. "Not long after we got engaged, she cheated on me with an ex. I should have been gutted, but mostly, I was relieved. We could finally acknowledge what we had wasn't enough. The hardest part was telling our families the wedding was canceled." He offered up a sly grin. "Good thing we did, since I already have a wife."

"Sorry about that." Sofia sipped her tequila. Already her muscles felt looser, though she wasn't sure if it was due to the tequila or the fact that Javier was opening up to her.

He topped up her cup. "What about you? Any near-misses or broken engagements?"

"No. I've been traveling so much that I never settled down. I've had flings. Fun experiences. But nothing serious. Lately, I've been wanting more." She locked eyes with him, hoping he'd see past the frivolity to the depth of her soul. "Maybe I'm being unrealistic, but I want to find 'the one.' I look at Olivia and her boyfriend, and I see how happy they are. They don't know what their future holds, but they want to explore it together. I want a love like that."

"We all want a love like that. Right?" When he held her gaze, she could have sworn he was about to reveal more. But he drained his cup and set it down. "We should get some sleep. Wakeup call is at six."

"Ugh. You archaeologists and your early schedules. When can we dive in the cenote?"

"We'll go around two, during the hottest part of the day. You'll have to spend tomorrow night here, but Dr. Molina should be back with the truck the next morning. I can take you to your hotel then. In the meantime, you're stuck in here with me."

"It's fine. Thanks for letting me stay." She was tempted to try kissing him to see if she could reignite their old spark. But for once in her life, she did the sane, sensible thing. It wasn't as though she'd come to Calakmul to win him back. Quite the opposite, she needed that divorce. "I'm not that much of a diva that I need a hotel room."

He rubbed the back of his neck. "Sorry I called you that. And I'm sorry I insulted what you do. That was out of line."

"It was. But I get it. I know I'm not saving the planet or studying a long-lost civilization. But the world can be a messed-up place and sometimes we need a little entertainment."

"Agreed. I was just being a dick. I respect you immensely, and I admire your willingness to embrace adventure."

His simple statement—that he *respected* her—almost brought tears to her eyes. But it was probably just her exhaustion making her weepy. Today's events had put her through the wringer. "I'd better get some sleep."

"Good night, Sofia."

"'Night, Javier."

But as she curled up on the blankets and drifted off to sleep, she wished she'd had the courage to kiss him.

CHAPTER 13

If the other students were surprised to see Sofia the next morning, they didn't remark on it. Good thing, since she had no intention of revealing the truth about her relationship with Javier. To make herself useful, she pitched in with the pot washing and labeling—simple jobs that didn't require an archaeology degree.

For most of the morning, Javier worked beside her and teased her with a familiarity that brought back memories of their shifts together at El Marinero. Whether it was due to the cenote incident or their late-night talk, the walls between them had crumbled into dust.

Around mid-morning, he went to confer with the crew in Trench B. When he came back, he was grinning.

"What's up?" she said. "Are the students asking questions about us?" If she'd been in their place, she would have been dying of curiosity.

"I think they've seen past your ruse of being a grad student, but they haven't demanded an explanation yet."

She laughed. "I'm pretty sure a real archaeologist wouldn't have been foolish enough to fall into a cenote."

"Probably not. Anyway, since you're here, they convinced me that you need to visit the other cenote. The fun one. I told them we'd go there after we're done diving."

"There's a fun cenote? One that's less creepy?"

"It's about a quarter mile away. Since it's closer to the surface, it's more like a swimming hole. It's a great place to cool off after the workday ends, but only if we're not behind schedule."

She clasped her hands together. "Please say we're not behind schedule. I want to go."

"Then we'll make it happen." He came and sat beside her. "As long as we get our work done."

She gave him a salute. "Yes, sir."

Sofia continued working with him until the midday break. After lunch with the crew, he announced it was time for the final dive of the season. She borrowed a wet suit and a set of scuba gear, and followed him to the cenote. In the light of day, the ropes and warning signs surrounding it were so glaringly obvious that her fall appeared even more idiotic. Thankfully, no one commented on it.

This time, when she descended into the cavern, she no longer felt like a damsel in distress, but a bold adventurer. Javier joined her, bringing an underwater drone called a DORY that he used to capture photos and videos. As they dove beneath the surface, Sofia stuck close to his side. Since the cenote branched into dozens of waterways leading to other sinkholes, she couldn't risk getting lost. The last thing she wanted to do was cause more drama.

During their dive, Sofia was in constant awe of the finds they encountered: human skulls, arm and leg bones, and lots of pottery, including an intact urn, perfectly preserved from the day it was made. When Javier motioned for her to follow him down an uncharted tunnel, she felt like a true badass. She could have spent hours underwater, but their oxygen tanks only lasted fifty minutes. Once their time was up, she reluctantly joined him in swimming to the surface.

After the students hauled them up to the top of the cenote, she wrapped Javier in a spontaneous hug. "That was awesome! Thanks for letting me come with you."

His affectionate smile warmed her from the inside out. "My pleasure. We got some great shots in that last waterway. I can't wait to look them over."

"Can you send me some of the pictures? Please? I won't post them if they're supposed to be top secret. I just want them for my collection."

"Sure. You can post them as long as you don't mention which cenote they came from. We don't need any tourists tromping around the site." He grinned. "Except you, of course."

She rolled her eyes. "I'm hardly your average tourist." *I'm your wife.*

Not that she'd say it. Not when the students were still within earshot.

Getting those photos would be a coup. Once she posted them on Instagram, Willa would shit herself with jealousy.

After they returned to the site, Javier told the crew they were free to go swimming. Sofia was so sweaty and sticky that she would have swum in her clothes, but one of the female students loaned her a bathing suit. Getting to this cenote involved a fifteen-minute slog through the buggy jungle, but the trek was worth it.

Sofia joined the others gleefully, jumping into the underground lake with a whoop of delight. When Javier plunged in beside her, she couldn't resist checking him out. Shirtless, he looked even better than he had in Vegas. But other than sneaking a few glances at his muscular form, she behaved herself.

Remember, you're friends, not lovers. And you're about to get a divorce.

By the time they made their way back to the excavation site, Sofia was tired but happy. Rather than put her wrinkled outfit back on, she grabbed the t-shirt and shorts Javier had lent her. Even if they were too big, they were soft, comfy, and relatively clean.

The thought of going back to her hotel filled her with a pang of sorrow. She wasn't ready to leave. But this wasn't her real life. It was just a fun little interlude. Hadn't Javier said he'd be leaving Calakmul soon? No doubt he was heading back to Chicago to work on his dissertation.

Besides, once she returned to L.A. and filed the divorce papers, she'd have a decent chance at landing a spot on *Recipe for Love*. Being on a reality show would be a new adventure, free of mosquitoes, jungle predators, and spooky underground caverns.

No matter how much she enjoyed being with Javier, she had to face the facts. Their lives weren't headed in the same direction at all.

CHAPTER 14

Going to bed at nine o'clock wasn't Sofia's style. If anything, she was the type to stay out until sunrise partying. But when darkness fell on the dig site, everyone retreated to their tents for the night. At least turning in early meant more time alone with Javier. But the longer she was with him, the more she remembered why she'd fallen for him in the first place.

A damn shame they had to get divorced.

Just get through tonight.

By tomorrow, she'd be headed back to her hotel. Once she was free of Javier's magnetic pull, she wouldn't be tempted any longer.

But as she sat across from him in the close confines of his tent, she couldn't deny how much she craved his touch. The flickering light of the camping lantern cast shadows across his rugged features. How could she let him go without trying anything?

He glanced up from the book he was reading. "Everything okay? You look like you're lost in thought."

"Just...thinking over my next few days. I'm going to extend my hotel stay one more night before I head back to Cancún."

"Are you visiting anywhere else on the peninsula?"

"Nope. I need to get back to L.A. and file the divorce papers."

"Right. Makes sense."

The silence that followed was so painful Sofia could hardly bear it. She wanted to bring back the intimacy they'd shared last night. "I'm not that tired. Do you want to do something? Like play cards?"

He set down his book. "What did you have in mind?"

"We could play poker and gamble for..." She grinned at him. "We could play strip poker."

Where the hell had that come from? The words had escaped her mouth so fast she hadn't thought to filter them. But now that they were out, she could think of nothing she wanted more than to watch Javier strip in front of her. Her pulse rate spiked when he reached into his knapsack and pulled out a worn deck of Bicycle playing cards.

"Five-card draw," he said. "The loser removes an article of clothing."

She stared in shock, stunned he'd agreed so readily. "Okay. Great. If we're going to do this, I'll need a little tequila."

But under no circumstances could she get drunk. If anything happened between them, she wanted to remember all of it.

He filled a tin cup with tequila, passed it to her, and dealt out the cards.

She glared at her hand in disgust. All she'd gotten were five low cards, without a hope of a straight or a flush. "Damn."

He cast her a smug grin. "Is there a problem?"

"No problem at all." She swapped out four of her cards but only ended up with a pair of threes.

When he displayed his hand, revealing two pair—sixes and nines—she took a deep breath and slowly removed her shirt. Or rather, *his* shirt. Underneath it, she was wearing the rose-colored bra she'd chosen when she'd set out for Calakmul yesterday. A lacy, barely-there bra that displayed her breasts prominently. As she imagined his mouth on them, her nipples tightened in anticipation.

Javier's jaw dropped. "Fuck me."

That's the idea.

It was her turn to stare when he lost the next hand and peeled off his t-shirt. She gazed at his broad chest, admiring the ridges of muscles and the dark swath of hair that trailed down his stomach. Though she'd ogled him freely when they'd gone swimming, they hadn't been alone. Now that no one was around to stop them, she wanted to run her hands along those muscles and taste his bare skin.

He arched his eyebrows. "You like what you see?"

Of course she did, but she wasn't about to admit it. She licked her lips and took another slug of tequila, shivering at the harsh bite of the alcohol. "Just deal the cards."

When she beat him a second time, she expected him to remove his shorts. Instead, he took off the gold cross around his neck and placed it to the side. "Wouldn't want to give you too much temptation."

Unfair. This time, when she lost, she had no choice but to remove her shorts. Underneath, she wore a tiny pair of panties that matched her bra. Panties that were now uncomfortably damp, due to the raging heat flooding through her.

Javier stared again, his expression even more slack-jawed than before. But he shook his head quickly, as though trying to clear his mind. After releasing a jagged breath, he dealt out the next hand.

This time, Sofia made no attempt to win. Now that she was so close to being naked, she wanted to push him over the edge. Though he'd dealt her a pair of kings, she discarded them and ended up with nothing. She took off her bra, tossed it aside, and rolled her shoulders. "Ahhh. That feels so much better."

The look on his face was priceless. Like he wanted to tear his gaze away but couldn't find the will to do it.

"You okay over there?" She cupped her breasts and tweaked her nipples, just to show him what he was missing. Bad idea because it only made her throb with longing. If he didn't touch her soon, she was going to self-combust.

He refused to break. "I'm just fine."

He was not "just fine." His eyes were dilated with hunger. His shorts did little to hide his obvious erection.

She tossed back the rest of her tequila and set down the cup. As she met his gaze again, her heartbeat quickened. The distance between them was only a few feet, but it could have been a mile. If she crossed it, and he rejected her, it would hurt like hell.

Javier set down his cards. "Sofia, I..."

"Yes?" *Say you want me. Please.*

"I can't do this."

"Play cards?" A ludicrous question, but she was giving him an easy out.

"No. I can't sit here and pretend we're just friends. Not when I—"

"When you want me with every fiber of your being?" She didn't think she could stand it if he turned her down.

When he nodded, she tossed the cards aside. "Then come over here and kiss me."

His relieved expression sent her heart soaring. He crossed over to her side of the tent but resisted touching her. His nearness was so tantalizing she could barely stand it.

"Wh...what are you doing?" she asked. "I thought you wanted me."

"I do. But first I want to get a good look at you. This way I'll have something to keep my fantasies going after you leave." He cupped her face in his hands and brushed his lips across hers with featherlight softness. "I've wanted to kiss you since the moment you walked onto my dig site."

"Liar." She trembled as his lips grazed her eyelids, her cheeks, and the curve of her neck. "You were furious with me."

"Only because I was flattered you'd come all this way to see me, just to find out you were here to get a divorce. You didn't actually want me."

"I do now." When his lips found hers again, she kissed him back. Gently at first, and then passionately, tasting tequila on his tongue. But he pulled away all too quickly.

"Let me turn off the lantern," he said. "The others are curious enough without us casting racy shadows on the walls."

"Wait." She reached for her messenger bag, pulled out a strip of condoms, and set them on the blankets beside her. "I don't know if you remember, but I always come prepared."

"I *do* remember. Thank you." He turned down the lantern and pushed her back onto the blankets. "Sound travels here. Can you keep quiet?"

"Of course," she whispered. "I'll be quieter than a mouse."

Though if memory served her correctly, she'd been very loud when they'd had sex in Vegas. Like, crying out his name, moaning in ecstasy, rocking the bed kind of loud. But for his sake, she'd try to show a little self-restraint.

Once the darkness enveloped them, she was lost in sensation—his lips covering hers, his calloused hands caressing her breasts, the warmth of his bare skin pressed against hers. He smelled of lake water from the cenote, and no scent on earth had ever aroused her so powerfully. With a quick tug, he made short work of her panties. She drew him closer, not caring that their bodies were slick and sweaty from the humidity. When he sucked on her nipples, she moaned into his shoulder. Keeping quiet was going to be a bigger challenge than she expected.

You're supposed to be over him, damn it. You're getting a divorce.

But right now, all she wanted to do was give way to the passion burning inside of her. His lips traveled a sensual path along her skin, making her squirm with need. When he parted her legs and found her sweet spot with his tongue, she was utterly lost. She didn't care that his scruff would leave a burn, not when it felt so delightful brushing the inside of her thighs. His hands tightened around her butt, holding her firmly in place as he delved in deeper, bringing her closer and closer to the edge.

"Yes," she whispered. "More of that. *Please.*"

She fisted the blanket beneath her as she urged him on with desperate, breathless pleas. As the orgasm skyrocketed through her, she shook with a pleasure so intense she had to muffle her cries with a pillow.

When he faced her again, he smoothed her messy hair away from her face and murmured her name softly. "Sofia, mi corazón. You tasted so good. Sweeter than any of my fantasies."

She pressed a kiss against his damp forehead. "I never stopped thinking about you."

It was the truth. For all the flings she'd had, whenever she was alone, he was always the one she'd dreamed of.

"I wish I hadn't left you in Vegas," he said.

Maybe his words were just pillow talk, but she took them to heart. "You didn't want me."

He nuzzled her neck. "I didn't want to be married. But I hated cutting you out of my life. I was madly in love with you."

Her heart billowed with happiness. "I wish I'd known." She smoothed her hands along his back, kneading his warm muscles with her fingers.

"I was afraid if I said anything, I'd get in too deep." He sighed. "Stupid, I know."

"Not stupid. I felt the same way. I wasn't just in love with you, I felt like we were soul mates, destined to be together. But it doesn't matter now. We're here, lost in the jungle, and we have the whole night together. And I have a lot of condoms."

"Perfect." He ran his hand along the curve of her spine. "May I have one?"

"Absolutely." She fumbled in the darkness until she found one. She handed it to him, waiting eagerly as he removed his shorts and boxers, then put it on. When he entered her, she let out a gasp of pleasure.

He stilled for a second. "I didn't hurt you, did I?"

"No, I'm good. It just feels so incredible." *Like it's meant to be.*

Then he was moving against her, thrusting hard, pressing her against the blankets. She clutched onto him tightly, trying her best to keep quiet even as she wanted to moan at the sensations he was arousing in her. As she got closer to her peak, she dug in her nails, urging him on, until her world exploded in a shimmering haze of stars. The pleasure soared through her, and she was cascading, tumbling, falling, but he was there to catch her. He gave a final, powerful thrust, followed by a loud groan. As if realizing what he'd done, he quieted immediately, but it was too late.

He started laughing. "So much for being discreet."

She giggled. "Here I thought I was the noisy one."

"I couldn't help it. You felt so good." He leaned his forehead against hers. "I hope we didn't wake anyone up."

"It's fine. It'll give them something to talk about tomorrow."

She lay beside him, slowly catching her breath. Outside, she could hear the faint jungle cries, but she felt secure and cozy in his arms.

Tomorrow, they'd have to face reality. But for now, he was still her husband and she planned to make the most of their last night together.

CHAPTER 15

When Sofia woke, she was groggy, stiff, and slightly sore. From outside, the sound of voices meant the archaeologists were already hard at work. She stretched out her arms, gave an enormous yawn, and put on Javier's t-shirt. She couldn't imagine what a mess she must be, her curls all tangled, her face wiped clean of makeup. But she didn't care.

Last night, she'd had sex with her husband. Three times. And it had been glorious.

Javier unzipped the tent and poked his head inside. At the sight of her disheveled appearance, his eyes danced with amusement. "Buenos días, Señora Sanchez-Castillo."

Señora. He'd never addressed her that way before. Like she was his *actual* wife. She grinned at him. "Buenos días."

He handed her a travel mug. "¿Un cafecito, mi corazón?"

"Sí, gracias." She cradled the mug and inhaled the rich aroma of coffee. "Smells wonderful. What time is it?"

He glanced at his watch. "Almost nine thirty."

"That late? I had no idea."

"No worries. I decided to let you sleep." He chuckled. "That six o'clock wakeup call was a real bear this morning, and I blame it all on you."

She laughed because he didn't look remotely angry. "Sorry."

"No, you're not. And I'm not either. Last night was incredible."

A warm flush heated her cheeks. "It was."

"I also came to tell you Dr. Molina returned with the truck a half hour ago. We can leave whenever you're ready."

Now? She wasn't close to being ready. She wanted to stay at the site—to help with the lab work, swim in the cenote, and hang out with Javier. Anything to extend their time together. "Do you want to wait until break time?"

"It's okay. Like I said, we're cleaning the dig site today. Getting ready to pack up before the rainy season sets in. Now that Molina is back, he can supervise."

"Okay. Sure." Emotion welled up in her throat, making speech nearly impossible.

What did you expect? It's what you wanted.

Sure, she'd wanted it initially. Now she didn't want to lose him again.

She told herself her feelings were just a result of really great sex. But she'd had plenty of great sex over the past few years, most notably with Ziyad in Morocco. No matter how much fun she'd had, she'd never felt like the sex had the potential to turn into something more. Nor did she want it to.

With Javier, it was different. She'd always wanted more with him. If given the chance, she'd be willing to put in the work to make it last.

But a relationship with him wasn't in the cards. She wasn't a part of his ten-year plan. And if they were still married, she couldn't be on *Recipe for Love*.

"Sofia? You okay?" Javier asked.

"Sure. I'll get ready."

"Great. I'll let the crew know we'll be leaving soon." He left, zipping up the tent behind him.

She changed out of Javier's shirt back into her original clothes, now hopelessly wrinkled. Even if her heart ached at the thought of leaving him, at least her brief visit had been memorable. Maybe this time they could stay in touch. If he was back in Chicago when *Recipe for Love* aired, he could watch her on TV and root for her to find "the one."

Who was she kidding? She'd take Javier over a reality-show hottie any day. Why look for "the one" in L.A. when the guy she wanted was right here? It didn't take a PhD to figure out that shit. But Javier probably didn't feel the same way. He'd loved her once, but that had been four years ago.

When she emerged from the tent with her messenger bag slung over her shoulder, Javier was talking with the students. She resisted the urge to blush in embarrassment. Even if she and Javier had tried to keep things quiet last night, they'd lost control too many times to count. If anyone had been awake, they would have gotten an earful.

But she faced the crew without shame. "It was great to meet all of you. Good luck with the end of the dig."

She followed Javier to the truck and climbed in beside him. As he pulled away from the site, she tried to control the painful emotions battering her heart.

"The Biosphere has some amazing wildlife," he said. "Do you want to stop and take pictures anywhere?"

For once, she wasn't in the mood. "No thanks. I took a bunch of photos on the way out here. Though if you see a jaguar, you can stop. That's the one animal I haven't seen."

As they drove along the bumpy road, the silence weighed on her. She wanted to say something—*anything*—to keep Javier close, but she couldn't find the words.

When he stopped the truck abruptly, she peered out the window. "What happened? Did you spot a jaguar?"

Javier turned to her. "No. I just..."

"What?"

He released a ragged sigh. "I know we made the right decision when we said goodbye in Vegas, but it was so hard to lose you. And now—"

"You don't want to let me go?" Her voice trembled out of fear she might be wrong.

"Not if I can help it. I'd give anything to have you back in my life again. But you've got that reality show waiting for you. This isn't a part of your plan."

She laughed. "If you know me, you should realize I rarely stick to my plans. I'm not wedded to the idea of the show. I just needed a next step. And I wanted to find 'the one.' But maybe he's already here."

His voice swelled with hope. "You think so?"

"I'm willing to find out. But what about your plan? The ten-year one? I'm not sure where I fit in."

"Maybe it's time I stopped trying to plan everything. Sometimes, the best things happen when you least expect them." He leaned toward her and kissed her tenderly.

Craving more, she grabbed his shirt and pulled him closer, deepening the kiss. This was what she wanted. Not a reality show or a fake relationship or thousands of new followers. *Him.* The man she'd never stopped loving.

When he broke their embrace, he regarded her with such affection that she all but melted. "So...I have kind of a wild suggestion," he said.

Her heart thrummed with anticipation. "What is it?"

"Would you be up for seeing more of the peninsula? Usually when my digs end, I head back to Chicago. But this time, I made plans to travel for two weeks. I'm hoping to hit the archaeological hot spots, like Chichén Itzá, Tikal, and Tulum."

She nudged him playfully. "Just ruins? Or could you squeeze in a little beach time?"

"I could be talked into beach time. I could be talked into anything if you'd come with me as my traveling companion."

She clasped her hands together, trying to contain the excitement bubbling up inside of her. "Your traveling companion with benefits?"

"That's the best kind."

Two weeks in the Yucatán with Javier? How could she resist? The area teemed with delightful photo and video opportunities. And if they traveled together, she'd get to know him even better. "Sounds amazing. What about after?"

"I'm not sure. But once I leave Mexico, I made plans to spend the summer in San Diego, working on my dissertation. I've been traveling so much that I could use some family time. My older brother had a baby girl two months ago, and I haven't even met her yet." He placed his hand over hers. "Any interest in going back with me?"

Sofia's heart raced. "Definitely. I know my parents would love it if I spent the summer at home." It would be a great base of operations for creating the foodie videos she'd had simmering on the back burner.

"I'd like that a lot. But I have to be honest—I don't know where I'll end up after all this."

"That's okay. Neither do I. Maybe we could figure it out together." She glanced at her messenger bag. "What about the divorce papers?"

He grinned at her. "What divorce papers?"

"The ones I—"

"All I know is that my sexy wife came all the way to the jungle to find me at my dig site, and now I can't wait to spend the next two weeks with her exploring the Yucatán."

His sexy wife. She liked the sound of that. "Then let's do it."

Who needed a reality show? With Javier by her side, her future held the promise of more adventures, more sex, and—most important—a lasting love with the one man she'd always wanted.

Something told her it would all work out just fine.

The End (for now...)

***

Did you enjoy Sofia and Javier's story? If you did, be sure to leave a review!

Also, if you sign up for my newsletter, you'll get a free short story, plus exclusive sneak peeks and updates on my future releases.

ABOUT THE AUTHOR

Carla Luna writes contemporary romance with a dollop of humor and a pinch of spice. A former archaeologist, she still dreams of traveling to far-off places and channels that wanderlust into the settings of her stories. Her books have been called "escape reads," perfect for perusing during a beachside vacation or a relaxing weekend at the lake.

Want to hang out with Carla, get exclusive content, and support her books on social media? Sign up for Carla's newsletter here.

JOIN CARLA ONLINE
www.carlalunabooks.com

Read More of Carla's Books
Field Rules (Romancing the Ruins #1)
Blue Hawaiian (Blackwood Cellars Series #1)
Red Velvet (Blackwood Cellars Series #2)
White Wedding (Blackwood Cellars Series #3)

OFFSIDES

A Standalone from the *First Down* Series

Jennifer M. Miller & Jenna Fields

ABOUT *OFFSIDES*

Torn between two college athletes, Rosie has a tough decision to make.

Will she take a shot at the soccer hottie she met online?
Or, will she give the star quarterback a chance to win her heart.

Her past could make her fumble.

Win, lose, or fall flat on her face,
Rosie has two chances at one goal—
Find the one she will love forever.

CHAPTER 1

"Roseanna Mariella Fernandez! Less talking, more working." Tia wiped sweat from her brow, then reached around me to grab a bottle of creamer.

"Uh-oh. She used your full name. Somebody's in trouble." Meghan Grace set a paper mug underneath the espresso machine and tinkered with the buttons.

I let my eyes roll at her sing-song voice. If I was in trouble, she was too, since she was the person I was talking to when Tia hollered.

When Tia poked her head out the drive through window, I read another crazy message I'd gotten the other day. "Sexy_Daddy_3000 said, is your passport Asian because I want to get in ja-panties."

She laughed.

"Okay, but what did you text back, because nothing gets past you without a smart quip, or kickass comeback?" Grey shuffled around me filling coffee orders as fast as she could.

"I sent him a picture of Papi and told him he had the wrong number. For the cherry on top, I copy and pasted a sermon on abstinence. En Español of course." A proud smile covered my face.

Grey pumped a few squirts of vanilla syrup into a plastic cup of ice. "I've got to hand it to the guy, that was pretty clever."

"You would not believe the lines men send me in this stupid app." When Tia walked by, I shoved my phone into my apron pocket. If she found out I was using a dating app, she'd kill me.

Then she'd tell my parents, who would resurrect me just to kill me all over again.

I could tell her the app was built to help young women find good Catholic boys who eat dinner with their families every Sunday night... Nope. Even then.

It wasn't that they didn't want me to date, they just hoped all of my focus was on finishing my last year of college.

"You're about to graduate with the highest honors mija. You're receiving recognition of excellent athleticism for your work with the band. Don't blow it all on some silly boy. Enfócate en tu escuela." I could hear my mother's voice from miles away.

"What's the wildest message you've gotten so far?" Grey topped a drink with whipped cream.

"I got one yesterday that said I'm jealous your heart is pounding inside of you and I'm not. That one was pretty gross. The day before that, I had to pretend to be my dad again when some random dude asked if he could send me a picture of his—" I cleared my throat, unwilling to say the word.

People on the internet never ceased to amaze me.

"That app is not going to lead to a real relationship. You know that, right?" Who was this chick and where did she hide my best friend? It was my job to give dating advice. Not hers.

"There is this one guy, Soccer Hottie, that I really like talking to." I Pretended to wipe the sides of the coffee machine, Tia's eyes and ears were too close for comfort.

"Is that the guy who kept you up all night last night?" Grey asked under her breath.

I raised a quizzical brow. I hadn't told her about the new mystery man, yet. Hell, I didn't tell her anything about last night. She had her own boy drama keeping her up.

"I heard your phone dinging until two A.M." She slammed a lid on a cup a little too harshly.

Oops.

Busted.

"Sorry. I'll make sure to silence my phone tonight. Anyway, He's really sweet. I think you would like him. His messages always make me smile. He asks me questions about my day and tells me I'm beautiful. They're always heartfelt notes."

"Uh-huh." Grey rolled her eyes.

"He's crazy hot, too. Built like an athlete ready to go pro, I'm talking abs for days, strong arms that can wrap a girl up and never let go. And, he's got these adorable dimples that I just want to poke with the tip of my finger."

"Just the tip?" Grey pulled her lips in to contain the laugh.

"No. He's not like that." Soccer_Hottie wasn't like the other guys who sent me dirty pick-up lines. It felt like he genuinely wanted to get to know me in our chats.

"Yeah. I'm sure he's awesome." Grey feigned indifference.

Whatever.

Maybe one day she'd meet him, and it would all make sense.

In the time we'd been chatting about the disastrous men I'd met online, Grey had made three coffees, toasted a bagel, and cleaned the counters.

Me?

Hah!

I hadn't even finished pouring the black copy some guy named Bill ordered.

"Who's next?" I stepped up to the cash register to take the next order.

"Hey, Grey!" Chase, Meghan's boyfriend, walked up to the counter wearing his stupid meet cute grin.

That boy was crazy in love with Grey. They were perfect for each other—long lost sweethearts separated by time and heartache.

Last year they found their way back to each other, but that road was filled with twists and turns, bruises, bumps and secrets that I can't even begin to describe.

Chase had practically moved in with us, he came around so often. He didn't bother me at all; I was happy Grey had someone special to love and be loved.

His best friend?

That was a different story.

Chase's right hand man, quarterback extraordinaire, tall, dark and sexy as sin...

Adam Lovett.

He stepped up to the counter beside Chase.

The hisses and whirs of the coffee machines faded away.

Had Adam seen me? En el nombre de Dios I hoped he hadn't. *Santa madre de Jesús lo vi.*

Wicked strong biceps that fit perfectly pressed against my ear. I nibbled on the tip of my fingernail, wishing it was him instead.

Light green eyes that closed right before he lost all control. I swallowed. Why were those smoldering green eyes locked onto me.

Why was my throat so dry?

"Hey, Rosie." His voice was deep and seductive and desperate.

For me?

My heart pounded against my ribcage. Could he see the steady beating beneath my thin white shirt?

My palms grew sweaty.

At any moment my knees would buckle, and I'd fall flat on my face.

No.

I can't let that happen.

Instead, I ducked beneath the counter.

CHAPTER 2

"Rosie?" Meghan knocked on my bedroom door. "Heads up, Chase is on his way over."

I shoved my gym bag over my shoulder and opened the door. "Have fun. I'm headed out to the gym for a little extra practice."

My halftime routines came second nature to me. I didn't need the extra practice, though it never hurt.

My mission was simple: avoid Adam at all cost.

Miraculously, I'd managed to avoid Adam for a few days.

One early morning, he'd popped into the coffee shop. I'd already hid from him in the break room and ducked behind the counter.

"Trash looks full. I'll take it out." I exclaimed to the entire coffee shop a little too loud.

Grey looked at me like I'd grown three heads. I couldn't really blame her, I usually asked the new girl to take it out.

Plus, the bag was only halfway full.

The heat of his stare locked onto my back. I yanked the bag free from the bin and tied the drawstrings.

"I can help," he offered.

I risked one glance from lowered lashes, and instantly wished I'd hadn't. Had he been waiting for me to look his way? Hoping for a magical moment for us to share?

Our eyes connected for two long seconds and the world stopped spinning. Desire and hot, heavy want filled the space between us.

He called to me and my soul longed for him.

Soul?

Wake the hell up and smell the Rosies.

That boy is off limits!

"No thanks." I ran out the side door as fast as my feet could carry. I stayed outside until I watched his car pull away.

***

With a little luck and a lot of caution, I'd successfully avoided Adam for a full week.

I knew I had to be extra careful running from class to class on campus. He was an agriculture major, and I had two science classes. My chances of hiding forever were slim to none.

Unfortunately, I was running a bit late for my early anatomy class, so I rushed down the sidewalk without a second thought.

Soccer_Hottie: Good Morning Beautiful

My phone vibrated in my pocket. When I paused to answer it, I couldn't stop the smile that stretched across my face.

Fiesty_Rose: Hola handsome.
Soccer_Hottie: When do I get to see your sexy face?

Flames rushed to my cheeks. I wanted to meet him. Soon.

But what if he didn't like me in person? What if I wasn't as beautiful in real life as I was in my pictures?

Screw that!

I'm hot as hell and he'd be lucky to have me in his life.

Soccer_Hottie: My place Saturday.
Soccer_Hottie: Come.

I imagined he whispered the word into my ear, in bed, right before a big release overcame my whole body. A chill spread through my arms and legs. It left my knees a little wobbly.

"Are you okay?" Strong arms wrapped around my center.

Huh?

I hadn't realized I'd closed my eyes.

I opened them to find my hands clinging to Adam's Biceps like my life depended on him to carry me forward.

"Adam?" I shook my head, trying to shake off the shock of his touch. "What are you doing?"

He blinked too fast. "You were about to pass out. Are you feeling okay?"

I did?

Crap!

But, how had I ended up in his arms?

"Did you eat breakfast today?" He ducked down to examine my face closely.

Why was he still holding me? Why did it feel so, natural?

"Rosie?" Adam ran his hands up and down my arm and I cursed myself for the way my body responded to his.

With one touch, he could calm me down completely.

I nodded. "I'm okay. I guess I forgot to eat breakfast."

He picked me up bridal style.

"Bájame pendejo. This is ridiculous!" I mustered the energy to swat at his arms.

He set me carefully on a bench nearby.

I'm going to be late for my class.

He kneeled down in front of me and slid his backpack off his back. He rummaged around for a few seconds before freeing a small package wrapped in tin foil.

"All I have is a bacon, egg and cheese biscuit. Should help you feel better, though." The smell of bacon kissed my nose. He handed me the package with a stupid smile that sent that goofy, familiar blush back to my face.

"Thanks." I unwrapped the foil and took a bite.

"I've been looking for a moment alone with you." He stared down at the groun.

Alone?

Why does he want to be alone with me?

I hoped he wasn't looking for a repeat of our spring break trip to the beach.

"Wh-Why?" I fumbled the words.

"I wanted to talk about that night on our trip."

Oh, no. Was it not as good for him as it was for me.

A million fears rushed through my mind.

"When I woke up the next day, you were gone." He picked at an invisible piece of lint on his shirt.

"Oh." I took another bite.

If my mouth was full, he couldn't expect me to say anything. *Right?*

"I just wanted to make sure you're okay with everything that happened. Things have been kind of weird between us since we got back." Why couldn't he look at me?

It didn't feel like shame or embarrassment. Worry, maybe?

He took a deep breath. "I just don't know where we go from here."

Where we go?

Where do you want to go? *Por favor diga en algún lugar que tenga más de estas galletas.* It had to be one of the best breakfast sandwiches I'd ever had.

I stuffed my mouth as full as I could.

He chuckled. "You've got a little biscuit under your lip."

Adam reached up with his thumb to caress my cheek. Stupid me, I leaned into his touch, desperate for more.

My phone pinged.

I ignored it and rested my cheek against Adam's hand.

Adam's phone chimed. "That's my alarm for class. Can I meet you later?"

He pulled his arm back and heaved his backpack back onto his shoulders.

"I have to work." I glanced down at my phone.

Soccer_Hottie: Pick you up at nine.
Soccer_Hottie: Be ready for me.

"Maybe another time." Adam leaned down, placed a lonely kiss on my forehead and the whole world stopped.

Like nothing had happened, he walked away.

My heart pounded against my chest. All the calm I'd felt when he was close, vanished.

His dark washed jeans and long white t-shirt turned into a blur. A strong, built, sexy as sin blur that I wanted more of, but seemingly couldn't have.

His best friend dated my best friend. That had to be against some crazy unwritten girl code somewhere.

And what if we built a relationship and then it went south? That would be a disaster. It would destroy Grey.

If Adam and I broke up, Grey would have to pick a side. So would Chase. What if she chose mine and he chose hers? Would they fight because of us?

She'd already been through so much drama with Chase. I couldn't be the reason for more animosity.

I guess I should have thought about all of that in my tequila haze on our beach trip. I should have played out the break-up scene before I crawled into bed with Adam.

But he kissed me this time.

This time, the responsibility is on him.

He ignited the fire.

Not me.

What did that kiss mean to him? To me?

He asked me where I thought we should go next, but he didn't tell me what he wanted.

What did I want?

My phone chimed again.

Soccer_Hottie: Wear a dress. Red is my favorite color.

I took a deep breath to steady my nerves.

What the hell had I gotten myself into?

CHAPTER 3

"Why are you out of breath?" Grey adjusted the strap of her apron.

"Today's been a disaster. I've been running late all day. We had a surprise quiz in chemistry, Adam kissed me, and I got a parking ticket." I clocked in on the closest point of sale system.

"You're not just gonna breeze through that thing with Adam like it didn't matter, are you?" She adjusted the bobby pins In her high knot.

It wasn't that big of a deal. He kissed me, so what? It was a sweet little forehead kiss, and it wasn't the first time we'd kissed.

Hopefully, it won't be the last. I scowled at my inner conscious.

I shrugged.

"Nope. Not gonna happen. Spill the tea." She shook a packet of green chai tea in the air.

I smiled. "It was just a quick forehead kiss."

She gasped.

I rolled my eyes and walked around the counter into the empty coffee shop. We still had some time before our afternoon rush.

Grey poured two glasses of water and followed me to a corner table.

"Forehead kisses are the cutest. You know, I think he's really into you." She took a sip of water and handed me the other cup. "Hydrate before the rush hour."

I knew he was interested in me.

That was part of the problem.

If I had a list of all the things I wanted in a guy, he would check every box—body of a Greek god, confident, smart, sweet, kind.

People looked up to him.

And apparently, he wanted me as much as I wanted him.

"I know," I whispered.

"What's holing you back?"

You.

Chase.

Our friendship.

"Well, there's this guy I met online." As soon as I mentioned the dating app, Grey released a long exasperated sigh.

"Ni siquiera lo conoces. What the hell, Grey?" How could she be so judgey? Soccer Hottie was different than the other jerks. I could feel it.

"Fine! What do you know about this guy?" She crossed her arms and leaned back in the chair.

"He plays soccer for our university. He's a junior. He's having a party this weekend and he invited me." I spoke with confidence and a little hope.

"Uh huh. What's his name?" *Damnit Grey!*

"Un nombre no es tan importante. Te mostrare." I pulled out my phone to text him. His name didn't matter to me.

Well, it did, actually. We hadn't gotten to that step yet.

We were taking our time getting to know each other, twenty-four question style.

Feisty_Rosie: if you're going to pick me up, I need to know your name.

"Hah! You didn't even know his name. How much can you really know someone you just met online?"

"You're not my mother." I jumped up from the table and rushed back to our workstation.

I tinkered around with the machines and cleaned the counter, for real this time.

Soccer_Hottie: Mateo

"Look," Grey started as she walked to the counter, "I'm worried about you."

"His name is Mateo. Stop worrying and give him a chance." I wrung out the rag and hung it over the sink.

Grey uncrossed her arms.

Usually, I was the overprotective one.

When had the roles switched?

"Let's make a deal." Grey waited until she had my attention. "I'll give Mateo a chance if you give Adam a shot, too."

What? Did she know what the break-up between Adam and I could lead to? Hadn't she considered it?

"Then we can double date." She winked.

I giggled. Why couldn't we double date if I ended up with Mateo? He was an athlete, too? Chase and Mateo would have tons to talk about.

"You know, we never really talked about what happened between you and Adam over spring break," Grey said and all of the air in the room disappeared.

The temperature rose at least two thousand seventy degrees.

What happened?

Could I tell her that after our night out with the girls, I came back to the house with Adam? Or that after everyone else went to sleep, he and I hung out for hours?

Should I tell her we took shots of tequila until all the bottles were empty?

***

Spring Break

"You're beautiful," he'd said after tucking my hair behind my ear. His voice was deep and filled with seduction.

"You're not so bad yourself." I ruffled his hair, thankful all the gel he'd put in it came off in the ocean.

He dropped his head on my shoulder.

"You smell so good," he slurred.

My off the shoulder blouse left the warmth of his skin pressed directly against mine.

Desire clouded my mind.

His nose rubbed against my neck, and I didn't try to hide the moan.

His touch ran up and down my neck from my ear lobe to my collarbone.

I pressed into his gentle touch. Anticipation swirled deep in my core.

"I want a taste." He groaned against my skin.

Yo también quiero eso.

"Do it," I whispered.

His lips skimmed my collarbone. Subtle kisses turned into teasing, mesmerizing laps.

"So good." He nibbled on my ear.

I clung to the timber in his voice and the dark, desperate sounds he made with each movement.

His touch left me hanging on the border of losing control or demanding to take it.

Without disconnecting his lips from my body, he stood in front of me. His hand dug into the velvet upholstery behind me.

I closed my eyes and leaned back.

The room started spinning.

Was it the alcohol making me dizzy, or him?

"Wait." I pressed on his hips.

He took a step back. How was he so attuned to all of my needs?

His chest heaved up and down. "What's wrong?"

There was something in the way he asked that turned me on even more than his kiss. Was it care or compassion? I didn't really know what to call it or why, but en el nombre del Padre, del Hijo y del Espíritu Santo, I needed to find out.

Fast.

"Could you get me some water?" I asked.

"Of course." Adam ran, literally, to go to the kitchen and back.

He handed me a glass of iced water.

"Thanks." I took a sip to calm the crazy storm in my heart.

"I'm sorry I went too far." He held my gaze until I looked away.

I finished the rest of my water in one gulp. "Screw it. Me voy a ir al infierno"

Faster than I probably should have, I dove into his lap, threaded my hands into his hair and slammed my lips against his.

His thumbs traced my spine and moved over to the arcs of hips, massaging them in slow, sensual circles.

I pressed forward, deepening our kiss, taking what I wanted.

His fingers dug into my hips and guided me, rocking me against the length growing in his pants.

I shifted my hips, grinding deeper into him. "Your stupid jeans are in my way. Quítatelos."

He must have taken a few Spanish classes, because he stood up with me in his arms.

My legs automatically wrapped around his waist and my lips reconnected with his.

The taste too sweet to let go.

He carried me to his room and threw me against the bed.

His eyes connected with mine. A bead of sweat glistened against his forehead. He bit his bottom lip.

Agonizingly slow, he pulled off his shirt. The hard plains of his abs made my mouth water. My fingers itched to trace all the lines.

His hands moved to his zipper and my heart skipped a beat.

I sat up on the bed. "I want to do it."

With a nod, he moved closer.

I shoved my fingers into his boxers and tore off both layers in one quick swoop.

"You like it rough?" He cocked his head. "Can't say I'm surprised."

With a wink, I jumped up and shoved him on the bed. "You'll have to wait and see."

Just as slowly as he had done, I pulled my shirt over my head. He gasped when I tossed my skirt to the floor.

I walked over to my purse and grabbed a condom.

Our bodies connected in a sultry rhythm.

His muscles contracted beneath me. My hands roamed all over the places they'd begged to go before.

For one night, the dreamy quarterback every girl on campus wanted belonged to me.

"Mine." I claimed him in the heat of the moment.

"Yes." His teeth clamped down on my nipple.

A scream snuck out of my throat and into the space around us.

He flipped me over and we danced beneath the sheets. A never-ending party of two lovers tangled up in each other, reaching the highest of highs over and over and over again.

Breathless and satisfied, we collapsed beside each other, lost in the passion of the night.

But when the sun rose, everything changed. I woke up in his bed, naked and confused. I questioned all the decisions I'd made and the effects they'd have on the people I loved.

Adam and I?

We could never happen for too many reasons to name.

So, like any other college girl after a night of shame, I wrapped myself in a towel, grabbed my clothes and snuck out of the room before he noticed I was gone.

I couldn't tell Grey all the juicy details of that night with Adam. I wasn't sure how to process that night on my own. How could I expect anyone else to do something I couldn't?

I could, however, learn more about Mateo.

I knew he played soccer for UGA and he lived on campus. That was pretty much it.

So, when our shift ended and we made it back to our house, Grey and I piled around the desk in my room and powered on my laptop.

We started on the college athletic page on the main campus website. I clicked on the team photo but couldn't really tell who was who. Instead, scrolled through the individual player photos.

"Ah-ha! Mateo Rodriguez!" I'd found him.

"That is some next level super spy shit." Grey looked over my shoulder.

I tried to shield the screen from her, but she swatted my hand away.

"Well, he is kind of cute," she shrugged.

"Hey!" Chase called from the living room.

"In a weird skinny soccer player kind of way." She laughed.

Once I had his full name, I moved to all the social media channels, starting with the Book of Faces.

"You really think he's on that platform? It's so old school." Meghan Grace leaned in closer to my computer.

I picked at the cuticle on my nails while we waited for the page to load.

Butterflies fluttered in my core.

What is wrong with me?

What did I really have to be nervous about?

"Wow! He does have a Book of Faces profile. Scroll down already." Grey snatched the mouse from me.

She'd moved so close to my laptop, I could barely see the screen.

Grey shook her head. "Who is that? Seriously, Rosie? I don't think this is going to work."

"All I see is your big fat head. Gah! Move." I shoved her aside.

All it took was once glance at the photos for my jaw to hit the floor.

A silent beat passed between Grey and I.

Page after page was covered with pictures of Mateo, but he wasn't alone. Each pose was different, and the outfits changed to reflect the season, but the same two people were in every photo.

Mateo and a dainty little Latina princesa, covered my screen.

Her nails were long and manicured. Her hand pressed against his shoulder or his chest in every damn picture.

Her jet black hair was longer than mine.

Shinier, too.

Bet that Cherry colored lipstick cost more than my entire bag of make-up. *Lord, the things I would give to have lashes as long as hers.*

I wouldn't have stood a chance if I tried to compete with her.

"Who is she?" Grey and I asked at the same time. Only, Grey asked with confidence, like the unknown girl had trespassed into her space.

My words were small next to Grey's.

Game day with my biggest fan.

I read the commentary in the post. The posts seemed so vague.

Your support means the world to me.

Her name wasn't tagged in any of the photos.

I searched for a link or a name or a profile.

Something—anything to learn more about the woman in all of his pictures.

"Adam is looking better already." Grey tapped my shoulder.

"Yeah, he is!" Chase stuck his head into the door frame and then popped back out of the room.

Feliz Navidad! From us to you.

Us.

The word sunk painfully low.

Whoever she was, she was part of him in some way. For some girls, that would have been an immediate turn off. Most people would have walked away and crossed him off their list of eligible bachelors.

For me, it was another look at something that I didn't have, but really, truly wanted.

No one had taken a photo of me and called me his biggest fan.

I'd never taken a holiday photo with anyone other than my family.

I wanted that. Someone who would wear matching outfits and pose with me on a rustic bridge or a field of sunflowers. Didn't I deserve a guy who was proud to have me on his shoulder.

Someone who wanted to tell the world about me.

"Look!" Grey interrupted my personal pity party.

"This restaurant keeps coming up in a lot of the photos. See the sign?"

I zoomed in on the photo. "Isn't that the Mexican Restaurant off Tillman Road?"

"I think so." Grey pecked away at her phone. "It's only about 10 minutes away."

I snorted. "What? You're not really suggesting we go there, are you?"

Right... Great idea, Grey. Let's walk right through the front door and demand answers.

"Well, it is dinnertime, and you're acting a little hangry." Grey placed a hand on her belly.

I popped a brow.

"Fine. I just want to be nosy. Remember our last restaurant fiasco?" Grey reminded me of the time we ran into her high school bully at the mall last summer. She happened to be our waitress, and I had her mascara running down her cheeks before the appetizer touched the table.

I shook my head. "No. Bad idea."

"Why? We're just two girls getting dinner after a busy school day. No one will know why we're really there." Grey smile mischievously.

I would know.

She would know. "What about Chase? Wasn't he planning to take you out?"

"Nope." Chase poked his head back into the door. "Coach called the starting offense in for a quick meeting. Good luck. Take pictures of the cat fight, Grey."

He kissed her cheek and said goodbye.

Before I could protest, Grey grabbed her keys.

The pit in the bottom of my stomach swirled in endless circles.

I tried to picture how our little lunch trip would play out. No matter how hard I tried, it didn't end well for me.

How could it?

CHAPTER 5

If my life had a playlist, the score from Star Wars, or maybe Jaws would have followed me into that restaurant.

If I closed my eyes and listened carefully, I'd hear my great abuela screaming for me to run the other way.

"Here. Add an extra layer." Grey handed me a tube of bright red lip gloss.

I only threw a little shade before I snatched the gloss and ran the brush across my lips. "Better?"

"Yep." She popped the damn p and I'd never wanted to slap her more in my life.

"Haven't we been here before?" I asked, remembering a chicken dish I'd ordered before. "Pretty sure I got sick the last time we ate here."

Grey opened the door. "Maybe. We're already here, though. No turning back now."

A cheerful petite brunette lead us to a small booth in the middle of the restaurant. Another woman dropped off chips, salsa and two glasses of water.

"Hola mija." The waitress spoke directly to me, ignoring Grey. "Amora cuidará de ti."

"What did she say?" Grey stretched across the table when the woman walked away.

"Our server's name is Amo—" I stopped when a man carrying a sizzling fajita skillet passed.

The mouthwatering fragrance of sautéed peppers, onions, and succulent beef tackled my senses. My stomach growled. "I didn't realize I was hungry."

"I could devour some fajitas right now. With sour cream and a little cilantro sprinkled on top." She dunked a chip in salsa. A dollop of sauce dropped onto the table.

"Tu Madre's is better." Grey took another bite.

I smiled at her attempt to try to speak a little Spanish. She'd been working on a few words and phrases.

I swallowed hard. My stomach would start eating itself if I didn't eat soon. I scooped a big glob onto a chip and overfilled my mouth.

Bad idea.

"Hola mi amigas." A high pitched, perky as hell, princessa practically skipped to our table.

"Hi." Grey smiled way too big and too damned bright.

I slammed my jaw together, crunching all the sharp bits of chip into my gums.

"I'm Amora. You look familiar. Are you students at Southern?" When she spoke, she bounced and her stupid black top exposed two inches of midriff.

Black lace peeked out from the low cut V-neck t-shirt, and I wanted to spit my mouth full of salsa at her.

Grey kicked me under the table. *Hard.*

What the hell? I shifted my snarl to Grey.

"We are." Grey rested her arms on the table. How could she look so calm?

Oh, that's right.

Her relationship wasn't hanging on the line.

Just mine.

"Is this tap water?" I pushed the cup away.

Grey kicked me a second time, and I gave her a "kick me one more time and I will snatch that leg out of its socket so fast you won't even have time to blink" glare.

"I think so. Would you prefer something else?" Princessa smiled like she had a heart of gold.

Made me sick to my stomach.

I opened my mouth to give a list of demands but Grey cut me off.

"This is fine. Could we order some queso and the chicken fajitas platter with all the yummy side things, please?"

As soon as the waitress turned to walk away, I kicked Grey under the table.

"Ouch!" She yipped. "What the hell was that for."

"For kicking me. Twice," I whisper yelled.

"You were about to make a fool out of yourself. You don't know who she is to him. It could be his best friend from grade school. Maybe they're cousins."

Yeah... kissing cousins.

I rolled my eyes and crossed my arms.

The booth became more uncomfortable with every passing minute. The wood carvings on the back of the bench looked fancy, but the tiny grooves pulled on my ponytail anytime I moved.

"Whatever." I took a sip of water.

What the hell was I doing? Why had I let her talk me into coming to this restaurant.

My stomach growled.

I avoided conversation and any form of eye contact with Grey. It wasn't too hard since her phone went crazy with notifications. Guessing by the giggles and smiles, Chase's meeting ended early.

Must be nice to have someone special in your life. Someone to talk to you while you wait for your food, to cheer for, to love.

Maybe I'd find that one day.

Hell, maybe I already had.

People talk about fate, like everyone is destined to be with one person for all of eternity. My mom says everyone has a soulmate—one true love like in the fairytale movies.

Out of all the people in the world, how was I supposed to find the one person made for me?

What if that person was Mateo, who was Amora?

Something deep in the back of my mind scream, *"What if it's Adam?"* I tried to silence that part of me. There was too much at risk with him.

Or maybe I'm just making excises because I'm afraid he won't care for me the way I might for him.

What I'm so distracted by these two guys that it takes me too long to find my real soul mate? Would he still be waiting for me, or when I did find him, would there be another woman, like Amora, in his arms?

How would I recover?

Walk away and kiss my only chance goodbye? Would I settle for someone else?

Fight for his love?

Absolutely not.

That's not me… if he loves me, it will be him that has to prove how much he cares. He'd have to earn his shot with me. Not the other way around.

But what if I wanted him to fight for me and he didn't?

CHAPTER 6

"Did someone order fajitas?" I heard the sizzle before her high pitched voice.

"Smells amazing." Grey's eyes grew three times their normal size.

There was so much steam I couldn't see any of the food on the plate.

"Smells burnt." I scowled and waved away the smoke.

I started coughing loud, dry, fake as hell, coughs that the whole restaurant probably heard.

I grabbed at my throat, milking every drop of agony written on Amora's face.

Grey quietly shook her head. "She's fine."

"Drink some water." She shoved my glass to the edge of the table. *Jerk!*

If only my eyes could throw shade at my friend and Amora at the same time.

"If you're not happy with the fajitas, I can have the kitchen remake it." She didn't shift her hips or cross her arms. She maintained an innocent angelic smile.

"We'll be fine. Thank you." Grey dismissed Amora.

"She's been nothing but nice to you. We're here to get information, not act like a petty petra." Grey pulled a tortilla out of the canister. She stabbed some chunks of chicken and peppers with her fork and placed them on the tortilla. She drizzled more than enough cheese and sour cream over top.

I stole a chip and watched in awe as she shoved the overflowing fajita into her mouth.

"Desacelerar. No se te va a escapar. I swear I can't take you anywhere." I nibbled on a chip.

"Me? You're the one acting like a spoiled brat." Grey took another bite like her comment was everyday common knowledge.

It wasn't, and she knew better.

"Whatever. Esta fue una mala idea." I grabbed my bag, moved to the edge of the bench, and planted my feet to stand up and walk out.

I knew this was a bad idea.

"Hola amigas." Mateo, in all his glory, blocked my exit path.

A familiar flutter buzzed along my skin.

My heart skipped a beat. Or two or three.

Our eyes met, but his shifted too soon.

"Amora said you weren't happy with your fajitas." Why did the first thing he said to me have to include *her*.

My heart and brain battled against each other. It wasn't the time or the place, my brain reminded me.

The organ beating in my chest demanded otherwise... *Right here. Right now. Tell me everything. I need to know who she is to you.*

Mateo set a plate of freshly made fajitas on the table then ran his hands through his dark brown hair.

"Don't I know you?" The million-dollar smile from all his photos stretched across his face. His lips were thin and soft and I wanted to run my finger along their edges.

"Sort of." My confidence wobbled.

"Grey." Chase?

What the hell? Guess his meeting really did end earlier than expected.

Grey slid into the booth, making room for Chase to slide in beside her.

Oh, no! No. No. No.

Donde hay uno siempre hay dos. Please tell me he's alone.

"Rosie." Adam.

This is not happening.

I've never wanted to be more invisible than I did standing in that restaurant. I was surrounded by people I knew. My best friend, her boyfriend. Adam. Mateo.

Yet, I felt so alone.

Adam High fived Mateo in some stupid bro hug greeting. "Sup, Mateo! You coming to the party after our game this weekend."

Mateo and Adam knew each other? Of course they did. Statesboro is a small town, and their both athletes. I should have predicted that they would at least have heard of each other.

"Can't." Mateo's glance shifted from Alex to me. He winked. "I've got a hot date planned."

I sat down before I toppled over.

Something in the room shifted. Not sure what, since I was still in shock. A shock that only intensified when Adam followed me into the booth, wrapped an arm around my shoulders and kissed the top of my forehead.

Mateo shrugged. "I'll grab two more waters."

I shrugged Adam's arm off me. He didn't fight it. He just let it fall with a small, sad smile, which made me wish I hadn't pushed him away.

As fast as my emotions had changed when Mateo walked in the room, the tiny hints of heartbreak on Adam's face knocked the breath out of me.

I grabbed my chest.

Adam took my plate and topped it with peppers, onions and chicken. He added a few chips on the side and slid it in front of me.

"You need to eat." Adam whispered so only I could hear.

When he sat next to me, my heart steadied. When he kissed my head, my mixed emotions melted away. How did he have so much control over me? When had I given him permission to weasel his way into my life?

"You'll be there, though. Right?" He asked.

"Huh?" Where did he expect me to be?

"At the party. You'll be there. Right?" He asked again. Though if I wasn't mistaken, he was begging me to go with him.

Not just to the party.

This was his way of asking me out. I could feel it in my bones. He wanted more than just one night.

And when I looked up at the smile that hardly touched his cheek and his glossy eyes, I couldn't refuse.

Silently, I nodded.

Because words would not escape me.

CHAPTER 7

The night before the big party, I locked myself in my room.

I had a decision to make, and it weighed heavy on my heart. I'd told Adam I would go to his after party. But I also told Mateo I would have dinner with him.

The Robert Frost poem came to mind. The one where two paths rested in front of me. A soccer hottie I barely knew represented one path, the famous quarterback I knew too well on the other.

Both choices scared me a little.

The risks were big. If I picked Mateo, I'd lose Adam and vice versa.

Even deeper than that, if I picked wrong, I'd end up heartbroken.

A knock came from the door.

Grey knew I needed space, but it was dinner time. She was probably stopping by to check on me.

When I opened the door to find Adam standing there waiting for me, my heart sunk. Tears welled in my eyes.

He brushed them away with his thumbs. "Don't cry."

He pressed his forehead against mine and I let it all out. All the fears I'd bottled up for way too long streamed down my cheeks.

"Hey." He pushed my chin up. "Talk to me. Let me fix this for you."

I hiccupped. He was perfect. So incredibly perfect in all the right ways.

Too good for me.

"What is it, baby?" He called me baby and I crashed into him. My whole body fell against his.

"I don't want to worry anymore." I finally pieced a few words together, though, I'm not sure they really shared the thoughts I wanted to express.

"What are you worried about?" He led me into the room and shut the door behind us.

I dropped onto my bed and pressed my face into my palms.

"Rosie. Eat first. Then we'll talk." He handed me a brown bag that smelled amazing.

Nodes of fresh garlic and Italian herbs hit my nose before I opened the container.

"Alfredo. I used my mom's recipe." He pulled a fork out of the bag.

Guilt mixed with the pasta in my stomach.

How could I sit here and let him take such good care of me, if I'm not really sure I want to be with him.

"Do you believe in fate?" I asked after a few quiet minutes.

"I don't know. Maybe. I think sometimes the thought of fate puts too much pressure on people to fall in love. Love doesn't always hit people fast and hard." He cracked open a can of soda and handed it to me.

"I guess I hadn't thought of it like that." I took another bite.

"My parents were friends first. My mom didn't agree to go on a date with my dad for years. Then one day, she was ready. They've been together ever since." His smile dried up all my tears.

"You're right. It is a lot of pressure." I sipped on the soda.

"Is there anything I can do?" He leaned back on my bed. His arms flexed under the weight of his body.

"Keep being you." I pressed my forehead against his and he wrapped his arm around me.

Being in his arms felt natural and safe.

Why was I so confused about my feelings for him?

I couldn't use Grey as a reason not to be with him. She wanted us to be together.

"There's my happy girl. I knew she was in there somewhere." He kissed the tip of my nose.

With Adam, time stood still. Nothing else mattered. When I stopped to think carefully about the choices ahead, I realized my heart only wavered, when I worried what would happen if he broke my heart.

My phone chimed. "Could you hand me that? My mom calls every Friday before a game. I can't miss her call."

Adam reached over and paused before he handed it to me.

He looked at the screen and gave a subtle nod.

He handed me the phone and walked to the door.

"Good luck at your game tomorrow." Heartbreak rimmed his eyes. It was the last thing I saw before he walked away.

When I looked at my phone, the hair left my lungs.

Soccer_Hottie: Hey, beautiful.
Soccer_Hottie: Can't wait to you tomorrow.

The end is only the beginning!

***

Join my newsletter for updates on the rest of the story!

***

Enjoy the story? Be sure to leave a review!
And, catch up on the latest Meghan and Chase drama.

ABOUT THE AUTHOR

Jenna Fields writes small town college, sports romance for Creative Words Press, LLC. Her friends would describe her as a lover of chocolate, tequila connoisseur, and mompreneur. When she's not writing, Jenna travels the globe with her family. At each destination, she draws inspiration for her next story.

Whether it's a budding flame between the star wide receiver and his coach's daughter, or a sexy track star and her dreadful ex, she always adds a healthy dose of humor and heart to her work.

You may be familiar with Jenna's alter ego: USA Today and internationally bestselling author, Jennifer M. Miller.

Jenna's bookish idols are Lucy Score, for her witty banter, and Meagan Brandy, for her angsty characters.

Read More of Jennifer's Books:
Books2read.com/jennafields

MERENGUE AND MURDER

By D. C. Gomez

ABOUT *MERENGUE AND MURDER*

Creating memorable events was Julia's specialty. Unfortunately, even all her experience couldn't prepare her to handle her cheating ex crashing the party and the dead body. Family gathering can be deadly.

Enjoy this fabulous humorous fiction filled with quirky characters.

PART 1

The stale smell of cigarettes lingered in the air, making Julia's nose tingle. It was strange to have an establishment that still allowed people to smoke inside, but the Knight's hall was privately owned. On the first floor, they held membership functions, like bingo, but the public could rent the second floor. They made their own rules, and Julia was not complaining. It was one of the few halls in Salem that still allowed people to bring outside food. With a capacity of two hundred people, the cost of three hundred dollars a night was a steal.

She swirled her drink around for the tenth time that hour, closing her eyes to let the music vibrate through her body. It had been almost a year since the last time she danced. She missed getting lost to the beat, but she refused to be seen on the floor alone. For that matter, she avoided as many people as possible these last few months. Tonight was no exception. She leaned against the far wall next to the bar, in the back nook. The location was discreet and gave her a splendid view of the rest of the hall when she had her eyes open.

"Are you done nursing that drink? Or do you need a nipple for it?" a man whispered from behind.

Julia spun around, almost spilling the drink on the guy.

"Slow down now," Gabriel said. "Dumping it on me doesn't count as finishing it."

"What makes you think I had any intentions of spilling on you?" Julia replied, staring up into a pair of breathtaking hazel eyes. "This is actually my fifth for the night."

Gabriel had the rare combination of light-colored eyes and jet black hair. Unlike his siblings, who all had the traditional brown color, like most Dominican. His eyes sparkled every time he smiled, giving him the appearance of a mischievous little boy. His jacket fit perfectly to his body, highlighting his muscular physique. Julia didn't bother checking him out anymore. Gabriel always dressed to perfection. Gabriel let his eyes roam from Julia's lips to her drink, and just smiled.

"Is it now?" Without waiting for permission, he took the glass from her hand and drank.

"Give me that back," she ordered, almost in a low growl.

"I'm surprised it's only your fifth," Gabriel teased, handing her the glass. "I thought only ten-year-old's drank virgin Shirley Temple."

"And what might you be drinking tonight?" Julia took his glass, just like he had done.

"Representing the culture, of course. Rum and coke." He beamed, and Julia rolled her eyes.

"Either you're going extra light on the rum, or the bartender forgot to add it." Julia handed him the glass, glaring up at him.

This was something extremely hard for her to do, since Gabriel was at least six feet two inches tall. She was barely five eight, with her three-inch heels.

"It's the rocks, they melted," he pouted.

Julia had the urge to squeeze his cheeks, but held back. They had known each other since high school, and for over a decade Gabriel had teased her like they were fifteen. She hadn't seen him much since she started dating Ivan. Normally, Gabriel avoided the couple like the plague.

"Admit it, you're just jealous you didn't think about ordering one first?" Gabriel tucked one of Julia's curls behind her ear. The unruly one refused to comply with her hair style.

"God, you are so right." Julia dropped her head to her chest. "It never occurred to me to order a rum and coke. Light on the rum."

"It just needs to smell like it, and the rest of your crazy family will leave you alone," Gabriel offered.

"The good news is that I'm working." Julia pointed to the crowd. "They can't possibly expect me to drink and make sure this event runs smoothly."

Gabriel put his hand on her forehead, taking her temperature. "Did you forget how insane your family is? Speaking of nuts, here comes your aunt. I'm out."

"What?" Julia turned around to watch her favorite aunt Carla maneuver her way through the crowd. "Coward."

"Self-preservation is more like it," Gabriel told her. "Nobody needs a grilling from your family while they're drinking. If you actually needed a wingman, I would absolutely have your back. This is not the case."

Carla reached the pair, just as Gabriel was moving away. "You don't have to leave on my account."

"Going to check on my parents," Gabriel told her.

"I'm so glad they could make it," Carla told him. "You are looking fabulous, as usual."

"Never as good as you." Gabriel winked, making Carla giggle. "You still owe me a dance, trouble."

"What dance?" Julia replied, but Gabriel had joined the crowd a few feet away.

"You are dancing with Gabriel?" Carla asked, giving Julia side glances.

"I'm not dancing with anyone." Julia turned to face her aunt. "What are you looking at?"

"Your hair is gorgeous. Why do you have it in that bun?" Carla pulled on the pins holding Julia's hair in place, before she could escape her aunt.

"Stop that." Julia finally slapped Carla's hand away. "I like my hair up. It's always up every time I'm working."

"Yes, but you are not working," Carla reminded her. "This is your aunt's fiftieth wedding anniversary. You are allowed to not be an event planner all the time."

While Carla was Julia's aunt, they were only ten years apart. Julia's family on her mother's side was huge, with ten siblings, and too close in age for her comfort. Her father's side was just as big, with eight siblings. Julia was grateful her parents didn't follow that backwards tradition and only had two kids. She couldn't imagine dealing with six more sisters. One was plenty.

"Somebody has to make sure everything goes according to schedule," Julia defended herself, and sipped her drink to avoid eye contact.

"What schedule?" Carla asked. "We are forty-five minutes behind, and half of your uncles are not here. Have you ever been to a Dominican party where people were on time?"

"A girl can hope," Julia replied.

"And why are you wearing a suit?" Carla pointed at the black slacks and black jacket Julia was wearing over a blue blouse.

"I'm working," repeated Julia.

"You are hiding," Carla corrected her. "Girl! Don't make me drag you out of this corner. You better go out there and start . . . oh shit!"

Carla stopped talking as she faced the crowd. Her mouth dropped, and she glanced over her shoulder to look at her niece.

"Julia, please don't panic," Carla whispered, covering Julia from the crowd.

"What is going on?" Julia got on her tiptoes to look over Carla.

"I swear I don't know who invited him." Carla held Julia with both hands. "But you must keep it together. Do you understand?"

"For the love of God, what are you talking about?" Julia didn't have to wait long for a reply.

Carla moved out of the way and pointed toward the front of the hall. Walking down the main aisle was her ex, Ivan. The two-timing. Worthless, drop-dead gorgeous love of her life was heading toward her aunt and uncle.

"What is he doing here?" Julia was trembling.

"Julia, get it together," Carla ordered. "You are a professional, and you can't go out looking like this."

"What?" Julia was barely breathing, as her heart raced faster and faster each second.

"Let's go."

Carla dragged her around the corner of the bar, toward the adjacent stairs. Unlike most traditional halls where the stairs led up to one main entrance, this one had two. The stairs split in two on a small landing, allowing guests to enter from either the left or the right. It also made it convenient to make it to the bathroom from the bar without being seen. Carla and Julia went down the small stairs, across the landing, and up to the other side. As soon as they arrived on the other side, Carla shoved Julia into the women's bathroom.

"What are we doing?" Julia whispered.

"Making sure that asshole knows what he's missing?" Carla stated, as she pulled the pins out of Julia's hair.

"My hair is going to look like shit now," Julia complained.

"Girl, please!" Carla was busy tossing Julia's hair all over the place. "Give me some credit. I didn't spend fifteen years doing hair for nothing."

Carla searched the bathroom and found a can of hairspray. Julia glared.

"Who leaves hairspray in a public bathroom?" Julia tried to get away from her aunt.

"A. This is not a public restroom, it's a hall. B. I'm sure they have enough events here to be prepared. Now stand still." Carla held Julia's hair in place as she sprayed it down.

Julia held her breath. Last time they used this much hair spray on a human being, it was probably in the eighties. She was only thirty-one, and definitely not old enough to have lived through that torture period.

"Perfect," Carla announced five minutes later.

Julia's eyes burned from the fumes. Before she could complain, her aunt turned her around toward the mirror. She didn't recognize herself. Normally, Julia wore her hair in a ponytail or even a bun, but completely straight. She took painful hours to tame her curls out of existence. Today was not the case. Her curls were on full display. She looked like a Latina Farrah Fawcett.

"Oh my God." Julia reached for her hair.

"Don't you dare touch it!" Carla slapped her hand down. "Enough with the hiding and playing it safe. That asshole slept with your best friend. It's time you show him he is dead to you. Now take that off."

"Take what off?" Julia couldn't stop staring at her hair.

"That jacket." Carla pointed at her. "You are not working or selling insurance."

Before Julia could complain, Carla had pulled the jacket off.

"Oh, that is too sexy." Carla admired the sleeveless blue top Julia was wearing. "Thank God you didn't have one of those granny shirts you like to wear."

"I'm not going out there," Julia informed her.

"You have to," Carla explained. "They must make speeches. And since you are the event planner extraordinaire, that's your area of expertise. All you need is lipstick, and you have that boy kissing your ass."

"Do I want him kissing my ass?" Julia asked slowly.

"Best way to reject him is after he begs for forgives." Carla pulled a lipstick from her pocket and applied it to Julia's lips.

"You have pockets in that dress?" Julia forgot all about Ivan by the surprise fashion-sense of her aunt.

"Of course," Carla bragged, pulling out a small money pouch and a knife. "A woman can never be unprepared."

"If I knew dresses came with pockets, I would have worn them a long time ago," Julia announced.

"That's great." Carla did one last check of her niece before pulling her out of the bathroom. "I'll take you shopping next week. Right now, take your sexy little butt over there and get this party started. Just don't make eye contact with Ivan."

"I thought that was the reason we were doing all this?" Julia asked, looking around the hall.

"No," Carla explained, holding her niece with both of her hands. "We changed your look, so he knows you are not mourning around for him. You ignore the shit out of him, so he knows you don't need him."

"Why me?" Julia whispered, but adjusted her top and raised her head. "Make sure you don't lose that jacket. It's custom fitted, and I need it for work."

"Fine." Carla stepped back in the bathroom and grabbed the jacket. "I'm going to put it in this room here."

Not losing sight of her niece, she tossed the jacket inside the small storage closet. Julia shook her head but didn't argue. At least fifty more people had joined the event. They needed to get started before the fire marshal arrived and shut them down.

"Are you sure I look alright?" Julia asked.

"You look hot as hell, now go." Carla gave her niece a little push.

Julia held her head high and marched toward the front of the hall. The DJ stood on a small stage on the far right side. Julia heard murmurs as she approached the stage, but never looked at any of the guests. She would lose her confidence if she did.

This is just another gig. You have done this a thousand times. Be professional, Julia reminded herself.

The DJ smiled at her and handed her the mic. "All set."

"Thank you," Julia whispered back.

Pressing a few buttons on his switcher, the DJ turned on the microphone and the spotlights on Julia. For the first time, Julia was grateful for the blinding lights. She couldn't recognize anyone in the crowd.

"Good evening, *Familia,*" Julia announced, and the claps and shouts from her family and friends filled the hall. Julia smiled and waved at the rambunctious group.

"Thank you so much for joining us on this very special evening," Julia started her speech. Switching between Spanish and English as she introduced the honor guests, the reception court, and, of course, the main couple, her aunt and uncle, Rocio and Duran.

Julia had years of experience both setting up events, and even being the master of ceremony. She let that training take over and conducted the event with grace and charm. They played videos of the couple; speeches were made, gifts presented, and finally, the dinner announcement. After dinner, the couple would cut a cake, do a dance, and the formal part of the event would officially be over.

"Great job, honey," Julia's mother said.

Julia was handing the microphone back to the DJ when her mother spoke. The sudden praise was a shock. Her family was of that old school generation in the Dominican Republic, where praises were rarely given. They show their love by the things they did, not by what they said. Julia and her sister, Anita, had been working with their parents to become more expressive. This was the first time her mother praised her in public.

"*Gracias Mami*," Julia breathed.

"I'm so glad you changed," her mother added. "You were looking like an old lady."

Julia swallowed hard. The praises didn't last long. But at least she received one.

"Did you see who is here?" Her mother leaned in to tell her.

"Who?" Julia had a horrible fear she knew exactly who her mother was talking about.

"Oh Julia," her mother said. "He came over last night and was so sad."

"*Mami*." Julia couldn't find the words to start her argument. "Please tell me you didn't invite him?"

"He wants to apologize," her mother said. "He is so sorry and knows he made a horrible mistake."

"*Mami*." Julia took a deep breath.

"Julia," her mother cut her off. "You are not getting any younger. You are one of the oldest in your generation that is not married or with kids. God, you are not even seeing anyone."

"*Mami*, I need to check on the food." Julia rushed away before she said anything she would regret.

Tears threatened to escape her eyes, but Julia forced them back. She would not break down during the party. It was a bad idea to move back in with her parents. There was no escaping her mother's nagging remarks. But she had no place to go after the break-up. She had spent all her savings on the down-payment for the townhouse.

She hadn't even unpacked when she found them on her bed. Julia took another breath to force the images away. She would not torture herself again. This was not the day.

"Julia," she heard Ivan's voice. "You look beautiful."

Her stomach turn at the sound of his voice anymore. But she didn't have the mental strength to deal with him at this time. Without slowing down, she glanced over her shoulder.

"Sorry, I'm busy," she told him and kept on walking.

The line for the food was piling up, and Julia rushed to the back. Only a few of her cousins had volunteered to serve food. She wasn't surprised. Nobody wanted to do manual labor when they could talk with their friends. After figuring out where the bottleneck in the line was being created, Julia jumped in. Her aunt Carla was busy at the end, ensuring everyone took silverware and napkins. At least somebody was paying attention to details.

After a long internal countdown to settle herself, she plastered a smile on her face. Julia offered chicken or pork to the guests. With the speed developed after years of facilitating, she got the line moving again. Family members gushed about how beautiful everything was and asked for help for their next gathering. Julia made mental notes on how to decline at a later date. Helping her family translated to a lot of long hours for no pay, and endless arguing.

"Why the sudden change of outfit?" Gabriel asked, bringing Julia back to her post.

"Let me guess, you prefer this version better?" She handed him a piece of chicken thighs and a piece of roast pork without asking.

"Not really," Gabriel said. "It's not really you. I prefer the ponytail."

Julia blinked. Seventy percent of her days she wore the long ponytail, like the one Arianne Grande usually rocked. She enjoyed the way it bounced as she walked. She didn't even mind the curls on it at times. Nobody else in her family cared for it. They thought it made her look too young. She could please none of them.

"Can I get two chickens instead?" Her uncle Victor asked.

Julia had lost her flow, and the line was piling up again. "Of course you can."

"Actually, give me the chicken and the pork, and I'll come back for seconds," Victor changed his mind.

Julia glared and place the meat on his plate. This was not a surprise to Julia. Victor enjoyed being difficult. If he could complicate a situation, he would, or just instigate chaos.

"Are you going to serve drinks or do people have to get it?" Victor continued.

"The soft drinks are free at the bar," Julia told him. "Just send one of your kids to get one."

"You could have somebody serve drinks to the guests," Victor added.

"Probably," Julia said, trying not to roll her eyes. "But I won't. Walking is good for people."

Victor was only fifteen years older than her, and she had a hard time taking him seriously. While the man was book smart, he had no common sense. The desire to choke him was something she fought daily. How her mother managed was beyond her?

"Victor, *compadre*, the line is getting long. Would you mind?" Her dad encouraged his brother-in-law along.

Julia gave her dad a grateful smile as her uncle walked down the line.

"Don't listen to him," her cousin Carlos told her. "You know he's nuts."

"I know," Julia replied, giving him extra pieces of chicken.

"You did great, by the way." Her cousin squeezed her hand.

At least in her generation, compliments were not a foreign thing. "Thank you, sweetie."

"Oh no," Carlos stopped.

"What is it?" Julia asked, glancing down the line.

"Beto is here," Carlos informed, as he made his way toward the new arrival.

"What am I missing?" Julia asked.

"Nothing special," her father commented. "The same family soup-opera. One of these days, we should sell tickets to the show. Let's just hope they don't start fighting."

Julia followed the action on the other side of the table, as Beto and Victor stared each other down. Beto was in his thirties, with short black hair, and the family black sheep. With several children of his own, they knew him to be a player as well. Julia shook her head and prayed they didn't cause a scene. This would be a horrible way to mark this monumental occasion. It wasn't every day that people stay married for fifty years. Even her own parents had their rocky patch.

PART 2

Julia's feet were killing her. It had taken over an hour to finish with the food and the additional family photos. They still had the cake and dance. Dominican parties wouldn't take forever if people showed up on time. Julia wanted to explain that to the crowd, but nobody cared. Everyone was enjoying themselves. That was an enormous victory. Julia nibbled on a piece of chicken leaning on the wall behind the serving table, waiting for the next set of events.

"Dear, what time is it?" Her parents' old neighbor Lucia asked.

Julia searched her pants but realized her phone was missing. She didn't have a watch either.

"I'm so sorry, Lucia," Julia explained. "I do not know. I need to find my phone."

"Did you lose it?" Lucia asked, searching around the table.

"No, I think it's in my jacket," said Julia, trying to remember where she had seen her jacket last.

"I don't know how we survived without phones," Lucia said. "I still remember when we only had one phone in the house. And it was a land line."

Lucia was so old, she probably still remembered when TV was in black and white. But Julia decided it was safer not to point that out.

"Those were different times," Julia added politely.

"Life was less hectic back them." Lucia added a few more pieces of chicken to her plate. "People were less stressed and had more time to visit."

That was a different way of looking at those times.

"That is very true," Julia said. "Excuse me Lucia. Let me see if I can find my jacket."

Squeezing from behind the table, Julia made her way to the small closet. Before she could reach the hallway, Ivan stopped her.

"Julia, please. Could we talk?" He asked.

"Is there anything to talk about?" Julia folded her arms in front of her.

"You know I love you," he pleaded. "You can't throw away five years of a relationship over one mistake."

"One mistake?" Julia bit her lips to avoid raising her voice. "This is the last drop of mistakes. Did you honestly think I didn't hear all the humors about all the other girls you were messing with? The fact that you went after my best-friend was a low blow. I trusted you."

"I was drunk, and she came on to me," Ivan defended himself. "You know how she is."

"This is not the place." Julia shook her head and walked back the way she came.

"There you are," Carla said as Julia reached the bar area. "Have you seen Victor? We need him for pictures."

"I haven't." Julia thought about it for a moment longer. "I actually haven't seen him since we came up for food. He never made it for seconds."

"That's odd," Carla told her. "You know that boy loves to eat. What's wrong?"

Julia was wringing her hands and looking over her shoulder. "Nothing."

"Nothing looks very disturbing then," Carla pointed out. "What happened?"

"Ivan keeps wanting to talk," Julia confessed. "To make things worse, mother invited him. So he thinks a reconciliation is inevitable."

"Lord help us, no," said Carla. "That man is a snake. He hits on anything that walks. You saw it."

"I can see it now." Julia looked over her shoulder. "I just don't know if I'm strong enough to keep saying no all night. I'm tired."

"Julia, you better find your strength, or you're going to be stuck with that asshole for life," her aunt prophesied.

"I don't even want to think about it." Rubbing her temples, Julia turned toward the stairs. "I need to get my phone."

"Where is it?" Carla asked, following Julia.

"Hopefully in the jacket you threw in that closet." Julia pointed in the closet's direction. "I really hope my jacket is not all covered in dust."

"Oh, come on, don't be so dramatic," Carla told her, as they climbed the stairs to the other landing.

Julia glanced in the hall's direction, making sure nobody was on that side. The area was clear, and both women quickly climbed the rest of the steps. Julia opened the closet door, but the room was pitch black. She searched the side of the walls.

"What are you doing?" Carla asked.

"This room is a lot bigger than I thought, and I can't find a light switch." Julia stepped inside the room, searching around.

"Maybe there is a string hanging from the middle for the light," Carla offered.

"Why wouldn't they place the light switch by the door?" Julia shook her head in disgust. "Stupid old buildings."

Stepping further inside the room, Julia waved her hand around, searching for a potential light switch. Her feet slammed into something solid.

"Ouch."

"What is it?" Carla asked from the door.

"I kicked something." Julia bent over to inspect what was on the floor. "What in God's name?"

Julia rubbed her hand with what felt like cloth. But it was solid, like a leg.

"I found it!" Carla shouted from the door, turning on the light switch. "You were looking on the opposite side."

As the lights went on, Julia rubbed the leg of a stiffened body.

"Oh, God!" Julia shouted.

"Shit," Carla added, entering the room and closing the door behind her.

"What are you doing?" Julia jumped to her feet and stepped away.

"Making sure nobody sees that in case he's dead." Carla pointed at the body.

"If he is dead, we need to call the cops." Julia backed farther away from the body.

"Let's not jump to conclusions," said Carla. "Let's find out if he is dead first. Go check."

"Check? Who? Me?" Julia was getting ready to run out of the room. "I'm not getting near that man."

"How are we supposed to find out if he is alive?" Carla was pushing her niece toward the body. "I have no idea what I'm looking for."

"What makes you think I do?" Julia was holding to the door handle as Carla pulled her away. "We just need to call the cops now."

"And ruin Rocio and Duran's celebration, I don't think so," Carla announced. "Anyway, go and find out who it is."

"I'm not getting near it." Julia was going to bolt as soon as she got away from her aunt.

"Fine." Carla held Julia by the shoulders. "We will do it together."

Julia was not moving from the door, but Carla pulled her along. Julia took quick shallow breaths as the two of them got closer to the body. As they reached the stiff body, Carla pulled Julia down next to the body. Julia was trying not to puke, as her heart race increased. Cautiously, Carla poked the man in the side, but nothing happened.

"Hey, you," Carla said to the body. "Can you hear me?"

The body never moved. Holding tight to Julia's hand, she moved the body with her free hand. Blood covered the floor where the man had been.

"Ahhh." Julia pulled back, but Carla held her steady.

"Breath Julia," Carla ordered as she continued to turn the body to face them. "Oh God, it's Beto."

"Are you sure?" Julia stopped fighting and turned to look. "Oh, I'm going to be sick."

"Don't you dare puke in here," Carla demanded. "We are not having your DNA next to this body."

"DNA?" Julia looked around the room. "They are going to find our fingerprints everywhere."

"We were looking for a jacket." Carla pointed at the bundle in the corner. "We saw nothing and heard nothing."

"We can't just leave him." Julia's hands were shaking. "What if someone finds him?"

"Yeah, that would be bad." Carla pulled Julia to her feet. "Grab you jacket and let's get out of here. I have an idea."

Julia didn't care what crazy idea her aunt had. She just wanted to get out of the closet with poor Beto. Making sure she stayed as far away as possible, she grabbed her jacket. As soon as the material was in her hand, she jumped for the door, but Carla stopped her. Carla cracked the door open and looked outside. After peaking out and making sure nobody was around, Carla squeezed them out.

"Don't make a scene, and finish the rest of the program," ordered Carla.

"We can't just leave him there," Julia complained. "What if someone goes in?"

"Relax." Carla's hand betrayed her confident attitude as they shook. "I'll make sure nobody goes in. Go"

It took several gentle shoves to get Julia moving. Her hands were sweating, and she was lightheaded. Wiping the sweat on her jacket, she steadied herself and made her way to the DJ stand. Julia never heard the murmurs coming from the crowd this time, or noticed Ivan walking in her direction. She pushed past him like a zombie, never even stopping when he spoke. Dropping her jacket behind the DJ she took the mic.

"Julia," the DJ asked softly. "You are pale. Are you okay?"

Julia slowly raised her face toward him.

"It's been a long night," Julia mumbled. "I think my sugar dropped. Let's get this done so people can party."

Pasting her rehearsed smile on her face, she centered herself. Julia had performed ceremonies after finding out a wedding cake had been destroyed, the bride had destroyed her dress, or the groom was too drunk to stand. This was nothing different. Dead body in a closet, just another minor inconvenience.

Please don't puke. Julia prayed.

"Dear family and friends," Julia announced in her most cheerful voice. "It's time for cake."

The crowd exploded in applause. You could always make everything better with cake. She escorted her aunt and uncle to the cake table and assisted with the staging of the photo. This was her terrain. Julia could manage this with her eyes closed. The crowd had thinned out, but on the opposite side of the room she saw her uncle Victor. He looked a hot mess. His shirt was untucked, his tie crooked, and his wife glared at him.

As soon as the photographer was done, Julia handed the duties to cut the rest of the cake to one cousin. In a family of over one hundred cousins, it wasn't a problem to find a few capable ones to work. Before anyone could ask questions, she made her way toward her uncle.

"What is going on?" Julia asked as soon as she reached them.

"What else?" Amelia, Victor's wife, replied. "He knows he is not supposed to be drinking. What does he do? Sneaks outside with a drink and falls on the sidewalk."

"Lord," Julia exclaimed, examining her uncle closer.

Victor's clothes were covered in dirt, and he had a bruise on his head.

"That was a nasty fall." Julia leaned in closer. "How did it happen?"

"I wasn't drunk," Victor hissed at the two women. "I just tripped over the stairs going down."

"He tripped because he was sneaking off with the drink and trying to run away from the kids who found him," Amelia clarified. "You are lucky you didn't crack your head open and kill yourself."

"Yeah, let's avoid that," Julia told them. "Have you seen Beto?"

"God don't mention that one to me," Amelia answered. "He came in drunk and just started arguments with everyone. Alcohol is going to be the death of this family. Let's get you some ice."

Amelia dragged Victor toward the bar, leaving Julia with more questions than answers.

"What they aren't telling you is that he cried like a bitch," her cousin Angel said softly from her side.

"And you know this how?" Julia asked just as softly as she turned to face him.

"Jul, I saw the whole thing," Angel snickered.

Angel was only fifteen, but already taller than Julia. With big brown eyes, and curly brown hair, Angel had all the aunts wrapped around his finger. He was smart but played the role of the family prankster.

"Please tell me you had nothing to do with that fall?" Julia questioned her cousin, who was smirking like the big-bad-wolf.

"I'm totally innocent." Angel raised both of his hands in defense.

"You haven't been innocent since you could walk," Julia corrected him. "Why were you outside?"

"Don't tell my mom." Angel glanced over his shoulder.

"Spill it," Julia demanded, crossing her arms over her chest.

"I was meeting my girl, Laura, when *Tío* Victor showed up." Angel adjusted the buttons on his shirt. "I might have been hiding on the side of the building. It's possible that's why nobody saw me."

"Where is Laura?" Julia was relieved Angel hadn't pushed their uncle but wasn't planning to get him off the hook that easily.

"She never made it," Angel explained, pouting. "Her girlfriend couldn't get the car from her parents."

"The horror." Julia shook her head, trying not to laugh. "Did you see anyone else outside?"

"Not in the front," Angel continued. "In the back of the building, Beto and Carlos were doing one of their business meetings. They had a couple more guys with them."

"Did they see you?" Julia bit her lip.

"Jul, please." Angel rolled his eyes. "I'm a ninja. Now I must do my ninja magic and begone. I just took *Tío* Victor's phone. Let me see how long it takes for him to notice."

"You are evil," Julia said, but patted his shoulder. At least her younger cousin still used the Spanish word for aunt and uncle, *Tío* and *Tía*, when addressing his elders.

The dancing part of the party had started, and the DJ was blasting modern Merengue songs. Like many Dominican parties, age didn't play a role in the celebration. Mothers dragged their kids to the floor, and couples joined in. The dance floor was quickly filling up with happy partygoers. Julia was losing track of people, and she desperately needed to find her cousin Carlos.

As Julia scanned the crowd, she found her aunt Carla busy dancing away with her boyfriend. Julia bit her lip to avoid screaming and marched across the dance floor.

"I'm so sorry," Julia said, pulling her aunt away. "I just need to borrow her for a minute."

"I'll be right back," Carla told her date, who smiled at the two women walking away.

It didn't take long for a lonely dancer to keep him company. Carla only smiled as she watched her ten-year-old daughter dance with her future stepdad.

"What are you doing?" Julia said, trying to keep her voice under control.

"I'm dancing with my man. What does it look like?" Carla replied.

"You were supposed to be watching the closet." Julia pointed in the room's direction.

"It's fine." Carla waved her niece away. "I got Joel watching it."

"Joel? Joel who?" Julia asked, looking around the hall.

"What do you mean Joel who?" Carla glared. "Your cousin, my nephew, who else?"

"Oh, that Joel." Julia turned her aunt around to face the hall. "Like that one over there, stuffing his face with cake?"

"What the hell?" Carla shouted. "He was supposed to be watching the door."

"You asked the sugar addict of the family to do something when cake was being passed around." Julia rubbed her face to avoid choking her aunt. "Do you honestly not know your nephew?"

"Stop being overly dramatic," said Carla. "It's been less than ten minutes. What could possibly go wrong?"

"Besides someone finding the body in the closet?" Julia stared at her aunt.

"Julia, can we talk?" Ivan had made his way toward them.

"This is not a good time, Ivan," said Julia, but never looked at him.

"Let me go check on our friend," Carla told her. "I'll be right back. Handle this."

Carla took off toward the closet before Julia could complain. Julia could not afford for Ivan to follow her around. She took a deep breath and faced her ex.

"We really need to talk," Ivan repeated. "We have a house together."

"There is nothing to talk about," Julia said as she faced Ivan. "I transferred the house to you months ago. You have your ring back. We are through. Why are you even here?"

"We are meant to be together." Ivan reached for her hands, but Carla grabbed her arms.

"Sorry Ivan," Carla said, pulling her niece away. "I need to steal Julia." Carla whispered in Julia's ear, "Our friend is gone."

"What?" Julia grabbed her aunt, and this time she dragged her with her. "What are you talking about?"

"He is gone," Carla repeated, as they rushed toward the closet.

"*Tia*," a young girl called after Carla.

"Give me a minute, Gloria," Carla replied. "I'll be right back."

"This is horrible," Julia whined.

"Tell me about it." Carla smiled at the passing family before opening the closet.

"Hurry up," Julia pleaded.

Carla propped the door open and pushed Julia inside. The light was on and the room was completely empty.

"How is this possible? Where is the blood?" Julia asked as Carla closed the door.

"Are you seriously looking for the blood and not the body?" Carla walked around in circles in the small room.

"Yes," Julia replied, rolling her eyes. "Obviously, the body is gone. But it was covered with blood. Who takes a body and cleans up after themselves? How long were we gone?"

"Not long enough for people to clean," Carla replied. "Are you sure he was dead?"

"Maybe, I don't know." Julia shrugged.

"You are not sure?" Carla turned to face her.

"Shhh." Julia stopped her from talking. "Lower your voice. He looked dead, but I'm not a doctor. I'm an event planner."

"I was stressing all night over this, and he wasn't even dead." Carla covered her face.

"I'm glad you were worried about his health," Julia told her.

"Of course I was worried," said Carla. "But you also know Beto's reputation. He has issues with everyone. Finding out who killed him in this family would be a nightmare."

"It couldn't happen to a better person," Julia added, trying to keep the sarcasm out of her voice. "But now what do we do?"

"First thing, let's find out if anyone has seen Beto." Carla took Julia's hands. "Breath. He is not dead, and there is a logical explanation for this."

"I hope you are right." Julia took a deep breath and closed her eyes.

"Let's go," Carla whispered.

Julia nodded as Carla opened the door.

"What's going on?" Ivan asked as soon as the door opened.

"Are you spying on people now?" Carla chastised him.

"Julia and I were in the middle of something," Ivan clarified. "Just a bit suspicious about why you're hiding in a closet."

"When I need to give you an explanation about my actions, I'll let you know," Carla informed him. "Stay in your lane, little boy. I'll see you in a bit, Julia."

Carla pushed Ivan out of the way and headed toward the main hall. Julia crossed her arms and glared. She wanted to be searching the hall for Beto, not having never ending conversations with her ex.

"Ivan, what do you want?" Julia asked. "Why are you here?"

"I love you." Ivan reached for her, but Julia stepped back.

"You have a strange way of showing your love," Julia replied. "Please leave me alone."

"Nobody is going to love you like I do," he added.

"That's a blessing," she mumbled under her breath.

"Here you are," Gabriel said from behind Ivan.

Ivan turned to face the other man. Gabriel walked past him and wrapped his arms around Julia. Not sure what he was doing, Julia embraced him back.

"Are you done saving the party with your aunt?" Before Julia could answer, Gabriel kissed her.

The warmth of his lips stole her breath away. Gabriel had the right combination of strength and tenderness, making Julia lose herself in his touch.

Gabriel pulled away slowly. "You still owe me a dance."

"Yes . . . I do," Julia mumbled, staring into Gabriel's eyes.

"What the fuck is this?" Ivan screamed.

Gabriel moved Julia behind him and faced Ivan. "Last time I checked we don't owe you an explanation."

"Why are you kissing my girl?" Ivan demanded.

"Your girl?" Gabriel turned back to glance at Julia. "Are you still dating this fool?"

"Not at all," Julia answered.

"Are you planning to get back with him?" Gabriel continued, not taking his eyes off her.

"When hell freezes over," she said.

Gabriel turned to Ivan. "You had your chance, and you blew it. Get lost now."

"This is not your decision, it's Julia's," Ivan told him.

"Interesting." Gabriel wrapped his arms around Julia. "She has been telling you all night to get lost, and yet you don't want to listen. But now it's her decision? Julia, honey, what do you want to do?"

"There is nothing to do," Julia replied. "We are done Ivan, goodbye."

"Is there a problem?" Julia's mother asked, followed closely behind by Carla.

"Well, it seems Julia has finally moved on and someone is not getting the hints," Carla informed her sister, smiling at Julia and Gabriel.

"Mrs. Garcia, you know Julia and I are meant to be together," Ivan pleaded with Julia's mother.

"Ivan, dear," Mrs. Garcia said. "It seems you are a few months too late. I recommend you move on as well."

Ivan pouted but held his tongue. Mrs. Garcia glared at the man, who dropped his gaze.

"Good night Ivan," Carla dismissed him.

Not looking at either Julia or Gabriel, Ivan stomped away. Carla and Mrs. Garcia watched him leave before speaking.

"I expect a visit this week," Mrs. Garcia informed Gabriel.

"It will be my pleasure, Mrs. Garcia." Gabriel bowed his head at her.

Mrs. Garcia smiled at her daughter before heading back to the hall. Carla hugged Gabriel and then Julia.

"It took you long enough," Carla told them, and left behind her sister.

"Lord help me," Julia said. "Thank you, but you didn't have to. You are taking your wingman duties seriously."

"What makes you think I was being your wingman?" Gabriel raised her face with his hand. "You are a bit blind at times."

"What?"

"Julia." Gabriel kissed her again. This time slower, taking his time with her mouth. He pulled away from her, leaving her breathless. "I have been crazy about you for years. Our timing has always been off. Now that we are both free, I refuse to lose you again."

"Are you serious?" All Julia could do was blink at him. "You know how insane my family is."

"Just like mine." Gabriel smiled at her. "Would you give me a chance?"

"I don't know," Julia teased, but raised on her toes to kiss him. "But you are a great kisser."

"Yes, I am," Gabriel replied, and kissed her back. "How about that dance?"

"In a few," Julia answered. "My feet are killing me. Do you mind if we sit?"

"Of course." Gabriel took her arm and walked them over to one of the empty tables.

The older crowd had slowly cleared off, leaving the younger generations to enjoy the music. Gabriel and Julia sat next to each other, facing the dance floor. The DJ was mixing between merengue and bachata at a smooth beat. Gabriel took Julia's hand and kissed it.

"Are you ready for another drink?" Gabriel asked.

"I would love one." Julia smiled.

"Shirley Temple?"

"Of course," she giggled. "I'm not brave enough for a rum and coke yet."

"I'll be right back." Gabriel stood and headed for the bar.

"Pshh." Julia heard the sound from the table next to her.

Angel was sitting alone, holding a large newspaper in front of his face. Julia looked both ways before addressing her cousin.

"What are you doing? Where did you get that paper from?"

"Shhh," Angel ordered. "I'm undercover."

"Undercover?" Julia turned to face her. "You just look even more suspicious with that. What are you doing?"

"I have info on your boy?" Angel turned the page on the paper without looking at Julia. "I heard you were looking for him."

"What boy?"

"You know." Angel glanced in her direction, winking. "The missing Beto."

Julia stood straight in her chair. "What do you know? And how do you know I was looking for him?"

"I know everything." Angel laughed. Julia realized he was trying to give an evil laugh, instead he sounded like Kermit the Frog. Not the most impressive laugh.

"Angel, spill it before I go over there and shake you to death." Julia was channeling her mother's mean look. The one that had made grown men cry.

The effect worked as Angel winced.

"Relax, Cruella, you don't have to get all evil over there." Angel dropped the paper. "It seems poor old Beto got caught kissing another woman."

"Beto kisses everyone. What else is new?" Julia scanned the hall for a potential Beto victim.

"He got caught by his current girl," Angel dropped the newspaper and made a drum roll on the table.

"Beto has an actual girlfriend?" Julia's eyes were wide with shock. "That boy is a hoe. Who would be crazy enough to date him?"

"Maribel." Angel announced.

"Damn!" Julia covered her mouth. "She is going to kill him. That girl is a nutcase."

"Too late for that," Angel added. "It seems she hit him over the head with a bottle. Eyewitness said the scene was spectacular. I'm not sure where she dumped the body, but I'll let you know."

Angel left the paper on the table and waved at his cousin.

"The boy should get a career in journalism or the tabloids. He would make a killing," Julia said out loud.

"Are you talking to yourself again?" Her sister Anita said, as she embraced her. "Congratulations are in order."

Anita was the perfect daughter in her mother's eyes, always involved with the family. Her sister knew how to dress for every occasion and looked like a cover model. She got married in her mid-twenties and was expecting her first child.

"Where have you been all night?" Julia asked.

"Don't be changing the topic, this is not about me." Anita sat next to her.

"Right." Julia beamed back at her baby sis. "Does everyone know?"

"Of course!" Anita waved her hands around the hall. "Scandals in a Dominican family travel faster than lighting. The fact that two of the hottest men in town were getting ready to go to blows for you, *Telenovela* material. A Latin TV station would make a killing with that story."

"That's not funny." Julia punched her sister's leg. "But why did Ivan talk to mom, anyway?"

"Besides the fact that we throw the best parties in town, and he is no longer invited," Anita pointed out the obvious.

"Yes, besides that." Julia needed more. Something more tangible than the booze and the music.

"Maybe he heard the rumors," Anita mused.

"What rumors?"

"That mom was planning to give you the business as a wedding present." Anita leaned against her sister.

"What business? The hair salon?" Julia shook her head. "That's not a present, that's a nightmare. Why would anyone ever think that? Anyone that knows me, knows I can't do hair to save my life."

"We know that," Anita said. "But people believe what they want to. Especially if it comes from credible sources."

"Anita, what have you done?" Julia tapped her fingers on the table.

"It wasn't just me." Anita raised her hands in the form of a peace offering. "The *Tias* also helped."

"Why?"

"Because you had been mopping around like a schoolgirl over that loser." Anita leaned back in her chair, rubbing her pregnant belly. "We wanted to see what he would do if he knew you were getting a fortune."

"Were you planning to warn me about this?" Julia couldn't be mad at her sister.

"We were waiting for the right moment, but somebody beat us to the punch." Anita stood up as Gabriel joined them. "Hi big brother. Welcome to the family."

Anita kissed Gabriel on the cheek and waved at her sister.

"I still want to know where you were all night," Julia informed her, but Anita just waved.

"Do I want to know what that was all about?" Gabriel asked, taking the seat recently vacated by Anita.

"The usual," Julia answered. "Getting caught up on the gossip, intrigues, and fights that go on behind every large family."

"There is never a boring moment." Gabriel took her hands again.

"Not around here." Julia leaned her head on his shoulder. "It seems you have the seal of approval from my family. How is your family going to take it?"

"Considering my mother adores you," Gabriel kissed her forehead. "We will be lucky if they don't start planning our wedding tomorrow."

"That is a huge possibility," Julia admitted

"You don't sound worried." Gabriel stared into her eyes.

"If someone wants to plan our wedding, I say we let them." This time Julia kissed him.

"We are not even on our first date, and you are okay talking about our wedding. Interesting." Gabriel bit her lower lip when he finished.

"Why fight the madness?"

Julia did not know what the future would hold, but this time she wasn't planning to hide from it. She could feel the stares of her family and friends. The gossip mill was in full swing, and probably the entire city of Salem already knew. After years of caring what everyone thought, she was done.

"Are you ready for that dance?" Gabriel asked softly in her ear.

"Yes. Yes, I am." Julia took off her heels and held Gabriel's hand.

"Is about time."

They stood together and made their way toward the dance floor, as the crowd broke into cheers. Julia waved at her family and friends, as she embraced Gabriel. She closed her eyes and let Gabriel move them to the beat of a fast merengue. She would worry about the missing Beto and the rest of the drama tomorrow. Tonight, she would dance the night away.

The End... for now

***

Enjoy the story?
Please leave a review and stop by my website to get a FREE copy of
The Origins of Constantine.

ABOUT THE AUTHOR

D. C. Gomez is an award-winning USA Today Bestselling Author, Podcaster, motivational speaker, and coach. Born in the Dominican Republic, she grew up in Salem, Massachusetts. D. C. studied film and television at New York University. After college, she joined the US Army, and proudly served for four years.

D. C. has a master's degree in Science Administration from the Central Michigan University, as well as a Master in Adult Education from Texas A&M- Texarkana University. She is a certified John Maxwell Team speaker and coach, and a certified meditation instructor from the Chopra Center.

One of D. C. passions is helping those around her overcome their self-limiting beliefs. She writes both non-fiction as well as fiction books, ranging from Urban Fantasy to Children's Books. To learn more about her books and her passion, you can find her at www.dcgomez-author.com.

MIA'S LOVE

Q Entertainment Series Prequel

Lynn Yorke

ABOUT *MIA'S LOVE*

Salvador Quiñones and Mia Marlowe are busy chasing their dreams of fame in 1980's New York City when they meet. Neither were prepared to fall for each other so hard and so fast. But they've both made a deal with the devil for success and now they have to decide if stardom matters more than love, and just what they would be willing to risk for either.

CHAPTER ONE: AFRO BLUE

April 1980

Every day started the same for Sal. Rise before the sun woke up and have some scrambled eggs, fruit, and toast to dip into his *cafecito*. Try to be quiet so as not to wake up his older brother Tito, who snored like a chainsaw on the beat-up couch in the living room that served as his makeshift bedroom by night. Haul his conga out the front door and down the four flights of stairs to the quiet street outside. That morning, his routine was no different.

Sal walked the several blocks to the park, nodding *"Buenos dias"* to the old timers who found it impossible to sleep past four am and were already on their stoops having their own *cafecitos*. In contrast to the weary men and women climbing down from the subway platform on the IRT 1 train after the night shift, who smiled a "good night", too exhausted to say the words.

It was spring in New York City, at the northernmost tip of Manhattan. Sal relished the calm before the city fully awoke, before the grimy heat that only a place made of concrete could produce descended upon him. Strolling into the park, Sal found Santiago sitting in his accustomed spot in the corner of the wide, open playground with his conga at the ready in front of him. The older man's dark brown face creased into a broad grin when he saw Sal approaching.

"Good morning. How are you feeling today?" Sal asked him in Spanish.

Santiago rose to hug him, clapping him on the back before sitting down. "Good, thanks. How's it going?"

"Good," Sal said.

This had been his life since he first touched a drum in his grandmother's sunny courtyard back in Havana before he could even talk. Memories of home hovered at the back of his mind as Sal opened the metal folding chair Santiago always brought for him. Settling with his conga and sitting quietly for a moment, he touched the flat, taut surface of the drum with his palm, feeling its energy waiting to be tapped. Sal admired the tall, swaying trees nearby as the sun rose steadily over the skyline leading towards the Bronx. He couldn't see the river that flowed between his new island home and the rest of the world, but he could smell it. It wasn't the deep blue-green of the ocean, but it would do.

Santiago rapped his hands against the side of his drum, the notes fanning across the playground and drawing the smiles of people walking on the other side of the tall metal fence that separated them from the sidewalk. Sal joined in, feeling the soul vibrating from the drum beneath his hands until it became his heartbeat, and there was nothing else but him, the old white-haired man by his side, and the music.

He realized just how much time had passed when he heard the pealing of the bells of the nearby parish church. It was already seven-thirty. Saying a hasty "*adios*" to Santiago, Sal got his drum back in its carry bag and hustled back home for a shower and a shave. The prickly growth on his jaw and his chin had to be tamed, every dark hair on his head perfectly combed.

Tito was up when Sal came out of the bedroom, already showered and dressed for the upcoming long shift at La Nueva China. Still sleepy, Tito rubbed his shaved head as he drank his *cafecito* at the table, while wisps of cigarette smoke curled between his fingers. His book of the day lay next to his plate, and he mumbled good morning. Tito was only two years older than Sal, but leaned back in his chair like a weary man three times his age. Having the responsibility of a mother and father rather than an older brother could do that to a person.

"You look sharp, Salvo. Good luck today," Tito said.

Sal smiled with gratitude despite his heart rising to his throat. "Thanks. I'll see you later."

***

The train ride down to Harlem was fast, as was the bus ride across town to the east side. Sal spent a fair amount of his free time there, visiting clubs and trying to get to know other Latin musicians who congregated there. But despite his comfort with his surroundings, gradually hearing less English and more Spanish, his nerves jangled louder as he got closer to his destination.

There. The red sandstone building whose address was on the card in his hand was suddenly looming over him as he stared up from the sidewalk. He took a step forward, knowing he'd make a great impression if he was early, but his foot faltered. Not yet. Suddenly parched, he needed something to drink. Another *cafecito* to rev him up and motivate him? Maybe not. More coffee probably wasn't the answer to calming the pulse pounding in his throat and chest. He needed something cool.

He pivoted and headed down the street instead, crossing at the corner to the bodega on the other side. Sal nodded and said hello with a big smile to the man behind the counter. Stroking the cat sitting on a stack of crates lazily guarding the premises against mice and men, Sal went to the back of the store. He examined the drinks displayed behind the refrigerator's clear sliding doors. And then he stood there, trying to trick himself into thinking this was about deciding what to get while his body cooled from the cold and ice formed in his bloodstream.

His world was about to change; he could feel it. One way or another, his future was about to happen. All he had to do was turn around and reach for it. But there he was, rooted to the spot, studying his own reflection on the cooler's glassy surface. A single drop of cold sweat trickled down his back as he stood in front of that cooler, losing his nerve like a little punk, when he heard a gentle throat clearing and felt movement behind him.

"Excuse me. I'm sorry, but I need to get past you."

And then Sal turned at the soft, hesitant voice and was stunned at the sight of the speaker. The voice didn't match the vibrancy in her golden-brown eyes, a light color that was striking against the smooth, deep mahogany of her face. Those eyes caught him off guard, made him forget momentarily that he had something else to be worried about. Now all he could consider was how her every feature came together in gorgeous symmetry, the soft nose with that delightful slope in the middle, and the pink lips that looked full and tender. They shone with the slightest hint of gloss. He wondered if the lip gloss was flavored and what it tasted like. Wondered how soft that big halo of brown hair felt and if it would spring back to shape after he'd finished plunging his hands into it.

But instead of spilling everything that was inside him or just stepping deeper into the warmth that he knew waited in that body–

small-breasted but with hips and an ass that seemed perfectly designed for his hands–he paused. Sal pulled his mind back out of his dick and concentrated on behaving like the gentleman his mother had raised. Or had tried to raise until he was fifteen.

"Which one did you want?"

"That one."

With a timidity that caught him off guard–yet another mismatch between her appearance and behavior–the girl took a hesitant step closer to point at the big glass jar full of *coco frío*. She stood back and watched him retrieve the clear bottle, palming it before handing it over. Sal saw her eyes run over him, his face, his hair, and then to the tall black bag next to him on the floor.

"My drum. I play the conga."

"But, *congueros* are usually —" She stopped herself, and he could guess what she'd been going to say. The African somewhere in his lineage wasn't showing up nearly as much as the Taíno and Spaniard.

"Handsome?" he finished for her with a grin.

She looked flustered. They retreated into silence, staring at each other until the bodega owner peered around the corner at the front of the aisle.

"You okay back there? Is something wrong?" the man asked.

"No. We just needed time to decide." Sal nodded at the older man, who shook his head and disappeared. Turning back to the gorgeous stranger, he said, "I'm Salvador Cobas Quiñones. You can call me Sal. What's your name?"

Sal leaned forward slightly, his gaze moving between her eyes and her mouth, and for the first time, she smiled at him. He caught his breath, steadying himself. Suddenly he wanted to know her, everything about her.

"I'm Mia Marlowe."

It was a movie star's name. He stood behind her while she bought her drink, soaking up the citrus scent wafting from her hair, and she stood aside as he bought the same kind. By then, his awareness of her had overtaken the ability to think about choosing something else.

Outside, she grinned at him and then said, "Well. Nice meeting you." His impulse was to follow her, and as luck would have it, they were going in the same direction, anyway. Mia slowed and gave him a curious look.

"I'm headed this way. I've got an audition." Sal gestured to the bag hung over his shoulder while he held the bottle of *coco frío* in its paper bag in the other.

"With who?" Mia asked.

"Sisco Diaz."

She shook her head, an amused expression on her face. Even her teeth sparkled in the sunlight like a toothpaste commercial. He tried not to keep staring at her mouth, but then found himself admiring the rock and roll of her hips in her bell-bottom jeans instead.

"Of course," she said with an amused headshake. "I'm headed there myself."

"For an audition? Let me guess. You're a singer."

"Not yet. I'm the receptionist." Mia's glance at him was shy, those golden eyes startling him again.

"But you *are* a singer. I can tell. And someday everybody will know your name, Mia Marlowe," Sal said.

Her laughter warmed him, made him nearly forget the cold terror he'd been experiencing back at the bodega before he turned and saw her face.

"We'll see. Here we are." When she stopped in front of the sandstone building, Sal did too. He took a deep breath as she gauged him with those beautiful, now profoundly kind eyes. "Ready?"

He nodded once. "After you."

Maybe it was gentlemanly to let her go up first, but it sure didn't help Sal's focus when he faced Mia's plump ass climbing the steps to the front door. It didn't seem as though she was purposely trying to attract his attention; she didn't need to. The stirring in his pants was going to embarrass him, so he pulled his gaze away, focusing on her espadrille sandals instead.

Sal took in the small reception area with its old, stately furniture and rose-colored paint. A dark-haired woman smiled at him pleasantly enough, and he grinned back.

"Carla. This is the *conguero* Sisco's expecting," Mia told her. "Salvador Quiñones."

"Hi. I'm Carla Di Donato, Sisco's secretary."

"Nice to meet you," Sal said with a smile.

The secretary's eyes flickered between them while she reached for her desk phone, and her smile broadened. Mia's complexion didn't betray any noticeable blush, but she looked flustered, her breathing a little rapid. Sal gawked at her until he heard a loud laugh coming from his left.

"I was about to let you know your appointment was here," the secretary said when Sisco appeared.

Sal turned and smiled at the other man. Francisco "Sisco" Diaz was a big man. He was in his early forties and muscular, although his middle was developing more than a hint of padding. Salvador had never seen what his hair looked like, even in old photos; Sisco had been shaving it off for years, exposing a pink scalp. Dressed in a button-down silk shirt open at the collar, his huge gold medallion gleamed from its spot nestled in thick, dark chest hair. With his light brown eyes and sensual red lips, a lot of women found him attractive. When he was out at a club, which is where Sal had more or less ambushed him for an introduction, he always had two sexy ladies clinging to him, one on each side like an old-school pimp.

Now Sisco was looking him up and down, nodding as if approving of his clothes, then shook Sal's hand. The older man's hand was unpleasantly clammy, and Sal quickly wiped his palm on his pants when Sisco turned to snap his fingers at Mia.

"*Nena*, you got my drink?" he demanded.

Sal found his gesture and that he addressed an employee as "girl" a bit rude. Mia's smile faded as she handed him the drink she'd bought at the bodega, and Sal's smile faltered when she sat behind her desk. She gave him a quick thumbs up and then dropped her gaze back to the neat surface.

Of course, she wasn't coming into the audition. That's not what receptionists were supposed to do. But knowing she wouldn't be there stole some of his peace, and he could feel the cold trickle starting again as he followed Sisco into the big room with the darker crimson walls and black lacquered furniture. It felt oppressive for such a large space compared to the small outside area.

Two men were already in the room sitting in big wing-backed chairs with their legs splayed while they spoke Spanish with Puerto Rican cadence and slang. One was long and lean, while the other was shorter and burly, with prominent red lips. Sisco went to lean against his large desk and folded his arms. All three stared him up and down, but they seemed pleasant.

"That's Fito Calderon, and that's Memo Gutierrez," Sisco said, pointing to the thin and the husky man, respectively. "If I hire you,

you'll be backing them up on their upcoming album and when they gig."

"*Mucho gusto.*" Sal shook their hands.

"All right. Let's see what you got," Sisco said.

Trying not to let them see how he inhaled and exhaled, Sal went to the spot on the carpet near the array of instruments where a lone chair was placed. He got his conga out of the bag, took more deep breaths, and began to play. He fumbled at first but gained his rhythm, beginning to relax into the playing. Then Memo called out another style, a different time signature, and nodded along when Sal played that. As he switched, he felt his confidence growing, and then they weren't asking him to do anything, just sitting back and staring at him with small smiles forming on their lips.

Now he was sweating but from excitement, from playing hard and loud with his whole soul pouring into the drum. They each got up, Memo retrieving a set of claves and Fito sitting behind a middle-pitch conga to jam with him. Sal lost track of time, falling into the beats the way he did with Santiago, and could have kept going, wanting to keep channeling the force that was winding through the room from their playing until Sisco finally laughed and shouted, "Okay, that's enough, that's enough!"

Fito's face was red from exertion, and Memo was grinning from ear to ear.

"What do y'all think?" Sisco asked them while Sal waited, trembling from the withdrawal of all that power that had flowed through his body.

"I think we've found our new *conguero*," Fito said with a huge smile.

"Okay, thank you." Sal was so happy he could have exploded, but he tried to play it cool. "When do I start?"

Sisco took him to sit at the desk so he could formally sign the boilerplate agreement while Fito and Memo hung out on the other side of the room.

"Come back Monday at nine o'clock. Just understand that even though you take most of your orders from Fito and Memo, you work for my label, which means you work for me. If you have any issues, you bring them to me first, and I handle them. It also means you don't play with nobody else not signed or affiliated with the label unless you go through me. Understand me?"

"I understand," Sal said, shrugging off another moment of discomfort.

He breezed through the contract, barely taking note of its contents, hasty to sign before Sisco found a reason to change his mind. Then he phoned the secretary, demanding she come in with her notary kit, and she watched them both sign the paperwork, giving him a long look before she put her official stamp on it. It was done. He was a signed studio musician. Grinning at everyone, Sal waited to see what they would say or do next. Take him out to celebrate?

"All right, kid. See you Monday," Fito said with a nod, then went back to chatting with Memo about.... baseball.

"Okay. See you then," Sal responded slowly, making his way to the door.

Sisco just raised his chin with a sarcastic smirk. "Yo. You said you work at a Chino-Cubano place, right? You half?"

"No. My Tío Juan is Chinese. He's my uncle through marriage."

"That's cool. Bring me some of them black beans and rice when you come back next time. And some pork fried rice, too."

That condescending smile was Sal's signal to leave. Trying to stay loose and not let Sisco's comments get under his skin this early into his signing, he bagged his conga and walked out. When he reached reception, Mia sat there, staring at him with her eyes shining. Carla was missing.

"I made it," he said.

"I heard. You were great. Congratulations." Mia beamed at him, and he understood for the first time what it meant when someone said their knees went weak.

"Thank you." He paused, not wanting to leave her, trying to think of some way to keep this conversation going. "What time do you–?"

Sisco's door opened. He seemed surprised and displeased to see Sal was still there, obviously in the middle of chatting with Mia. Crossing the area with an arrogant bop, Sisco went around her desk and leaned over her shoulder to peer at the desk calendar. The smile that had been on Mia's face dwindled, and her shoulders stiffened. She looked up at Sal, and the eyes that had shone moments ago were now full of embarrassment, almost apologetic. Immediately, Sal knew something was going on between his new boss and the beautiful girl, and disappointment exploded in his chest, scattering charred ashes everywhere.

"What do I have next?" Sisco asked, running his thick finger over the paper. He took his time, his face mere inches from the cloud of Mia's afro, then lifted his eyes to Sal. "Oh, you still here? Let me walk you out."

Mia's eyes lowered when Sal followed Sisco downstairs and outside into the bright sunshine of the late morning. It had grown cooler, and Sal shrugged his jacket on while Sisco shoved his hands into his pocket and looked up and down the quiet street from the stoop like a king surveying his lands. Ready to sink his teeth into everything that moved and grow richer and fatter from its bounty.

"*Oye.*" At Sisco's demand for his attention, Sal turned to him and waited. "I consider myself a decent guy to work for. The pay is good. You'll get perks and the chance to play with some of the best musicians in the city. If you're smart, and I can tell you are, I'll teach you how things work behind the stage, what it takes to own something like this for yourself someday, if that's what you want."

"I hadn't really thought about it. I just want to play and someday lead my own band. That's good enough for me," Sal said.

"That's fine, but you gotta always think a step ahead. Do more than survive from day to day. Nobody successful ever stops at *good enough.*"

Sal mused over his words, thinking this advice sounded a lot like what Tito always said about his music career. He felt a surge of appreciation that Sisco saw his potential beyond playing music. But Sisco didn't stop there.

"The thing is, to get this far, you need discipline. And around here, that means you're gonna have to respect house rules, just like all the other artists who work for me." He looked at Sal to make sure he was listening. "I need you on time and ready to go one hundred percent from Day One. That means no cocaine, no horse, no pills. I don't have a problem with a little Mary Jane or having a drink or two when you're in public, but that's it. If you get sloppy, throwing up on yourself or swinging on people, that makes the label look bad. It makes *me* look bad. And I can't afford to look bad, you dig?"

Sal drank a little occasionally, but that was all. Tito's rules on that were even stricter. So far, so good. He nodded. "*Claro.* I won't do anything that reflects badly on you or the label."

"Good. Also, and I'm fucking serious about this. Don't shit where you eat." This time Sisco's eyes seemed smaller, speculative, like a cobra deciding if Sal was a mouse, and if so, would that mouse make a satisfying meal?

Even with his great command of English, that was a new one for Sal. "I don't understand," he said, his brows drawing together.

"The only other thing besides alcohol or drugs that can make a man lose his mind and fuck up his game is pussy. I don't like telling grown men how to act, but I've seen it happen, so the rule is no relationships at work. Not with the label's female artists or any groupies that come to the recording studio. Not with anybody that works in there no matter what they do." When Sisco turned his head to nod at the door to the building, Sal's fist clenched on the strap of his bag. He knew exactly who Sisco was referring to. But he kept listening, all the while plummeting from the heights of victory he'd felt not so long ago. "You're a good-looking cat. Probably gettin' up under skirts left and right, huh?" A falsely hearty chuckle followed that assumption.

Sal tried to smile like he always did when men talked shit like that. It was embarrassing to admit that he actually wasn't getting up under skirts. Not that girls didn't offer or he didn't want to accept. He was too busy between work at the restaurant, perfecting his skills, and trying to meet the right people to help his career. And then there was Tito, who scared off any girl he tried bringing around like their disapproving *Abuela* standing by the door with a headscarf and a broom ready to sweep them right the fuck out.

"Yeah. I was like that when I was your age. Feels like a long time ago, man. A *long* time ago. But I realized everybody's gotta settle down at some point. Find that good pussy that makes giving up all the other pussy worth it." Sisco sighed, taking on a bemused grin. He leaned toward Sal as though confiding in him and looked up at the window of the second story, making it even more obvious who he was speaking of. "I found my good pussy. And I'm not ever letting her go."

The weather suddenly turned when a bank of clouds appeared out of the blue and drifted across their patch of earth and concrete, obliterating the sunshine. Sal shivered at the drop in temperature in that shade, at the look in Sisco's eyes, now almost dreamy as though he were picturing fucking that girl. Dominating her and calling it love. And Sal understood what this entire conversation had been about all along.

His jaw tensed, disgusted at the crass way Sisco had referred to Mia. Sal no longer pretended to smile.

"My brother says gentlemen don't talk about their women and what goes on between them in private. I kind of stick to that."

He gripped his bag tighter, staring at the view across the street, and waited for Sisco to turn around, get the contract and rip it into confetti after what he'd said. Instead, Sisco's eyes widened, and he laughed. This time it was genuine, as though he was too shocked by the lecture on old-school manners by some kid to be outraged.

"All right, youngblood, that shit was funny. I'll give you that," Sisco said, holding out a fist. Reluctantly, Sal knocked it with his own. Ritual complete, Sal descended the pink stone steps to the sidewalk and fought the impulse to wipe his hand on his pants for the second time that day. It felt dirty. As he walked away, he heard Sisco's last words. "Everything I said goes into effect right now. Don't be late next time."

CHAPTER TWO: SECOND TIME AROUND

It was a Friday night, and Mia was prepping to go out while her younger twin brothers were screeching and chasing each other through her family's two-bedroom apartment. She had to push them out of the bathroom more than once while doing her hair alongside her stepsister, Cherise.

Her stepmother Pam watched them get dressed for their night out, her normally full lips pressed in a thin "O" around her cigarette.

Cherise was only a year older than Mia and had been in stiff competition with her since childhood. That night, as every Friday night, the battle was for time and space in the bathroom. She was busy pulling a hot comb through her shoulder-length hair between trips to the stove while Mia picked her voluminous afro into a perfect halo. Cherise returned, coughing dramatically when Mia finished her do with a lung-tightening blast of hairspray.

"You're in my way," Cherise grumbled when their elbows bumped. "Can you even fit your big head through the doorway?"

Ignoring her, Mia swiped on some cherry gloss, smacked her lips loudly, and gave Cherise a parting smirk. The disdain was mutual. As little girls, when their parents had gotten married, Mia had been excited to have a sister, but Pam going easy on her natural child and her annoyance at being saddled with Mia eventually ruined that.

"I don't know why you let those girls go to the Skate Key," Mia overheard Pam grumbling to her father, Robert. "You know nothing but hoodlums go there looking for ass and trouble."

They had this conversation every Friday. Pam had decided Mia was "fast" after she'd had the nerve to fill out during early puberty at eleven. That was why Pam had quite a long list of activities Mia could not do and places she was not allowed to go. Their parents had decided long ago that Robert's domain was at work, but the household was Pam's. There was one venue left Robert insisted was fine: the Skate Key, the premier uptown roller-skating rink blocks away.

Her best friend, Tonya, was waiting for them in the lobby of their building. The elevated 1 train rumbled by. Despite summer being right around the corner, it was chilly, and Mia was glad she was wearing her brown suede jacket over her denim overalls and tee-shirt. The minute they were outside, Cherise picked up speed and walked ahead, ditching them as she always did despite Robert's order to stick together.

"I barely made it out tonight," Tonya said. "My mother found out Alonzo was there when she wasn't home. She wants me to stop seeing him."

"Are you going to?"

"I'll show you what I'm gonna do."

There was a phone booth on the sidewalk next to their building. With a devilish grin, Tonya ducked inside, pulling the two-paneled, clear door shut and digging into her pocket for change. Mia rolled her eyes, folding her arms and facing the street, keeping an eye out. They were on the border of the huge blocks that made up the projects. Once they crossed, they left its protection.

Mia tried not to pout at the prospect of Tonya's boyfriend showing up. She couldn't help but think about the black-haired boy she wished would show. Salvador, who'd been rehearsing with Fito Calderon's band for a whole month, seemed to duck her whenever she spotted him coming or going.

***

A frisson of pure and unexpected pleasure had rippled through her the first time she'd laid eyes on Salvador Quiñones when he'd turned around in the bodega's aisle, and their gazes had connected. She'd been tongue-tied at how gorgeous he was. Mia was average height for a woman, and he was a few inches taller, but the wingspan of those shoulders was broad, the black dress shirt stretching across the muscle. His hair was as black as his shirt, thick and straight like a wave made of silk. That sweep of hair led away from the inky marks of his eyebrows and the angled planes of his high, sharp cheekbones beneath lightly tanned skin.

She could imagine running her fingertips down the smooth line of his strong profile and across lips that looked soft, fuller on the bottom, and dusky pink. Above those lips and around his jawline was a dark shadow that would be a full mustache and beard if left unchecked for a few days. But it was the eyes that arrested her, captivated her. They were dark and narrow under spiky ebony lashes. Once she fell into them, there was no escape.

It probably hadn't taken over ten seconds, but time seemed to stop while she absorbed him. He'd stared right back at her with the sort of intensity that would ordinarily make her turn and run, but she didn't want to. It was pleasant there, standing and soaking in the heat radiating off him.

Every instinct told her to get closer to the primal power he exuded whenever she saw him, inviting her to draw strength from it. And it appeared as though he wanted to get to know her better too, but Sisco was making it impossible, spending even more time lounging over her desk than before. He glared at Salvador every time he saw them together, even if all they were doing was exchanging an innocent "good morning" or "good night". Sal took the hint and kept his distance.

Frustrated, Mia wouldn't force the issue. She understood he was there for his career like she was, and ruining his chance over a girl he barely knew wasn't smart. It made her ache to know she'd probably never get to feel those lips on hers, but she understood. Nobody messed with Sisco and survived, career-wise. Or otherwise.

***

Mia and Tonya met their friends at the rink, had hotdogs and soda in the eating area, and then got their rental skates. The place was packed. Huge strobe lights colored the oval in pink, gold, and purple. She and Tonya skated, arms locked, even doing some spins in the center of the floor. Until, of course, Alonzo showed up with his curly brown hair and catlike green eyes, and Tonya forgot she existed.

"I'm gonna go take a break," Mia announced.

She was returning to the seating area when she turned at the appearance of a dark-haired young man, broad-shouldered and lean-hipped. Dark, piercing eyes were searching the crowded space, his strong profile vaguely reminiscent of a hawk seeking prey. *It couldn't be*, Mia thought as she slowed to stare at him.

He was with another man, also young but taller, watching the crowd with a dour, closed-off expression under a shaved head. They were both wearing button-downs open to offer glimpses of black tank undershirts, terribly and misogynistically referred to as "wifebeaters" by the folks she knew. Apparently, violent assholes had an unofficial uniform. She hoped that wasn't true of all men who dressed that way because she was pretty sure now that one of those guys was Sal. The other man with the shaved head looked like he could be the brother he'd mentioned in one of the brief conversations they'd had.

She'd mentioned to Sal that she and her friends came to the Skate Key most Friday nights. He'd responded that he didn't know how to skate, so she assumed she'd never run into him there. This was a nice surprise. Better than nice. It made her flush all the way down to the tips of her toes.

Heart pounding, she got over her typical shyness and rolled over to where he and his brother stood at the desk. His back was turned while he told the attendant his shoe size, but the brother saw her. He was handsome, in a different way than Sal, with a slightly darker complexion and a full mustache. Intimidatingly thick dark eyebrows arched over cocoa-brown eyes, lighter than Sal's. Obviously uninterested in skating, he stood with his back to the attendant's desk with folded muscular arms and stared at her as she approached. There was no smile on that face, but he dropped his arms, seeming more open, until Sal turned around and saw her, then grinned. She was dazzled by that smile, barely noticing anything else.

"Hey. You're here," Sal said, and she had to try with all her might not to melt right there in front of him.

"Yes. Typical exciting Friday night," Mia responded with a small laugh. "You finally made it."

"Yeah, we made it. This is my brother, Tito. Tito, this is Mia from work."

Tito was now frowning at her. The shift in his expression and his posture was sudden and off-putting. Mia had no idea what she could have done wrong in under ten seconds unless his stare at her big hair and full lips meant she was somehow "unsuitable" for friendship with his brother. He crossed his arms again, shifting his gaze to the crowd.

"Hi," she said to Tito with a small wave.

"What's up?" he mumbled in response. "Salvo, it's too crowded. We shouldn't stay long."

Sal rolled his eyes and sighed. "I told you, you didn't have to come."

Tito quirked one of those thick brows and pressed his lips together, reminding Mia suddenly of Pam. "I'm gonna get a table and something to eat."

"Okay." But instead of joining him, Salvador looked at her. "If you're ready to get back out there, I'll go with you."

Mia's flush spread to every part of her body. Feeling uncharacteristically giddy, she said, "Okay."

Tito abruptly turned and strode away while Sal found a spot on the bench outside the rink to tie his skates. It was clear he didn't have much experience skating after he'd walked awkwardly to the entrance and clung to the outside half wall once inside the rink. He tried looking nonchalant and cool as always, but when his foot slid and his legs began to separate, the alarm on his face was comical. Mia suppressed a giggle, skating beside him while he inched along unsteadily.

"I'm glad you decided to try it," Mia said loud enough so he could hear her over the music. "I guess your brother doesn't skate."

"No. Tito can't risk falling on his ass in public. He's too cool for that." Sal shook his head, then gripped the wall again when his legs started going in different directions. "So.... this is how you have fun?"

This time, Mia couldn't hold back a gentle laugh. "If you come around enough, you get better. Here."

Boys had taken her hand to skate before, but this was the first time she was the one to reach out. But Salvador did that to her, made her want to try things she normally wouldn't. Made her feel things she otherwise didn't. He made her braver, and she liked feeling that way. When his fingers locked with hers, the sizzle burned brighter, higher, the warmth of his palm touching hers so intimately. He smiled at her, his gaze grateful and sensual at the same time. This close to him again, she inhaled his scent of coconut and rich coffee and found she was the one who needed to hold on before she swooned and crashed.

She was able to lure him from the security of the wall, and they rolled along together over the smooth surface of the rink. "I Wanna Be Your Lover" by Prince played as Sal slowly got his bearings, managing to keep his legs together.

"I love this song," Mia remarked.

"I have the album. That guy is amazing," Sal said with enthusiasm. "I heard he played every instrument in the recording."

"That's impossible. No one's that good," Mia scoffed. "I'm surprised you'd listen to him, though."

"Why, because I play Latin music?" Sal shook his head. "I listen to everything. If you want to be the best musician you can be, you have to see how everything is connected. Jazz, R&B, blues, hip-hop. All these styles come from the same mother. It all starts with the drum."

There went that sensation of wanting to swoon again. Fervently, Mia replied, "I'm so glad you said that. I feel the same way. My friends always ask me why I'm working at a Latin music label when I want to sing R&B. I know the styles are different, but we have so much in common."

Sal was doing better with each turn they took around the oval. He even looked like he was enjoying himself as he began to sway a little bit like she did, keeping time with the music and getting into the flow of the crowd. He stumbled a bit if somebody in front of them did a fancy spin or tricks, but she kept him up on his feet. At one point, Cherise danced past them, going backward with her secret boyfriend, giving her a wicked "I'm gonna tell on you" grin, and her friends rolled by in a group with wide-open mouths. She'd skated with boys before, but no one who looked like Sal or whose side she wanted to cling to all night.

They took a break to get some drinks, and Mia introduced him to the group, girls and guys she'd known since she was little. Sal was pleasant and charming with everybody until Mia said, "Maybe we should go check on your brother."

Mia had spotted Tito staring at them whenever they rolled past his section. A gorgeous Latin girl with huge hoop earrings and bright red lipstick was sitting with her arm draped over his shoulder, but his eyes were locked on Mia, and they were grim. Maybe it shouldn't have mattered since she'd probably never hang out with Salvador outside of work again, but she wanted his brother to approve of her.

"What's up? Having a good time?" Sal asked, his demeanor shifting to seriousness even while he still smiled.

"I don't think I like the atmosphere," Tito answered. His eyes flicked over their shoulder, and they turned to see a group of guys all wearing green shirts, hats, or bandanas.

Sobering, confused, Sal turned back to Tito. "I thought those guys were your friends."

"They want to be my friend, but I don't want to be theirs." Tito lifted his chin in their direction, and the guys threw up signs with their fingers in return.

Mia knew who they were and knew they were to be avoided. Of course, one of them was Cherise's secret boyfriend.

Sal sighed. "Okay. Give us another half hour and then we'll go."

Tito nodded, his fists on the table, still looking stiff and annoyed while the girl played with his earlobe. A song by Shalamar had just begun. Mia loved that album. Loved that Salvador showed up, and they had time, real time, to relax and have fun without the restrictions and anxiety at work. It really was a second chance for their friendship, or at least Mia hoped. And on this second go around the rink, Sal's movements were fluid and sure, but he still held her hand and wouldn't let go. He only stopped when everybody decided to leave.

The group of friends splintered off in twos and threes as they walked back home. Tito was just behind them, Cherise and Tonya in front. The night had grown even cooler, and Sal's side offered a comforting source of heat as she kept close with her arm through his.

Mia said good night to him at the bottom of the wide steps to her building while the others politely looked away, except for Tito, who stood with arms folded like a watchful eagle.

"I'll see you at work Monday," Sal said.

Tiny points of light reflected in his eyes, lights that seemed to shine at her. He seemed reluctant to go, and she didn't want him to, wishing this night with him could last forever.

"See you Monday." Mia waved, and when she could finally bear to leave him, she still waved until she was inside the building. He watched her the whole time with a smile until the security door closed.

Mia was floating on a cloud made of pure bliss. She swore she couldn't feel the scuffed surface of the floor as first they dropped Tonya off at her door, then went higher up to their apartment. The night swam in her mind in a flow of wondrous impressions and sensations; Salvador's scent, the colors that played across his face, the unbridled happiness she felt being able to talk to him and touch him all night. Being touched by him. She could still feel the press of his palm against hers like a secret kiss.

But then Cherise unlocked their front door, and Pam stood there, in her robe and slippers, shaking her head.

"I saw you out the window with that Spanish boy. You know the rules of this house. No dating."

"I'm not dating him. He works at my job. He just happened to be at Skate Key. It wasn't planned," Mia said, pulling off her jacket wearily.

"Is that true, Cherise?" Pam asked, her eyes swinging to her daughter.

"I guess." Cherise looked tired and bored with this conversation, but Mia was grateful she'd backed her for once. "He came with his brother."

"Oh." Pam seemed mollified by that answer, but before she turned to go down the hall to her bedroom, she pointed a finger at Mia's face. "I still don't want him coming around here again, understand?"

Mia looked down and nodded. "Yes, ma'am."

***

But Pam wasn't in control at the studio. She wasn't there to curse or complain as a friendship began to blossom between Mia and Salvador. They started leaving the office separately at lunchtime for "errands", meeting up again in the nearby park to have sandwiches and talk. They never discussed why it had to be that way; it was unspoken that it was because of Sisco and his irrational jealousy.

Then stolen lunchtimes extended to dinners at his aunt and uncle's restaurant, a tiny place in the Forbidden Zone across the street from their public housing complex where Pam had said it was "too dangerous" to go without her or their father. Pam had exaggerated as usual. Mia felt safe with Sal and his family, enjoyed their easygoing laughter, except for Tito, who didn't seem to care for her all that much.

She and Cherise had come to an arrangement so she could see Sal while Cherise saw her boyfriend. They told Pam they were going out together, then split up the second they were out of sight of the window. With more freedom, early dinners turned into movie nights. Soon, Mia started rising earlier in the mornings to see Sal play with the old man, Santiago, whose wizened ebony face reminded her of her late mother's father.

It was like a vision from an old dream when she'd been safely cocooned in her mother's arms. She hadn't realized how much she'd missed being held like that, loved like that, without condition.

One day, while watching the light move across Sal's face as he played, his eyes rapturous, it dawned on her that she was happy again for the first time in a long time. And it was because of him. But with that happiness came a craving for him that was growing too big, too strong, too quickly. Mia knew he wanted her, too. As inexperienced with physical love, as she was, it was obvious from how he stared at her, his eyes drinking her in when he thought she wasn't paying attention. She could feel the longing rolling off him like a blast wave when he leaned over her desk to look at something in the comics she had stashed in her drawer or when his thigh touched hers in the darkness of the movie theater. He always seemed to need to make contact with her, and she relished that. But he never went further than those surreptitious touches. Never kissed her, never told her he wanted more.

"I'm fine with that," she told Tonya, who listened to Mia talk about Sal with frustrated sympathy. "You'll always be my ace, but it's nice having a guy as a friend."

"Stop fucking lying," Tonya exploded after hearing that for the tenth time as they lounged in Tonya's bedroom, listening to music. "Here. Take these. Go to his house when his hot, angry brother isn't home."

Mia gawked at the small squares of foil Tonya had shoved into her hand. "I don't know what to do with these."

"Pam never talked to you about it?"

Mia twisted her lips at her. "Please. She thinks I'll get pregnant just by looking at a boy."

"God, I have to do everything around here." Tonya left the room in a huff and returned with a banana on a tray. She settled back on the bed, brushed her straightened bangs out of her eyes, and picked up the yellow fruit. "Okay, this is what you do."

CHAPTER THREE: FAME

"We're gonna have to find a new lead singer."

Fito made this announcement at the start of a rehearsal two months before the band was scheduled to appear at the upcoming Latin All-Stars Spectacular at the Roseland Ballroom. It was going to be history-making, a big night for the New York City Latin music scene. This news was met by a burst of complaints ("¡Ay, coño!) interspersed with laughter and rude jokes.

The bassist Carlito twisted his lips at Fito. "What happened to Ginny?"

Fito didn't seem to want to answer the question. He and Ginny had been sleeping together and acting like no one knew when it was so obvious.

"The cute little blondie at Tower Records is what happened to Ginny," Memo said.

"Never mind that. What's done is done. We need a new *cantante* to redo Ginny's vocals and get her up to speed for the show, which, as you know, is in late August. That means we don't have a lot of time. I've already called everybody I can think of, and they're busy or just don't like me."

"*Ay, pobrecito,* nobody loves your skin and bones?" someone crooned to him. More laughter ensued.

Sal's heart beat double time at this revelation and call to action. This was finally it, the way to get Mia the chance Sisco was dangling over her head like a carrot. He rarely took center stage when addressing the group, feeling a little too green and intimidated by their seniority, but this was the moment. "I might know someone," he offered. All eyes turned to him in his spot near the wall.

"Who do *you* know?" Fito asked with mock indignation. But he was waiting for an answer all the same.

"I can't say yet. Let me talk to her and ask."

"That's why I like you. You take the bull by the balls and find *solutions,*" Fito said, pointing at him with pride, then clenching his fingers together as though around actual balls.

"By the horns. The expression is by the.... never mind." Sal went quiet while the others began tossing names of girlfriends and groupies.

After the discussion and the rehearsal, they broke for lunch. Mia would already know to leave for the park the second the music stopped. Entering the park, he spotted her right away. She was hard to miss. Her hair was parted and brushed into two neat afro puffs. He teased her when she wore it like that, calling her Minnie Mouse, but secretly he loved how cute she looked. And to be honest, it was a bit too easy to imagine gripping them, one in each hand, while she rode him like a bicycle. Or a bull, for that matter.

She was waiting for him on their usual bench near the tree-shaded playground, where tired moms and doting *abuelas* fanned themselves and ate flavored shaved ice from a cart to keep cool.

Sal tweaked Mia's cheek and sat beside her, almost too excited to eat. She was halfway through what looked like her typical Tuesday lunch; Pam's leftover Monday night roast beef.

"What happened at rehearsal this morning? Sisco came downstairs and threw a fit in his office. I think he even broke something," Mia said, daintily wiping her mouth with her napkin.

Sal watched her sip orange soda from a can, tortured at the sight of her lips on the rim. He dreamed about those lips opening to his. And he'd tried not to, really tried hard not to think of that mouth lowering onto his swollen cock. Nope, he couldn't let himself think of that or any of the things he'd love to try with her.

Switching focus, he said, "That's what I want to talk to you about. Kingpin was pissed because Ginny quit on us."

"Kingpin" was the code name for their boss, in case they were ever overhead talking shit about him.

"Fito cheated on her?" Mia asked, already knowing the answer.

"Yeah. Big surprise. But that means we need a new *cantante*."

Mia finished her sandwich, swallowed hard, and washed it down with her drink. Her golden eyes were even more luminous in the afternoon rays washing over her face. In their amber depths, he saw anxiety first, followed by quick calculation.

"Sisco will say no," she concluded with a shake of her head. Balling up her tin foil, she arched her arm and tossed it into the nearby trashcan with one neat bank shot. "He's *been* saying no."

"But he hired you because you're good. You said that's how you met him when he heard you sing at that club."

"Yes, and that was months ago, and nothing's changed. He won't..." Mia's voice trailed off. And as always, Sal refrained from asking specifics about the nature of their relationship. He didn't want to hear her say she'd let that man's greedy fingers touch her body. He couldn't handle the images it would cause to fester in his mind like mold. "Anyway, I'm not signed, and even if I was, I don't speak Spanish, so I don't see how I could sing it and sound authentic."

Sal turned to her, resting his arm along the bench behind her shoulders and leaning in earnestly. "Mia, Fito is the one who gets the final say on who's in the band and who isn't. Sisco can't keep holding you back. You wanted a shot, and this is it. You can do it."

"What about the language?" Mia asked after a long pause, where she searched his eyes with hers. Sal's chest opened at that look, inviting her all the way inside.

"I'll help you. I'll write the lyrics in English, so you know what they mean. It'll help you get the emotions right. And I'll write them again and break them down like they'd sound in English so you can memorize them that way. We'll speak Spanish in front of you at the restaurant so you can pick up the accents. Then you can really start learning the language."

"That sounds like a lot in two months," Mia said dubiously.

"It really isn't if you do it every day. Spanish has rules. Once you remember them, it's easy. You want hard? Look at English. Bear with me. The bear went into the forest. I ran outside my house with my ass bare-naked." Sal grinned, nudging her shoulder with the back of his hand.

At his teasing, a slow smile spread across Mia's face. He was so close, he could see the flecks of black fanning out from her irises in the middle of that honey-gold. Before he could stop himself, he ran his finger from her shoulder up the line of her neck to her round cheekbone. Damn, he'd give anything to just lean in and taste those lips, knowing he'd find a sweet combination of cherry gloss and orange soda.

"Thank you, Salvador," Mia said. Her voice was quiet but so sincere that it made him ache with the need to pull her closer.

"You don't have to thank me," he said. "I'd do anything for you, Mia."

Abruptly, he straightened, pulling his hand away. He feared he'd said too much. Sisco's shadow still loomed over them, even in this beautiful, sunlit world away from his domain. But if Mia found success apart from the would-be king, if they both did, there would come a day when Sisco was in their rearview mirror, and they could do whatever they wanted. But first, they had to get her in front of Fito and a microphone.

CHAPTER FOUR: EVIL WAYS

Mia primped her hair and adjusted the collar of her sleeveless dress as she stared at herself in the ladies' room mirror. She'd gone through this ritual about three or four times. Each time she'd turn to leave, she would notice another flaw. Hair not fluffed enough. The buttons were done wrong. Her wide eyes, big like a deer with its foot caught in a snare. None of that was cute. None of it mattered when her voice was a squeak at the bottom of her throat.

"Mia, come out." It was Carla on the other side of the white door. "You've been in there for fifteen minutes, doll face. Time's up."

Slowly, Mia opened the door. Carla looked good in her green polyester pants suit with the scarf tied around her throat. The brunette had been working at the label in its various iterations since the late sixties, back when it belonged to her uncle Tony Rizzo. They'd produced doo-wop records and crooner ballads back then. She'd probably still be there when Sisco and the rest were long gone. Carla gave Mia a sympathetic yet stern look, her arms crossed.

"They're waiting for you. Are you nervous about singing or about *him*?"

"Both," Mia whispered. Her voice was a little stronger than a squeak, but by no means stage-ready.

Carla put her arm around Mia's shoulders and walked her up the stairs to the second floor. Before they entered the rehearsal space, she made Mia stop and look into a mirror mounted on the wall.

"Look at yourself, Mia. Who's in that mirror? Is she a girl with nothing to say that anybody wants to hear? Is she gonna let a guy with zero talent of his own tell her the only talent *she* has is lying flat on her back? Is that accurate?"

Mia saw her own face sharpen in response to those words. They weren't meant to hurt her, but they hit home. "No. It's not."

Neither said anything else. Carla brushed her hair in place with her fingers and wiped a smudge of pink lipstick off the side of her lip, then sailed back down the stairs, her footfalls soft on the carpeted steps. Mia turned to face the door, took a deep breath, squared her shoulders, and entered.

Salvador was in his spot with his drum. His eyes widened when she entered. The tightness around his mouth eased into a grin, and his shoulders visibly relaxed.

Mia turned to Fito, who was at the piano playing scales. Memo raised a bushy brown eyebrow at her but said nothing. The rest of the band continued fiddling with their instruments, but straightened up when Fito called her.

"Mia, Mia, Mia. Finally, our princess has arrived," he said, standing up and taking a grand bow. He sat back down. "Okay. Let's take it from the top."

Salvador had already told them what she would sing, "Ay, José", originally performed by Graciela Perez with Machito's orchestra. The song required range, attitude, and sexiness that average everyday Mia didn't think she possessed. But Sal had insisted it was the best song for the audition, short and sweet.

Mia stepped in front of the microphone. She'd been in the rehearsal room before running errands or dropping in to listen when she had a minute, but she felt claustrophobic as they all stared at her, waiting till she gave Fito the signal that she was ready.

When the door opened, she smiled, thinking Carla had found the time and was coming to show her support. But when Sisco strutted in, giving her and Fito a dirty look, her heart sank faster than a stone in a scummy pond. She looked swiftly at Sal, whose face and body tightened again instantly with wariness.

"Sisco. You almost missed it. Have a seat over there," Fito said, not fazed. He'd told Mia he'd cleared her audition with Sisco first, but had brushed it off when she asked how Sisco had handled the news. She gathered it hadn't gone well, as evidenced by how many times he'd slammed his office door that morning.

"Thanks. Glad somebody invited me," Sisco answered. He sat directly opposite her, and she burned under the stare that scrutinized her. A hush fell over the room as tension thickened the air. Someone coughed awkwardly in the back. "All right. You think you can sing. Go ahead."

Glancing at Sal, Mia saw his nostrils flare slightly as he cut his eyes at Sisco. Fito just nodded at her encouragingly and counted the beats to the opening notes. Her heart was hammering in her chest and throat, vibrating throughout her body but she would not allow herself to be intimidated. Carla was right. Sisco's only talent was being a bully, and she couldn't let him win.

At first, her eyes remained on Salvador, but as the music compelled her to open her mouth and sing, even she was surprised at the strength in her voice. Switching focus, she withdrew into herself, controlling her breath and stomach muscles, reaching up for the higher notes without strain, projecting power that fanned across the room. When she looked back at Fito, he was grinning broadly. Salvador was gazing at her with pride; they'd practiced this song incessantly, but this was the first time she'd sung with live music. His awestruck expression never lifted as he tapped his drum in the song's leisurely beat.

And Sisco....his face was flushed, heavy with lust layered with bitterness and anger. Under that stare, she felt naked and ashamed. But she allowed herself to feel that only for one second. Just one. That awful sensation was replaced with a sense of triumph as she finished singing and swayed to the music as it continued. Their eyes locked, and when she wouldn't look away like she usually did, like he was expecting, she saw the first flicker of doubt on his face. Sisco leaned back, giving up his aggressive posture, and just nodded with a grin.

A warmth spread from her belly until it showed on her face. She wasn't smiling with Sisco but at him. Even if he somehow managed to convince or coerce Fito not to take her on, she'd shown Sisco that he wasn't in control of her, and he never would be.

Salvador didn't smile when Sisco stood up and stalked out of the room without another word. Shifting his gaze back to Mia, he nodded and smirked. With the oppressive presence gone, the band stopped playing and erupted into excited chatter as Fito came over and shook her hand.

"Gentlemen, meet our new *cantante, la Señorita* Mia Marlowe."

Then, even though she was supposed to be cool and professional, a mature, sexy songstress who could dominate a crowd, Mia laughed and ran to hug Salvador. Before either of them could quell the enthusiasm, he picked her up and swung her around. He held her against him, hugging her, then looking into her eyes, with his pearly smile on full display. They were pressed chest to chest, and his face was so close to hers that their lips would touch if either moved an inch.

"Take it easy there, kids," Memo exclaimed, and they all laughed.

"Thank you so much for this opportunity. Thank you!" Mia said to him and Fito as Salvador finally let her slide out of his arms. She tried not to think about how she still tingled with the electric pulse of being held against him or that he'd been hard against her.

"*Preciosa*, you're not going to be thanking me when you're splitting your time behind the desk and the microphone. You've got the talent. Are you sure you're up for the pace? You've got a lot of catching up to do with the songs," Fito said, his hands on his slim hips.

"I won't disappoint you, I promise."

"That's what I like to hear," Fito said, pointing at her. "Okay. Salvador said he's going to work with you on your Spanish. Practice, practice. Come to rehearsal at six tonight."

"I'll be there."

When Mia returned downstairs, she experienced that floating sensation again, almost better than the night Salvador had first walked her home. Carla was standing near the window, looking out onto the busy street. The sidewalk below shimmered with heat; above, the rooftops had a baked appearance, bleached tan, white and gray. They hadn't had rain in two weeks.

Mia was going to share the news when she glanced at her space. The items on her desk, the black telephone, the green-shaded secretary lamp she loved, pencils, and pens, were all on the floor. The desk calendar was ripped to shreds with gouges through the paper and cardboard backing. That's when she saw her ornate silver letter opener, the one her father had given her as a gift when she started working there. He jokingly said, "'Cause you can't trust those musicians."

The irony of those words as she stood with her scattered items haunted her. She turned to Carla.

"Were you here when he did this?" Mia asked her.

Carla nodded, her arms crossed as she faced the window. "I think you should go home early today. Get some rest. And maybe," she said, turning to look at Mia. "It might be time for you to move on."

Trying not to show Carla how she was quivering, Mia shook her head. "Fito just hired me. I'm so close to getting what I came here for in the first place. I can't quit now. Aren't you the one who said I shouldn't let him win?"

"That's before I saw him use that letter opener of yours," Carla said with wide eyes, pointing to it on the floor.

"Then why are you still here? You don't seem to be afraid of him no matter what he does," Mia countered.

"Because he doesn't want an old broad like me, thank God. And because I was born Carla Marie Rizzo. I know you don't know my family, but that name means something. He's nuts, but he's not *that* nuts." Her eyes were deep chocolate, and they were clear. "You're not me. You do need to worry. He's been infatuated with girls before, but I've never seen him like this."

"I can handle him."

Mia dropped the subject, overwhelmed by the swing of her emotions from frightened to powerful, elated to deeply unsettled. With a sudden horrible thought, Mia rushed around to the drawer and sighed in relief when she found her comics were there intact. If he'd messed with those, she was the one who was going to use that letter opener next.

She probably would be nuts to stay after that, she thought, bending to pick up her things from the floor. But he wasn't going to win, period. Mia did decide some time off would be good so she went and told Salvador she was going home for the afternoon and would be back in time for rehearsal that night.

***

Mia was up with the dawn and went to sit with Sal while he played with Santiago, paying deeper attention to the structure of the music and how it changed and flowed. Afterwards, they took the train down to Harlem. When she walked into headquarters after giving Sal a head start, she was surprised to see him still standing in reception. He wasn't staring at the noticeably empty space where the calendar used to be but at an enormous display of bright red roses in a crystal-cut vase sitting right in the center of her desk. Sal's eyes moved to her face, curious, and she thought, a bit jealous, judging by how thin his mouth looked.

"Looks like you have an admirer," he said, gesturing to the card tucked amongst the flowers.

Mia looked at Carla, whose face betrayed disappointment at seeing her. She shook her head and pushed away from her desk to pour herself a cup of coffee in the breakroom. Walking to her desk, Mia put her purse in her drawer and plucked the card wedged between the roses, crimson as fresh blood. She was reluctant to touch it, feeling more foreboding than pleasure. The paper was thick, creamy, and felt heavy in her hand. Taking a deep breath, she pulled out the card while Salvador watched for her reaction. She kept her face neutral as she read the message scrawled in Sisco's surprisingly fine script.

"Mia. Congratulations on the gig. I always knew my girl was going to do big things for me. We'll do big things together. I love you always, baby."

She became aware after several minutes that Sal was standing there, waiting for her to say something. Mia swallowed down the shock, the sense that she was skirting on the edge of a volcano with its pit roiling and bubbling. It was an even greater shock to realize it wasn't Sisco's rage that frightened her more. It was her own, deeply buried, rising to the surface but still contained.

"Who are the flowers from?" Sal asked, his eyebrows so furrowed they nearly touched.

Mia crumpled up the note in her fist and threw it in the trash. The flowers and the vase followed the note. She met Carla's gaze, then Salvador's.

"A nobody."

CHAPTER FIVE: HUMAN NATURE

It was another Thursday, and the workday was over. Mia was on her way to La Nueva China restaurant, anxiously peering around the block to make sure Pam or her father wouldn't see her going in that direction rather than home.

"*Hola*, Mia," Tío Juan greeted her with a wave from the counter. He beamed at her, and she smiled back, asking how he was in Spanish.

"Mia, *ven*." Tía Mavis got her attention from the kitchen doorway, beckoning to her. She began speaking rapid Spanish, no English, just as Sal had insisted. Mia gathered she wanted help to get something from a high shelf because Tito had gone somewhere.

"How was your singing?"

Mia wasn't sure if she got Mavis's question right. She responded in chopped-up Spanish, trying not to feel embarrassed at her slow progress, and said she was doing well singing the songs for the album. After almost two months, Salvador's phonetics had helped enormously, and she was copying the accent better. She wouldn't fool a native speaker in a conversation, but she was pretty decent on the recording.

"*Hola*, Mia." Sal appeared, kissing her on both cheeks, which, for some reason, he did whenever they spoke Spanish but never when it was English.

When Tito appeared, he only grunted in her direction, reserving the conversation for his family members. She tried not to care that he still hadn't warmed up to her. She'd finally had to voice the question at the back of her mind since their first meeting at Skate Key; did Tito not like her because she was Black?

"No," Sal had said with wide eyes. "The girl he was in love with back home in Havana was black."

"Oh. Well, what happened?" Mia asked after a moment.

Sal had shrugged, looking away. "It didn't work out."

Mia guessed that whatever happened that "didn't work out" had left Tito embittered toward anyone who looked like that girl, which was sort of its own form of prejudice. But she couldn't force him to like or accept her, so she dropped it, being as pleasant as possible when he was around.

That night, the restaurant emptied by eight o'clock. Mia was having such a fun time listening to Tía and Tío tell stories about their early days in New York that she didn't want to leave. Not until an ugly surprise landed on the doorstep when Sisco appeared. Mia wasn't sure if he'd known they'd be there or if he was as unhappily surprised as they were. The look of outrage on his face was enough.

"What the fuck are you doing here, Mia? You know I've got a policy about motherfuckers dating at the office," Sisco had said, looming over their table.

Staring up at him with wide, startled eyes, Mia said, "We're not dating. We're just friends." The look on Sal's face, a mixture of hurt and resignation, made her ashamed.

Sisco stood taller, his gaze hostile and settling into something that was more than a little frightening, like listening to a Rottweiler beginning a low growl in its throat as it started showing teeth. That moment when it's freeze or fly, and the room was so small there'd be no way around him either way.

In the time since he'd given her his bouquet and "love" note, Sisco had grown more erratic, swinging from upset whenever he heard her singing upstairs to murmuring praise at her for how she moved him when she sang. How he wanted her to sing for him, alone. Despite everything, she'd clung stubbornly to the belief that she could control this situation, until now.

Mia looked at Sal, wondering if she'd see the same fright she was feeling. She went mute when she saw his eyes were pitch black and every bit as hostile as Sisco's. A muscle ticked in his jaw, set at a sharp angle.

"We're not at work right now, and we're not finished our dinner, so, if you don't mind." He gestured toward the kitchen with a flat palm. "My Tío Juan will get you whatever you need, but you should hurry. The kitchen is about to close."

Sal's voice had been steady while he delivered this speech, nothing betraying either anger or fear. His tone was neutral but firm, the way he always spoke to Sisco, not intimidated by his size or his power to make or break careers. And Sal's quiet self-possession, his protectiveness, made her belly flood with a sinuous, liquid heat she'd never felt before. But she also understood how dangerous it was for Sal to disrespect Sisco, especially in public.

"Yo, I don't give a fuck where we are. Get up, Mia. Now." Sisco took a step closer to Mia, but Sal rose with his chin lifted, blocking his path.

Mia's throat squeezed, comparing the two of them. Sisco was a hulk with a height advantage, but Sal had muscle and was pretty solid. If there was a fight, it would be ugly. Before either could say another word, Tito walked out of the kitchen. A machete was tucked into his apron, and his lips were set in a line.

"Is there a problem?" he asked, staring at Sisco with his arms hanging loose at his sides.

This time the size match was even. Tito's face was impassive, but his eyes blazed. Sal was utterly still. Juan came from around the counter, wiping his steak knife on his own apron and keeping it in his hand. Sisco looked at them with contempt, but she saw unease in his shifting glance for the first time since she'd met him.

"This place is a fucking dump. You surprised me, Mia. Thought you had a little more class." Sisco popped his collar, and his stare swung back to Salvador. "I'll see *you* tomorrow."

Everyone but Tito seemed to breathe again when Sisco lurched out the door. Mavis rushed to the window to watch and make sure he was gone. She locked the door.

"That was your boss?" Juan asked in Spanish. He sighed and shook his head. "He's crazy. Maybe you shouldn't go back tomorrow. Or ever." With another shake of his head, he went back behind the counter.

"We can't just not go. We've got meetings and rehearsals," Sal argued.

"Salvo—" Tito began.

"It's cool, Tito. I can handle him," Sal cut him off. He seemed more annoyed with his brother than he had with Sisco.

Later, after they closed the restaurant and Tito went his own way, Sal walked Mia home in silence. They both paused when she took out the keys to her family's apartment.

"I'm sorry for what happened. I feel like it's my fault," Mia finally said.

"It's not. There's only one person to blame for his behavior, and that's Sisco. I've never asked you this because I didn't want to hear an answer I didn't like, but is there—was there ever anything between you two? Because he's said things that made me think there definitely was." His voice was quiet and his eyes, already dark, were depthless, as though they'd swallowed all the light in the hallway.

"No. Never. When I met him, he was all business. He promised to give me a chance. But once he made it clear what he really wanted, I said no. I stayed at the label, hoping that someday someone who really believed I had talent would walk through that door. And then you showed up." Mia stared into that deep-ink gaze, looking back at her with open longing. He overtook her again, and that sensation knocked down what was left of her reserve. "Salvador. If it wasn't for him, would you want us to be more than friends?"

Sal was so close that she could feel his warm breath skip across her cheek. Mia shivered, touching the warmth of his chest through his shirt. "Yes," he whispered, bathing her in his coconut scent and his heat. "I don't care what he does anymore. You're mine, Mia. All mine. I love you."

The way he spoke and his look of pure devotion washed over her. Her response rose to her lips all on its own, from the deepest place inside her. There was no doubt, no hesitation when she said, "I love you too."

Mia was suspended, trapped in that delicious moment where he was all that existed. Sal slid his hand up her cheekbone, cradling her face. One more second, then their lips were touching, with such tenderness it made her tremble. He exhaled, pulled her in tighter, and she parted her lips to allow the kiss to deepen. She loved feeling his rapid heartbeat against her breasts and the bristle of new growth on his jaw under her fingertips, loved the way he held her, made her feel wanted and cherished in a way she'd never experienced.

Suddenly the door swung open, and they jumped apart. Pam stood in her robe and pink sponge rollers, glaring at Sal.

"Good evening, Mrs. Marlow," Sal said politely, looking more nervous in her presence than he had with Sisco.

"It's late. Boy, what are you doing in front of my door at this hour?" Pam asked, folding her arms across her chest.

"Making sure Mia gets home safe."

"Mm-hmm, well, thanks, but you can leave now. Go home."

"Goodnight, Mia." Sal's eyes on her were worried.

"Goodnight, Salvador."

Once he was gone, Pam pulled her inside and pushed her towards her bedroom. "I thought I told you I didn't want that boy coming around again. You are determined to get knocked up with some little light-skinned baby, aren't you?"

Something in Mia just snapped, emboldened by Salvador standing up to Sisco, no matter the outcome. "I'm not fifteen like you were, Pam. I know better than that. Trust me, I don't want your life."

Mia braced herself, waiting for Pam to get her belt for the back-talk, but she stood there, her chest heaving. She could see that her verbal blow had landed as Pam's eyes widened. Pam actually looked hurt.

"Why have you hated me all these years?" Mia asked before she could halt the words. Her throat thickened with tears. "I was just a little girl. What could I possibly have done to make you dislike me? Is it because I looked like my mother, and you couldn't handle knowing you weren't first?"

Pam gripped her own elbows, shaking her head. "No, Mia. It was because of what *I* had before I met your father. When I was fifteen, I had a boyfriend who said he cared about me, then turned around and ditched me the second I told him I was pregnant. My mother threw me out because she was more worried about church folk looking down on her for my 'sins'. We had to stay with a neighbor, Miss Mabel. She was so sweet, but she was too old to be taking care of a baby, and I couldn't afford anybody else. She'd forget she left the stove on or let strangers in the house. Every day I'd be terrified to leave Cherise, not knowing what would happen while I worked my two jobs cleaning at a hotel and waitressing in a bar with grown men trying to feel me up. Am I hard on you? You're damned right I am. I *have* to push you to do better than I did. You are so smart, Mia. And you're talented. If you don't succeed, then I'll know I failed. It's not that I don't love you. I just can't bear to see you go through what I did."

Frozen tears she would never allow to fall glinted in Pam's eyes as she went down the hall to her bedroom and shut the door.

CHAPTER SIX: BLUE VELVET

The next morning, Sal stood in front of headquarters, preparing to face Sisco. He would have preferred to be anywhere else in the world at that moment, but he couldn't leave Mia to deal with Sisco alone. He'd spent half the night replaying the scene at the restaurant and remembering the queasy fear that had gripped him, despite showing everyone a brave face.

Then the memory of the incident had given way to fantasizing about the sweet expression on Mia's features when she'd said she loved him. That delicious kiss had him aching and twisting in his sheets. After all these months trying his hardest not to touch her, denying them the pleasure he'd known they both craved, one kiss wasn't enough. He was dying to see her for another dose of her sunshine, no matter the cost.

Carla was alone in the reception area, as usual. "You're early this morning. It's not even eight-thirty," she said, looking up from the big book opened on her desk to check her watch. "Excited for tomorrow, kiddo?"

"Yeah. Is Sisco here yet?" he asked, rubbing his sweaty palms on his slacks.

"He's in his office with Fito and Memo."

Carla went back to her book while Sal took a seat. The building was otherwise silent. She cursed under her breath when her summons came through on the phone. Rolling her eyes at Sal, she said, "The master calls. Just when I was getting to the good part." Holding up the book with a shrewd grin, Carla handed it to him before going to the mahogany door with her pencil and notepad.

Our Bodies, Ourselves was written on the cover in green lettering and a photo of women holding up protest banners. "What's this?" Sal asked with puzzlement. "Is this like a science book or a political thing?"

"Just give it a skim. You'll both thank me later."

He had no idea what she meant by that. Shrugging, Sal took the book to the small alcove with the padded bench where Mia sometimes perused her collection of old Black Panther comics on her breaks. He read the intro, and his eyes could have popped out of his skull. Tito had given him "the talk". It was mainly about not getting a girl pregnant, but nothing about what led to that point or how to please one in the process. The book was about women's bodies, sex, and what they liked. And there were drawings, like classy porno scenes. In the few encounters he'd had, the girl had seemed into it, but he'd never been sure if he was getting anything right. Dammit. According to this book, he'd probably been getting it wrong.

His face burned while he flipped through the illustrations and the advice, wondering what Carla needed it for since she was already married and had grown kids. Then he thought about Mia and what she might like. Suddenly desperate to know more, he read as much as he could, hastily dropping the book when the office door opened and Fito and Memo emerged wearing uncharacteristic scowls.

Fito spotted him and beckoned him over. "I tried calling you, but your brother said you left already. The meeting's canceled for this morning."

"Is there a problem? We're still on for the show, right?" Sal asked, looking from one face to another. Carla regained her seat at her desk, shaking her head.

"Just somebody being stubborn, as usual. The organizers announced they want to do a taping and sell it after the show, but Sisco's giving them shit about the distribution rights. Like we're so big time, he thinks threatening to pull out is going to cost them more than it costs us. Sick of his shit." Fito had never looked so angry. He pulled Sal toward the door to the lobby. "Just go home, kid. Relax, get some rest, and come to my house tonight. We'll jam a little bit down there. Bring Mia, but tell her I don't want her singing. She needs to save that voice for tomorrow."

"All right, we'll come over tonight."

On the way out, Sal met Mia about to ascend the stairs. Fito grinned and winked at them as he left, tipping his hat to Mia. Sal stopped her, leaning in for a kiss but she put a staying hand on his chest.

"No, *amor*. No more hiding." Pressing his lips against hers, he no longer cared if Sisco or anyone else saw them together.

"Why are you and Fito leaving? Did something happen this morning?" she asked with concern after he pulled back and stroked her satiny cheek.

"Sisco pissed Fito off, so Fito canceled the meeting and told us to come for rehearsal later at his house. I'm gonna bet Sisco's in an even worse mood than last night. Maybe you should call Carla and tell her you need to rest for tomorrow. Let's spend the day together. We'll go wherever you want. Do whatever you want."

Willing her to agree, pleading with his eyes, his chest was full when Mia nodded with a soft smile dimpling her cheek. They rushed around the corner to the nearest phone booth so she could make the call. It didn't take long, but Carla must have said something because Mia's smile turned embarrassed.

"Carla already saw us from the window. She said we'd make terrible spies."

Sal laughed in agreement. "Does she know about us? I get the feeling she does." He thought of the book on her desk and flushed.

"Yeah. It's come up. She, um, made me read this book she has stashed in her desk."

"Let me guess. The white book with the green letters and the ladies on the cover?" Sal said, quirking his eyebrow.

"That's the one." Mia paused as they stood outside the phone booth, looking uncertain and excited. A combination that set off a throbbing inside him. "Did you look at it?"

The air around them condensed into a soft bubble as though they were in the phone booth together. Mia's gaze rose, held his, and he fell thoroughly under her spell. He wasn't aware of reaching out to touch her hip until he felt the brush of the blue denim under his fingertips, almost as soft as velvet.

"Yeah. I've thought about us doing some of those things. But I would never want to pressure you if that's not what you wanted," he blurted.

Mia's eyes turned even softer. When she put her hand in his, he felt a jolt of lust and longing so strong it overwhelmed everything else.

"I've thought about it, too. But I've never done *it*. I probably wouldn't be that good at it."

Sal's insides tightened to know she'd want to share something so important with him. "Mia, you're good at everything you do. I'm not worried about that. I just want you to be sure you want me to be your first. It should be special for you."

"Are you saying I should wait for someone else?" Mia asked with a slow, teasing smile.

His eyes widened. "No."

"I thought so. Where can we go?"

CHAPTER SEVEN: LET ME BE YOUR ANGEL

The apartment was quiet when Salvador unlocked the front door. Mia followed him in, laying her purse on the table. Just to make sure Tito wasn't home, he checked the kitchen and the bathroom. She'd been there before, briefly, when they were hanging out, and Sal needed to pick up or drop something off. It was cramped, and the walls were an unremarkable beige. Tito's clothing strewn about the living room made it messy, but peering down the short hallway, she could see Salvador's room was neat at least.

Sal returned while she looked at the shelves near the door. Black and white pictures of their parents, young and smiling, adorned one level. Another showed Tito and Salvador as little boys with big grins and missing teeth. There were a lot of books about music, English classics, some novels she owned, and a thick, dog-eared Spanish-English dictionary. She paused at the stacks of horror paperbacks and pulp fiction.

"Those are Tito's," Sal said with a headshake. He seemed nervous suddenly, his arms crossing as he stared at her.

She knew he wanted her as badly as she wanted him, but he wasn't making a move. Deciding somebody had to get this started, Mia took a breath and reached out. His expression changed from nervous to needful, and he opened his arms, stepping in to meet her halfway. This time, their kiss wasn't gentle like the night before; this was deeper, more urgent, tongues exploring with boldness.

"Are you ready?" Salvador asked, his arm around her waist. Mia nodded with a breathless grin, and they were in his bedroom within a few strides.

Sal shut the door behind them but paused again at the side of the bed, staring at her the way he had the very first time they'd seen each other. But she realized the look in those eyes wasn't quite the same. Back then, they didn't know each other; only curiosity and lust existed. Now they were best friends, and there was adoration in his gaze, overflowing when she touched his face.

"I've dreamed about this moment since we met, Mia," he said. "But are you sure you want this? We can wait."

"I want this," she whispered. "I want you, Salvador."

At her words, she felt his relief, but his body tightened in a different way. His kiss was hotter while he pulled off her clothes, his mouth traveling from her lips to her throat, where he nibbled and then moved lower to taste the hollow at her collarbone. He squeezed her breasts when they were free of her bra and took each nipple in his mouth, alternating between them while she tried getting his shirt off. It was impossible to do both, and she laughed breathlessly until he lifted his head and smiled.

He pulled his shirt over his head and dropped it on the floor alongside hers. Mia sucked in a breath at the beauty of his firm chest and immediately reached to touch it, running her hand along his pecs. Sal trembled when she touched his nipples, his eyelids lowering, and she was surprised to realize a man could enjoy that. Mia gripped them with more purpose, and he groaned, and that slight sound thrilled her. When he did the same to her, she gasped, and they did that for a time, just exploring each other with their hands and taking off what was left of their clothing until they were fully nude. Her own responses surprised her. She'd always envisioned her first time happening in darkness, under covers, anything to stay hidden. But she wanted Salvador to see her, really see her.

Salvador's cock was fully erect. It wasn't her first time seeing one, but this was the first that would enter her body. She shivered at the thought of what was about to happen. While she loved that it was thick and veined, she was intimidated.

"Um, how is this supposed to fit? I don't think I'm this big inside," she said dubiously.

Sal grinned. "It'll work. The book said we can get you ready. Lie down."

"Well, if the book said so," Mia said with a raised eyebrow, and he laughed lightly, with an undertone of excitement.

Mia got on the bed, and he followed, pushing her to lie on her back. Sal's hands traced her body in a line that scorched a fire trail across her skin. He leaned down to kiss and tease her nipples again between his fingers, then skimmed between her thighs to stroke upward to her pussy. It felt strange to have someone's hand other than her own petting the softness there, then parting the crease to explore. When he touched her clit gently and began to rub around the hood, Mia gasped, opening her legs wider.

For a while, she focused on that while he stopped kissing to watch her reactions with that intense gaze. He pressed one finger inside her opening, then another, breathing almost as heavily as she was when she moaned softly. Mia felt wetness on her hip when Sal's cock brushed it. She grasped it, experienced enough to know how to stroke back and forth firmly yet gently. The look on his face at her touch made a corresponding pulse go off in her body.

"You're really wet," he said, his voice hushed in the quiet of the room. "The book said that's a good sign."

She laughed, and he looked down at the quiver of her breasts, groaning before leaning down to suck her nipple again. "I think so. Maybe it's time to put a rubber on."

"Okay, but the book also said we should try to make you come first. Have you come before?" he asked.

"By myself, yeah."

"Shit, I'd love to watch you do that, but that's my job today."

His fingers inside her moved quicker, and his breath was faster. She was alarmed when he moved down her side and between her legs. He inhaled, and despite her sudden worry he wouldn't like her scent, it seemed to make him more excited. Mia's pulse fluttered in her throat like a wild thing trapped under her skin while he leaned in, replacing his talented fingers with his mouth.

Her eyes were on the ceiling fan, whirling above them in lazy sweeping circles, and she gripped the sheet underneath her when he did the same to her clit with his tongue. Each wet stroke grew bolder while he became more confident and the sensation of it was the most intense pleasure she'd ever felt. It rose higher, an unbearable tension that twisted and coiled until it burst in a shower of rapture. The cry that tore from her sounded like another person, another Mia, someone free that she had only suspected was inside her.

After a while, as she descended from that glorious high, she became aware that Sal was looking up at her with a huge grin.

"I got it right?" he asked, and she laughed, still shivering.

"Yes."

Sal moved up, kissing her, and she was curiously aroused to smell herself on him. She sucked on the tongue that had given her such exquisite pleasure and wanted to return the favor, even though she wasn't sure just what to do. She and Tonya hadn't covered that in the lesson. Sal lay back, his eyes closing, while she reached down and took his cock in her hand. He moaned when she licked the head, tasting his flavor and liking it. She didn't get much farther than wrapping her lips around it for a few seconds; she sucked once, and that was all he could seem to take. He reached over to the bedside table and pushed her off gently to unroll the rubber on quickly.

Sal reversed their positions, so she was lying down again, then gripped himself and rocked into her gently, slowly, withdrawing, then pushing in deeper until he was fully seated. His eyes were heavy-lidded, gazing into hers with a dark lust that thrilled her, turning the stinging pain of his cock stretching her open into a deep, unfamiliar delight. It felt strange, it hurt, but it was the best hurt she'd ever felt because it was Salvador inside her.

"Okay?" he panted. His face was flushed darker, and his mouth was parted as he began to move, picking up speed when she nodded.

"Yes, yes, it's good," Mia moaned. "Please..." She didn't know what she was asking for, only knew she needed more of this.

"You're so sweet, Mia," he whispered, his breath starting to hitch as he thrust his hips deeper. "So sweet. Look how good you're taking me, just like I knew you would. *Damn.*"

Sal pulled her thighs open wider, his strokes a perfect rhythm like her pussy was another drum under his command, beating her just right, not too hard but enough to wring more cries from her. Sweat rolled down his temple, and she wiped it away. He groaned her name, and she was fascinated watching his face crease when he tensed and then shook, falling into her arms with a low guttural cry.

When he pulled out, she still hurt, but her entire body buzzed. Salvador fought to slow his breathing by her side, pulling the rubber off and rejoining her until they were lying face to face. The bubbling excitement had simmered down to a dreamy haze of pure tenderness as he stroked her cheek with a look in his eyes that made her own water.

"How do you feel?" he asked.

"Wonderful." She pressed his hand closer. "Happy. How do you feel?"

Sal's eyes caressed her along with his hand. "In love, with you."

CHAPTER EIGHT: SUPERSTAR

The next morning, Sal walked out into the living room to find Tito already up. He took a drag of his cigarette as he regarded Sal with a mixture of pride and concern.

"It's your big day. How are you feeling?"

"Good. Nervous but good."

Salvador brewed some coffee, his stomach too noisy to handle anything else. His hands had never shaken before, but the liquid in his small tin cup was trembling when he lifted it to his mouth.

"Listen," Tito began after a silence. "Yesterday, I went to smoke a cig on my break and realized I was down to my last one. I came home to get the extra pack I kept in the drawer and saw a girl's purse on the table. Your door was closed. I'm gonna guess you were in there with Mia."

Sal blew out a breath. "If you're going to tell me I shouldn't have, please don't. It's obvious what the problem is. You're jealous."

Tito froze. "Jealous, how?"

"Ever since we left home, it's just been us, even with Juan and Mavis nearby. I think you're worried I'll go off with her and leave you behind, but I won't. She'll add to our family, not take anything away."

Shaking his head, Tito frowned. "That's not what concerns me right now. What about what happened the other night with Sisco because of her? Why didn't you come to me and let me know what was going on?"

"Because I figured you'd blame her like you just did. And I don't need you to handle anything. I can manage Sisco myself," Sal declared in frustration.

"He's not just some punk you can brush off, Salvo. I talked to some people who know him or know of him, and I heard things about how he deals with people who don't give him what he wants. He might be wearing a suit instead of colors, but make no mistake, little brother. He's a fucking gangster."

"Yeah, the guys in the band told me those rumors too, but they still work for him. It can't be as bad as you're suggesting, or he would've been locked up by now."

Tito sat back with a humorless laugh. "Shit. After everything we've been through, are you really this naïve? It's like you don't remember how we got here. Why we're not at home with Mami and Papi."

There it was, the unspoken thing welling up from the forbidden depths of memory. Tito never wanted to talk about it, wanted to bury it, but Sal did remember. He'd been there when Tito faced down a man like that, a man with government connections who wanted the girl he loved for himself. Carmencita. And when that man had come for him, and Tito defended himself, he'd been forced to do something that had damaged his soul. In desperation, their parents had urged them to flee, to find shelter and a new life in the States. And after everything, Carmencita refused to go with Tito. She hadn't loved him enough. And they'd lost everything.

His voice low, Sal said, "Don't think I've forgotten a second of it. You did what you needed to do, but this is different. Sisco's a businessman first. He's got too much to lose to go that far."

Tito's stare was stark, but he nodded. "Well, I guess you know more than me. Just watch your back."

"I should get going. Here's your pass." Sal plucked the ticket and VIP pass from the bookshelf, showed it to Tito, and then placed them back in their spot. "I'll see you tonight."

He went to the front door to pick up his conga but paused. Sal returned to the table and hugged Tito's shoulders. Tito held onto his arm for a time, causing Sal's vision to blur. Before he went for the door a second time, Tito said, "Regardless. Proud of you, man." Grinning at him, Sal left.

***

Twilight had descended. Sal was in the dressing room, but they only had limited time before they had to hustle out onto the stage. His hands were still shaking, but Memo squeezed his shoulder and pounded the jitters out with a slap on his back.

"You're gonna be okay, kid," Fito said, giving him a second pounding.

"Can you encourage me without breaking my back?" Sal exclaimed, and they laughed.

He only relaxed when he saw Tito come in, dressed to impress for a change in a charcoal shirt and black slacks. They hugged, and Tito greeted everyone. They both turned to stare when Mia rushed in moments later, followed by Tonya and Alonzo. She was absolutely stunning. Her hair was parted on one side and drawn into a billowing ponytail wrapped with gold wire at the base. It matched the shimmering gold sequin halter jumpsuit and sandals she wore, setting off her rich, dark skin to perfection.

Glancing at them, Tito offered her a rare "hello" and retreated to the side to give them a moment.

"You look amazing," Sal said, floored at the idea that just yesterday he'd held her in his arms, in his bed, and she'd been so sweet and innocent, and now...she was a full, flowering goddess. A goddess who looked like she was about to collapse in tears.

"We're gonna go find our seats," Tonya said, giving Mia a hug. "You're gonna be great. We'll see you after."

When her friends left, Sal asked, "What's wrong? Did something happen at home?"

"No, it's not them. It's me. I can't do this. I just came to tell you and Fito, but now I can't even face him. Tell him I'm sorry, and I–I just can't."

More tears bubbled up in her wide eyes, an even deeper gold than her outfit, and she backed away out of the dressing room. Sal followed, ignoring the frantic traffic going back and forth down the backstage hallway. He was in the presence of stars he'd worshiped, but for the moment, he forgot to be in awe of them. Even when the deities known as Mongo Santamaria and Celia Cruz passed by with friendly nods, all Sal cared about was the frightened face of the girl who was about to cut and run.

"No, Mia. You can. And you will."

"I can't," she moaned, the sound so different from the pleasures of their sweet, stolen afternoon. "I'm going to embarrass myself in front of all those people. They're gonna wonder who the hell let me up there. I'm so sorry. I'm so–"

"Stop apologizing and get it together." His voice was brusque, and she blinked with surprise. Sal hated speaking to her that way, wanted nothing more than to swaddle her in tenderness and tell her it was okay to just go home. But he couldn't do that. "Mia, this is your chance. It's happening now, whether or not you're ready. Baby, I

MIA'S LOVE ❧ **348**

need you on that stage with me. What am I gonna do without my girl, huh?"

Mia shook her head, but she laughed a little. "All they need on that stage is you. You look so handsome."

She ran her hands down the collar of his silk maroon shirt. Sal shivered at her touch, needing more. It was a struggle not to kiss her and ruin her perfect, red-painted lips, but there wasn't time.

Groaning, he pulled her hand off his chest and held it instead. "Later. Right now, we all need you to get out there and do your job. It's not just a dream anymore. It's your job. And it's time for us to go to work. Baby, you are gonna blow everybody away."

A girl carrying a clipboard ran down the hall to the dressing room doorway. "Five minutes!" she called. The voices in the room grew noisier as everyone began filtering out. Fito looked at them with a raised eyebrow, the question clear in his expression. Sal could feel Mia's trembling, almost the same way she'd trembled in his arms, but he let it rise instead of tamping down the lust that surged in him. He needed this power, this energy coursing through every vein and firing up his muscles. It was better than adrenaline.

The awareness of being watched managed to pierce that internal body armor. From beyond her shoulder, he saw Sisco staring at them with a bottle gripped in one fist. His eyes were red with intoxication and dull rage. The eyes of a beast swiftly losing touch with his humanity. A slow grin oozed across his lips. He raised his free hand, formed into the shape of a gun, and cocked his finger in Mia's direction. He mouthed, "*Pop, pop.*"

Sal's blood froze, understanding the message. Tito's warning hit him full force, and he was sorry he hadn't listened. His jaw settling, he knew what he had to do. But first, the show.

When he turned, Tito was there, putting his arm around Sal's shoulder and the other around Mia's as he led them after the band members down the hall. Tito hugged him, murmuring, "You're gonna be great, Salvo." And then he stood back while Sal and Mia stepped out on stage.

Instantly, he was blinded by the glare of the stage lights aimed up at them; the crowd beyond was a dark mass interrupted by sparks of white and blue light. It was so hot up there; it hadn't felt this hot during the rehearsal, and he immediately felt the trickle of sweat down his back. Polite applause began, not quite as enthusiastic as it would be later when the bigger names showed up, but it was humbling to be on the receiving end just the same.

Alternating between English and Spanish, Fito greeted the crowd, who clapped again. Mia stood on her mark, just to Sal's right, squinting at the audience and then at him. Everything went quiet as the lights dimmed, creating a sensual atmosphere. Her jumpsuit glimmered in the soft glow. Sal couldn't stop staring at her as slowly her transformation began. She held the mic stand in one hand, closed her eyes, and began to sing in perfectly accented Spanish.

There was a hush when her voice rang out in clear, crisp notes. Even Sal was stunned at the power of it, realizing it had been there under the surface all along. It was finally set loose. They all started playing, each instrument joining in until the harmony overcame everything else. There was no more anxiety or fear. No worries about anything or anyone that wasn't a part of the fantastical magic they were creating. Fito looked at them, grinning from his spot behind the tambores like he was in paradise.

In the end, their set was only six songs, but when Fito named them one at a time, the crowd's appreciation was more than polite. It was a roar of approval. They clapped and cheered hard when it was Sal's turn to be introduced, and his heart swelled with pride as he bowed. But for Mia, there was a standing ovation. The look on her face at their acceptance, to hear how much the crowd loved her, was the best moment of his entire night.

And it might be her last good memory of their time together. He had to make it last for her forever. As they all left the stage, he grabbed her hand, squeezing it tight, and whispered in her ear, "You were wonderful."

"Come on, guys, let's celebrate!" Fito exclaimed as they walked backstage.

But Sal knew he'd run out of time for that. He pulled Mia along, away from the streams of people waiting to congratulate her and shake her hand, and she let him, suddenly shy again despite her triumph. As though she'd burned through all that enormous power on stage and was now depleted. Looking around, he pulled her down a different corridor and found a small supply closet, fortunately, unlocked.

"I love you, Mia," he murmured, all the lustful energy he'd poured into his performance redirecting again, back into needing her.

For the second time, and quite possibly the last time, he pulled her clothes off in the tiny, dimly lit closet and hastily pushed his pants and boxers down. There was no caution, no hesitation, no question of what he was doing right or wrong, just the raging desire to draw satisfaction from her beautiful body and give himself up to her. She held on, showing him how much she needed this connection again.

"I love you, too. Oh, *Salvador*," she breathed when he found her breast and sucked her nipple inside his mouth.

There was nothing in the closet to lean on but a rolling cart. Sal pushed it against the wall and sat her on it, rubbing the head of his cock up and down her crease. She gasped, moaned, and then covered her mouth with her hand when he pushed deep into her with a sudden thrust. At first, she held onto his shoulders with one arm while he found his rhythm, until they created one together, until her pleasure mounted, her breasts shaking with every motion he made.

His own pleasure was rising too quickly. Sal withdrew, despite her hushed protest, but she stopped complaining when he got down on his knees, inhaled her, tasted her, and sucked on her. Couldn't get enough of her tangy nectar and how she made him feel, knowing he was pleasing her. The hair he'd combed and styled to perfection was ruined when she suddenly tugged on it, a small, sharp cry escaping between her fingers. She was still desperate for him when she pulled him up and urged him back inside, her hot pussy a sweet, dripping haven.

"Mia," he moaned against her throat.

He didn't care if he wasn't quiet, didn't care if the cart's wheels were squeaking crazily or if it left chips in the wall from banging into it. Everything was condensed down to how she felt enveloping his cock, the sheen of sweat on her skin under the single lightbulb. He grinned, his breath hitching, staring at her lush mouth while she panted. She was purity to him, whole and giving, but he still felt a dirty excitement knowing people were strolling by the door, unaware of them and what was happening in this tiny, now sacred space.

That last thought did him in, and he pulled out abruptly, finishing himself off with a stroke, shooting pearl white lava all over her lower belly. He collapsed on her, the cart taking his full weight while they shivered and held each other. But there was no more time left for relaxing the way they had the day before. He was instantly alert to the reverberations of the music coming through the walls from the next act on the stage.

"Looks like I made a mess," he said, running a finger over the sticky wetness he'd left on her skin.

"Good thing this is where they keep the towels," Mia replied.

Sal chuckled. "I guess we got lucky. Let me help." He ripped open a roll of paper towels and cleaned her off with gentle yet thorough swipes. "There. All clean."

Pulling up his pants and zipping them, he waited for Mia to get her jumpsuit back on and smooth down her hair. But faced with the prospect of what might be waiting for them, Sal hesitated before opening the door. Peering down the hallway in both directions, he saw it was all clear. He gathered her back into his arms, breathing in her skin's sweet, body-butter scent.

"I want you to know when I say that this was the best night of my life, I'm not talking about the show. It was this. It's you. It's all because of you." Sal cradled her beautiful face in his palm, absorbing every beloved feature. "My Mia. My superstar. Now I want you to go find Tito and let him take you home."

"Why would I leave with Tito?" Mia asked, puzzled. "You're not going to an after-party without me, are you?"

"No. I just need to take care of something for Fito," he fibbed. "I'll come find you as soon as I'm done."

Kissing her again, he ushered her out the door, hating to do this, but needing to know she was safe. She still looked confused, but she didn't argue. Then, inhaling, filling himself with steel, he looked around the room. On a shelf, he found a box of tools, and in it was a screwdriver. He picked it up, looking down at it as though the hand holding it wasn't his own. This wasn't him. This was actually ridiculous, thinking he was going to defeat a man like Sisco with something this insignificant. But Sisco wasn't leaving him much choice but to settle this problem once and for all. Armed and ready, he set off to look for Sisco and face him head-on. To keep Mia safe from him. For Mia's love.

But he didn't find him. Not in the crowd, not in the men's room or the downstairs lounge. Not in the balconies on the upper level, swilling champagne and playing the big shot like he otherwise would. A mixture of relief and anxiety overtook him as he searched for Sisco and found ... nothing.

Sal went backstage to the dressing room, but by then, another band was in there waiting for their turn. In and out, no time to waste. He caught up to Fito and the others outside on the sidewalk, signing autographs for a slew of new fans. Mia was with them, signing autographs and looking serene and professional, like she'd been doing this for years. Marveling at her once more, Sal squeezed his way through the crowd.

"Where's Tito? Why didn't you go with him?" Sal asked, peering over heads to look in all directions.

"He was gone. I'm ready to go if you are," Mia said, still smiling at the fans and scribbling her name.

His heart lodged in his throat at her words. "All right. Let's go home."

"Hey, what's this? You have to come to celebrate with us. We're going to the Copa for a little disco." Fito did a hip-swivel, and Memo groaned.

Sal shook his head. "We're tired. We'll see you next week."

"I'm leaving too. I can give you a ride if you want," Memo offered.

Tito wasn't there when Sal and Mia entered the apartment a half hour later. Even though it was still early, she was exhausted from the energy expended and the interaction, and her battery had run down to just about zero. After a quick shower, she put on a shirt he offered her and collapsed onto his bed, asleep almost the second her head touched the pillow. Sal lay with his eyes open in the dark, watching the occasional sweep of headlights from passing cars drift across the wall. He only allowed his lids to close when he finally heard the front door unlocking and the sound of Tito's keys clattering against the porcelain dish on the bookshelf.

***

Soft kisses along his jawline woke Sal the next morning along with a strong dose of sunshine. Mia's face, free of makeup, was the most gorgeous thing he'd seen. The smell of coffee brewing hit his nose, then his stomach, and he stretched, wrapping his arms around her.

"Making my *cafecito* for me? You're gonna be such a good wife when we get married," he said.

Mia laughed. "I don't see no ring on this finger." She held up her left hand with a twist of her lips.

"Give me a minute. I'll fix that."

"Anyway, I haven't been to the kitchen because I don't have any pants. I hope Tito won't mind that I stayed here."

"Don't worry about Tito," Sal said.

"Okay." Mia leaned down to kiss him again, then got up and left the bed. "I still need pants, though. Do you have something I could wear?"

Dressed in a pair of his track pants, Mia went to the bathroom while he went to seek out Tito in the living room. His brother was at the dining table, lit cigarette in one hand, coffee cup in the other. He sat calmly, reading his book. It wasn't until Sal reached the table that he saw Tito's eye swollen shut under a darkening bruise and a bandage taped to the side of his neck.

His heart-stopping, then picking up speed again, Sal stared at him. "What happened? Tito?"

"I cut myself shaving," Tito replied and took a sip, still looking at his paperback. In his black tank top, body stiff, he looked ancient, impenetrable as a stone. He finally turned to Sal. "You were great last night. You and Mia." The one good eye watered, and he turned back to his book.

Sal set down his cup, reaching over to pull his brother into a hard embrace. Tito held on for a long time. Tears swam in Sal's own eyes, gratitude indistinguishable from sorrow.

"Thank you, Tito. Thank you."

EPILOGUE: THE BLUEPRINT

Three months later...

Sal was lounging in reception, listening to Carla go on about the book she was reading by somebody named Susan Sontag when Mia rushed in carrying a thick envelope.

"Is that it?" Sal asked with a grin.

"Yup!"

Immediately, he got up from his chair and followed her and Carla to the mahogany door, giving it a hard knock. They heard "Come in!" from the other side and entered.

Fito was sitting behind the black lacquered desk with his feet up. He was putting the phone down when he saw what Mia was carrying. A huge grin splitting his face. He pointed to the tv on its rolling cart.

"Let's see this magnificence," he said, rubbing his hands together.

Mia went to the VHS player, a top-of-the-line model, and pushed the tape in the slot. She turned the television to the right channel and came back to Sal, struggling with him for a seat on the chair until he pulled her onto his lap. He knew she didn't enjoy flaunting their newlywed love quite so openly, but she'd just have to deal with it.

"Oh my God, I look like a freaking Oscar award," she said with a laugh. "The sound is good, though."

They were watching the Roseland performance, their first appearance on a big stage. Sal thought he looked good playing, but Mia was as dazzling on tape as she'd been in person.

It was because of the show that their album *Canción de Mi Vida* debuted at the top of the Latin charts. When it became known that Mia was an unsigned artist, offers to meet with agents who represented R&B, Latin, and pop stars began rolling in. The agents were only brave enough to make an attempt because the obstacle that had stood in her way had vanished the night of the show.

The manner of Sisco Diaz's sudden departure had come as no surprise to almost anyone who knew him. One minute he was around, making life hell for everyone he encountered, and the next, he was gone. No one was brokenhearted over it, not the artists he'd withheld royalties from since beginning the label, or the wife he'd left in the Bronx with two kids and no support, or the gentlemen on Arthur Avenue to whom he owed quite a lot of money. It was presumed he was somewhere in Puerto Rico, but if no one saw him again, it would suit them just fine.

Fito had taken over management of the label temporarily until Sisco was found. If Sisco was found. That was just fine with Sal, Mia, and pretty much everyone.

Sal and Mia headed uptown at the end of that day, after rehearsing for a club gig. They stopped at her family's place to celebrate the twin's birthday, then crossed into the Forbidden Zone, as Mia still referred to it, to the new apartment they'd gotten together. Sal loved it, with its views of the leafy park and the little courtyard in front where he set up his conga to play for the neighborhood kids whenever he had a minute. They'd had a small wedding a few blocks away at the church on Broadway before her father would agree to them living together; they would celebrate with a big party next summer, planned by Tía Mavis, Pam, and Tonya.

The following night, they went with Tito to the movies to see a creepy story about a family living in a haunted hotel. It had first played months ago but had returned for a limited run to the tiny theater nearby that showed horror movies on Saturday nights.

"Man, fuck those ghosts. I would've left the first time some weird shit happened," Tito said with a shake of his head when it was over.

Back at their place, Sal was quiet while Mia and Tito discussed the movie's solid points versus the novel. Turning to him, Tito asked, "Why so quiet? You didn't like it?"

"It was good. I've just been thinking about something Fito said to me after rehearsal," Sal said. They both lifted their eyebrows, waiting for the follow-up. "Well, he was talking about how lucky he's been in life. He didn't really have a plan, but things fell into his lap."

"And... that's a good thing, right?" Mia asked.

"Yes and no. It's great when things work out without effort, but it might not hurt to think ahead a step or two. Maybe it's better to make a blueprint and leave space for luck when it comes instead of relying on it. Mia, what's your plan?"

Mia grinned. "We've talked about it. Be a successful singer and performer. Write my own songs. Spend my money on comics." When he twisted his lips at her, she laughed. "Be a supportive, loving wife to my handsome husband and have a few kids when the time is right."

"Sounds good. But what are the steps to singing success? You need an agent. You need to learn notation to write the songs for your band. You need to have it in your contract that you own your masters. Get a lawyer to check everything before you sign, so no one can control you or cheat you. Tito, what's your plan?" he asked, turning to his brother.

Tito frowned. He rubbed his fingers along the raised line on the side of his neck in an unconscious gesture. "Shit, I don't know. Tio keeps saying he wants me to take over La Nueva when he's ready to retire. I could see that happening."

"But is that what you want?"

"It's something," Tito said with a shrug. "You got a better idea?"

"I do," Sal said, leaning forward. "I form my own band after another year or two with Fito's orchestra. Mia can sign with him as an R&B artist or with whoever she wants, as long as they offer a good contract and treat her right. Then down the road, we form our own label. Be good to our talent. Not abusive."

Sal knew they'd understand the reference to abusers. They never mentioned Sisco by name. He was a ghost whose power over them was diminishing a little every day.

"What exactly would I do for a record label?" Tito asked. "I don't play. I don't sing."

Sal knew what Tito's skill set was. "Be my right hand. Look out for me. The way you always have." After they sat silently for a while, Sal said, "Think about it."

"It sounds like a good plan, Salvo. I think I raised you right." Tito smiled.

"And you, *amor*?"

Mia nodded. "I'm on board, Salvador."

Sal grinned at his brother, whose eyes now held a spark of hope he hadn't seen in a long time. And Mia... there was nothing but love and contentment in her smile. And his heart had never felt so full.

***

In the morning, Sal rose with the sun. He ate his toast and had his *cafecito* quietly to not wake Mia. He'd kept her up pretty late, trying out more of those illustrations from their own copy of Carla's sexy science book. It had gone pretty well, if he said so himself.

At the park, Santiago was waiting for him in their usual spot. They greeted each other with hugs, and Sal drew his coat tighter around his body in the brisk air as a flock of pigeons battled for the remains of Santiago's toast. Then the old man's hands tapped his conga, and the notes made the pigeons startle and fly off.

Sal emptied his mind, his palm warming on the smooth surface of the drum, and played.

The End

***

Enjoy the story? Be sure to leave a review! Also, sign-up for my newsletter for exclusive sneak peeks, and updates on my next release.

ABOUT THE AUTHOR

Lynn Yorke writes across romance genres, including contemporary, suspense/thriller, science fiction, paranormal, dystopian and action (including the kind where the heroes and villains wear spandex) and loves featuring diverse characters as a reflection of her family background and upbringing in New York City. Whatever gets the heart racing, she wants to write it, sometimes all in the same story! Yorke enjoys travelling, films, music and fresh air in the park. She resides in New York City with her family.

Sign up for Lynn's newsletter here
https://landing.mailerlite.com/webforms/landing/v1lot8

JOIN LYNN ONLINE
https://lynnyorke.com/

If you'd like to follow up with Salvador and Mia's daughter Melody, look for her story in the novella "K-Pop Love" in Sinfully Wicked: A Limited Edition Collection of Contemporary Romance.

OWNED BY THE JOCK

Imani Jay

ABOUT *OWNED BY THE JOCK*

Amy
"Tiago Silva: our local, star basketball player, and the object of my naughtiest fantasies...
He's freaking gorgeous, tall, broad, ripped, cocky as all hell... and a student at the college I work for!
Nothing can ever happen between us. Period.
But, when his intense dark eyes travel along my curves, I have trouble remembering all the reasons I can't be with a man a couple of years my junior."

Tiago
"I got my eye on voluptuous, brown-skinned Amy Kane from the day she was introduced to my cohort as our career counselor.
Her no-nonsense buns and severe-looking glasses only make me want to pull up her tight skirt and pop the buttons of her blouse!
She keeps saying no to my advances, but the hitch in her throaty voice whenever I'm near, and the flame in her big brown eyes tell me otherwise..."

Once burnt by a man she trusted, Amy closely guards her heart and body. Especially against the college star athlete coveted by legions of groupies!
Tiago might be a few years younger but he's an ambitious young man who knows what he wants & gives his all to get it! On the court, in class & in matters of the heart...
So, how long can a girl resist the advances of the hot college jock intent on making her his?!
Read along to find out!

This is a full story with a cautious BBW, a Latino jock who's all kinds of naughty, no cheating, no cliffhanger & a guaranteed HEA!

WARNING: if you don't like scorching hot sexy times, and a hero ready to play dirty to get his gal, this is not the book for you!!

ACKNOWLEDGEMENT

Thank you, awesomest reader ever, for taking a chance on another one of my books! And to my tribe, my writing family, all the amazing ladies and gents who listen, advice, support...

Thank you all for helping make this lifelong dream of mine a reality.

CHAPTER 1:
AMY

Yes, I know: he'll be here in fifteen minutes! I frantically click on the snooze option of my email's meeting reminder.

He is Santiago Daniel Silva. Senior in my hometown's small UC (which also happens to be my place of employment), in the software engineering program, star of the basketball team, and the object of my most carnal desires. Tall as a sequoia and ripped as fuck, with soulful eyes, a pillowy mouth, and the bronze skin of his Aztec ancestors.

***

I didn't notice Tiago the first time we were introduced. I was newly appointed as the career advisor to our university. My entire first day of work had been spent going from one department to the other. The IT students were the last ones I visited, and everyone melted into the blur of too many faces I'd met that day...

But the second time I saw Tiago? I noticed him, alright! He was leading our team to victory in a regional game. Covered in sweat, bouncing on his feet with an agility his tall powerful frame shouldn't have allowed. Intense gaze constantly on the ball and the other players' moves. He was a titan on the court: both mighty and agile. I watched in trance as he made one basket, one pass, one rebound, one swipe after another. His strong muscles glistening under the projector lights. All six feet seven of brawniness exposed for my eyes to feast on. The defined biceps, corded forearms, wide chest, muscular back and mighty legs. The tattoos ornating his brown skin. His short cropped hair looked fuzzy and soft from afar, making my hands itch to run through it. The dimples piercing his cheeks with each smile or laugh. I sat on the bleachers with a group of my colleagues, but it was as if everyone and everything had faded away. Everyone, but the gorgeous giant playing ball like a beautiful symphony.

I left the stadium dazed and aroused, walked into my apartment with stiff nipples and damp panties, and barely locked the door behind me, fell on the couch, pulling my bra down to play with my breasts, and sticking my hand down my underwear. Rubbing at my clit, running my fingers through my wet folds. Pulling soft moans from my lips. Eyes shut tight, hanging on to images of Tiago Silva, I came like never before! And my obsession has only grown stronger, scarier.

Every time I see him, my body reacts as if Tiago is the one giving me those solitary orgasms. I've even stopped going to his games, but that's no use. His presence is burnt behind my eyelids. I envision images of his big hands all over my body. Fantasies about the deep voice I've only heard on the campus radio and local TV stations, whisper naughty things in my ear. Too many nights, I wake up hot and bothered from dreams where I can smell and taste Tiago!

This obsession worries me: I'm a twenty five year old woman. I should be focused on my career, not some big shot college baller who's years younger than me. OK, it's just two years, but still: I will not lust after one of the students, damnit!

***

Damnit! He wears glasses! Thick black rimmed glasses, that combined with his couple of days old scruff send him in a completely different stratosphere of hotness. The faded jeans and fitted sweater combination does nothing to help his case: his thigh muscles roll under the fabric as he makes his way through my office door, and the woolen fabric loosely molded to his chest is at once a miracle and torture to my eyes. I'm fucking screwed.

I clear my throat to invite Tiago to take a seat. His long ass legs barely fit in the space between my desk and the visitor chair. A space that perfectly suits normal sized people, but not this giant. Makes me wonder what other part of his body might be oversized... *Bad Amy, no!*

"You requested an appointment, Mister Silva." I prompt.

"Call me Tiago, please." He responds with a big bright smile that reveals strong white teeth, forming a beautiful contrast with his tanned skin. And the dimples appear. *Oh Lord, did I just come? I think I came!*

"What can I do for you, Tiago?" Fake it till you make it: this appointment is supposed to last a half hour at the most, I can and I will survive The Hotness!

"Well..." he scratches his strong, square, scruffed jaw. Giving me a lopsided grin, hot eyes travelling over my torso.

Gah, kill me now!

"I'm here to answer any question you might have, and to assist in any way I can." I say, hoping he'll come out with it already.

"Well, you see, my question is a bit unusual..."

What?...

"Would you like to go out with me?"

WHAT?!

"Hum... I don't... What?!"

"Go out, on a date, you and I." Asshole is still muddling my mind with his panty melting grin, dark eyes twinkling with mischief. Leaning forward, elbows resting on his thighs, fingers crossed under his chin. His latest championship ring glinting on his finger. Intense gaze never leaving mine.

Is this really happening or am I in one of my Tiago dreams?

"I don't think..." I slightly shake my head, unable to form a coherent sentence.

"Hear me out: you're not my teacher. I have recruiters blowing my phone and email, so you don't even have to worry about me work wise."

I know my eyes are as wide as saucers and my jaw hangs slack. He did not!

"Just one date. I promise you'll have fun. And if you don't, I'll never bother you again."

I take in a deep breath, square my shoulders and ask: "Is this some kind of joke? Did you make a bet with the other jocks?"

He flinches at my demeaning tone. The flirty smile fades away and a cold mask takes over his expression, a muscle jumping in his jaw.

"It's a simple yes or no answer, Ms. Kane. No need to get nasty."

I gasp, jump from behind my desk and stomp to the door, opening it wide for him. "You can leave now, Mr. Silva."

Tiago rises from the chair with such force that it rattles on its legs. In one wide stride he's right in front of me. His impossibly tall frame shadowing me, broad shoulders blocking the sunlit window behind him. He stands so close I can see the freckles spread across his prominent cheekbones, the scar in his eyebrow. Face furrowed, mouth a thin line, nostrils flaring. Eyes burning a hole into my skull. Heated waves emanate from his body. Clean soap and pure male scent filling my nostrils.

"I noticed you on your first day, when they introduced you to our cohort. I think you're fucking beautiful."

I gasp with shock this time. And Tiago takes advantage of my surprise to lay one of his big, strong hands at the side of my waist. Sending an electric current through my body. He slowly removes his glasses, sticks them in his pocket and leans closer, bringing our faces mere inches apart.

"I haven't really seen you since then. Maybe from afar at some of our games. Never got a chance to approach you." Tiago licks his lower lip, the gesture capturing my attention. The poke of his pink tongue over the plump flesh, captivating... "There is no joke. No bet. Just a woman I can't get out of my head."

He bends down and presses his firm lips to mine. In a chaste kiss. Absolutely making my brain explode! I lift my hands and take handfuls of his sweater for support before my knees give out...

"Go out with me." He croons against my mouth. All fresh breath and soft lips. And I let out a whimper, which makes his cocky grin reappear, hitching one side of his face. "Please." He adds.

This time the kiss is all consuming! Tiago's hot mouth opens up and his lips attach to mine. I'm flooded with heady sensations, my conscience having completely vacated the premises! When my lips start moving in sync with his, he maneuvers me aside to close the door. His powerful body presses my soft curves against the wooden panel. Hard muscles against feminine forms. He pushes a strong leg between my quivering thighs, resting it firmly against my pulsating pussy and starts rubbing. I follow suit, wantonly grinding myself on his hard muscles. Tiago slides his big palms higher up my body, maddeningly grazing at the sides of my breasts. Almost making me shake with a mix of pleasure and desire. Our mingled moans and groans arouse me even more, and I know if this keeps I'm going to come... When we hear a knock on my office door!

***

Tiago detaches his mouth from mine and connects our foreheads. Our breathing heavy, his leg still trapped between mine. The hard pipe of his dick nestled against my belly...

"Who is it?" I croak out.

"Amy, it's me. You wanna grab lunch?" My colleague and next door office neighbor, Sandra asks loudly... from right behind the door!

The few inches of wood separating us, the realization of what her reaction would be if she saw me in this position... at work... with a student!! It all comes down crashing and I shove Tiago with both palms, gritting between clenched teeth: "get off me!"

He takes a step back, hands raised in mock surrender, his cocky grin making a new appearance. Burning dark gaze taking me in, marking me like his mouth, hands, bulky body and thick erection just did.

"No thanks, honey. I'll take my break later," I say out loud to Sandra.

"You want me to bring you something?"

God bless well intended people!

"No, thank you. Not hungry yet." I reply with agitation, eyes glued to the tent in Tiago's jeans, telling me there is something I'm hungry for, alright. *No, Amy!!*

"Okay. See you later, then." Sandra throws, her voice sounding further.

We listen to her heels click away, till there's no sound left but that of our calming breaths. Tiago takes a step toward me, and I swiftly regain the safety of my position behind my desk.

"No, out! This never happened, and will never be discussed. Or attempted. Ever again!" I deadpan, having regained some semblance of bravado.

"Of course," he concedes too easily, before adding: "about that date...?"

"Out, I said!" I'm almost hysterical in my need to put some distance between myself and the giant sex on a stick!

Tiago chuckles and makes his way to the door, rearranging himself in his pants. "I'll see you around, *princesa,*" are his ominous departing words!

I slump in my chair and bang my head on the desk. I'm screwed.

CHAPTER 2:
TIAGO

Yeah, I'm an asshole. I know. Blindsiding Amy like that in her office? Not my most gentlemanly move. But, in my defense, I've been trying to get close to the woman for fucking months!

***

The way she looked that first time I saw her stole the top spot in my spank bank. From the tight skirt that stopped at her knees, revealing long shapely legs, to her full hips and incurved waist my hands itched to grasp on, an ass you could bounce a quarter off of, and a blouse that hinted at a generous pair of tits. All prim and proper, with her cat-eye glasses and hair neatly pulled into a bun. And that fallen angel face! Huge, expressive, chocolate brown eyes I could picture staring up at me while she'd be down on her knees, worshipping my dick. A rounded nose, and fire-engine-red painted mouth I just knew I had to ravage. All that deep brown skin to feast on, and curves for fucking days: how could I not want to wreck her?

When Amy spoke, introduced herself in that goddamn sultry voice, shared about her role and how she could be of assistance: her eloquence and clarity drew me in even further. I felt the instinctual need to mess up her orderly exterior.

Well, mission accomplished! The way she looked when I left her office: top untucked and skirt bunched up her thick thighs, cotton soft hair mussed, delicious lips swollen, sporting the mark of my kisses, nipples about to pierce the silk of her blouse, and fighting to regulate her breathing. Amy looked fucking magnificent. And now, I know the volcano that lies under her reserved surface.

***

I've been obsessed with Ms. Amy Kane for most of my senior year, but holding it in. Studying, practicing basketball, playing, focusing on the path to my future. *And fuck, it feels good to know I'm almost there*! Just a few weeks and I'll graduate, with honors and a number of job offers already aligned. I kept my head in the game, worked hard and I'm so close to my goal I can almost taste victory. I've sacrificed so much to build the man I am and the life I want. I had a modest upbringing in a family of Mexican immigrant farmworkers. My parents taught all five of us, Silva children, integrity, discipline and dedication.

For years, my life has been nothing but long hours of study and practice to keep my grades high and my scholarship. I've led a sparse social life, no time or interest in a steady girlfriend. Not that I've been a monk, far from it. *Shit, there have been more groupies, cheerleaders and one-night-stands than I care to count.* Meaningless encounters, just an exchange of pleasure, a way to blow off steam. I've been consumed with school and sports, and to be frank no one has retained my attention. Well, till Amy. Beautiful, tempting, fascinating Amy Kane. Of the dark skin I want to lick all over, throaty voice I long to hear call my name in pleasure and round ass I fantasize on spanking. She'd be the perfect reward for my efforts.

***

I set my head back, letting the hot jets of the shower run down my body. It feels good, relaxing. I needed this, to release some of the tension. Left palm flat against the tiles, I close my eyes and wrap my right hand around my erect dick. *Fuck, I cannot think of this woman without getting hard!* And having tasted her? Having felt her full breasts against my chest and had my rough hands all over her soft body. Gotten drunk on her scent and high on her deliciously pained moans? I'm going to do everything in my power to feel the sheath of her warm wet pussy contract around me! Not even a minute of pumping and I come in long, luscious spurts. My fingers contracting almost painfully on my cock. My throat letting out an involuntary groan of her name. *Shit, I gotta make this woman mine!*

***

You know what they say about the best laid plans, right? Yep, they're meant to go to shit. For ten days I've been trying to get a hold of Amy! I've called her office, emailed her, requested a meeting through the UC's online calendar, inconspicuously hung around her building. Nada. I knew she'd try avoiding me. Never thought she'd succeed with such force. I've done everything in my power, short of straight up stalking her, and my sick mind -or maybe it's my dick doing the thinking?- has started considering criminal offenses.

It's the end of the basketball season, and our team is not playing till a week from now. For the first time in a long while, there's no pre-game warm-ups to worry about. No bus ride to God knows which UC. Just a late afternoon Friday, classes done and the start of the weekend.

By pure force of habit, I take a detour by Amy's office building on my way to the students' parking lot. At this point, I have nothing to lose and for once I'm not in a hurry to get to class, practice, or back home after a long day that beat my ass. So, I follow a wild hunch and make my way to her office.

CHAPTER 3:
AMY

I'm so tired! Beat by days of avoiding Tiago... Ignoring all forms of communication from him. Getting to the office at the ass-crack of dawn, working through lunch, and skipping town before the after classes crowd hits the parking lot by the admin building. I'm physically, mentally, and emotionally drained!

But today is worse. I don't even have the strength to make sure he has a game, or to check if I'm safe staying in the office this late in the afternoon. That's how bad today is. I don't even care if Tiago corners me again, because today I have much bigger fish to fry. The family event I've been cowardly ignoring for months has arrived... It's tonight and I have no way of escaping unless I become suddenly gravelly ill, or a meteor shower descends on the Central coast!

I bring the tips of my fingers to my temples and start rubbing circles, closing my strained eyes. As I rest my head back on the armchair, I hear a knock.

"Come in," I respond, without looking up. Not caring who it could be at this point.

The door opens and a few seconds pass before the gravelly voice that's been haunting my dreams inquires: "you're OK?"

Of course! What else?!

I take my time to lower my hands from my face and swirl in my chair, facing the intruder. Santiago Silva stands before my eyes in all his glory. Tall, broad, and obscenely beautiful. His thick brows are furrowed in concern, full pink lips tight, intense gaze traveling over my features, searching for the answer to his question.

"Mr. Silva, what a pleasant surprise," I reply sarcastically.

"I asked you a question," is his rude-ass retort.

"Well, I don't remember returning any of your meeting requests. Yet, here you are. Seems neither of us is getting their way today."

He sighs deeply, drops his backpack on my visitor chair and strides towards me. *Oh boy...* I shake my head, lifting my palms to ensure we maintain an absolutely necessary distance between our bodies. I have enough mess to deal with tonight! Tiago ignores my gesture as he squats right in front of me, laying his big hands on my knees. The warmth of his touch spreads all over my body. His somber eyes bore into mine. I stare back in fascination, gorging on his handsome features, appreciating the casual outfit that showcases the piece of art that's his athlete's body. The white cotton t-shirt that hugs all the right parts of his chest and upper arms, and grey sweats I'm going to have to stare at on his way out... *Yeah, I won't lie to myself.* Our personal spaces mingle, his amazing scent filling my lungs. Tiago's somber eyes take me in and the annoyance on his face makes place for concern. I can imagine what he's seeing: the same face the mirror has reflected to me for days. Deep bags under my eyes, an air of exhaustion...

In a tender gesture this time, he takes my chin between his thumb and forefinger and asks: "What's wrong, *princesa?*"

I scoff at the term of endearment.

"Not a princess, young man."

Tiago looks at me with huge eyes, his lips trembling for a second before letting out a deep rumbly laugh! He gets up, resting his behind on the corner of my desk for support. Wiping off tears of amusement. "Young man?" He finally asks, once his hilarity has calmed down. "Just how old are you? Let's have it."

"A lady never..." I start.

"Nope," he interrupts. "If you're going to use our age difference, the least you can do is be open about it."

I grumble, purposefully unintelligible: "*twenfi...*"

"Excuse me? I don't speak mumble." He teases, cupping his big tanned hand over his ear.

Gah! Even his ear is sexy!

"Twenty-five," I articulate this time and he bursts out laughing again! I can't help but smile a little. "Fine, it's only two years." I concede, crossing my arms over my chest. "But I'm still part of the admin staff."

"Of the university where I I have less than a month left as a student?" He replies, raising a challenging eyebrow. "You're going to have to find better." He smirks, eyes twinkling with mischief.

"I'm not attracted to you...?" I ask. Can't even spit out the lie convincingly!

"Is that a question, *princesa?*" His cocky smirk is firmly in place.

I roll my eyes. "Stop calling me that, I'm absolutely not a princess."

"*Absolutely not* is pretty strong..."

"Well, try growing up dirt poor in the Seaside projects. You sure won't feel like a princess."

He nods before adding: "fair enough. Try growing up actually sleeping on dirt because that's how poor your family is."

I watch him closer. For the first time, getting a glimpse at the man behind the hot jock. A slice of his truth. What his childhood must have been. How hard he must have worked to become who he is. Tiago's serious expression only holds for a few seconds before the cocky grin returns.

"What did your parents do for a living?"

"They run a grocery store."

Tiago shakes his head. "Migrant farm workers beat storekeepers on the dirt poor scale, *princesa*."

"You're annoying," I state with a smile.

"I'm right and you know it. Now tell me what's bothering you."

Goddammit, he completely distracted me from my troubles!

"Who said something's bothering me?"

"It's written all over your face and you were rubbing your temples when I came in. Barely noticed it was me. After avoiding me for days, all of a sudden you let down your guard. Something's up."

"Fine, I'll tell you. But only because I need to talk about it!" I declare vehemently.

"Sure. Now spill." Tiago arranges himself comfortably on the corner of my desk. Long legs stretched out, feet crossed at the ankles. The soft fabric of his sweats molding his powerful thighs. Arms crossed, biceps bulging. Olive skin in perfect contrast with the immaculate cotton of his t-shirt. The veins of his forearms, the intricate tattoo running down one arm in a full sleeve. His corded neck put in display by the position of his head turned sideways to face me. The deep brown eyes observing me intently, full mouth I remember tastes divinely delicious, strong masculine features. My mouth is as dry as the desert and it's not just because I'm embarrassed by the story I'm about to tell.

CHAPTER 4:
TIAGO

I have to muster all my self-control to keep my hands to myself. To not take Amy in my arms and hold her close to my chest to chase away her troubled look, or crush her lips with mine, let her rub herself all over me like she did last time, to make her forget all about her worries. No, I will listen and help if I can. I need her trust, if I want more than a passing fling with this woman. She resists our mutual attraction, but can't deny it. I won't give her an excuse to make us a casual fuck. I want so much more from Ms. Amy Kane.

She sets her head back on the leather seat. Legs crossed at the knees, her tight black skirt rising a bit, revealing a patch of dark brown skin I yearn to run my fingers over, my mouth, my tongue... Her sigh is long and charged with emotion. Amy's eyes stay closed for a few seconds. The silk of her blouse following the movements of her chest, the heavy breaths that make her tits rise and fall in rhythm...

"My cousin married my ex today and I have to go to their wedding reception in a couple of hours," she blurts out.

What?!

I sit up straighter. "What?"

"My cousin..." Amy starts reiterating, but I cut her.

"No, I heard you. Seriously?"

"Yes!"

"Why?" I ask, incredulous. "Why would you go to that?"

"Because that's the right thing to do. Because we're family. Because I want to show them I don't care."

I rub my chin and notice her eyes greedily follow the movement of my fingers on my stubbled jaw. I let my hand linger, slow my pace and observe as her gaze grows heavy-lidded. She's so into me! We're going to have so much fun.

"OK, you need to elaborate."

"There's not much to say. Maybe six months ago, I met this guy through common friends. We started dating. I thought things were going well. Took him home to a family thing. He dumped me on that very day, when he dropped me off at my place. Few months later, I find out him and my cousin hit it off at the family event and were dating. Flash forward another couple of months, they send me an invite to their wedding reception."

"Dang, that's cold."

"Not helping!" Amy complains.

"Sorry, sorry!"

She shakes her head, eyes full of defeat. OK, we can't have that. I get off the table and come stand in front of Amy, encasing her face with my big palms, I tilt her head up and bend at her level, bringing our mouths close enough to drop a quick peck on her full, soft lips. She lets out a sigh of content, encouraging me to keep on with my kisses. Our lips caressing, molding, closing over each other. Then she wraps her hands at the back of my neck, the tips of her fingers languorously stroking my hair. I don't know who gives the first swipe of tongue, but in a matter of seconds we go from a delicious kiss to flat out mouth fucking... Amy's amazing taste and scent invade my senses. And my dick takes this as permission to come out and play: standing at attention to pitch a tent in my sweats. *Shit, we can't do this!* Not here, not like this... not when Amy's worried sick and most likely still confused about what she wants from me, from us. I know I'm going to hate myself for this later, but I detach my lips from Amy's and walk to the door.

"What are you...?" She asks before realizing I'm just turning the lock.

I come back to her comfortable leather office chair and settle in, installing Amy in my lap. She throws me a suspicious look, most likely wondering what I'm up to and maybe hoping for something to happen between us...

I lean back into the plush leather, one arm loosely wrapped around her curvy waist and ask: "You sure you want to go?"

She nods, her defeated air returning. "I have to. I don't want it to look like I'm bitter or jealous."

"OK, but are you? Bitter, jealous, hurt...?"

Amy looks up to the ceiling, eyes getting a bit misty. She twists her mouth to the side, her posture growing rigid.

Shit, well played Silva!

"Hey, come here. I'm sorry, didn't mean to upset you." I pull her against my chest and she buries her face in my shirt. Inhales deeply then shakes her head, raising her eyes to mine.

"No, you didn't upset me. I'm just... It's hard to accept that the same guy who dumped me after a few months, asked my cousin to marry him after even less time."

I let my gaze travel over her features. Searching for signs of heartbreak, but if I'm reading her right: this is more of an ego wound. I run my hand over her soft curly hair, squeeze Amy tighter against my chest.

"I'm guessing you're single..."

She nods her silent acquiescence.

"Would it help if you went with a plus one? Someone who's obviously into you. A sexy, athletic, successful guy?"

Amy twists her lips to the side again, but this time it's to repress one of her beautiful smiles. My dick twitches and she opens her eyes big, brows raised!

"Hold you horses, cowboy!"

I chuckle and move her perfect ass to one thigh instead of directly on top of my crotch. "Stop wiggling around and nothing will come poke you."

Amy stares at me for a few seconds, hand over her mouth, shaking her head with incredulity. She's fucking funny and I'm glad I'm able to take her mind off her worries. She takes a deep breath, a small smile still lingering on her lips, before asking: "you'd really come with me?"

With a straight face, I reply: "oh you thought I was the guy?"

Amy mock-slaps my chest and I take her hand in mine, laying it over my heart and resting my much larger palm over.

"I'd be honored to be your date at your ex and cousin's wedding reception," I deadpan.

She rolls her eyes, unable to refrain a smile. "I can't believe I'm agreeing to this. And, just so we're clear: I don't need a pity date," Amy ruins the mood by getting all defensive again.

"First of all, you do." When she opens her mouth to cut me off, I raise a hand signaling I'm not done. "And second, I've wanted to take you out since the first time I saw you. This is actually you taking pity on me."

With her sweet ass on my thigh, palms flat on my chest, upper teeth worrying her bottom lip and her sharp gaze studying my face for any sign of cunningness, Amy sits straight and still for a moment before agreeing. "OK, but no chatting around to your buddies."

I almost lift her from my lap to drop her juicy behind in the chair and walk out of there. But manage to remind myself: she's probably wary of the entire male population and barely knows me... Also, if what I've experienced so far keeps coming, I will not be deterred that easily.

"Amy, I'm younger than you by a couple of years. Not a pimply teenager who constantly needs to brag to his friends."

"I apologize. That was... I'm sorry. Thank you very much for offering your company. That would be very helpful."

I simply nod, my face relaxing a bit. Still pissed at her remark though, and worried Amy might keep bringing back our age difference.

I'm startled when she runs the delicate tips of her fingers over my brows! Soothing the furrowed lines. She then drops a soft kiss on my mouth, before repeating: "I'm sorry, Tiago."

Fuck! The caress of her mouth and my name on her lips are enough to erase all irritation and worry. I grab Amy by the back of her head and deepen the kiss. My tongue plunging and plundering. My other hand seizing a palm full of soft, squeezable ass-cheek and kneading. She whimpers into my mouth, moaning my name... *Fuuuck, that's the most enticing sound I've ever heard in my life!* I open my legs wider, making her slide in the middle, right atop my hard dick. Amy puts her small hands back around my neck and starts rolling her hips. I buck up into her and the friction is all at once delicious and maddening. An excruciating pleasure. I feel the hard tips of her nipples rub against my chest through the thin layers of our clothes and her bra. Our mouths devour each other, molding, detaching, angling, hungrily sucking and drinking in. Teeth grazing...

CHAPTER 5:
AMY

I smooth my palms down the fitted fabric of my cocktail dress. I look fabulous, if I dare say so myself. Hair curled in lose strands, face made up in a sexy but classy fashion. My faux-lace black dress embracing my curves, tight and revealing enough to show off my generous forms but tasteful. I spritz myself with an exquisite perfume, and I'm wearing a pair of black heels that showcase my toned legs.

The perspective of showing up with Tiago, of spending the evening on his arm, makes me giddy with excitement. Which is completely crazy: I've been dreading this party since I received the invite in the mail, then endured the phone calls from my cousin, parents and everyone and their mother.... The guy's a sorcerer! I better be careful before I find myself in deeper than I've bargained for. Like earlier in my office. We went at it like horny teenagers and I ended up straddling his lap, rolling my hips up and down his thick shaft... Senses filled with everything that's Santiago Silva: nestled against his hulky body, my mouth gorging on his impossibly delicious taste, filling my lungs with his tantalizing musk, squirming at the sound of the groans escaping in his deep rumble. I'm ashamed to admit I would have gone much further, hadn't Tiago pulled the brakes. Yeah, I'm probably going to end up sleeping with the guy. Not sure I'm up for anything else, but I don't see how we can resist the insane attraction between us. On those unsettling thoughts, I hear the doorbell and grab my things to rush out: there's been more than enough *intra muros* interaction between Mister Silva and I for a good while!

***

Holy smokes, the man cleans up nicely! I can die peacefully, now that I've seen Santiago Daniel Silva in a suit. *How...? Why didn't anyone warn me?!* Tiago is absolutely delectable. Tall, broad, his powerful frame impeccably dressed in a perfectly cut charcoal gray suit. His crisp white button-down, free of a tie, open at the collar, revealing his strong, tanned neck. His buzz is slightly overgrown, but he made the effort to shave and his dimples appear even more prominent on the smooth skin of his cheeks. The scar at his eyebrow gives an edge to his otherwise polished appearance. A shiny pair of black leather Oxford lace-ups, and the glint of a chunky watch complete the ensemble. I'm absolutely, one hundred percent ready to hand over my panties right this second!

"Looking good, Mister Silva," I purr wantonly. *Yep, panties ruined and about to drop!*

"Well, thank you, Miss Kane. You look absolutely stunning, yourself."

"Thank you," I return, twirling on my heels to show off my attire. Backless dress and all...

Tiago takes my free hand in both of his and watches me for a few seconds, a wicked grin on his full lips.

"It's not too late," he finally lets out.

"For what?" I ask, brows bunched up.

"To ditch the reception and spend the weekend locked away from the world." He bends over and croons at my ear. His warm breath making me shiver and the spicy cologne he's wearing muddling my thoughts.

"Tiago..." I breathes, holding on to his muscled forearm.

He nips at my earlobe, huge paw coming down to squeeze my ass and I let out a small whimper, my pussy spasming over the scrap of my thong. His mouth traces a burning hot path from the sensitive skin at the back of my ear, descending along the side of my neck, to end with a kiss at the crook of my shoulder.

"Wouldn't want to ruin your lipstick," he says with a wink when his head comes back up.

And all I want to do is pull Tiago back close, climb him like a tree and let him lock me away for the weekend! *Oh Lord...* I shake my head at him and he chuckles.

"Fine, I'll behave," is his big fat lie, as he guides me towards his gleaming black truck.

***

Once settled in the car, Tiago turns my way and enquires: "are we telling any particular story about us."

I shake my head. "No, my sister and best friend will be there. I told them about the hot student who asked me out, so... just the truth. You asked me out, I agreed."

Tiago gives me a raised eyebrow as he maneuvers the car out of its parking spot. "You've been talking about me?" He asks.

"Uh, yeah. It's not every day some guy keeps locking me in my office for make-out sessions," I deadpan.

"Some hot guy," Tiago repeats my words.

"Some hot guy," I concede with a smile, shaking my head.

He takes my hand, bringing our interlaced fingers over his thigh. "You should know, I talked to my family about you. And, don't freak out, to my best friend."

A sense of unease creeps into my happy bubble. "Is this best friend a student at the UC?"

He nods, sending me a brief glance. "It's OK, Amy. I promise. I just wanted to share with someone who knows me and who's good advice. He's not the kind to gossip."

I take a deep breath to calm my nerves and push away the dreadful sentiment. "OK, if you trust him, I trust your judgement."

Tiago smiles softly. "That means a lot. Thank you."

I nod and smile back. He inputs the address of the reception venue in his phone and the GPS guides us to our destination.

***

The reception hall is packed. I recognize most of the bride's side of the party: some of my cousins, aunts, uncles and family friends.

Pulling Tiago by the hand, I make my way through the crowd, stopping ever so often to exchange hellos, kisses and hugs. Feeling curious gazes scrutinize our couple. Quite a few people in my family were present at the gathering where my ex, Dan and my cousin Tima met, Dan having arrived on my arm... So, inquiring minds are certainly curious about my reaction to their wedding and who the hell I brought tonight. I hold on tight to Tiago's hand, keep a smile plastered on my face and advance resolutely. When we make it to my family's table, elegantly dressed in a sensible cocktail dress, my mom observes us while trying to hold in an amused smile.

Making me whisper in her ear, as I hug her: "Arrêtes, maman." *Stop it, mom.*

She's in on the secret of my non-relationship with Tiago and I know she can't wait to see how I'm going to handle this big hunk of a guy. My mother thinks her kids are the salt of the earth. She told me from day one, the breakup was my ex's loss. Claimed it was good riddance and room for better things to come. Well, she seems to approve of my current choice of companion. But of course, I have yet to meet a female who doesn't fall under Tiago's charm.

"Tiago, meet my family. This is my mom, Coumba. My dad, Abdel, my sister Astou and her husband Nick." I offer, standing at his side.

Tiago extends a polite hand, introducing himself in is deep baritone, with a courteous smile. I exchange eyerolls with my sister and mom at my dad's bunched up brows. My super protective daddy is the sweetest, but his scary face is kind of wasted in this instance. He really doesn't have to worry: I know what I'm doing, I'll be fine. *Right?*

We settle into the two vacant seats next to my sister and her husband.

"Great season so far, man." Nick engages Tiago with enthusiasm.

Our UC's basketball team is the pride and joy of our small town. The entire population gets in a frenzy, the years we have players talented enough for a chance at the college championship. Nick and Tiago appear to hit it off and get into an animated discussion. I nervously let my eyes roam around the room.

"They're over there." Astou points out, low enough for my ears only.

Her hand coming to squeeze mine. I squeeze her back, my eyes following the direction she indicated. My cousin and her spanking new husband occupy a beautifully decorated table set up on a platform, surrounded by their close family and friends. She looks gorgeous in her wedding dress and even I have to admit Dan looks pretty dapper. I still want to punch in his stupid face but I can't deny the truth: these two make a great couple. I swallow a lump in my throat and lift my glass with the rest of the room to toast at the speeches. Tiago covers my free hand with his, under the table. He pulls my fingers into his strong ones and rests our joined hands on his muscular thigh. His warmth invading and soothing. I turn a grateful smile to his handsome face, getting lost in his dark gaze for a beat.

"You're OK?" He bends over to whisper into my ear. His warm breath making me shiver and turning my nipples into hard pebbles. The scent of his woodsy cologne filling my nostrils and triggering sensations I have no business feeling sitting this close to my parents.

I nod with a small sideways smile. Taking stock of my emotions, I realize I do feel OK. Not great, but not devastated. It's not a good feeling seeing the man who rejected you, tie his destiny to someone else. Even worse, when he met that someone while in some form of attachment with you. The fact that someone is a family member, regardless of us not being close, definitely didn't help. But, I realize I'm fine. Better than I thought I'd feel, seeing them together, being faced with the reality of their union. I don't know how much of it is time heeling all wounds, or me showing up here on the arm of a man I share a mutual attraction with, but either way I'll take it.

"I think I'm ready to go congratulate them." I let him know with a brave smile.

CHAPTER 6:
TIAGO

When I push from my chair, Amy lays her delicate hand on my shoulder, shaking her head.

"No, I need to do this alone. Thank you, though." Her smile is more assured than a few minutes ago.

Fuck, she's gorgeous! I can see where she gets it from. Both Amy and her sister take after their beautiful mother: the big brown eyes, fine features and curly hair. Their dad is an elegant gentleman, who gave Amy her deep brown skin. I'm happy to get to see her outside of school. Amy might be slightly off because of the circumstances, but I can tell this family is a tight knit. Just like mine. Amy's brother-in-law is a really cool guy. Not sure if he knew she was bringing me or if he recognized me when we were introduced, but he made me at ease. These are good people. This woman might just be perfect for me.

***

"I'm going to go check on Amy." I say in the general direction of the table. Words of acquiescence meet my declaration.

She's been gone for a solid fifteen minutes now. Which is starting to concern me. I can see the bride and groom's table from where we're seated. I watched Amy get in the greeters line and lost sight of her at some point. I'm here to make sure she's OK and I'm doing just that.

After crossing the vast reception hall from one side to the other several times, being stopped by fans to discuss our odds for the end of the season and a few women trying to hit on me, I find Amy standing at a window in a deserted hallway. She has her arms wrapped around herself, eyes lost through the darkness outside. Her expression not exactly sad, but pensive. I close the distance between our bodies, coming to stand flush against her. My tall frame towering over Amy. Calloused fingers running along the side of her face.

"You okay?"

She nods, offering me a dazzling smile, making my heart beat a tad faster and my dick stir in my slacks.

Eyes riveted to mine, Amy elaborates: "I feel surprisingly good." She takes a deep inhale, before adding: "I thought I'd be devastated..." For a second, a slight furrow marres her gorgeous features. Before a bright smile, full of relief clears her face. Amy looks at me with a tender expression. "Thank you."

She lifts on the tip of her toes and presses her full mouth to mine, making my cock twitch again. I lay my hands at Amy's waist and pull her closer, partly carrying her supple body. She opens her mouth and our parted lips come together in a long, wet, deep, maddening kiss. We both tilt our heads to the side, for a better fit. Our tongues tangle and roll and lick. Our lips suck and pull. Our teeth graze and nip. I languidly fuck her mouth, the way I want her to imagine I'll be plunging in and out of her sweetness. She tastes amazing. Her floral scent with just a hint of patchouli goes to my head. Her full, luscious forms mold to my hard muscles like we were made for one another. My huge palms grab handfuls of her thick ass, and I squeeze and press her even closer. The apex of her thighs rubbing against my hardness. Soft moans of pleasure escaping from her mouth, and mingling with my own possessive groans.

"Let me take you home," I whisper in her ear, nipping at her tender lobe.

Amy sighs with pleasure, eyes close, hands roaming the tense muscles of my back. "We... we have to go say goodbye to my family."

"Fuck..." I murmur. *I had completely forgotten about the rest of the world.*

I take Amy's mouth again, losing myself in her delicious taste. And we go at it like kissing is getting out of business, like two teenagers eager to savor every second before curfew. The sounds of the party are but a far, vague mingle of voices and music. We're cut off the world, in our own bubble in this dimly lit, deserted hallway.

But, said bubble bursts when a loud masculine voice exclaims: "what are you doing, Amy?"

Our lips come apart, but our bodies stay close. We turn our heads in unison towards the intruder. It's the groom, perfect...

"This is my wedding, Amy. What are you doing making out with some dude in a corner?"

Guy has some nerve, I'll give him that. I prepare to rip him a new one, but Amy beats me to it.

"It's your wedding, right? So, go find your bride and mind your own fucking business, you asshole." She spits in his face, eyes glaring, magnificent in her irritation.

"Well, there's no need to..."

"Fuck you, Ben. You hit on my cousin while we were seeing each other. I don't care if we were not serious. I don't care that she's the love of your life. You're not a decent person, so don't you dare try to lecture me," she continues, ignoring his attempt.

I'm standing tall, broad chest expanded, eyebrow raised, just waiting for the piece of shit to give me an excuse to intervene. But, I guess it's the first time Amy tells him how she feels, because poor guy looks like he's struck by a twelve ton truck. Eyes wide and mouth gaping.

Amy pulls me by the hand and starts toward the reception. "Let's go say bye to my family, babe. Time to get out of this place."

I can't help but turn to the guy with a cocky smirk. He still looks devastated. I bring my eyes back to Amy's swaying hips and button my jacket in hopes the flaps will hide my erection.

CHAPTER 7:
AMY

I'm pretty sure my family is as smitten with Tiago as I am. My mom and sister gave him heart-shaped eyes as he politely wished them goodnight. And my dad and brother-in-law exchanged warm handshakes with him as goodbyes. If they knew the same hand was all over my ass just a few minutes before...

Tiago and I hold hands walking to his car. His large, warm paw engulfing my smaller fingers. He opens the passenger side door for me, his gentlemanly manners growing on me. The ride to my house is mostly silent, soundtracked by a radio station's nightly R&B selection. The air in the truck's cabin is saturated with his fragrance. All I want to do is jump Tiago: straddle his lap, once more lay my mouth on his, run my hands over his shirt and pop the buttons open. Lightly scratch the golden skin of his strong chest. Kiss down his neck, taste the soft skin where his pulse is beating erratically. Grind myself against his thick erection. Undo his belt and pull his pants and underwear out of the way, just enough to reveal his cock... *Shit, shit, shit! I need to get myself together!* I turn my gaze outside my window, inhaling deeply, trying to move my thoughts from Tiago's bulging crotch. From his flaring nostrils, from his hands tightly gripping the steering wheel. From his intense silence since we left the venue. The streets of Monterey are mostly deserted at this late hour. With just a few groups of students coming in and out of bars and clubs. There's barely any traffic on the brightly lit road and we make it to my place in no time. Tiago parks, comes to get my door and walks me to the entrance. The quietness still heavy between us.

"Would you like to come up?" I ask with a tempting smile.

He gives me a sexy grin of his own. "Yes, I'd love that. But, I also want your phone number. And I want to make sure we're on the same page."

What?

"What do you mean?"

"I want more than coming up for one night."

Not this again. I shake my head slightly. "It wouldn't be smart for you and I to see each other other than casually, Tiago."

"You're wrong, sweets." He leans over and takes my mouth in one of his devastating kisses, making my pussy pulsate with want. "You taste so fucking good... he murmurs at the seam of my lips, driving me completely crazy.

"Tiago..." I manage to let out, lips still moving on his succulent mouth.

"Yes, sweets," he groans out.

"If you're not gonna come, I need you to stop fucking my mouth."

He chuckles low and sultry, making my skin explode with goosebumps.

"Alright, *princesa*. Give me your number and I'm out of here."

With shaking hands, I pull my cell phone out of my clutch, unlock it, access the contacts and hand it to Tiago. I appreciate him not making a comment about my trembling fingers or even taking a gloating air. He simply inputs his digits and calls himself. I hear his own phone vibrate in his pocket and he cuts the call, returning my device.

I pointedly look at his tented pants before asking: "are you sure?"

His smile doesn't waiver as he responds: "positive, *princesa*. Now, go get some rest. Tonight was intense."

I nod and start climbing the stairs. "Tiago," I call and he stops his progression toward his car, turning to face me. "Thanks for coming with me tonight. It meant a lot."

He simply inclines his head, blinding me with another dazzling smile and my knees go weak.

***

I wake up from another sex dream starring Tiago. One that's much more realistic than any I've had so far. Now that we've heavily kissed several times and pawed each other like teens in rut, my libido is out of control! I can barely close my eyes without being assaulted with fantasies of Tiago. Alone in the locker room, after a shower, in nothing but a white towel. His bronze skin gloriously exposed to my eyes, shiny droplets of water calling for my tongue to lick him all over. Dark hair damp, eyes twinkling with mischief. White towel lifting under the push of his erection... *Fuck, why does he have to be so hard-headed? I* bet we could get out of each other's systems if we had sex. This crazy, intense thing between us is nothing but hormones and a long dry spell on my part. I don't get why Tiago insists on dating me. Well, I won't be deterred that easily.

I grab my phone from the nightstand and look up Tiago's name in my contacts. Weird, his name's not there... I go to the last issued call and burst out laughing. He named himself 'Loverboy'.

"Hey Loverboy," I purr into the microphone with a smile

A chuckle accompanies his response. "What's up, *princesa*? Did you sleep well?" His breathing is a bit labored and I can hear sounds of nature indicating Tiago's probably outdoors.

Shoot! "Is this a bad time? It sounds like you're outside."

"No, you're fine. Just coming back from my morning run."

"Ugh, athletes."

Another deep chuckle that hits me straight in the belly. "Not only athletes run, sweets."

"You're right, sorry. Ugh, fit people."

This time, he laughs out loud, making my grin grow wider. "What are *you* doing, little miss judgmental?"

"Laying on my bed. Just woke up..." I purposefully let my voice trail.

Tiago marks a beat before asking: "what are you wearing?" In a hoarse tone.

"You don't want to know, Mister 'I'm Only Interested In Dating'," I taunt him further.

"I never said that, *princesa*. What I'm interested in is you. All of you. Dating, talking, laughing..." Tiago marks a pause before finishing, "fucking," his deep voice coming out gruff, charged with desire.

I'm stunned silent for a few seconds.

"Amy?"

I clear my throat. "Yeah, I'm here."

"Thought I lost you there for a sec," he says cockily.

"No, I'm here," is all I can repeat, mind filled with images of Tiago Silva *dating, talking, laughing and FUCKING me!*

His deep chortle resonates again, the bass of it feeling like a caress all over my skin.

"I'm wearing cotton pajamas. Shorts and a t-shirt. With hearts all over. Nothing fancy or sexy."

"You in shorts? Definitely sexy. Fuck!" He ends with a short cuss.

"What are you wearing?" *I'm an absolute masochist: I need a visual to pair with the low, breathy voice.*

"Running pants with basketball shorts on top and long sleeves. You wanna see?"

"I do," I answer unashamedly.

"Come buy me breakfast," he tempts me.

I only have to think for a second before jumping off my bed. "You're on. Meet at First Awakenings in thirty?"

His amused voice confirms: "Meet you at First Awakenings, *princesa.*"

CHAPTER 8:
TIAGO

I arrive at the breakfast place hair damp with perspiration, cheeks reddened, breath still labored and eyes intensely roaming the crowd of patrons. My fast beating heart has little to do with my morning run. *Get it together, man! She's just a chick.* But, I know she's not just a chick. She might be the one. Beautiful, funny, smart, strong willed, and capable to get my dick hard with a simple smile.

"Tiago?"

I turn around and there she is: fresh as a button, beautiful, a sight for sore eyes. My eyes can't make up the saying on her gray cotton t-shirt, all I see are her full, round tits, molded by the thin material. A pair of washed blue jeans seem painted on her full curves, making my mouth water. I want, no I *need* to sink my teeth into this round ass, these thick thighs, kiss down her soft stomach, nustle my face between her generous breasts. Her big curly hair frames the face that's been haunting my dreams for months. The happy smile Amy gifts me makes me want to throw my resolve to the wind and fuck her brains out without any promise of a future from her. But I can't, I won't. I'm determined to see this through. Date the fuck out of Amy Kane and figure out if we're meant for each other.

"Hey," I croak out, starting to feel self-conscious about my appearance. But, Amy doesn't bat a lash as she hugs me and raises on the tips of her toes to press her lips to my cheek. I'm immediately assaulted by the impossibly sensual scent of her perfume, the press of her generous breasts on my arm and the side of my chest, the feel of her full lips on my skin. *Fuck, I'm screwed!*

Amy tries stepping back but I surprise her by hooking an arm around her waist, making her gasp softly. Her big brown eyes lifting to my face in wonder, mouth slightly parted. I bend over, my eyes never leaving hers and brush my mouth to hers, murmuring: "good morning, *princesa*."

Her smile returns and she shakes her head. "Stop, you panty collector."

"What did I do?" I ask, my hand still wrapped around her side. Fingers grazing the soft skin between her shirt and jeans. My cocky smile returns when I feel her shiver under my touch.

"Oh, I've heard all about your groupies, Big T." She lifts an eyebrow, teasing me by using my nickname on the court, and yeah, with the ladies.

I shake my head, still not letting her go or moving from the restaurant entrance. "That was before you, sweets. I had no serious interest in any of those girls."

"And you have serious interest in me?" She pushes, her expression of incredulity almost insulting.

My lips crook up to the side and I bend again, whispering to her ear: "I have all kinds of interests in you," I nip at her lobe before finishing, "including serious."

Amy lets out a girly giggle that tells me I'm not the only one to be affected beyond my comfort zone, here. And we stay like that, my arm wrapped around her middle, one of her hands lightly resting on my chest, lost to the world, drowning in each other's eyes, hearts fast beating, heads filled with images of what we'll do to each other once alone...

When a loud call interrupts our moment. "Hey Amy, I thought that was you!"

I turn my head to the side the voice came from, at the same time I feel Amy taking a brusque step away, breaking our embrace. I recognize the woman facing us, she's also part of the University's admin.

"Hey Sandra," Amy lets out in a shaky voice.

"How are you girl? Saturday breakfast, huh?" The lady throws me a side glance, eyes lit with curiosity. "Hi, I'm Sandra. We've never officially met. I'm a big fan." She says thrusting her hand at me.

I shake her hand, giving her a polite smile. "Nice to meet you, thanks for your support."

Amy looks between her colleague and I with panicked eyes. "Wow, talk about small town. Did the whole campus decide to grab breakfast here today?" She laughs nervously.

I watch her closely, trying to convey with my eyes that this is okay, she doesn't have to hide us, we're not doing anything wrong. That *I* would never do anything wrong to her. That she can trust me, and give this insane attraction between us the chance to grow into something big and real. But I guess my eyes can't say all that...

"Well, I'm ordering my food to go. It was nice running into you two. I'll see you Monday, Sandra." Her face turns to me, but her gaze doesn't meet mine. "Mister Silva..." she gives me a head nod and rushes inside the restaurant.

CHAPTER 9:
AMY

I messed up. I look through the restaurant's glass door and see Tiago is still standing in the same spot. The spot we were occupying just a few minutes ago. Hugging, staring into each other's eyes languorously, almost kissing... And now, now I've ruined it all! Sandra was on her way out of the restaurant, so she didn't linger after my awkward departure. Just ping-ponged a dubious look between Tiago and I.

Tiago... His face is closed-off, but he wasn't able to immediately mask the flicker of emotion on his features. Pure, unadulterated hurt. *God, did I mess up!* I pull out my phone and text him: *'I'm sorry. I panicked.'* I watch as Tiago pulls his cell from his running pants pocket, thumbs through the screen, then lifts his hardened gaze back to mine. He holds my stare for a beat, before pocketing back his phone, pulling the hood of his sweater over his head and starting a light jog towards the street. I quickly lose sight of his departing form in the small crowd of weekenders. My incredulous eyes come back to our now empty spot. *How did I manage to screw things up so royally in the span of a couple of minutes?*

***

'Tiago, it's me... Amy... again. I just want to talk, honey... and apologize. Call me back... please.' I sound pathetic, even to my own ears. I've called and texted him every day since the disaster of last weekend. *I want, no I need to apologize to Tiago.* He's done nothing to deserve my lie. I was taken by surprise, completely unprepared. I hadn't even considered the possibility of us running into someone from the university. *Such a fucking idiot!* Mind muddled by Tiago's blazing gaze, his tall, muscular form, high cheekbones, full mouth, golden tan and big hands. I really didn't think things through. I knew from the beginning I didn't feel comfortable going out with one of the students, but resisting Tiago ended up being impossible. In my mind's eye, I can still see his gorgeous smile and hear the deep

rumble of his laugh. So handsome, confident, manly... Nothing like the kid I thought I was dealing with at first.

I fluff my hair and nervously run my clammy palms over my jean-clad legs, pulling on our UC's team jersey to make sure it falls nicely. This is my last attempt. I promised myself: I'll go watch him play and try to talk to him one more time. That's it. I owe it to Tiago, if only for accompanying me to my cousin's wedding. I owe it to myself to act like a decent person... and maybe see if things can be salvaged? I've got to be honest, here: I've got it bad for this man. Not only are my wet dreams filled with reruns of our hot kisses, but I've spent the past week fantasizing about all that could have been. Dates, more kisses, getting to know him, talk, even more kisses, laugh together, again kissing... and at some point finally getting Tiago alone in a room where we could ditch our clothes and get our hands, mouths and hopefully other body parts better acquainted. I missed all that, I ruined all that. So now, I want to at least make things right.

***

The stadium is vibrating with cries of fans, sounds of horns, claps and stomping each time one of our players is called from the locker room. My heart beats a mile a minute, waiting to hear the only name that matters to me tonight, and there it comes: "Aaaannnnd, straight from the Salad Bowl of The World, our forward, our captain. I give you Big T, Tiagooooo Silvaaaaa!" The crowd goes bonkers, girls shrieking at the sight of the giant of a man walking through the two lines made by his teammates and high fiving them in passing. He is glorious. From afar, the projector light makes him look like an unattainable star, when a week ago he was the one calling me 'princesa'. My stomach drops and my throat constricts. I wonder if I'll ever hear that word again... With difficulty, I swallow the lump in my throat and clap so hard my palms hurt. I'm too far, a speck in the crowd, for Tiago to see or hear me, but I want to give him all my support. This is an important day for him, for the team, for our university and small town. Winning the regional championship could mean big things to come for all of us. More exposure, more opportunities. And a lot of this is thanks to Tiago. Before he joined the team, we hadn't made it to semi-finals in several years. Of course it's been a combination of factors, but Tiago's skills, hard work and his natural talent for leading have been a definite factor in our current success. So, we're all here hoping for a happy ending... some of us more than the others!

CHAPTER 10:
TIAGO

Bounce, pass, score, run, block... repeat. The game is almost over and the score is tight. We're only five points ahead, they could catch up at any time. Just a few seconds left on the timer, now... Aaaannnddd we make it! The final buzzer resonates like a cry of victory and the entire stadium descends on the court to cheer and celebrate with us. *We did it!* Five years of hard work have paid off. We went from being a team no one really worried about, to the first contender to the regional title. And tonight, having won the semi-finals brings us one step closer to making history for our small UC. I'm exhilarated, laughing and yelling with everyone else, even if part of me is still sore.

The sweetness of this hard earned victory can't completely take away the bitter taste in my mouth. The taste of rejection, humiliation and hurt. Hurt, pissed at myself and angry at the world. It felt like the same old song all over again: "Sorry, T. I really like you, but my parents wouldn't approve. you understand, right? Not that they're racist or anything", or "come on, man. You don't have a better pair of sneakers?"

It was the same story and I can't believe I was dumb enough to not see the signs, to believe Amy could be my girl. That she saw me for who I am and not some dumb college jock to fuck on the side, use as her pretend date and keep hidden away.

I shake myself and pull my biggest, fakest grin. I won't let the memory spoil our moment!

***

I take a sip of my drink and laugh at my teammates' rowdy jokes. We're sitting center stage in The Tavern, the current hot spot in our small college town's quasi non-existent night life. And everyone and their aunt has been buying us rounds. Those of my guys who drink are plastered, and the few of us who don't consume alcohol watch them make fools of themselves with amusement. I flick my wrist, taking a look at the time. Eleven thirty. It's time I call it a night if I want to be up tomorrow for my run. I clap a few hands, slap some of the guys' backs and start toward the bar entrance. Out in the street, I take a deep inhale of the fresh night air, relieved to be out of The Tavern's stuffy atmosphere. Tucking my hands in the front pockets of my jeans, my leather jacket protecting me from the coolness, I turn in the direction of my apartment, just a couple of blocks away.

A soft feminine voice I'd recognize anywhere calls my name from behind me. My head whips around in an unconscious gesture, and there she stands... Amy. More beautiful than in my poor recollections, tempting, enticing, alluring, fascinating... and not for me. Of course, she'd wait for me at night, in the dark, far from the crowd. Where no one could see us together. I feel my face harden and my jaw clench.

"What do you want?" I ask her, chest filling with a sharp pain. Not only because of the memory of her betrayal, but from seeing Amy. Being so close to her, all I'd have to do is extend my hand and we would touch. I'd feel her soft skin again, hear her moans, pull her tightly against me... *Fuck, quit it Silva!*

"Hey Tiago," she answers, voice still calm and gentle. "How've you been?"

"What. Do. You. Want. Amy," I deadpan, staring her down with a coolness I don't feel.

"Right."

I watch her throat work as she swallows on nothing with apparent difficulty.

"I wanted to apologize for the way I behaved. Honestly, I just panicked. I was unprepared to be open with the university's staff about you and I, and..."

I interrupt her: "you already said all that in your messages. Is there anything else?"

She flinches and I want to punch myself, but I don't let it transpire.

Amy takes a deep inhale, nodding. Before carrying on: "I also wanted to ask if there's still a chance." She finishes, lifting her chin in a determined manner. Regaining some of my respect.

"A chance for what?" I ask, in perfect asshole style.

For a few seconds, she just stares at me and I think she's going to drop the ball, let it slide, once more spit on the possibility of an us. But she doesn't...

"A chance for us to be together," Amy specifies bravely.

I study her for a bit before spitting out: "come here."

She advances to stand at a foot's distance, my tall frame overshadowing her.

"Why did you come talk to me at night, in an empty street?" I growl in her face.

Amy's gorgeous eyes flutter with confusion, as is she hadn't considered this.

"I was at your game, and inside The Tavern. I... I guess I was gathering the courage to come talk to you. This is the only time I was able to catch you alone, Tiago."

I scrutinize her gaze, trying to read her, to sense if I should lower my guard. Forgive and move on. My hand comes out and wraps around her waist before I've fully formed the thought, and I bring Amy flush against me. *Fuck!* That wasn't smart... Her full curves mold to my hard muscles like we were made to complete one another. The close sight of her parted lips, big, expressive eyes, wild hair... Her full tits crushed against my chest. the small, incurved waist held in my arms. *Fuuuckkk!* Not fucking smart.

"Are you horny? Did you come after me so I can take care of you?"

She shakes her head, making the big curls framing her face bounce with the movement.

"When was the last time someone made you come? Ate you up?"

Amy's head moves with vehemence, denying my claims.

"It's not like that, T. I'm honestly sorry. I didn't think, and... I just want to be with you. Give us a chance." Her eyes go wider, as if she's surprised herself with those last words.

I scoff with derision, twisting the knife in the wound, unable to let her words in, only hearing my stamped pride. "I can fuck you in the alley, if you want. Promise to make it good for you."

Amy's gaze finally switches to the determined woman I fell for. "I know I was a dick, but don't push it, OK? I don't even know how many times I apologized. And I mean it. I made a mistake. I'm honestly sorry. Don't ruin us, Tiago."

I let out a dark bark of a laugh. "I'm the one ruining us? That's grand."

"Listen, you big oaf of a man," Amy retorts, "this is my career we're talking about, I will not be perceived as unprofessional. You're leaving in a few weeks, I have to stay and work in this university. I can't ruin years of work for a fling."

I open my mouth to protest, but Amy raises her open palm to my face, effectively silencing me.

"This is a great opportunity for me, UCM is a small but great school."

At her completely logical explanation, the frustration starts sipping out of me.

"I'm also worried about you, Tiago. You could get in trouble." Amy's earnest expression continues to melt away my anger.

But I'm still upset. She cut me deep, where it hurts the most. Took me back to my poor brown kid status, the one girls loved messing with in private but never brought out into the light. The guy other players all wanted on their team on the street court, then ignored come Monday morning at school. I don't know that I can trust her, but my mind, body and heart won't let me pass up this chance.

CHAPTER 11:
AMY

One minute, I'm staring into Tiago's dark eyes, silently begging him to believe me, and the next his delicious lips fall on me in a hard, punishing kiss. He takes, and takes, and takes. Royally screwing my mouth with long, deep, wet strokes of his delectable tongue. Rough brushes of his full lips, the abrasion caused by his unshaven jaw, the steel pipe of his dick pressing against my belly, his big fingers digging into the flesh of my waist, the hard planes of his body plastering me as if to fusion us. This is both wonderful and an insanely painful torture. Not a physical pain (although, tell that to my pussy clenching on nothingness...), but a need so powerful it hurts!

I'm also worried. The single brain cell I have left functioning tries analyzing if this is okay behavior, or some form of punishment on Tiago's part. I'm lost and turned on like never before in my life.

"You hurt me," are the first words out of his mouth, when Tiago detaches from mine.

"I'm sorry, honey."

He shakes his head. "It's gonna take more than that, sweets."

I nod, strengthening my resolve. "I understand."

Tiago watches me for a beat, expression inscrutable, before taking my hand and turning us back to the bar. A bar that's filled with my colleagues and his college mates.

"Let me buy you a drink?" Tiago asks, his scarred eyebrow raised in a challenging gesture.

I don't have to think about it twice and nod my assent, briefly squeezing his hand with my much smaller fingers.

The dimples make a brief appearance and I feel like falling to my knees. *Oh, how I've missed them!*

Tiago's expression sobers up: "I need you to be sure, Amy. We can't keep going back and forth on this."

"I'm positive," I answer immediately.

He nods, just once, and pulls me by the hand back into the crowded bar. I take a fortifying inhale, preparing for the stares, the sarcastic smiles, the comments... But I'm surprised when people simply greet us in passing. We're obviously together, in a more-than-friends type of way, but no one seems to care, either staff or student. Was it all in my head? That's what Sandra told me. After our disaster encounter at First Awakenings, her and I had lunch together the following day at work and her advice was: "girl, please. That boy is fine and he's into you, you better tap that." I'd blushed and prayed it wasn't too late...

Tiago settles on one of the bar's high stools and pulls me in the space between his legs, loosely wrapping his long arms around my waist. At first, I'm rigid but progressively start relaxing when no one comes at us with torches and pitchforks. I stand close enough that my back rests against his front. My fingers curled around Tiago's wrists, gently running over his bronze skin. He orders our drinks and we barely speak, just enjoying one another's presence. Soaking in our bodily warmth, the simple fact of being together, this close, after so many days and after thinking it was over.

Tiago rests his chin on my shoulder, one arm stretched on the bar, his other hand resting on my thigh. And I forget all about the crowd around us, my fears, the pain I inflicted on him, on us. All I care about in this instant is the fierce drumming of my heart, resonating throughout my body. The blossom of hope filling me to the brim, and the ardent desire licking its languorous flames between my legs and at the peaks of my breasts.

Our moment is interrupted by a sultry feminine voice calling TIago's name. He turns to the intruder and I watch as his features switch to a cold mask.

"Hannah," Tiago nods at the stunning Nubian princess standing at our side, before placing his chin back on me.

She sends me a brief gaze and I attempt a small smile that's completely ignored.

"I was wondering if you had time to talk," she insists in her throaty tone, moving closer to Tiago.

He raises his head again, leveling her with an icy stare. "Do you not see me with someone?"

Outwardly unfazed, the gorgeous Hannah replies: "maybe I can come by your place tomorrow?"

He stares her down for a beat before turning to me. "We're out of here, *princesa*. I think we've socialized enough."

"Uh, sure. Bye," I throw at Hannah over my shoulder, feeling bad for her.

Once outside, Tiago has me tucked to his side, one arm wrapped around my shoulders. I revel in the scent of him I've missed so much. The woodsy cologne and male aroma I thought I might never get to experience again. I snuggle closer, enjoying the feel of his big, strong body.

"So Hannah, uh?"

"We used to fuck on a steady basis. Hasn't happened in months. She needs to get over herself."

"Oh... okay." I feel my eyes grow wide.

"I just got you back, and you and I have things to work through. That's what I choose to focus on. What I will not do, is waste my time and energy, or yours, dealing with a bratty girl who thinks the world revolves around her, just because she was born with good genes."

"Great genes! She's gorgeous," I add, playing devil's advocate, while thinking Tiago's speech was all kinds of hot.

He shakes his head. "Don't try to distract me. You, young lady, have some groveling to do." He follows this with a wink and a teasing smile, the deep creases of his dimples peeking under his stubble covered cheeks. Dark brown eyes twinkling with mischief, making me wonder what he has planned for me. His impeccable bone structure making my pussy shed tears of lust.

CHAPTER 12:
TIAGO

Amy is in my house. She's walking around my home, from one room to the other, a huge smile on her face, looking like a kid in a candy store. Running the tips of her manicured fingers over the spines of my books, along the wooden pieces of furniture. And ever so often, turning to throw me one of her heartwarming grins. Almost two weeks ago, I thought I lost her and all possibility of an us. I sense we're in the same state of wonder. A mixture of disbelief, hope and dread. My greedy eyes follow the sway of her full hips, stealing peeks while I'm supposed to choose what music to play. I love having her in my space. My small, cozy home. The two bedroom house, ten minutes drive from campus. My sanctuary.

After eighteen years spent living crammed up, first with other families in farm labor complexes, then with my parents and siblings in the modest three bedroom that was all they could afford, once retired from migrant work. I needed room to breathe, and I never compromised. From my first year living on my own, I worked extra hours, saved on my scholarship and did what I had to do to make it happen: create a shelter for myself, where I could have silence, all my stuff and privacy. So many important things I lacked growing up.

I shake myself out of my serious thoughts, feeling the side of my mouth hook up when I select a song on my phone and cast it to the sound system. At the first notes of *'Boo Thang'*, Amy cracks up laughing and comes join me on the couch, setting her sweet ass a mere foot from me. As her chuckles die down, I hook an arm around her waist and pull her close.

"So, you wanna be my boo thang?" I croon in her ear, kissing the soft skin under her lobe and sliding down her neck, feeling the tremor shaking her at the contact of my lips, at the nip of my teeth. *Fuck she feels good, tastes even better...*

"Tiago..." Amy exhales my name like it's a reverent prayer. "We need to talk, baby." Her voice comes out breathy, head thrown back, neck arched, giving me full access.

My tongue dips in the small hallow at the base of her throat, where her pulse beats erratically.

"We'll talk." Tongue roll. "Later." Soft bite, followed by a moan. "I've waited too long to taste you." Suction of my lips on her tender skin. "To get you alone."

Amy rolls her hips and writhes. I detach from her for a second, and she hooks her fingers into my flannel, pulling to get me back close. I smile, biting on my bottom lip, loving her eagerness. But, not ceding till I position myself exactly where I've been wanting to be for months, now. Stark between her legs. I'm on my knees on the thick, plush carpet, between Amy's legs, and I almost come just looking at her. Big hair mussed, splayed out like a crown on the back of my dark brown leather couch. Eyes glazed over with lust and never leaving me, taking in every single one of my moves. Full lips parted and glistening after each pass of the tip of her tongue. Her heavy breasts rising and falling in rhythm with the deep inhales stretching her white cotton shirt. Her small hands fisted at her sides. Hips rising from the couch in uncontrolled, jerky movements. Breathtaking.

I bring my shaky fingers to the waistband of her jeans and let my eyes do the asking. Amy nods briefly and I proceed to unbutton, unzip and pull her pants down her long, shapely legs. The vision of her thick thighs makes my mouth water. I force myself to admire her delicate, dark red painted toes, running my hands over her calves, taking handfuls of her thighs, kneading and worshiping her full flesh. Letting the tips of my fingers run over her soft, dark brown skin and pull more trembles from her luscious body. I finally allow myself to look at the apex of her thighs and feel my nostrils flare. A tiny scrape of deep blue lace barely covers her pussy.

I'm an athlete, a disciplined man, used to controlling myself, but I know I'm only hanging by a thread in this moment. I hook my thick fingers at the sides of her underwear, slide to the center, the contact with her bare shaven skin making my dick jump in my jeans and sending Amy into a jolt. When my fingers meet at the center of the piece of lingerie, I hold tight and pull, the sound of ripping filling the air and mingling in harmony with our heavy breathing. As the fabric comes apart, Amy's full lower lips become exposed to my hungry eyes and I dive in.

CHAPTER 13:
AMY

I'm absolutely, one hundred percent sure I've died and gone to heaven. The sensations between my legs can only be otherworldly. Or Tiago's a fantastical creature. It's one of those two things. Because this pleasure, this overwhelming succession of wave after wave of ecstasy, cannot be of this earth.

Head buried between my thighs, huge hands cupping my ass, Tiago threw my legs over his broad shoulders and went to town on me like it was his life's sole mission. First, he ran the tip of his masculine nose along my slit. His torrid dark gaze never leaving mine. Then, he took a single lick. A taste. A tease. Right on my clit. No fumbling, no poking around, uh uh, nothing. Straight to the bundle of nerves. And straight to the most intense micro-orgasm of my life. I had no clue then, but this was just the first of a long list of "never before" for me.

After that first swipe of his amazing-feeling tongue, Tiago dug deep... He lapped between my folds, getting me wetter and licking my juices clean. He kissed my lower lips like he'd done to my mouth so many times, long, wet and heavy. Ran his tongue from my clit to my opening. Fluttered the tip of it on the hood, driving me bonkers, making me shake with pleasure. Stuck his tongue deep inside me, fucking me with it. All this, while his fingers dug deep in the full flesh of my ass, parted the rounded cheeks, teased at my hole. I felt myself leaking all over his face, the scruff of his cheeks scratching inside my legs and adding to the sensations.

After another tsunami has left me ashore, I lift on my elbows and croak out: "I want to see you."

I'm half-dead after three or four successive orgasms. I've lost exact count of the number of times Tiago has plunged back between my legs after making me come. I gather the little energy coming back to my body and pull off my shirt and bra, throwing them on my small pile of clothes. Tiago stands to his feet and starts unbuttoning his red and gray checkered flannel. The vision of the sturdy fingers that were filling me just a moment ago sends another tremble through my pussy.

He towers over me in all his glory. Tall, strong and fucking turned on. His dick tenting the comfortable jeans he's wearing. I fall on my knees at Tiago's feet and raise my eyes to his face. His bottom teeth sunk into his full lower lip, he jerkily discards the shirt and gets to work on his fly. The pants fall to the carpet in a muffled sound and are kicked away impatiently. Tiago fits his large palms at the sides of his black boxer briefs and drops them in an instant, his socks following suit.

His cock springs out and my mouth opens in awe. He's magnificent. Long, thick, with a beautiful smooth crown, engorged veins and a generous drop of precum leaking from the tip. My mouth grows dry and I swallow with difficulty, taking in Tiago's impossibly perfect physique. *Thank God for basketball!* He is R.I.P.P.E.D.! Muscles, on top of muscles, on top of muscles. I had no clue. This man should walk around naked all the goddamn time! It's a crime to hide this masterpiece under clothing. Bulging pecs with a dusting of chest hair, defined abs outlined by the most enticing jet black happy trail, thick biceps and thighs... and the tattoos! Sleek, intricate swirls and lines of dark ink cover one of his arms from shoulder to wrist. A couple of sentences are imprinted on the skin of his rib cage, the writing too fine for my eyes to decode in the dim light. Tiago's dick jumps, making my scrutiny focus back on that part of his anatomy.

His eyes eat me up like his mouth did earlier. He licks his lips and wraps his long fingers around his length, starting to stroke in languid movements, the tip mere inches from my mouth. Tempting me, inviting my kiss. And I cede to his call, close the distance between our bodies, wrap my lips around his soft skin and hard flesh. Start licking, kissing and sucking the head into my mouth, bathing it with my saliva and moans of pleasure. And alternating between rubbing my thighs together and spreading them. I circle his shaft with my hands, stroking up and down, while my mouth goes lower. Tiago's pubic hair is trimmed short and the scent of his intimate musk is clean and alluring. My tongue darts over his sack, I take his balls in my mouth one at a time, pulling a groan from him, his big hands framing my head, fingers digging into my hair.

When I've had my fill playing down there, I trace a wet path from the base of his cock to the tip, sucking at the soft skin, rolling my tongue over it, rubbing it over my lips. One of my hands pinches my nipples, alternating between the two, while the other one traces my wet slit from top to bottom in a slow, unrushed motion. Savoring the orgasm built, keeping myself on the edge. I know we're both about to come and want to make this last for as long as possible. My plan falls through when Tiago abruptly lifts me in his arms, wraps my legs around his waist, large palms taking hold of my ass and takes my mouth in a incendiary kiss. Lips, tongue, teeth, he goes at me like he's about to devour my ass! At the same time, lifting me up and down to rub my pussy the length of his cock, in a loud, wet, delicious friction.

All the while walking us toward the back of the house. Tiago opens a door without letting go of me or detaching his mouth. I peel off my eyelids, just the time to see we're in a clean and tidy masculine room, furnished with heavy dark woods and navy colors. He sets us on the bed without breaking contact, then stretches his arm toward the nightstand.

"I want to be inside you," Tiago breathes out, forehead resting on mine. His big body surrounding me, its weight resting on his elbows.

I can only nod, lips parted, mad with desire.

"Tell me you want me inside you," he presses, probing at my entrance.

I let out a pained moan, before whimpering: "I want you inside me, Tiago. Please, now."

The beautiful smile that takes over his face sends a jolt of pleasure between my legs and I almost come. Tiago pulls open his nightstand drawer and grabs a string of condoms. Ripping one from the lot, he tears the packet open and sits back on his haunches. Velvet eyes glued to mine, he gives himself a few strokes, the pleasure of which, and our advanced state of arousal, making him clench his teeth, his neck muscles visibly tightening, muscled thighs trembling. Tiago rolls the condom over his dick and motions to me with two fingers. He stretches his long ass legs, arms at his back, hands flat by the edge his huge California King size bed.

"Hop on, *mi reina*."

"Oh, I'm a queen, now?"

Tiago shakes his head, gifting me another dazzling grin. One that would have incinerated my panties, was I still wearing any.

"Bring your sweet pussy over here and climb up your man's dick."

My eyes grow wide and I do as I'm told. Scurrying over on my knees, I straddle his lap and position myself over his straight pointing cock. The thick head parts my folds, sending an electric current along my spine. I lower myself inch by delicious inch, and as Tiago's hard flesh invades me, wave after wave of pleasure starts coursing through my body. Hands gripping his bulky shoulders like my life depends on it, I stare into his gorgeous eyes, taking in his striking features, incredulous at the intensity of the sensations running over me. Tiago grabs me by the waist and pulls me down in one powerful motion, ending the torture I was imposing on us both. I sigh, long and trembling, forehead pressed to his, our gazes connected, heavy breathes mingled. He holds me in place for a long beat, pulsating inside me, our open mouths connected in a gasp of incredulity.

Finally, finally, finally, Tiago bucks into me with a fierce: "Fuck, you feel good."

I nod frantically, framing his face with my hands and taking his mouth. My lips and tongue rolling and dancing in measure with our hips. I bounce on his cock, while he grinds his hips into mine. The friction of his pelvic bone on my clit adding to the unbelievable sensations. I scratch at his shoulders and bite on his full lips. Tiago spanks my ass cheek, the sound resonating through the slap of our skins, the wet noises of our sexes, the hungry kisses we're exchanging. The sting of the naughty gesture sending a jolt of pleasure through my clit and throwing me overboard. I come, and come, and come... creaming Tiago's cock and balls, moaning and writhing on top of him, sucking his tongue into my mouth, and repeating his name in an insane litany. Just when I think my climax has culminated, he sends me through a new wave of pleasure as his dick starts twitching and jolting inside me, his fingers digging into the tender flesh of my hips and making me bounce frantically on his lap. We come together, our loud cries mingling and enhancing the experience.

We're finally laying down, spent. My head resting on Tiago's wide chest, hand on his shoulder, his fingers softly sifting through my hair, soft lips on my forehead. Our sweat covered bodies molded like they'll never part. The air in the room saturated with the scent of our lovemaking. I laboriously raise my head, dropping my chin on the backs of my hands and give Tiago a saucy smile.

"Well done, young man."

He lets out an amused chuckle and pinches my waist. "You were not too bad yourself, grandma."

After we each take a turn to the restroom and get ready for the night, Tiago gathers me in his arms under the blankets, and spoons me to sleep.

***

I wake up to the sounds of chirping birds and far away traffic. Peeking through one eye, I realize Tiago cracked open his bedroom window, letting in the refreshing Spring air. I turn to his side of the bed with a smile, but all I see is an empty pillow. I sit up slowly, paying attention to each and every deliciously sore muscle in my body. The tender flesh bringing back to mind all the acrobatics the crazy man put me through last night. And I smile to myself. He felt so incredibly good. The best. Like never before. I shake my head, a vision of Tiago's naked body flashing behind my eyelids, and my pussy starts pulsating at the memory of our amazing night together. I shake my head again, trying to clear it of the flashbacks. Tiago pinning me against the wall, bending his knees to take me from behind, pulling on my hair, spanking my ass, biting my neck, drilling into my wetness. My nails clawing at his back, his muscled ass, his chest, my teeth sinking into the same body parts. My lips wrapping around his cock, while he feasted on my dripping cunt... I bury my face in my hands, wondering how I'm going to face this man!

Hearing the ring of the doorbell, I walk to the living room and slip into Tiago's flannel as I gather my things, not wanting him to find me naked. I put my clothes in a neat pile on top of my purse and get to the door.

"Who is it?"

All I hear is a muffled response, and when I check the peephole, it seems the person has their finger on it. Thinking it must be Tiago acting silly, I open the door and come face to face with... Hannah... the vixen from last night.

"Hi," I greet, my voice firm and cordial.

She raises an artfully drawn eyebrow and stares me down from head to toe. "So, he took you home."

"Tiago's not here. You might want to come back later," I state in a calm voice, not addressing her remark.

When I try closing the door, she slips the tip of her high heeled boot in, preventing my move.

"Yeah, I'll come back later. I always do," she retorts, a catty smile on her arresting face.

"Excuse me," I request, still in a composed tone, looking pointedly at her shoe that's still blocking the door, and still not responding to her nasty comments.

"I hope you enjoyed your ride, cause I'll make sure it was your one and only."

"Excuse me, I'm gonna close the door, now," I reply, refusing to engage.

She scoffs and flips her long braids, catwalking her way down the entrance stairs.

I feel the sting of tears blur my vision and close the door behind her, rushing to wear my clothes and get the hell out of here!

CHAPTER 14:
TIAGO

I'm gonna kill Amy. There's no way I'm letting this one slide. After the night we shared, the unbelievable connection I know we both felt, the communion of our bodies and minds. A bond beyond words... She pulls a disappearing act on my ass?

I left her sleeping deeply and softly snoring. Mouth open, a bit of drool dripping at the side. Her big hair tied up in an old do-rag I'd unearthed from the depths of my closet, dating from my hip-hop phase. Dressed in nothing, her glorious forms enticing me and calling me back to bed. One round hip lifting the white sheets. Cute, painted toenails poking out of the covers. I'd almost foregone my daily run, and only years of discipline and ingrained routine finally pulled me away from her.

I ran faster than I had in years, to the rhythm of my rapid beating, foolish heart. Head filled with plans for the day, tomorrow, the day after that, the coming weeks, months... years. So, it's no wonder I got fucking pissed when I got home and found my place empty. Not a trace of Amy. As if last night had never happened. Just another figment of my imagination. I call and text her. She doesn't pick up, doesn't call me back, doesn't answer my messages... I begin to worry, and decide to pay little miss vanishing act a visit.

***

I'm fresh out of the shower, dressed in sweats and a T, my feet haphazardly stuck in the first pair of socks and sneakers I could grab. I drove the twenty minutes distance between my house and Amy's building in ten... Parking my car on the street, I take a quick jog up her entrance stairs and press on the button for her name on the intercom.

She answers after a few seconds: "yes?"

My heart starts settling now that it seems nothing's happened to Amy, and she hasn't evaporated from the surface of the earth.

"May I please come up?"

Silence for a beat, followed by the sound of the buzzer. *Thank fuck!* Before coming, I checked the text Amy sent me all those weeks ago, before our pretend wedding reception date. The one where she gave me her full address, to come pick her up. I climb up the flight of stairs to Amy's floor and knock on her door. She opens and stands aside to let me in, looking good enough to eat in a flowy white cotton dress. Her full tits looking fabulous in the round neckline of her dress. I quickly move my eyes to her face, refusing to get distracted by her appetizing forms. But the vision my eyes encounter is not one that'll help settle my emotions. Amy has been crying! Her eyes are puffy and red, the light in them dim.

"What's wrong, *princesa?*" I ask with fervor.

She scoffs with derision. "Nothing's wrong. Everything's just peachy. Or at least the way it's supposed to be."

I take a step closer, attempting to read her sour tone. "What happened, sweets?" I attempt again. "You fell asleep in my arms with a smile on your face," I remind her.

"Your girlfriend came to pay you a visit this morning at your place, while you were God knows where," she spits out, eyes lighting up with a fierce fire.

Okay, emotion is good. This I can work with. "Who's supposed to be my girlfriend? Because you're the only woman I've been interested in for months now, *mi reina.*" I speak softly, as if addressing a wild animal or a young child. Attentive to not brusque Amy.

"Your Hanna," she grits out.

A smile of relief and amusement takes over my features before I can refrain it, shit! And I watch as Amy's face hardens, and she points to her door. "Get out, you arrogant bastard! I was right about you from the beginning!"

I immediately school my features and advance toward her in one long stride. Planting my face just inches from hers, I say: "she's nothing and nobody to me. We fucked because she's hot and she was after me for a while. I cut her off ages ago, even before I started becoming obsessed with you."

Amy watches me closely, mouth still pinched, eyes guarded but I can perceive a flickering light in them.

"Swear, *bebé,*" I whisper close to her tightened lips.

"She said she always comes back, that she'd make sure last night was my only time with you."

"Sweets, Hannah never even spent the night at my house." I lay my large palms on Amy's shoulders, watching carefully for her reactions. "No one ever has. That house is my sanctuary, you're the only woman I've ever wanted in my space."

She blinks up at me, eyes getting misty.

"Amy?" I question, not sure why she's crying now.

"I'm not this woman... this ninny! You're turning me into a mess," she says in a loud voice and I'm not sure if she's still pissed or not.

I risk a smile, and Amy squints at me.

"Are you sure this girl knows the score? I don't have time for cat fights, Tiago!" She says vehemently after a long sigh.

"She knows, sweets. She was just trying to scare you off."

"What she did was piss me off," Amy retorts, crossing her arms over her ample chest.

And this time, I look my fill and chuckle, now feeling comfortable to get into her space. "She doesn't deserve your time or energy, *bebé.*"

I cup her face in my hand and Amy closes her eyes, letting her head rest into my palm. I rub at her soft skin with my thumb and bend to press my lips to hers. She lifts on her toes and returns my kiss. Deepens it. Wraps her wrists around my neck, pressing her soft forms to me, and making my dick twitch in my pants.

"Fuck," I murmur against her lips. "We need to talk, sweets."

Amy nods, wraps her small fingers around my hand and pulls me to her couch. My eyes take in the small but elegant interior of her studio. Soothing colors, comfortable furniture, interesting knickknacks and beautiful art on the walls. My brain jumps the gun, once more: her feminine touch will definitely complete my taste. I sit on the white leather couch and pull Amy on my lap, ass snuggled against my crotch, my dick nestled against her two fabulous globes. My nostrils filled with the soft scent of her perfume, and the undertone that's all Amy. For a moment, I just hold her tight, her head resting in the crook of my neck, her legs stretched the length of the couch, the side of her body laying at he center of my chest. My arms wrapped around her full, soft body, hands gently rubbing her skin.

"You scared me," I finally let out. "I came home from my run and you were gone without a word. And you wouldn't answer your phone... I thought something might have happened to you," I whisper against her temple.

Amy lifts her head to look at me, emotions battling through her gaze. "I'm sorry, that wasn't my intention."

I simply nod.

Amy takes a deep inhale, then like the queen she is, she tells me in a firm voice: "here's what I want, Tiago. If it works for you, great. If it doesn't, you need to tell me now."

I nod, eager to find out her heart's desire for us.

"I want you. Just the two of us. No groupie, no friends with benefits, no 'she's not important'. I want to nurture this thing between us." She lets the tips of her fingers run over my features. "I want to be you're true *reina*, the only one."

I take her hand and drop a kiss on her fingers. "You already are and you didn't even realize it. I'm falling in love with you, Amy."

Her full, pouty lips part, letting out a soft gasp, and her eyes grow huge. "Oh honey," she breathes out, "I'm falling for you, too."

Our mouths collide in the most hungry, worshiping, tender and erotic kiss ever. Amy positions herself to straddle me, pulling her dress up her thick thighs and giving access to my erection to rub against her panties through my sweats.

I throw my head back on the couch. "Fuck, you feel good!"

"No, you feel good, baby," Amy murmurs against my parted lips, her tongue plunging deeper, wilder. Each stroke and lick driving me mad.

I pinch at her pebbled nipples, triggering a long moan of pleasure. Bringing my hand between us, I push her underwear aside and rub two thick fingers along her slit, opening her for me, coating her folds with her juices, from clit to entrance. Our mouths still glued together, tongues battling, lips molded, her moans and my groans marry in perfect harmony. I starting tracing circles over Amy's clit with the pad of my thumb and pushing the tips of two fingers inside her. She bites on my lip, hard enough to hurt, but the pain only sends a jolt to my cock. I pump my fingers in and out of Amy's hot pussy, caress her clit, fuck her mouth with my tongue and roll her nipples with my other hand.

Amy's only seconds away from coming apart in my arms, when she cries out: "Fuck, I love the way you make me feel."

My mouth stretches in a cocky grin and I work harder to make my girl feel good. It only takes a few more strokes for her orgasm to explode. Amy whimpers against my mouth, hips bouncing on my hand as I continue pumping inside her, till the very last lick of the fire consuming her body. When she's done, I remove my hand from between us and lick my fingers clean, staring into her wide opened eyes and grinning wickedly. I pull the top of her dress down, followed by the fabric of her bra and give a long lick, suck and swirl of my tongue to each breast. My dick's about to poke a hole in my sweats, but now that I know we're on the same page, I'm in no hurry.

I take Amy's chin between my fingers and ask: "I've got two questions, *princesa*. First, do you have condoms? And second, how attached are you to your place?"

Her mouth falls open and I take the opportunity to ravage her with another searing kiss.

EPILOGUE

"I can't believe I agreed to this. There's no way I'll survive today. First, the reception on campus, then dinner at my parents? What the hell was I thinking?!" I ramble away in a stressed voice, sitting in the passenger seat of Tiago's truck.

"Relax, *princesa.*" He takes my hand and rests it on his muscled thigh after a squeeze, eyes still focused on the road. "Your colleagues were more interested in me fundraising for the UC with my business contacts, than in us being together." Tiago brings my fingers to his full lips, dropping a soft kiss on my skin.

"I can't say the contrary. God dammit, the dean has no scruple," I mumble.

"And, you know your family loves me. Just make sure to wave your hand a lot, and to get your ring in a good lighting." He throws me a wink.

I giggle. "Stop, you're dumb"

He grins wide, making my heart beat faster. "Worked with my mom and siblings."

I smile fondly. As soon as Tiago had announced our engagement, his family had gone crazy! Organizing one gathering after the other to introduce me to all their relatives. Making me fall deeper for my big-hearted, big-brained jock. I love seeing where Tiago came from, the people who made him. Watch him get roasted by his sibling. Tease his mom, kiss and embrace her. Have animated discussions with his dad about sports. The food is always delicious and the company amazing. I know my family will be excited too, I'm just nervous.

"And if you're a good girl," Tiago's voice cuts through my thoughts, "when we get home, I'll do that thing with my tongue and fingers..." He promises in a low, gravelly voice.

I feel my cheeks heat up. "Santiago Daniel Silva, this is not the time to mention the thing!"

"Just trying to help you relax, sweets. You know, get your mind off heavy things," he winks again.

Unbelievable... " Fuck you T," I deadpan.

"In a few hours, *mi reina.*"

I can't help but laugh, hit his arm and let out a happy sigh. Yeah, he's got me in any situation. Tiago is my friend, my lover, the guardian of my heart. One day soon, he'll be my husband. And I hope, in a not too distant future, the father of our kids...

The End

ABOUT THE AUTHOR

Imani is a lover of romance novels! She's been devouring them since she was a young girl (long before she was supposed to venture into steamy stories.) Imani is all about the feels, the sexy times, and most of all the characters! She loves a broody hero, a soft dude, a sassy woman or a shy wallflower...

Her entire life, Imani would daydream of swoony encounters. One day she decided to start writing the stories she always wanted to read; stories with heroines who look more like her, and hunks from all over the world.

What to expect from Imani's stories? Steamy insta-love romances with a diverse cast of curvy girls and their hunky alphas.

FIND IMANI ONLINE:
https://www.facebook.com/authorimanij

More Books by Imani Jay:
Owned by the Aussie
Owned by the Billionaire

FOREVER WITH HIM

Zaria Knight

ABOUT *FOREVER WITH HIM*

Eighteen-year-old orphan Diego Herrera is at a crossroads. A scholarship ensures that he'll have a better future. But it also means leaving behind the life he's rebuilt with his childhood best friend and stepbrother, Alonso. Diego's loved Alonso since he could remember. But their love is strictly forbidden.

I can still remember the summer when I knew, without a shadow of a doubt, that I was always going to love you. That my heart, mind, and body, right down to my soul, is wrapped up in loving you, Alonso. Even though I know we can never be together. Why does something so forbidden feel just right? Can you tell me why I can't stop?

***

"Felicidades! Come join the party, amigo!"

I closed my journal quickly as a masculine voice bellowed out congratulations to me. It was risky to be pouring out my heart onto a piece of paper, but it was better than getting too drunk and saying it out loud instead. My English teacher said it would be a great way to express myself, and my counselor agreed. But that was only if I could hide what was inside of it.

My stomach lurched. I was afraid it would be Alonso, the subject of my journal entry. But thankfully, it wasn't.

Glancing up, I saw a stranger's bearded face instead. He looked to be at least in his mid-thirties or forties, wearing tight blue jeans, a red plaid shirt, and brown cowboy boots. Probably a ranch hand.

Beside him was one of my best friend's cousins, who shoved a can of beer into my face with a grin.

The matron of the family-owned ranch was strict about liquor, though no one else in the family cared. But unfortunately, I forgot the reason why she was so anal about alcohol. Probably something to do with one of her sons who was the family's black sheep—the why didn't really matter that much.

We weren't supposed to be drinking on the property. Of course, they didn't care as long as a certain someone didn't see us.

Still, I mouthed no, getting up, being sure to shield my journal in the process. I didn't need anything to give me liquid courage, only to fuck up and say something I really shouldn't be saying.

"So happy for you," I heard someone else say.

He pulled me into a hug, a little tipsy. It took me a second to realize it was Rodrigo. He had a huge mustache the last time I'd seen him. He owned the ranch Alonso and I had our joint graduation party on.

"Thank you so much," I murmured, pulling away.

I never expected to have a graduation party on a ranch. Hell, I never expected to graduate at all back then. But Cottonwood Cattle Ranch was the only place big enough to hold all of us. And I couldn't lie and say it wasn't a gorgeous location.

However, the smell of cow manure was hard to ignore, which didn't but the warmth of the bond fire and the free flow of delicious smelling Mexican and Dominican dishes made up for it tenfold. I scooped up a plate of carnitas tacos to take home, anxious to get on my bike and ride into town to meet some other friends.

My eyes scanned the yard, and so many new faces greeted me with smiles. It amazed me that so many people could be so close-knit. If my would-be adoptive abuela had it her way, the López and Pérez families would all become my family too.

Something any former foster kid should be excited about. Only I had to go and fall in love with my would-be stepbrother, complicating everything, which was ninety-nine percent of the reason I was desperate to get away.

But I wouldn't be so lucky, it seemed.

Groaning, I tried to avoid the stare of the one guy I didn't want to see at this fiesta.

"Diego," Alonso called out to me, grinning wide. Some men I assumed were his uncles turned my way, beckoning me over.

I shoved my journal into my backpack, dragging my feet as I came over.

"Congrats! We're so proud. Are you going to college? Here, in Texas?" They shot off questions rapid fire, patting my back, shaking my shoulder, brimming with pride.

"Thank you. Yes! Actually..." My throat was getting hoarse from trying to answer them all, feeling a bit claustrophobic.

Most of Alonso's extended family were either farmers or ranchers. A good chunk had agricultural degrees. But there was something special, in their eyes, about us branching out and doing our own thing.

I was going to school for social work, hopefully. And Alonso for sports medicine. It was stereotypical of me to go into my line of work. I knew that even back then. I was yet another traumatized kid who grew up to try and help those in my situation in the future.

"Ah," I tried to change the topic, pulling away, trying to find an easy out.

They were all so expressive and touchy, especially Alonso. Something that didn't matter pre-puberty when wrestling or the slightest tap gave me a raging hard-on.

Then Alonso finally swooped to my rescue, shooing his uncles away.

"Let's get out of here," he leaned over to whisper, eyes twinkling.

I didn't have time to speak as he yanked me around the corner of the house, towards the barn, and out of sight.

He pulled me close, lacing his fingers through mine as soon as we were inside. I could feel the air shift, the look in his eyes deepening, trained on my lower lip. I turned away as he leaned forward, his lips landing against my neck. I knew I couldn't afford to get another hickey, especially now with his whole family right outside and so close.

"Ahh..." And yet, I stayed, sighing as his teeth grazed my neck, big hands clenching my cheeks.

I was already lost in the feeling of his touch. Because, unlike everyone else, I craved it.

He dragged my lower half against him, his hard-on digging into my stomach because of our height difference. He smelled like wood, neat and clean, unlike our surroundings.

The thing about Alonso that always turned me on is how much he made it seem like he wanted *me*. All of me, like he would swallow me whole if he could.

He nipped at my lips, tongue tracing and teasing me.

"I'll be quick," he murmured as one of his hands reached down to toy with my belt buckle.

It was then that I snapped back to reality, remembered where the hell we were and freaked out.

"Stop!" I gritted out.

I pushed Alonso away, ignoring my own erection. His shock was plain to see, a tent in his pants and confusion written all over his face.

Alonso didn't need to speak for me to hear the silent plea of, "Why?"

And I couldn't answer him. How many times had we snuck off during family gatherings, after school, and on the weekends?

Countless times. And not once did I say no. And, more than once, I initiated it. I was the one madly in love with Alonso, after all, not the other way around.

So what made this time any different? I couldn't put it into words, but it just was. It felt wrong for the first time since we started our little fling.

"Diego, wait," he said, reaching for me as I grabbed my backpack, "Don't go. I'm sorry! I don't know what's wrong, but I'm sorry…"

It's not you; it's me.

As cliche as the saying was, it was true. But I couldn't get myself to say that out loud. So, like a coward, I ran away from him and my overflowing emotions.

Cousins, aunts, and uncles blurred together as I did my best to slip away. It was starting to get dark, and our grandmother would be around to pick us up soon. Unfortunately, she was feuding with her sister-in-law, so she only stayed long enough to give us presents and have some food before leaving to "do some grocery shopping."

But fortunately for me, that meant she wasn't there to stop me and ask me what was wrong.

The only reason I had another way to leave was because I often came down to the ranch to clear my mind. Rodrigo let me ride my bike or laze around on the property, as long as I did something like watching his youngest children in return.

Finally, I reached my bike, huffing, and puffing. I wasn't the athletic type. Nevertheless, I got on it, pedaling as fast as my legs could take me. The sun beat down on my back brutally, but I didn't care.

And then I hit the road, away from the ranch, no destination in mind other than I needed to get away. Preferably forever.

**

After that disaster of a graduation party, weeks passed by in a flash. Before I knew it, there was only a month left before I would start my first year in college. Instead of moping around, that time in my life should've filled me with excitement, hopping from one graduation party to another as I said goodbye to my old friends and hometown.

Looking forward to the future should've been front and center in my mind.

Getting wasted, smoking, and studying should've been my top priorities. Those were the only things that should've been on my mind back then. I should have been in a festive mood instead of a shitty one.

But all the "should'ves" in the world wouldn't change the past. It simply wasn't the reality for me, so I pressed on, trying to keep my head up.

But despite my best efforts, all I could feel was a heavy sense of dread, more oppressive than the dry Texas heat beating down on my back.

It crept along in the corner of my mind, spinning in a loop, something I could not shake off. I tried and failed as I walked down the quiet road leading to my home away from home. Located on the outskirts of Houston, just a few minutes away from Sacred Heart K-12, the rural community of Fort Haven was as familiar as breathing air.

And now it was all slipping away, a part of my life I would cherish but would need to give up.

Three years ago, when I was just a freshman in high school, I found the courage to come out. Not out of the closet, though I knew I was gay since I was a kid. I always knew I was different. But back then, I came out in another way, out of my shell and out of the shitty house I'd called home for fourteen years.

Back in Houston, I never felt free enough to be myself. Only one person was worth staying there for, and I was desperate to follow him once he moved to Fort Haven.

I'd do anything to get out.

Thank God for miracles, however slight.

When my dad decided to leave me alone for a two-week drunken bender, with my mom following him soon after, I bounced from a group home to a foster family and finally into the arms of Lilianna and Alonso.

She loved me like a son and treated me better than I ever knew possible. And yet, I crossed a line that should've never been crossed with her real grandson, and I didn't know how to re-lock Pandora's Box.

"Hola, Abuela," I called out as I entered *Raíces* that steamy summer night, a small, family-owned Dominican restaurant with an apartment attached on top.

My eyes drifted around the restaurant to find *Raíces* empty, closed at least two hours earlier than normal. I frowned, walking past the colorful mural I'd passed a hundred times before: a green and yellow parrot against a red, blue, and white background symbolizing abuela's roots back in the DR.

The cash register counter also contained the colors of the Dominican Republic's flag, assembled from hundreds of *Coca-Cola, Jarritos,* and *Kola Real* bottle caps repainted and repurposed.

My adoptive grandmother, or Lilianna as I tried to call her back then, was a master at taking trash and turning it into treasure, a lot like how she took my shitty life and made it shine like gold.

A lone plate of mofongo sat on the counter, the smell of garlic, fried plantain, and pork filling my nose. I smiled, walking towards the register and reaching for a plastic spoon. I took a massive chunk out of the home-cooked meal, savoring it as I read the note beside it.

It read, "¡Felicitaciones! Estoy tan orgulloso de ti," in perfect cursive.

It filled me with pride to know that she was proud of me. Despite the odds stacked against me, I graduated on the honor roll and got a full-ride scholarship out of state. I tutored over the summer to stack some cash, too, so I wouldn't burden her until I could get a work-study job at my new school.

The last few years had been everything but easy, and she had been my rock.

So how had I let her down so badly? What the hell made me make out with Alonso the night of our graduation party?

"Ah!" My eyes snapped up, dropping my spoon as if whoever came downstairs could read my thoughts.

Sure enough, the reason for all my trepidation stood in front of me, all six feet of lean muscles, caramel-colored skin, and curly black hair. Alonso's dark gaze never left mine as he hopped the last two stairs straight down to the ground floor.

I backed away from the counter, nervous, knowing that Lilianna would be out for the night playing bingo with her girlfriends. Fridays were always a party after dark, especially when Alonso and I were alone.

"Hey," he whispered after a long while staring, my voice trapped by my constricted throat.

"...Hey," I finally managed to squeeze out, tugging at the tip of my white button-up shirt.

I yanked off my sweater, the private school uniform feeling stifling at that moment.

Alonso had just returned from baseball practice not too long ago; as the team's ace pitcher, already scouted by a D1 university, he tended to practice year-round. I could tell by the water droplets polling at the nape of his neck as he reached inside the restaurant's display refrigerator for a drink.

Alonso wrapped a white towel around his neck, wearing a form-fitting, long-sleeve top. I could imagine his muscles underneath. Not that I had to anymore ever since we went to second base not too long ago.

"Where have you been?" he asked between sips of cherry soda.

I gulped, eyes darting away. What could I say? That I had been avoiding him since our graduation party? Since he got the news that he was going to Texas State, and I abruptly decided to attend the University of California instead. I realized I couldn't contain myself any longer, no matter how much we fooled around. He was straight, I was convenient, and I was living under his roof. It was wrong on many levels, even though it felt right when I was in his arms.

"Just...out." The answer didn't seem to satisfy Alonso.

"Whatever..." He slammed the display shut, throwing his glass bottle in our recycling bin before turning to go upstairs.

I couldn't blame him for getting angry. I'd boxed Alonso out of my life because I was at an emotional crossroads. I had even hurt Liliana after I told her I wasn't interested in being adopted.

He never used to be so moody until we crossed the line. Back then, it seemed like we were either at each other's throats or in each other's pants. We were still inseparable, as always. Only the tension between us was sexual, always lurking under the surface.

I had an inkling that Lilianna knew I was gay. I couldn't put it

His skin-tight uniform made me blush. I shouldn't have felt the way I did about him, but I couldn't help it.

Alonso turned around and stared at me as if to say, "Come on."

There was nowhere to run now. No friend's couch to sleep on or after-school tutoring session to keep me distracted. Just my crush and I were under the same roof, alone, for the first time and many weeks.

Shit.

Out of options, I finally gave in. I pointed my eyes towards the ground and marched along, each step heavier than the last.

Each squeaky step to our apartment filled me with even more dread and anxiety. We had it to ourselves until morning. Which meant I needed to find the courage to break it off now. The first kiss had been an accident, a game of gay chicken that went too far. I never expected Alonso to reciprocate my feelings for him. Still, somehow stolen kisses became secret touches, all culminating in this night–the night I crossed the line with my stepbrother.

That was not unlike every Friday night since I moved in with Alonso and Liliana.

But that night wasn't like any other. That night I was going to say goodbye for good.

To petty high school drama. To the memories of a hellish group home filled with people who never loved me. To the taste of abuela's cooking. To the warmth being in a loving family provided. All things I could learn to live without, if only for a little while.

But what I was afraid to let go of, the love I nurtured since we were kids, hanging in the air, always unspoken but undeniably felt.

We entered our room. It felt so much smaller than it did back then. The TV feels too close to our beds, separated by a small dresser. I knew Alonso was about to move the dresser so we could push them together.

The walls were covered with our heroes: baseball legends, anime posters, and a small photo wall featuring our friends.

I couldn't bring myself to look at that photo collage. To look at Yvette kisses Alonso's cheek. A picture that should've been taken down months ago.

That is if we were in a real relationship and not whatever the fuck we were doing. I had no right to be hurt when I took advantage of his loneliness. When Alonso's girlfriend of two years broke his heart right before we all went to college, I was there like I had always been and took a chance.

In a way, I was worse than her at that moment. I'd known him longer, came on to him first, and broke it off just as fast as his speedball, the one taking him to Texas State.

"Come on. We don't have all night," he said, voice distant, deeper. "Or are you going to run again? Just tell me if you don't want this. Don't leave me guessing, okay?"

He always tried to force it lower when he was mad. Despite how tall he was, Alonso always had a gentle voice.

I shook my head no as he dragged the dresser from between the beds. He looked up at me then, the towel slipping from his neck, confused.

"Isn't this what you wanted? Isn't this why you came back tonight instead of crashing with your friends," he asked in a sneering tone, emphasizing friends.

They weren't my friends at all. They were mainly smoking buddies that helped me forget. Not that he had to rub it in my face.

"No. Listen to me. I'm... I'm going to do a program. It's for first-generation students. Which means I'll be moving onto campus early... I'm leaving next week."

I could feel the air getting sucked out of the room. Alonso darted upward, bushy eyebrows bunching up, thoroughly confused. And who could blame him? No one knew how hard I worked to get out, not even Liliana.

"So... So you're just going to up and leave. Just like that, huh? Fuck us, I guess."

He was on me in a flash, fist tightening around my shirt's collar. But as always, he sent mixed signals. He reached up to cup my cheek, gritting his teeth. It looked like he didn't know if he wanted to punch me or kiss me, and frankly, I didn't know which I deserved.

We both knew this relationship was a dead-end before it even began. But like stubborn idiots, we said screw the consequences for a while.

But it was time to grow up. Liliana was talking about adopting me, for fuck's sake. It was now or never. The party was over. We had to face reality.

And yet...

"Alonso," I began, pressing my cheek into the palm of his hand. "I have to go. I don't have a choice."

I said what I needed to say, but there was no conviction in my voice.

"Bullshit!" he shouted, dragging me towards his face until I was on the tips of my toes. "Bullshit, and you know it."

I closed my eyes as he leaned forward and made his decision. His lips were wind-chapped and rough, but it didn't matter to me. Each kiss from Alonso felt like heaven back then. I buried my hands into his thick, curly black hair, opening my mouth as he forced his tongue inside.

He always had a magnetic energy that threatened to swallow me whole. I moaned against his mouth as he grabbed my ass, dragging me back to the bed.

He flopped down, taking me with him so I could straddle his hips. We were on each other like animals, buttons popping one by one, as I struggled to get undressed. First, I had to stop Alonso from tearing my shirt into bits. Then I reached for him and helped him tug his compression gear off, nails digging into his chest.

"You're such a fucking liar," he grunted as he tugged on my belt buckle. "You said you loved me, Diego. Is leaving me with this bullshit goodbye what you call love?"

Ouch. Alonso's words hit me like a ton of bricks. My chest heaved, shaking my head no even as I struggled to come up with something to say.

I had slipped the last time when we almost went all the way. I just had to say something as stupid as "I love you" and mess it all up before I could get home base.

Didn't you say this was just for fun? That we're just fooling around?

It's what I should've said. But once again, what I *should've* felt and *should've* said didn't matter in the face of what I did next.

Instead of addressing him, I got to work doing what I knew how to do: drown out my emotions with drugs, drinking, and sex.

My tongue darted against his nipple, trailing kisses down his stomach. I yanked at his belt this time around, trying to get him to take off his pants.

He didn't comply. Instead, he forced me to get on my back, snatching my pants off before I could stop him. He also made quick work of my boxers before bending forward on the bed.

Since we didn't push our beds together, the space was narrow, and I was forced to lie still. Alonso's eyes never left mine as he took my throbbing cock to the hilt.

His mouth was so warm and so fucking wet. One of his hands gripped my inner thigh, while the other wandered upward, exploring my stomach.

I panted as he toyed with my nipples, head bobbing back and forth. I knew I wouldn't last long. I had a bad habit of blowing my load too quickly when he sucked my dick.

But I couldn't help it. Alonso was my first for everything: my first kiss, my first make-out, my first blow job. And now he would be the one I lose my virginity to, too.

Not that I minded. I couldn't even begin to count how many nights I'd laid beside my best friend in our extra long twin beds, imagining what Alonso could do to me, how he would taste, how he would smell if he would flash that toothy grin Alonso always had when he was having fun. Suppose he would want me if I were ready.

"Ugh!" My cheeks clenched, my back arching as I blew my load in the back of his throat.

He sucked it up greedily, which surprised me. He said he hated sucking dick more than anything. Why he was so eager that night was a mystery to me.

Once I finished, I sank into a puddle, exhausted. All the tension I had balled up was gone all at once.

"Turn around," he whispered, nipping at my neck as he crawled over top of me.

Alonso's broad shoulders blocked out the light from our ceiling fan. I realized immediately that this was the first time we'd done it in the light. No pillows over faces or fumbling around in the dark this time around. He'd sucked my dick and saw every vein, every hard plane versus the soft curves of the girls he was used to pulling.

His cock peeked out from the hole in his pants, stiff as a metal bat. When was the last time he'd been so hard after the fact? I couldn't remember. I usually got him off and wanted more afterward, but it was like his brain would turn back on and realize that I was a guy.

Not this time, I thought with a sigh.

I pressed the palms of my hands against his chest as he sank down, this time whispering in my ear, "Turn around, now."

He got up as I shifted around. Alonso dragged my legs so that they were off the bed and got behind me. Then, he grabbed two pillows and pushed them under my stomach.

I gulped, knowing what was about to happen. I could hear rustling, the ripping of a condom, and the hard squeeze of lube, followed by the cool sensation of it landing on my skin.

The pillows held my butt in the air as he spread my cheeks. I tuned out the rest, focusing on the feeling of his hand wrapped around my swollen shaft, pumping it softly, still trying to milk me even though I had nothing left to give.

I whimpered as he clutched my cheeks, whispering sweet nothings in Spanish as he lined the head of his cock against my hole. He kept trying to get me to calm down, unable to push inside, but the anticipation was eating me up inside.

Finally, it seemed as though he gave up, laying on top of me, forcing me down into the bed. Until he said those magic words that changed everything.

"Te quiero mucho. Te amaré por siempre, Diego."

And just like that, the dam broke. All my petty excuses for why we couldn't be together melted away. All my attempts to put up a wall between us shattered.

They evaporated like smoke as he clung to my waist and then my hips, sinking into me slowly.

We were becoming one before I knew it.

I clenched my teeth as his cock hit me deep. He pulled out to the tip, only to plunge back in, now giving me time to rest or resist.

"Alonso! Alonso!" I cried out, the pace punishing, though he was going so slow, so gently.

But everything was too new. My toes scraped against the floor as Alonso dragged me back to meet his thrusting hips, balls deep, to the point I didn't know where I started and he would end.

"Diego, please. I want you to look at me."

I gasped as he pulled out completely. He turned me around gingerly, and I couldn't hold back my moaning. I covered my hand with my arm to avoid staring into his dark eyes, overflowing with everything: love, hate, fear, confusion, and everything in between.

He spread my legs, holding my right thigh to keep my ass parted. Then he pressed insight, each inch harder to take than the last until he was nestled deep inside of me again.

"Faster," I whimpered. "Harder, please."

And I meant it. I couldn't take it anymore. I needed him to fuck me, not treat me like some doll.

He followed my command, his hips slamming against mine as he picked up the pace. It hurt, the sensation of fullness to the point of bursting, unlike his fingers or any toy.

But it also felt so warm and right, my cock slick with cum as his stomach glided against it with each stroke.

I fisted my cock, stroking myself into a frenzy, as Alonso lost his rhythm, drowning me in love.

"Te quiero, te quiero..." his soothing voice caused me to drift in and out of sleep, coming down from my high, our stomach coated in streaks of my cum.

Finally, Alonso pulled out and grunted as he ripped off his condom, vicious white streaks landing on my stomach and chest.

He collapsed shortly after that, both of us a complete and utter mess.

I wrapped my arms around Alonso's shoulders and breathed in his scent. He wrapped his hands around my waist, brought me closer to him, and squished together on my bed.

"Alonso?" My voice lifted in question.

"Yes?"

"I love you, too, Alonso. I love you so much; I just don't know what to do from here."

"... We'll figure it out. Just don't up and leave me. I'll always be there for you, you know? I want to be there for you."

It was all I needed to hear. So we lay in each other arms for a long while, both of us knowing at some point we would have to make everything look normal, to come out to Liliana, to decide if we were going to figure out a way to go to the same college after all.

I didn't know what the future would bring. But, I was happy to live in that moment. To find forever in Alonso's arms, even if it's only for a night.

The End

***

Did you enjoy this short story? If so, please leave a review! If you want to read Diego & Alonso's extended love story, make sure to stay tuned for the full-length novel *Always His* here:

authorzknight.com/forever-yours-trilogy

ABOUT THE AUTHOR

Zaria Knight is a USA Today bestselling author. She writes diverse steamy and erotic contemporary and historical romance for all orientations. Keep in touch on social media @AuthorZKnight. Or visit www.zariaknight.com.

You can also email zaria@zariaknight.com.

Newsletter:
www.authorzknight.com/newsletter

More Steamy Contemporary Romance:

Pre-Order Cowboy's Haven (Fort Haven Valley, #1) inside of Texas Heart: A Collection of Gay Cowboy Romance
books2read.com/texasheart

Shades of Love: A Limited Edition Boxset of Black, Multicultural, and Interracial Contemporary Romances (PRIDE Anthologies)
books2read.com/shadesoflove

Pre-Order SOL & Receive FREE eBooks:
bit.ly/solfreebies

Lighting Her Flame: A Kwanzaa Kisses Holiday Romance
books2read.com/lightingherflame

His Best Friend's Curvy Sister
(Curves on Demand)
books2read.com/curvysister

Made in the USA
Middletown, DE
24 October 2022